THE AUTHOR

Dr. Robert T. Golembiewski is Research Professor of Political Science and Management, University of Georgia. His major interest is to "build knowledge of behavior into organization theory," and he has pursued this goal in both business and government organizations where he has served as researcher and consultant.

The author or editor of more than forty books, Dr. Golembiewski is found by surveys to be one of the most-cited and highly ranked in research productivity in his field. Other books by Dr. Golembiewski include *Organizing Men and Power: Patterns of Behavior and Line-Staff Models; Learning and Change in Groups; Reviewing Organizations; Men, Management, and Morality: Toward A New Organizational Ethics; Public Administration as a Developing Discipline* (two volumes).

A graduate of Princeton (A.B.) and Yale (M.A. and Ph.D.), Dr. Golembiewski has received significant recognition for his scholarly work. He has served as Distinguished Visiting Scholar at the University of Calgary. He is a Fellow of the NTL Institute of Applied Behavioral Science.

HUMANIZING

PUBLIC

ORGANIZATIONS

Perspectives on Doing
Better-Than-Average
When Average Ain't At All Bad

ROBERT T. GOLEMBIEWSKI

LOMOND

1985

Library of Congress Catalog Number: 83-81972

ISBN: 0-912338-43-1 (Clothbound)
      0-912338-44-X (Microfiche)

Printed in the United States of America

Published by
Lomond Publications, Inc.
P.O. Box 88
Mt. Airy, Maryland 21771

— To —

Dr. George S. Parthemos:

A classical scholar, and a
scholar of the classics.

1921-1984

TABLE OF CONTENTS

List of Tables vii
List of Figures vii
List of Exhibits viii

Introduction 1

Part A What is Tough About Public Sector Change? 11

Chapter I Theorizing About Why Public-Sector
OD Can't Be Done: Some Real
And Confounding Constraints 13

**Part B How Well Does OD Do in Public-Sector
Change?** 43

Chapter II Tracking the Effects of Confounding
Constraints: Experience With Planned
Change in Public-Sector Settings, I 45

Chapter III Estimating The Success Ratio of OD Effects:
Experience With Planned Change in
Public-Sector Settings, II 73

Chapter IV Evaluating Applications of Flexible
Workhours: Experience With Planned
Change in Public-Sector Settings, III 93

**Part C Why Does Public-Sector OD Need to Do
Better-than-Average** 131

Chapter V Toward a Political Theory for OD, I:
The Ideational Poverty of
Democracy/Administration
Couplings 133

Chapter VI   Toward a Political Theory for OD, II:
                Administration that Reinforces
                Democratic Ideals 195

**Part D How Can Public-Sector OD Do
        Better-than-Average?**................................231

Chapter VII   Seeking Guidance from Experience at the
                Interface, I: Intervention Guidelines
                Relating to Environmental Texture 233

Chapter VIII   Seeking Guidance from Experience at the
                Interface, II: Intervention
                Guidelines Focusing on
                Intervenor Behavior 291

Index..367

LIST OF TABLES

TABLE   PAGE

1 Constraints on Specific Urban OD Interventions 52
2 Incidence of Common Constraints on OD Applications 65
3 Common Constraints Mentioned as Facilitators 65
4 Public-Sector OD Applications, 1950-79, N = 270 79
5 Incidence of Eight Classes of OD Activities in
   Public-Sector OD 80
6 Degree of Success of 270 Public-Sector OD
   Applications 82
7 Summary of Impact of OD Interventions on
   "Hard Criteria" 84
8 Overview of Panel of Public-Sector Studies Reporting
   Specific Flexi-Time Effects 98
9 Summary of Attitudinal Effects Reported by Employees
   in All Available Public-Sector Studies 107
10 Summary of Attitudinal Effects Reported by Employees
   in All Available Public-Sector Studies 110
11 Summary of Five Behavioral Effects Reported in
   All Available Public-Sector Studies 113
12 Summary of Public-Sector F-T Studies Reporting on
   Measured Productivity 120

LIST OF FIGURES

FIGURE   PAGE

1 Some Critical Problems Relevant to Federal OD
   Programs 15
2 A Model of Management 32
3 Differences in Workplace Democratization and Degree
   of Control by Employees 201
4 Major Subsystems of Members' Traits in Organization 204
5 A Model of Management 259

FIGURE   **PAGE**

6 The Three Domains Encompassed by Human Service
  Organizations 261
7 A Topological Approach to Marginality 309

LIST OF EXHIBITS

EXHIBIT   **PAGE**

1 Varieties of Democratic Forms or Levels in
  Complex Systems 141
2 Five Ways to Respond to Employee Needs 198
3 Some Contrasts of Positivist Science and Action
  Research 208
4 Arraying OD Designs by Four Major Classes of
  Attitudinal and Behavioral Supports 221
5 Features of Over-bounded and Under-bounded
  Systems 254
6 Different Attributes of Human Service Organizations
  and Business/Industry 260
7 Four Levels of Strategic Orientation to a
  Socio-Political Context 298
8 Predicted Effects of Standard Team-Building Design,
  Using Friedlander's Group Behavior Inventory 307
9 Typical Effects of Standard Team-Building Design 308

INTRODUCTION

This book spans a critical gap between dominant thoughtways and the evolving capabilities of a value-loaded technology. Specifically, this volume deals with two propositions:

- Planned change in public administration does not have much of a chance, to judge from most of the available literature.

- A value-based technology—variously called Organization Development (OD), or Organizational Effectiveness (OE), and sometimes encompassed by the rubric, Quality of Working Life (QWL)—not only promises opportunities for enhanced and responsible freedom in organizations, but even now has a tolerable success ratio in inducing planned change in both small and large systems.

Detailed support of the second proposition will establish the obtuse character of the first. In short, this book sees not only a substantial potential for change in public organizations. Moreover, these organizations can be "humanized," in the sense of becoming more responsive to the needs of their members.

I. A SENSE OF THE PESSIMISTIC LITERATURE

Specifically, several bodies of literature see two chances for conscious and timely public-sector change—slim and none. Allow two examples to serve our present illustrative purposes. Thus some observers have developed impressive catalogs of the reasons why public-sector organizations resist change. Examples are done with greater or lesser erudition,[1] but they commonly push their argument so far that fair-minded readers might reasonably wonder how public managers managed to move beyond quill pens. In this view, public managers can be moved, but only kicking and screaming and long after the reasonableness of the change in question has been obvious to almost all. To be sure, dramatic evidence supports some of this imputed recalcitrance. Consider the U.S. Navy's ponderous denials of the demonstrated usefulness of "continuous-aim firing," which allowed the British to improve the accuracy of their naval gunnery tenfold for nearly two decades before American naval officials "bought into" the idea.[2]

Perhaps even more influential over the last decade or two have been those observers who have applied economist-like reasoning to organizations, and in the process developed another sense in which that discipline can qualify as "the dismal science." Such observers start with some simple propositions: e.g., public managers strive to aggregate as many positions and budget dollars as possible. And from there, only a few logical arabesques are required to establish that all the worst we always believed about public bureaucracies is not only true in fact, but also seems to be unavoidable because of human nature.

Things may seem to change, one may fairly summarize this neo-Malthusian tradition of work, but in reality they remain essentially the same. Public organizations will tend to grow to strain the available resources, in this view, if not beyond that point.[3] At times, such efforts are playful and inventive, as in Parkinson's Laws which (as fate appropriately provided) were authored by the Raffles Professor of History.[4] At other times, such arguments have become the justification for Reaganite variants which essentially propose that, while smaller may not be better, smaller seems less expensive and may be the only way to beat down the self-aggrandizing tendencies inherent in public bureaucracies.

II. FOUR BASIC THRUSTS IN AN OPTIMISTIC VIEW

This volume accepts the pessimistic literature concerning change in the public-sector, but only in one particular. Essentially, three of the four basic thrusts below stand apart from the pessimistic literature. These thrusts can be introduced as four questions that serve to structure this book. They constitute the A, B, C, and Ds for approaching change in public agencies, as it were:

A. What Is Tough About Public-Sector Change?

B. How Well Does OD Do in Public-Sector Change?

C. Why Does Public-Sector OD Need to Do Better-than-Average?

D. How Can Public-Sector OD Do Better-than-Average?

Together, these four thrusts at once demonstrate that we can today do pretty well in inducing greater opportunities for responsible freedom in public organizations, despite the rockiness of the terrain. The analysis also suggests why it is important to do even better, and sketches a set of guidelines for doing so.

A. What Is Tough About Public-Sector Change?

Plenty, and the tough features probably will get worse. In this elemental sense, this volume agrees with the literature briefly referred to above.

This first theme gets plenty of emphasis from friends as well as disinterested observers, so it needs only brief treatment below in a single chapter. The focus there is on constraints against grasping what public-sector change seeks to reach. These constraints inhere in the institutional setting, and have inspired a rich folklore on the attractions of "getting along by going along."

Note that even in this first thrust, this book goes only part of the way with the pessimistic literature. The two sources see much the same reality, in short, but interpret it differently. The pessimistic literature often despairs of change, as in the case of economist-like arguments that make major assumptions about human nature. This volume also sees critical short-falls in the capacity and competence to adapt efficiently and effectively, but those short-falls are seen as having more complex roots. Thus a technology has not been available until quite recently to act on widely-shared values; administrative institutions and traditions developed willy-nilly and early in our two-centuries-plus of nationhood; and awkward mixes of our political philosophy and administrative ways-and-means often were made to do, unreflectively and under the pressure of events.

This volume seeks to emphasize both political philosophy and technology—in short, to accelerate a process of a better fit between ideals and practice.

B. How Well Does OD Do in the Public Sector?

Here this book definitely parts company with much of the literature. Now is definitely not the time for rose-colored glasses, but grounds for real optimism exist. Things are neither as bad now as they appear in some versions of bureaucratic reality, and the future is even more promising. Substantial light already appears at the end of what is admittedly a very long, and big, and dark tunnel. So pie-in-the-sky, bye and bye, is not the present message.

A developing and increasingly precise technology-cum-theory exists for midwifing conscious change. The focus here is on Organization Development, or OD, which has received substantial and growing attention in recent years. Convenient sources provide both introductory and substantive content for that body of technology and theory. This analysis will build upon this available work, but will not dwell on it. For present purposes, OD will be circumscribed only briefly: it rests on a relatively-explicit set of *values* concerning the character and quality of individual and group relationships—their "organization culture" in current vernacular; it is an *on-going process* of change that targets basic *organizational improvements*, rather than specific programs like Management by Objectives; and it relies on *systematic diagnosis* that will permit choice of *planned interventions* designed to induce people and groups to move toward an ever-closer approach to OD's basic values.[5] The key words are italicized here, and will receive diverse illustration and amplification in the fullness of this book.

Given that this volume departs from the common wisdom according to even some advocates of OD[6] as well as observers who are at best lukewarm about the technology-with-theory, substantial attention will be given to what seems an "average" success rate. Three chapters grapple with the task:

- an initial chapter seeks to provide perspective on how confounding constraints, credible and intimidating in the abstract, in fact effect a large number of OD applications in a wide rage of public-sector settings

- a succeeding chapter focuses on several measures of "success rates" obtained with a substantial catalog of *different OD applications*

- a concluding chapter summarizes the range of effects of *one kind of OD intervention*—flexible workhours or Flexi-Time—and compares results at a substantial number of public-sector sites

C. Why Does Public-Sector OD Need To Do Better-than-Average?

Although the cumulative record in this cluster of three chapters is substantial, even eye-catching and surprising, shooting the same average will not suffice, for several reasons. Hopefully, the human quest for a fuller sense of meaning and a better grasp of reality will generate dissatisfaction with "doing OK," even if OK is pretty good. Moreover, it seems safe enough to forecast that we will need to run faster to stand still. There seems no real promise that our lives will slow down so as to accommodate any lack of will and skill.

This volume urges on the reader yet another motivator to do better, in addition. In effect, we have postponed major issues of political philosophy, and OD provides one useful approach to getting at those issues. This is no matter of convenience, please note. Our present condition is something like the evolution of the plane. Propeller-driven planes did pretty well but they got bigger and especially went faster only by piling up the air in front of them, so to speak. That was no big problem for awhile, but in time that piled-up air became a barrier. Surmounting that barrier required a redesign of both the airframe and its power plant.

Something like this is occurring in our approach to governance. We have pushed problems ahead of us as we made real progress, and we succeeded in the long-run in not only creating a barrier to future progress but also in jeopardizing our achievements to this point.

Hence two chapters below constitute in effect a primer on political theory for OD. In sum, these chapters propose that "doing better-than-average" in OD in the public sector requires dealing with major barriers posed by our dominant political theory. Two very long chapters of this book seek to chip away at that barrier via a demonstration previously not attempted in any detail.

The burden-of-proof in those two chapters is heavy. Basically, the chapters argue that the two historic ways of coupling Administration and Democracy in our political theory have been paradoxical and disingenuous. In introductory preview, an autocratic Administration was subordinated to, and put in the service of, republican institutions.

The fit never was very comfortable, and of late it chafes more and more. That much we know, and can demonstrate in great detail.

The task that remains is one of disciplined radicalism. The radical goal is to move decisively toward a more compatible pairing of the two central concepts, Democracy and Administration. The discipline derives from several sources. The movement should occur in tempo with the growing competence and confidence in OD, as expanding practice and theory permit doing so with some safety and predictability. In addition, the focus is on approaches that demonstrate a promise of meeting employee as well as organizational needs.

Part of this task of conceptual reconstruction seems obvious enough. In earlier elaborations of Democracy and Adminstration·we generated intellectual problems with our heads—and, I judge, with our fears—and we must try to unmake those problems in the light of what we now know, in the context of conditions and knowledge that have changed substantially since those natal days. This involves doing better than we did then—"then" being the turn of the present century for most practical purposes, but with clear precedents that in essence extended back to the early 1800s.[7]

This book proposes that various OD designs now permit an approach toward a new concept of Administration which fits more comfortably with our republican traditions. Much remains to be learned about OD applications in the public sector, but more than enough practice and theory have been accumulated to get that future work off to a great running start.

D. How Can Public-Sector OD Do Better-than-Average?

A final cluster of two chapters seeks to respond to these multiple motivators to do better in public-sector OD. Those chapters seek to assimilate past OD practice, for the explicit purposes of transcending that experience and improving on it.

How to do better, specifically? The two chapters in this cluster emphasize a large number of guidelines for the OD intervenor in the public sector. These guidelines come in two packages, as it were. The chapters describe the "texture" of the public-sector environment, and then draw implications from experience as to how intervenors might behave successfully in that environment. These are not easy tasks.

III. THE BOOK'S DOMINANT DUALITY

Viewed from another and briefer perspective, this book reflects a dominant duality concerning OD in the public sector. This book is an end in several central senses; and yet I have the undeniable sense of another beginning as I write these words.

A. Coming to an End . . .

In what senses is this book an end, at least of Round I? The preview above of the contents suggests some such closure—a definite even if tentative and far-from-complete staking-out of what it will take to humanize public organizations.

B. Contributing to A Beginning . . .

Perhaps more essentially than being an end, and certainly in addition to it being an end of something, this book constitutes a take-off, another beginning. Perhaps better said, this book signals a kind of Round 2 in a very serious fight, perhaps *the* fight. If we cannot humanize our public worksites, in sum, it seems at least doubtful whether our republican political traditions will thrive, perhaps even survive.

So the stakes here seem high enough to make credible the investment represented by this book, despite very real costs of trying to provide an overview of OD state-of-the art in the public sector.

Four major components of the cost/benefit analysis deserve brief note. *First*, the tone of this book is up-beat—an informed realism with an optimistic thrust, hopefully. Most of the existing public-sector work on OD has a far more sober quality, even when it is not unredemptively depressed. From the perspective of this book, this downcast literature stands a good chance of snatching defeat from the jaws of victory.

Second, no one has put together the comprehensive case for public-sector OD. To be sure, I made a modest effort several years ago,[8] but the literature—and my thinking, I trust—have made major leaps since then. Moreover, that earlier effort did not have the support of the bulk of the work underlying this volume, which was still in-development as that earlier book was being written and began wending its way toward publication.

Third, any work that is a beginning/end has mixed attractions. The "good news," of course, is that this book may help make some useful things happen, and sooner than they might have. The "bad news?" Even if the basic thesis here is correct, developments quickly will both overwhelm and undermine what is set down here. If the basic thesis is inappropriate, of course, this book will only add to the confusion and babble.

Fourth, so why undertake such an effort? A synthesis like this one has its many faults, to put it directly, whose many painful features are very real but still remain less painful than not attempting the synthesis. To paraphrase Churchill's comment about representative government, the approach here taken is the worst possible option, except for all the other major options. What are some of these faults?

- work in the several areas-to-be-synthesized will be uneven

- the attempted integration will be characterized by jagged "seams" and "gaps" because "things don't quite fit"

- materials initially used for one purpose will be modified or adapted for another, which may test the patience of assiduous readers who read "something like it" someplace else; but that must be risked because such materials can be omitted here only at major cost to the full argument

- parts of the synthesis will be "old hat" for some, and too detailed or technical or abstruse for others

But so be it.

FOOTNOTES

[1]For a thoughtful example, see Herbert Kaufman, *The Limits of Organizational Change* (University, AL: University of Alabama Press, 1971).

[2]Elting E. Morrison, "Gunfire at Sea: A Case Study of Innovation," in Elting E. Morrison, *Men, Machines, and Modern Times* (Cambridge, MA: MIT Press), 17-44. This article first appeared as "A Case Study of Innovation," in *The Engineering and Science Monthly* (April 1950).

[3]An early expression of this point of view is in James M. Buchanan and Gordon Tullock, *The Calculus of Consent* (Ann Arbor: University of Michigan Press, 1962). For

an elaboration and extension, see Anthony Downs, *Inside Bureaucracy* (Boston: Little, Brown, 1967).

[4]C. Northcote Parkinson, *Parkinson's Laws* (Boston: Houghton Mifflin, 1957).

[5]To sample the available general sources, see W. Warner Burke, *Organization Development* (Boston: Little, Brown, 1982); Wendell French and Cecil H. Bell, Jr., *Organization Development* (Englewood Cliffs, N.J.: Prentice-Hall, 1978); Robert T. Golembiewski, *Approaches to Planned Change*, *Vols. 1* and *2* (New York: Marcel Dekker, Inc., 1979); and Edgar H. Huse, *Organization Development and Change* (St. Paul, MN: West Publishing Co., 1980). For a concise review of OD's reach-and-grasp, from which the present characterization borrows, see Glenn M. Parker, "OD: Back to Basics," in Matt M. Starcevich, editor, *Organization Development* (Washington, DC: American Society for Training and Development, 1984), 9-14.

[6]Concerns about—or perhaps even despair concerning—public-sector OD interventions get reflected clearly in W. Warner Burke, "Organization Development and Bureaucracy of the 1980s," *Journal of Applied Behavioral Science* 16 (September 1980): 423-437.

[7]See Robert T. Golembiewski, "Organizing Public Work, Round Three: Toward A New Balance of Political Agendas and Management Perspectives," in Robert T. Golembiewski and Aaron Wildavsky, editors, *The Costs of Federalism* (New Brunswick, NJ: Transaction, 1984); 237-270.

[8]Robert T. Golembiewski, *Public Administration as A Developing Discipline* (New York: Marcel Dekker, Inc., 1977), esp. *Part 2*.

PART A

What is Tough About Public Sector Change?

CHAPTER I: Theorizing About Why Public-Sector
OD Can't Be Done: Some Real
and Confounding Constraints

CHAPTER I

THEORIZING ABOUT WHY PUBLIC-SECTOR OD CAN'T BE DONE: SOME REAL AND CONFOUNDING CONSTRAINTS

Although the balance has been rectified of late, the early literature contains as much armchair theorizing about why OD applications in the public sector present unique if not insurmountable problems, as the literature contains examples of OD applications. Even when an application succeeds, plenty of theorizing encourages looking at that success as a fluke, as the exception that proves the rule, or as showing only that even a blind pig will sometimes find acorns if only it roots around long enough.

A good deal of this hand-wringing derives from ignorance about the OD literature, but do not disparage the power of armchair theorizing. Some people love some theories so much that they cannot be shaken loose from them, even when experience suggests the theory is inadequate or just plain wrong. The Germans had a phrase for it. So what if the facts, if experience, contradict a theory?: "... *desto slecher für die tatsache.*" That is, so much the worse for the facts.

This chapter looks at two basic and related ways of theorizing about the public sector that have made it so much the worse for OD. The focus, in turn, will shift between

- the broad institutional features characteristic of the public sector

- the related but narrower management system of public agencies operating within the broad institutional framework

I. INSTITUTIONAL CONSTRAINTS ON OD APPLICATIONS[1]

If somewhat arbitrarily, this analysis distinguishes institutional features of the public sector as "structure" and "habit." In broad terms, structure and habit interact so as to complicate OD applications in the public sector. We isolate them here only to simplify analysis.

One significant if preliminary point needs underscoring here. This chapter describes these constraints rather than wishing they did not exist. Indeed, many observers maintain that not only *is* public-sector OD more difficult than that in the private sector, but also that *it should be*. Effectiveness, representativeness, and responsiveness are far more significant in the public sector, these observers argue, and they often require sacrifices in conventional efficiency. Indeed, this line of argument proposes, even substantial inefficiency is a cheap price to pay for a polity that is representative and responsive. For example, some observers point to the significant role of political parties in our scheme of government, and they also would emphasize that at certain points their development was aided by (if not critically dependent on) graft and corruption.

Note also that the focus here is on the Federal government. However the tone of the presentation as well as many of the details apply with substantially-equivalent force at many levels of government.

A. Structural Constraints on Approaching OD Objectives

Public agencies present some distinctive challenges to OD programs, as compared with business organizations where most experience with OD programs has been accumulated. Five structural properties of the public institutional environment particularly complicate achieving the common goals of OD programs.

1. Multiple Access to Multiple Authorities

As compared to even the largest international businesses, the public environment in this country is characterized by what might be called, following David Truman, unusual opportunities for *multiple access to multiple authoritative decision-makers*. Multiple access is, in intention if not always in effect, a major way of helping to assure that public business gets looked at from a variety of perspectives. Hence the purpose here is to look at the effects of multiple access rather than to deprecate it. Figure 1 details some major points of multiple access relevant to OD programs in four interacting systems—the executive,

FIGURE 1. Some Critical Publics Relevant to Federal OD Programs

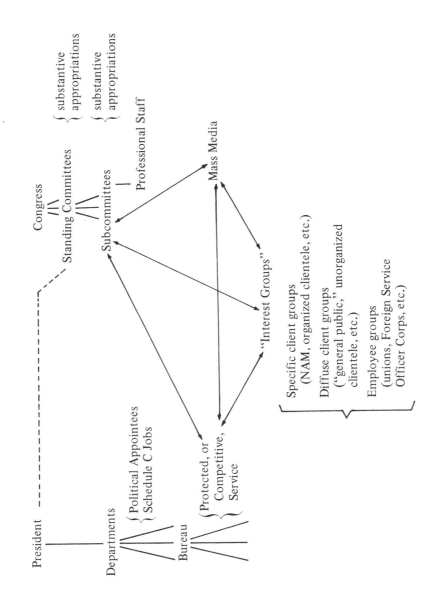

legislative, special interests, and mass media systems. This may be thought of as an "iron quadrangle," and it refers to those multiple sub-systemic units—the "little groups of policy neighbors"—that are so critical in public policy-making.[2] Indeed, some argue that these hardy clusters "run the government," in effect.

Multiple access has its attractive features in beginning OD programs in public agencies. For example, one large OD program was inaugurated in an economical way: top departmental career official sponsoring an OD program had developed a relation of deep trust with the chairman and the professional staff of a Congressional appropriations subcommittee, and that relationship quickly, even mercurially, triumphed over lukewarm support or even opposition from the department head, the then-Bureau of the Budget, and the predecessor of the present Office of Personnel Management. So it became "go" for Project ACORD, or Action for Organization Development, in the U.S. Department of State.

But multiple access can cut two ways. Funds for that very OD program "became unavailable" after its inception, despite strong support from both career and political officers at the top levels. In short, the successful counter-attack was launched by agency personnel in the protected service, an interest group representing these employees, members of a concerned substantive committee of Congress, and the media.

The two themes of the counter-attack were common to several reactions against OD programs. *First*, ordinary decency required allowing the dedicated civil servants affected to complete their careers in peace and in the traditional ways, rather than being subjected to an unwanted program that was seen as having problematic value.[3] *Second*, the use of sensitivity training in the OD program was disparaged as violating the privacy of organization members, or worse.[4]

Viewed from the perspective of top-level political and career officials intent on inaugurating a public OD program, the iron quadrangle in Figure 1 inspires substantial pessimism about a fair trial, in the general case. Specific conditions may raise or lower the odds, since the several links in the counter-attacking forces above can be variously strong or weak. For example, a public agency may have a very positive image, which gives its top officials an important edge in presenting their case to Congressional committees, the mass media, or the general public. Similarly, top political and career officials can induce—or can capitalize on—organized clientele opposition to policies and procedures and use it to force changes at the protected levels. Or political resources and professional skills may provide agency executives with substantial power to control their environment.[5]

Whether the iron quadrangle is more or less integral, the design and implementation of OD programs in public agencies has given that constellation short shrift. Perhaps this is because most early experience with OD programs has been gained in business organizations, where nothing even remotely like the iron quadrangle exists at managerial levels. Consistently, also, most OD experience has dealt with the more straightforward authoritative situations: e.g., with non-union contexts where by definition a major competing authoritative source for employees is not present.

2. Variety of Interests and Reward Structures

Again as compared to business organizations, the public arena involves in all OD programs a greater variety of individuals and groups with *different and often mutually exclusive sets of interests, reward structures, and values.* In the case outlined above, for example, the appropriations subcommittee was interested in improved operations and reduced costs. But the substantive subcommittee was concerned more with safeguarding program and personnel with which they had developed a strong identification. And never the twain did meet, although both committees were "in Congress." Role conflicts between legislators and administrators also seem to have been significant. For example, one Congressman explained his opposition to an OD program in these terms: "Improvement of efficiency is OK, but messing with people's attitudes sounds subversive to my constituents." The agency's top administrators felt no such constituency pressure, and their view was that attitudes toward work had to be changed.

Note two points. Such incongruencies of expectations, rewards, and values also occur in business organizations, of course, as in labor-management issues or when an active board of directors asserts itself. In my experience, however, they occur there in less intense and exotic forms. Moreover, although one can easily make sport of the public sector as "chaotic" and "disorganized," those features can contribute to government's openness and effectiveness in the broadest sense of increasing the popular support for a regime.

A conclusion need not be forced. All OD programs have to stress the development of viable "interfaces," that is, relations between individuals or groups with different values and interests. This problem is enormously complicated in public agencies undertaking OD programs, and has received little explicit attention in concept or in practice. For example, in only very few cases has the development of an explicit interface between legislative and administrative interests been attempted as part of an OD program, apparently in part because of the constitutional separation of powers.[6]

The point does not suffer for lack of supporting evidence. The failure to build such interfaces was a major contributor to the death of an urban OD program. Departmental officers rejected the idea of attempting to build into an OD program an explicit interface between a substantive sub-committee, an appropriations sub-committee, and the agency. Tradition, jealousy over prerogatives, and separation of powers were blamed, and with good reason. But it also seemed that departmental officials preferred things as they were. The lack of integration between sub-committees, perhaps, provided alternative routes of access for friends-and-neighbors; and that "looseness" also gave departmental officials some room to operate.

Hopefully, the paragraphs above do not get interpreted as unavoidable inevitabilities. Those paragraphs seek to emphasize the need to build interfaces, as well as the difficulty of doing so. Those interfaces can be, and have been, built. The substantial success rates for public-sector OD reviewed in the next three chapters imply such success, for example. And two other clusters of chapters dwell on why and how even greater success can be accomplished.

Nonetheless, the present point still remains: the OD intervenor will do well to emphasize the building of interfaces, as well as to give priority to those situtations in which a strong mutuality of interests predisposes building bridges across sometimes-troubled waters.

3. Command Linkages and Competing Identifications/Affiliations

The "chain of command" within public agencies, as compared to business and service organizations, is more likely to be characterized by *competing identifications and affiliations*. Again the difference is one of degree, but it approaches one of kind. Consider only one aspect of the integrity of command linkages common in business organizations. In them, typically, "management" is separated from "labor" only very far down the hierarchy, at or near the level of the first-line supervisor.

Moreover, the common identification of all levels of management often is stressed. "Management," moreover, commonly does not enjoy the kind of job security that can come from union contracts. One of the effects of such carrots and sticks, without question, is the more facile implementation of policy changes at all levels of organization.

Hierarchy has its effects in public agencies as well as businesses, but the chain of command seems less integral. Thus a unique family of implications alternative to the hierarchy exists at levels both low and high in public agencies, the apparent underlying motivation being to maximize the probability that evil will not occur, or at least will be found out. That is, the chain of command at the Federal level is subject to strong fragmenting forces even up to the highest levels, where political and career strata blend into one another. For example, the ideal of a wall-to-wall civil service is approached closely in practice, and it provides a strong countervailing identification to the executive chain of command. Career officials are "out of politics," but their commitments to programs may be so strong as to inhibit or even thwart executive direction.[7] Similarly, President Carter encouraged whistle-blowing in Federal agencies, ostensibly as simply another method of assuring that the public business gets done in ways that maximize the visibility and porosity of the process.[8]

That the public institutional environment permits (indeed, encourages) a fragmenting of the management hierarchy at points well up in the higher levels may be illustrated in three ways. *First*, the "neutrality" of civil servants has been a major defensive issue in at least two Federal OD programs in which I have participated, and OD efforts have been painted by many career people as sophisticated but lustful raids on a chaste protected service. *Second*, Congress is an old hand at creating countervailing identifications so as to enhance its control over administration,[9] for which the Constitution and tradition provide a solid rationale. *Third*, the Executive has also played the game, sometimes unwittingly. Consider the presidential-inspired Federal Executive Boards, some of which achieved a substantial measure of potency in the 1960s. Basically, these Boards were intended to be a horizontal link between field units of Federal agencies, as well as vertical links between the presidency and top career field officialdom. The FEB's provided career field managers with a potential way to supplement or even avoid departmental reporting relations, by-passing both career employees and political appointees. Indeed, President Kennedy may have intended them as just such a by-pass around "the feudal barons of the permanent government" whom he saw as major obstacles to change. [10]

A conclusion flows easily. Congress often encourages slack in the executive chain of command to facilitate its oversight of the President and his major appointees; and the Executive as well as the protected service often uses the same strategy. The integrity of the executive chain of command suffers, consequently.

How to evalute this sieve-like quality? From one perspective, the sieve permits numerous points of access, which has its attractive featues in a representative system which rests on the consent of the governed. Looked at more narrowly, this public sector quality certainly does limit the ability of public executives in initiating (for example) OD programs. [11] Witness the furor over the mere handful of Schedule C jobs removed from the protected service during President Eisenhower's first term to permit greater executive leverage. The question remains as to whether President Carter was more successful in his efforts to create a mobile core of senior administrators, which proposal was tied to attractive rewards intended to stimulate cooperation. [12]

Whatever the future brings us in this particular, one major conclusion seems safe enough. The motivation to avoid "spoils politics" helps explain much caution in such personnel matters, but managerial rigidity is the other side of the coin. Herbert Kaufman concludes that although extensions of the civil service were intended to provide upper-level political administrators with capable help, the latter have often been driven to "pray for deliverance from their guardians." [13]

4. Weak Linkages Between Political and Career Levels

Exacerbating the point above, the *linkages between political and career levels* are weak as a consequence of a variety of features of the public institutional environment. [14] This slippage between managerial levels significantly complicates beginning and implementing OD programs, and severely challenges the linkage of executive management with operating management.

The generalization concerning weak linkages in the managerial chain of command is meant to apply in four distinct senses. *First,* political and career levels often are weakly linked due to the brief tenure of the former.

Second, the job of linking the political leadership and the permanent bureaucracy must be handled by a tiny group of executives having diverse allegiance to the chief executive.

Third, there is reason to suspect significant slippage between the top officialdom and lower levels. For example, what lower-level careerists see as necessary protections of tenure, top career officials often perceive as cumbersome limitations on managerial flexibility. And both can be *correct*.

Fourth, the executive often weakens its own managerial linkages, as it seeks sometimes-unreconcilable political and administrative goals. Thus the unionization of public employees has been encouraged by presidential executive order. But one of the groups of Federal employees to organize were inspectors in the then-U.S. Civil Service Commission, which would be seen as "management" in most business organizations.

OD programs consequently are faced with the issue of somehow interfacing political and career linkages which powerful forces—constitutional, political, and historic—tend to pull apart. Consider only one dilemma. The general rule-of-thumb is that OD programs should begin "at the top" of organizational hierarchies, or as close to the top as possible. The rationale is obvious: that is where power often can be tapped-into most conveniently in business organizations. Respecting this rule-of-thumb in public agencies raises multidimensional dilemmas.

Basically, "the top" in public agencies is more complex than in most businesses. Initiating an OD program at the level of the political leadership maximizes formal executive support, but it may also raise complex problems. Support of the OD program is problematic because of frequent personnel changes at that level,[15] because of possible well-entrenched resistance from the permanent service, because legislators may fear that any strengthening of the executive chain of command would only mean fewer points of access and sources of information, and because employee associations may resist executive direction. Relying more on support from those in the protected service maximizes the changes of permanent support, and it may raise Congressional trust in the program. But this approach also may encourage executive resistance.

The OD specialist faces real dilemmas, then, in choosing the "top" of the hierarchy at which to direct his interventions. I have participated in change programs that have taken both approaches to seeking a power-base, and they show only that avoiding Scylla seems to imply meeting Charybdis. The ideal is to appeal to both the political officialdom and the permanent service, of course, but that is a demanding ideal indeed:

5. Public Sector As a Serious Merry-Go-Round

Reinforcing these first four structural properties of the institutional environment within public agencies function, a "cycle of governance" can be distinguished in our political-administrative history. Periodically, as Kaufman notes, three definite emphases in the overall goal of public administration seem to alternate: [16]

- *representativeness*, which implies a primacy of legislative inputs into administration, but can also be reflected in determined recruitment patterns mandated by an aggressive judiciary

- *politically-neutral competence*, in which the emphasis is put on ways to shield public agents from diverse influences—legislatures, political executives, political parties, and so on.

- *executive leadership*, in which the needs of political executives—presidents and governors, plus their institutional selves in executive offices—dominate

Kaufman does not advise thinking of these emphases in all-or-nothing terms. Rather, he sees complicated mixtures of them operating all of the time, with some periods being characterized by a definite emphasis on one or another of the trio. A definite central tendency—a mood, or zeitgeist, or whatever, as with the "imperial presidency"—may develop. "At different points in time," Kaufman explains, "enough people (not necessarily a numerial majority) will be persuaded by one or another of these discontents to support remedial action—increased representativeness, better and politically neutral bureaucracies, or stronger chief executives, as the case may be." This choice-process has no end, since no totally-satisfying resolution of the involved macro-issues has been invented or—probably better put—no always-satisfying resolution is possible. Thus Kaufman observes: ". . . the constant shift in emphasis goes on."

This three-phase cycle of governance has obvious and profound implications for OD, especially for comprehensive applications that have long lead-times. Thus OD seems most compatible with an emphasis on a professionally-competent and politically-neutral public service. But legislators and political executives will not simply play dead-dog forever, however tidy and convenient that might be to some. Indeed, they *should not* play dead-dog, if we mean to preserve our representative system in anything like a viable form.

The basic target of public administrative arrangements keeps changing kaleidoscopically, as it were, with various intensities and durations. Some such effect often operates in business organizations—as in oscillations between relatively centralized and more decentralized patterns—but the public sector has no close competitor in this regard.

An In-Process Summary

In summary, these five structural properties of the institutional environment of public agencies complicate attaining the objectives of typical OD programs. Consider the objective of building trust among individuals and groups throughout the organization. Technically, viable interfaces should be created between political officials, the permanent bureaucracy, Congressional committees and their staffs, and so on and on. Practically, this is a very tall order, especially because the critical publics tend to have mutually-exclusive interests, values, and reward systems. Indeed, although it is easy to caricature the point, Congress has a definite interest in cultivating a certain level of distrust within and between government agencies so as to encourage a flow of information. This may seem a primitive approach but, in the absence of valid and reliable measures of performance, it may be a necessary approach. No OD program in a business organization will face such an array of hurdles, that much is certain.

B. Habit Constraints on Approaching OD Objectives

The "habit background" in the public sector interacts in complex ways with these five structural properties so as to create serious obstacles to approaching OD objectives. "Habit background" is perhaps better illustrated than defined, and illustration certainly comes easier. Five aspects of this habit background are considered below, by way of illustrating their impact on OD objectives. These five aspects do not comprise an exclusive list, and they are conceived of only as general patterns and behaviors which give a definite flavor to the public institutional environment sketched above. But no OD intervention can neglect these five constraints inherent in the public-sector habit background.

1. Limited Delegation and Layering

In my experience, public officials tend to favor patterns of delegation that maximize their sources of information and minimize the control exercised by subordinates. Specifically, many public-sector officials seek to have decisions brought to their level for action or review. The most common concrete concomitants of this tendency are functional specialization and a narrow span of control. One of the major consequences is a large number of replicative levels of review. [17]

"Layering" of multiple levels of review is not unique to public administration—indeed, it inheres in generally-accepted organization theory—but it is supported by forces more or less unique to public agencies that have been powerful enough to substantially curtail innovation of ways to centralize policy and to decentralize operations. [18] The protection of the "public interest" is one such unique factor, for example. The rationale is familiar. [19] Political officials of short tenure often cannot rely on established relations of confidence with personnel at lower levels, nor do they exercise as much control over career rewards-and-punishments as is common in business organizations or in the military. However, the legislature will hold the political officials responsible. Consequently, political officials seek to maximize information sources and minimize the control exercisable by subordinates. This tendency is reinforced by law and tradition so that it permeates down the hierarchy throughout the permanent bureaucracy. The tendency is often referred to as "keeping short lines of command."

Keeping chains of command short implies constraints on approaching OD objectives in public organizations, based on my experience as well as the logic of the situation. Consider only two OD objectives:

— to locate decision-making and problem-solving responsibilities as close to the information sources as possible; and

— to increase self-control and self-direction for people within the
organization.

To the degree that the rough distinction above is accurate, public
agencies will experience difficulties in approaching both objectives. The
prevailing habit pattern in public agencies patently constitutes a tide to
swim against in these two particulars, although there are outstanding
exceptions to this generalization.

2. Legalities and Legalism

Again only as a description of what exists, legal patterns make
approaching OD objectives severely more difficult in public agencies
than in business organizations. [20] The point applies in two major
senses. Thus patterns of administrative delegation are often specified in
minute detail in legislation, basically so as to facilitate oversight by the
legislature. To be sure, we are a considerable distance beyond the first
Morgan case, which seemed to argue that only administrative actions
personally taken by, or under the direct supervision of, a department
head were constitutionally defensible. But flexibility in delegation is
still a major problem. Perhaps more important, a corpus of law and
standard practice exists which also makes it difficult to achieve OD
objectives. For example, considering only those employees on the
General Schedule, salary and duties are tied to a position classification
system whose underlying model emphasizes transdepartmental
uniformity and compensation for individual work. [21]

The legal habit background complicates approaching OD values.
Thus efforts to achieve OD objectives may run afoul of the possibility
that relocating responsibilities in one agency is considered to have
systemwide implications, with consequences that complicate the
making of local adjustments. As one official noted of an OD effort in
such straits: "I feel like I have to raise the whole civil service by my
bootstraps." Relatedly, one common OD objective seeks:

— to supplement the authority associated with role or status with
the authority of knowledge and competence.

This is hard to do to the degree that a specific pattern of delegation is
required by law. The same point applies to any rigidities due to the

duties classification common in public agencies in the United States, and especially to the concepts for assigning authority and for organizing work underlying the duties classification. Job enlargement begun as part of OD programs has run afoul of such concepts, for example.

At the bread-and-butter level, existing legal patterns also inhibit approaching OD objectives. Consider the common OD objective which proposes:

— to develop a reward system which recognizes both the achievement of the organization's mission and organization development.

Existing law and practice severely limit the search for such a reward system, although the 1979 changes in our public personnel policies motivated by President Carter seek some such outcome for senior civil servants.[22]

In general, in any case, rewards for exceptional performance—in money payments or in higher-than-normal GS levels for personnel in the civil service—are now possible, but they still are exceptional in practice. Equal pay for equal work, in sum, still practically means that exceptional work is not rewarded exceptionally. Management in business organizations typically has far greater control over reward systems, and especially at managerial levels. Specifically, the top public administrative salaries in the Federal government seem to be capped by a curious if potent resolve: those salaries should be no higher than those paid to top legislative staff on Congressional committees. Legislative vs. executive prerogatives clearly inspire such a convention.

Perhaps even more of a problem, neither existing law nor practice promise much in the way of support for various group compensation plans. Experiments in industry with some such plans have yielded attractive results.

3. Need for Security or Secrecy

The need for security or even secrecy in public agencies as against business organizations is more likely to be strong enough to present obstacles to approaching OD objectives. Military and defense agencies come to mind first, but they hardly exhaust the list. The "need for security" as used here can concern national security, it can be induced by a general anxiety born of a need to make significant decisions whose results will not be manifest for a very long time, or it can derive from felt-needs for protection from such outside forces as a Congressman with fire in his eye.[23] The need can also be real, exaggerated, or even imagined in various combinations.

Consider one case, which seemed to reflect some of all of these components. Agency personnel were exposed to sensitivity training, one of whose major purposes is to increase skills in being open about both positive and negative emotions or reactions. The training staff provided several settings in which these intentions might be approached, one of which was a "park bench." During one week of sensitivity training some time was set aside each evening for a meeting of all participants in a large room whose center contained the "park bench." But agency personnel seldom used the arena, although there was a good deal of nervous laughter from the periphery of the "park." After some three abortive tries of an hour each, one participant approached me. "I see the point of the thing," he said, "but a park bench is all wrong." Suddenly, the dawn came. "Park benches" were seen as stereotypic sites for sexual assignations and/or for exchanging secrets with enemy agents. Without doubt, some participants thought the "park bench" a silly notion, and hence did not participate. For most participants, however, the symbolism was so compelling that they could not use the "park bench." Moreover, many agency personnel were so closed, distrustful, and fearful of taking a risk that they could not talk about their guiding symbolism, even if they were aware of it.

This greater need for security cannot be established concretely, and it will certainly vary from case to case and agency to agency. But this much seems patent: to the degree the need exists so are OD objectives more difficult to reach. Consider only this OD objective:

— to create an open, problem-solving climate throughout the organization.

An open climate and a great need for security or for secrecy do not mix well.

4. Procedural Regularity and Caution

For a variety of reasons, government personnel are also rather likely to stress procedural regularity and caution. Perhaps better said, even if agency personnel are convinced that certain heuristics provide solutions that are "good enough," this conviction may conflict with other (and especially legislative) needs for external control. For example, sample checking of vouchers was widely accepted as an efficient-enough administrative approach long before relevant publics in Congress and the General Accounting Office recognized it as appropriate for their control purposes.

Good reasons support this bias toward procedural regularity and caution in public agencies, of course, and so much the worse for OD objectives. For example, the bias patently runs against the grain of the OD objective which seeks:

— to help managers to manage according to relevant objectives rather than according to "past practices," or according to objectives that do not make sense for one's area of responsibility.

The underlying rub, of course, is that a "past practice" making little or no sense administratively may seem an utter necessity from the legislative point of view. To be sure, the dictum "where you sit determines what you see" applies to all organizations. But the needs and identifications of administrators and legislators are likely to differ more than in the case for (let us say) the executives and middle managers of a business organization.

5. Sense of the "Professional Manager"

The concept "professional manager" is less developed in the public arena, in rough but useful contrast, and that has major implications for successful OD applications. OD has few attractions for "spoils management," or for what might be called "political management."

What evidence suggests a less-developed sense of the professional manager in the public sector? The fact that the emergence of degree programs in public administration lagged behind the burgeoning of business schools—by several decades, at least—suggests the conclusion.[24] So also do the Jacksonian notions deep at the roots of our basic public personnel policies. For example, the "career system" notion has been a difficult one to develop in this country at the Federal level. No small part of the difficulty derives from the value we place on an "open service" with lateral entry. Hence the tendency of our public personnel policies to emphasize hiring for a specific position rather than for long-run potential.

Derivations from these taproots have had profound impact. For example, to simplify a little, massive Federal attention to training was long delayed by the wrigglesworthian legislative notion that, since the Federal service was hiring people who already had the abilities to do the specific job for which they were hired, there was little need to spend money on training. [25] The relative attractiveness of public employment at the Federal level at least through World War II provided the proverbial finger in the dike, but conditions changed much faster than did public policy. Instructively, also, the system of regional executive development centers manned by the U.S. Civil Service Commission began as late as 1964, and then only with a miniscule budget and against substantial congressional opposition. Roughly, business has a 10-20 year lead over government in acting on the need for training. Not very long ago, in contrast, the Federal government was considered *the* model employer.

The relatively lesser stress on the "public professional manager" implies significant problems for approaching OD objectives. Thus one common OD objective proposes:

— to increase the sense of "ownership" of organization objectives throughout the work force.

No sharp contrast is appropriate. But a definite bias of public personnel policy limits such a sense of identification with, and commitment to, public agencies. If there is one thing most civil service reformers did not want, it was a public work force who "owned" the objectives of their agency. The only "owner" was the public; the model employee was a politically-neutral technician who repressed his own values in return for guaranteed tenure. Only thus could an elite and unresponsive bureaucracy be avoided, goes a major theme shot through our public personnel policies and institutions. This may seem like an extreme point of view, but it has many reflections in practice and scholarship. Consider Victor Thompson's *Without Sympathy or Enthusiasm*. This would seem a curious title for a book prescribing a public managerial role-model, and I can hardly imagine it being written for a business audience. But Thompson emphasizes that many see such emotional flatness as the major bulwark against a technocratic take-over of what only the public owns.

II. MANAGEMENT-LEVEL CONSTRAINTS ON OD APPLICATIONS

After having looked through a macro-scope in the section above, let us strive for a view of greater resolution that has less scope. We focus on the management level, in contrast to the institutional level just emphasized. On occasion, some might see great overlap between these two "levels." Not to worry on that score here. The distinction only serves as an organizing convenience. Again, or still, the focus remains constant: What public-sector features imply that OD can be done there only with far greater skill and good fortune, if at all?

Estimates of the differences between public and business management vary among observers, but few deny that institutional locus has an appreciable impact. For example, the late Wallace S. Sayre concluded that "business and government administration are alike in all unimportant respects." [26] Others note that critical differences typically exist between how the public and business sectors view the critical issues—those concerning people, purposes, and organization. [27] Generally, the differences make OD applications in the public sector more chancy, more complex, as three perspectives on those differences suggest:

- the different "games" characteristic of the two sectors

- the different conditions the two sets of administrators typically encounter

- the different cultures characteristic of the public and private sectors

A. Differences in the Ecology of Games

From a basic perspective, the "ecology of games" tends to differ in the two loci. Broadly, the several parameters of the games differ in: the number of interests legitimately involved; the range of applicable facts and values; the visibility of issues and of the processes of their resolution; the degree to which technical or scientific determinations (when applicable) are subject to the processes of broad consensus-testing and development; and so on.

How to develop the fullness of this theme without herniating the reader? Two approaches will get some attention.

At quite a general level, Eddy and Saunders provide useful guidance as to how public-sector OD can be more difficult than applications in the private sector.[28] Perhaps the foremost obstacle to public-sector OD inheres in the probable incompatibility between political systems and the concept of the ideal organization underlying most OD efforts. Political systems seem *distributive* in thrust, they explain, in the normal order of things. For example, political systems often fixate on win-lose games, as in distributing a finite amount of resources among competing interest groups. Gains for one group typically imply losses for another, so strategies and tactics may emphasize mistrust, a certain exuberance in describing reality, and decisions that are more responsive to aggregations of power than to people or even problems. Multiple checks-and-balances in the public sector also often operate so as to create veto-points. Typically, no single, effective point of initiation exists.

OD ideology stresses the *integrative* character of the ideal organization, in contrast, which is more consistent with prevailing attitudes about well-functioning organizations in the private sector. As Eddy and Saunders explain: "Emphasis is placed on commonality of purpose, collaboration, and win-win relationships. Ways are sought to minimize win-lose competition among operating units, and to enhance shared problem solving and planning." Hence the "potential incompatibility" between the "ideal organization" in OD ideology and the way political systems operate, and are *intended to operate.*

Let us seek greater specificity via Weisbord's six-box model of management in the public sector.[29] Figure 2 sketches that model, and the reader should understand that each box has both a formal and informal aspect. That is, the organization may solemnly legitimate certain specifics that, in reality, never get done and never were intended to be done. Or some very important things may actually happen even though they are not formally provided for; indeed, they may be explicitly prohibited.

Using Weisbord's model, Goodstein argues that public agencies differ markedly from business, in the aggregate.[30] Actually, Goodstein

FIGURE 2. A Model of Management

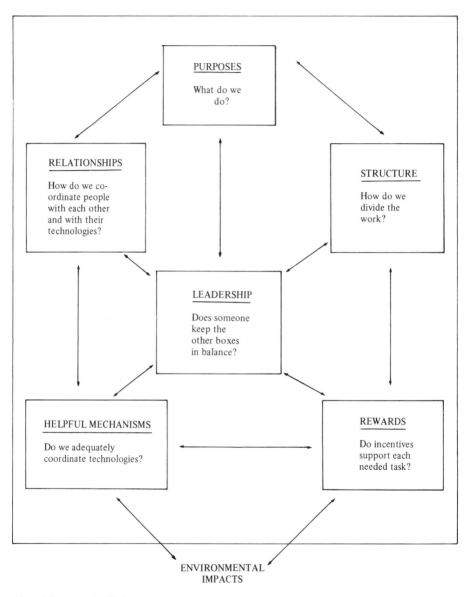

Adapted from: Marvin Weisbord, "Organizational Diagnosis: Six Places to Look for Trouble With or Without a Theory," *Group and Organization Studies,* Vol. 1 (December 1976), p. 430.

restricts his analysis of "human service organizations," or HSOs—
schools, welfare departments, and the like. So his focus is narrower
than all public agencies, but his analysis still reveals the genre.
Basically, Goodstein argues that—begin where you will with the boxes
in Figure 2, providing you go all the way around—HSOs differ in at
least degree and probably in kind from other organizations, especially
because they are necessarily so reactive to powerful environmental
forces that often get exerted in multiple directions. To illustrate, HSOs
often will not know what business they are in. Legislatures may impose
a set of policy compromises on one or more agencies that attract a
sufficient constituency only by lumping together irreconcilable
objectives. Witness that while the Rural Electrification Administration
was trying to make farm life more bearable for all, respecting one
legislative mandate, the Department of Agriculture in keeping with
another legislative mandate was trying to depose people from some of
the very farmland that REA was assiduously making more attractive.
Businesses are far less likely to experience such confusion about goals,
as their carping about OSHA, Affirmative Action, and so on, imply.
And the ripples-of-effects spread broadly. As Goodstein concludes:[31]

> ... in most human service delivery systems the goals are not clear, managers
> have difficulty in deciding whether or not the contributions of staff facilitate
> the goals, and, further, see themselves as unable to provide rewards because
> of the limitations of the bureaucratic system in which they find themselves.
> Thus, most workers in the human services area feel that their efforts are
> unrewarded, and this has very severe negative consequences on performance.

B. Differences in Dominant Conditions

Public managers also tend to face conditions that differ in at least
degree, and sometimes in kind, from those facing their private-sector
counterparts. To rely on Bower,[32] public managers more frequently

- deal with definitions of goals or purposes that are set or
  influenced by multiple external authorities—such as legislatures
  or courts—at many levels of government, that share neither
  common power-bases nor priorities

- operate within structures mandated or designed by external and
  very distant authorities

- work with people whose careers and even immediate job performance are beyond the present management's control or even ability to influence

- face the need to achieve their goals in brief time-frames, due to short-lived political majorities or the abbreviated tenure of political appointees

Each of these points of difference could be spun-out in detail, but one example concerning locus may illustrate and amuse. I recall discussing managerial differences with the head of a large hospital sponsored by a religious order. One difference was elemental and profound: "You can't fire a nun," the executive articulated the basic factor limiting her decisions.

C. Differences in Characteristic Cultures

Whether the public and private sectors vary only in degree or in kind, they may usefully be thought of as "two cultures," if one does not push the point too far and remains willing to allow for exceptions. With apologies to C.P. Snow, then, consider only four features which tend to differentiate the private-sector culture from the public sector.

First, public-sector organizations tend to permit less wriggle-room, which often becomes not only a condition but also a crutch of employees. Although considerable lee-way may exist in public agencies at start-up, they are more likely to get more imbedded sooner and deeper, in what the vernacular marvelously refers to as "red tape"—system-wide personnel policies and procedures, complex relationships with monitoring legislatures or interests that mold and shape the agency, and so on. Many people disparage these restraints, or at least their severity and incidence in the public sector, while others praise them as necessary to permit even a tenuous degree of popular control through elected representatives.

This greater degree of restraint has kaleidoscopic effects, however viewed. It can bound behavior, as intended; but this restraint also often limits when it might better not, as when conditions require change. Moreover, this constraint can exert its influence even when it does *not exist*, through the expectations and past experiences of organization members shaped over the years. The point can be illustrated economically by emphsizing one kind of actor at a critical interface in local government—the city or county manager, who is in effect a hinge between political officialdom and the more-or-less permanent career bureaucracy. Typically, a city manager comes into a jurisdiction, more or less inheriting a workforce; he is role-defined as the agent of a policy-making council or other legislative unit; with expectations of moving on after (say) 3-5 years of service, either for a better opportunity or because of a political change; and the manager often arrives with significant mistrust of real or imagined local enemies temporarily taking a low profile. Such factors can have profound effects on managers, even when the conditions to which the factors may be appropriate no longer apply. For example:

> A new public agency had its executive levels staffed largely by ex-city managers, many of whom had yearned to "start up their own organization." The new freedom proved more bane than boon, however. Start-up proved more emotionally-draining and risky than the new executives had anticipated. And the past experiences of the new executives proved substantial hindrances on what they—now set free, as it were—did, and when, and how. The effects were mostly unconscious, and the limits were essentially mental rather than legal or historical; but they were nonetheless real for it.

> It took perhaps 12-18 months for things to shake themselves out. Several managers could not cope effectively with their new freedom, successful though they had been as managers. Major personnel changes were made; and several other members of the original executive team had to reorient their attitudes and behaviors, which proved a long and difficult task. And by then, some agency policies and practices had become more or less set in the same old concrete.

Second, the public sector has fewer external supports or reinforcers for effort, inventiveness, and risk-taking. The point can be bawdlerized easily, so let us be careful. Many public employees do work long and hard; and many private-sector employees twiddle away their hours. On balance, however, the public sector has fewer non-psychic reinforcers for extraordinary effort. Thus the eminently-just principle of "equal pay for equal work" often has come to mean in practice that holders of the same or similar public-sector jobs should be paid approximately the same, given some *minimum* level of performance. If seniority weighs heavily in promotion, as it very often does, public-sector employees can by their own efforts seldom significantly influence the reward-and-punishment system. Various forms of preferential hiring—veterans' preference, points for service-connected disability, and so on—

exacerbate such tendencies.

Very often, good and substantial reasons motivate such public personnel policies, but their negative effects still must be reckoned with. Not having to make decisions about bonuses or awards for superior performance does avoid charges of favoritism and arbitrariness, for example, but that also means superior performance will rest largely on psychic rewards and reinforcers. Looked at from another perspective, the lack of flexibility with reward systems may go a long way toward explaining the often-observed fixation of public officialdom on symbols of status, appurtenances of overt power such as titles, and so on.

Third, public-sector work provides special encouragement for the Dr. No Syndrome at management levels. Especially because much government work is regulatory and is, or should be, charged with a sense of the public interest, it often becomes all too easy to fall into the habit of generating reasons why actions cannot work, should not be undertaken, will be objected to by certain power figures, real or alleged, and so on and on. One case of public/private sector interaction illustrates forces in definite opposition, especially because the case was one in which the regulatory agency was bound and determined to provide super service. Space permits only characterizing a few of the polarities represented:

- public officials knew they were moving well in advance of their normal expectations, and had little patience with private-sector officials who stewed that each day of review meant a reduced competitive advantage

- public officials in their own view were raising significant issues long after their private sector counterparts had concluded a nit-picking phase had begun

- while public sector officials were nearing closure on their job, and hence feeling less pressure about delays, private-sector officials were with heightening anxiety looking forward to a very long process of training, promoting, and marketing, and even minor delays in authorization were seen as having profound effects on that effort

- while officials of the firm worked overtime to meet agency rush-order requests for data, certain major political activities preoccupied key public officials in the regulating agency, and decisions went unmade

- the two reward systems were significantly out-of-synchronization. Early action might be reflected in bonuses for key private-sector officials and profits for the firm, as well as in a spiritually-significant vindication of their long research and development effort. Public-sector officials were substantially cut-off from such positive inducements of early action. If anything, in fact, their system had a definite bias toward delaying action, which would at least provide the defense that "we tried everything we knew" should something somehow go amiss.

- the perceptual filters of the public-sector officials differed substantially from their counterparts, especially in the breadth of technical and political issues admitted to analysis, and in the tendency to test technical detail as to implications for multiple reference groups.

Note also that the character of regulatory activities can generate some exotic species of the Dr. No strain, to risk a very bad play on words. We can here only illustrate the wicked double-binds and objective dilemmas that can pose no-win situations for both regulator and regulated, creating chasms even when both may yearn for helpful integration.

In one regulatory agency, a certain authorization was delayed for 18 months beyond the target-date which was itself set so as to provide more-than-ample time for developing appropriate documentation. Despite impressive evidence that authorization should be granted, the official-in-charge was having marital and other problems, as was widely known, and his work piled sky-high.

As fate would have it, new and unexpected evidence of the inadvisability of the authorization surfaced, and the official to some suddenly appeared prescient rather than derelict in duty.

The official was then variously honored, even though concern was more appropriate as to why anyone caught-up in personal problems for so long had not been put on leave, why the work had not be reassigned, or why the official had not been warned or even dismissed.

The impact on other agency personnel was both profound and predictable—legitimation for almost any delay was available, and the regulated howled, albeit mostly inwardly because the regulator had a powerful counter-argument against any plea for expedient action.

The Dr. No Syndrome is ubiquitous in government, but only occasionally will specific countermeasures be taken. For example, one public agency felt it necessary to hammer away at a counter-theme: Find a way to move the project ahead. Such counter-themes can expect significant opposition, often for solid historical reasons. Perhaps paramountly, in regulatory matters, many will argue that an arm's-length if not adversarial relationship is required for a fruitful specialization of functions and to avoid sweetheart arrangements. Even where regulation is not dominant, moreover, the Dr. No Syndrome may be observed widely. For example, public officials often have to fit narrow time "windows" under next-to-impossible conditions. When the time is politically ripe, action must come quickly, even though the costs of miscalculation can be great and may not be evident for years. But even if the great leap into the abyss of the unknown is hazarded, and even if the heroic is accomplished, a new political broom may soon sweep away the foundations before they have stabilized.

Fine-tuning is needed, as is clearest to see after requisite fine-tuning has not been achieved. Occasionally, public officials go galloping off in search of some will-o'-the wisp, let's say the New Society of Lyndon Johnson. The desire to do good, and the requirement that it be done quickly if not yesterday, can create some fearsome progeny which must somehow be dealt with. More commonly, as a direct consequence of having galloped off one time too many, experienced public officials are not easily aroused to take a giant step forward, in the absence of substantial proof that a giant step backward will not soon be expedient. Dotting every i and crossing every t thus becomes a common strategy.

What may appear foot-dragging to the outsider, that is, will often appear to the insider as necessary conservation of effort and stabilizing behavior that avoid having to undo later what was undertaken too quickly at great cost. The implied concern of the public administrator may be stated in these terms: Let's make sure the political system really means it.

This description does not imply that the Dr. No Syndrome is often or even usually bad, or that it is unique to government. A quality-control specialist in industry often will have a Dr. No role, to illustrate, and with overall benefit to firm and customers. The points here are that the Dr. No role is substantially more characteristic of the public sector. Moreover, whether with good, bad, or indifferent effects in the long-run, the Dr. No role contributes a special quality to the public-sector culture.

Fourth, relatedly, "developing a record" tends to be more important in the public sector. In part, the reasons inhere in the special trust of public office. In part, also, officials may devote much energy to preparing JIC or CYA defenses, given that some attack from some quarter, soon or later, for good reasons or trumped-up ones, is more probable in the public sector.

This need to "develop a record" gets expressed inward as well as outward. Although the magnitudes may stagger, we are aware of the howls of anguish induced by government demands that others supply a record. Thus the chairman of a large pharmaceutical firm complains that *more* man-hours get devoted to filling-out required government forms and reports than his firm devotes to research on cancer and heart disease.[33] He provides chapter and verse. A new drug application for an anti-arthritic compound sat 120,000 pages tall. The chairman emphasizes that only a fraction of those pages—perhaps 30,000 or so—were important to the government's evaluation of the drug.

As they do unto others, moreover, so is done unto government employees. Kaufman concludes that they get even worse than they give. Kaufman illustrates how the oppressors get variously oppressed: "Understandably (government officials) see themselves as experts in their fields, yet many of the constraints on them are the work of people they regard as uninformed amateurs. Career diplomats who must answer to legislators with no experience in foreign affairs, urban specialists who must defer to interests from back-country farm regions, and professional military officers challenged at every turn by civilians with slight knowledge of military strategy and tactics, for example, grind their teeth in frustration. If people outside government think that they are victims of irrelevant obligations and prohibitions, they should see what those inside have to put up with—at all levels, too."[34]

FOOTNOTES

[1]This section depends substantially on Robert T. Golembiewski, "Organization Development in Public Agencies," *Public Administration Review* 2 (July 1969): esp. 369-377.

[2]Lawrence C. Dodd and Richard L. Schott, *Congress and the Administrative State* (New York: John Wiley & Sons, 1979), esp. 10-11.

[3]The theme also appeared in mass-circulation news stories and editorials which argued against Project ACORD in the U.S. Department of State, for example. Stewart Alsop, "Let the Poor Old Foreign Service Alone," *Saturday Evening Post*, June 1966, 14.

[4]For example, sensitivity training has been criticized as "amateur group therapy." For an incisive distinction between training and therapy, see Chris Argyris, "Conditions for Competence Acquisition and Therapy," *Journal of Applied Behavioral Science* 4 (June 1968): 147-178.

[5]See, generally, Francis E. Rourke, *Bureaucracy, Politics, and Public Policy* (Boston: Little, Brown, 1969); and Laurence E. Lynn, Jr., *Managing the Public's Business* (New York: Basic Books, 1981), esp. 3-17.

[6]For sensitivity to such interfaces in city government, see Cecil H. Bell, Jr., and James E. Rosenzweig, "OD In the City," *Southern Review of Public Administration* 1 (March 1978): 433-448. For an overview of a successful effort at such interfacing in a large jurisdiction, see David H. Kiel, "An OD Strategy for Policy Implementation: The Case of North Carolina State Government," *Public Administration* 42 (July 1982): 375-383.

[7]For a summary of the programmatic commitments of career personnel, see John J. Corson and R. Shale Paul, *Men Near the Top* (Baltimore, MD: Johns Hopkins Press, 1966), 23-51.

[8]See James S. Bowman, "Whistle-Blowing in the Public Sector: An Overview of the Issues," in Robert T. Golembiewski and Frank Gibson, eds., *Readings in Public Administration* (Boston: Houghton Mifflin, 1983), 248-257.

[9]Joseph P. Harris, *Congressional Control of Administration* (Washington, DC: The Brookings Institution, 1964).

[10]Arthur Schlesinger, *A Thousand Days* (Boston: Houghton Mifflin, 1965), 681.

[11]The central issue is developed with humor and insight by Gordon Chase and Elizabeth C. Reveal, *How to Manage in the Public Sector* (Reading, MA: Addison-Wesley, 1983), esp. 63-92.

[12]Generally, see Frederick Thayer, "The President's Management 'Reforms'," *Public Administration Review* 28 (July 1978): 309-314.

[13]Herbert Kaufman, "The Rise of A New Politics," in Wallace S. Sayre, ed., *The Federal Government Service* (Englewood Cliffs, NJ: Prentice-Hall, 1965), 58.

[14]Dean E. Mann, "The Selection of Federal Political Executives," *American Political Science Review* 58 (March 1964): 81-99.

[15]One ambitious OD program, for example, was unable to overcome the rumor that several political appointees were negotiating terms of private employment. Agency personnel were encouraged to inaction, since these officials would "soon be riding their OD hobbyhorse" someplace else. These officials did leave. But all claim that the stories were seeded by career personnel who opposed the OD program, and that it was only the intensity of such "dirty fighting" that encouraged the political appointees to seek private employ after the rumors began.

[16]Herbert Kaufman, "Administrative Decentralization and Political Power," *Public Administration Review* 29 (January 1969): 3-4.

[17]Before a reorganization inspired by an OD program in the Department of State, some layerings of review were so numerous that "it could take as long as six months for an important problem to reach the Deputy Under Secretary. Now it takes an average of two days." Alfred J. Marrow, "Managerial Revolution in the State Department," *Personnel* 43 (December 1966): 13.

[18]Such innovation has been the major trend in large businesses over the last three or four decades. See Robert T. Golembiewski, *Men, Management, and Morality* (New York: McGraw-Hill, 1965). Strong pressures for just such innovation over the last decade have been widely felt in public administration. Aaron Wildavsky provides a case in point in his "Black Rebellion and White Reaction," *The Public Interest* 11 (Spring 1968): 9-12.

[19]Appropriately, consult Hugh Heclo, *A Government of Strangers: Executive Politics in Washington* (Washington, DC: The Brookings Institution, 1977).

[20]A very useful discussion of the antimanagerial thrust of much legislation is provided by Harris, *Congressional Oversight of Administration*.

[21]Robert T. Golembiewski, "Civil Service and Managing Work," *American Political Science Review* 56 (December 1962): 961-974.

[22]E.g., see John R. Dempsey, "Carter Reorganization: A Mid-Term Appraisal," *Public Administration Review* 39 (January 1979): 74-78.

[23]Great needs for "security" as here broadly defined can rigidify an organization and curb the effectiveness of its members. To the point, see Chris Argyris, "Some Causes of Organizational Ineffectiveness Within the Department of State," Center for International System Research, *Occasional Papers* (No. 2, 1967).

[24]Revealingly, it was not until 1946 that Cornell developed the first two-year master of public administration program comparable to the MBA long given by schools of commerce or business administration.

In the last decade or so, public administration and affairs programs have proliferated at the graduate level, but that progress has been uneven. Overall, see Robert T. Golembiewski, "The Near Future of Graduate PA Programs: Some Program Minima, Their Common Violation, and Some Priority Palliatives," *Southern Review of Public Administration* 3 (December 1979): 323-359.

[25]Paul P. Van Riper, *History of the United States Civil Service* (Evanston, IL: Row, Peterson, 1958), 429-434.

[26]Quoted in Joseph L. Bower, "Effective Public Management," *Harvard Business Review* 55 (March 1977): 132.

[27]*Ibid.*

[28]William B. Eddy and Robert J. Saunders, "Applied Behavioral Science in Urban Administrative/Political Systems," *Public Administration Review* 31 (January 1972): 11-16.

[29]Marvin Weisbord, "Organizational Diagnosis: Six Places to Look for Trouble With or Without A Theory," *Group and Organization Studies* 1 (December 1976): 430-447.

30Leonard D. Goodstein, *Consulting with Human Service Systems* (Reading, MA: Addison-Wesley, 1978), 103-113.

31*Ibid.*, 109.

32Bower, esp. 134.

33Richard D. Wood, "Paperwork, Paperwork," *Washington Post*, 12 (July 1976).

34Herbert Kaufman, *Red Tape*, (Washington, DC: The Brookings Institution, 1977), 26.

PART B

How Well Does OD Do in Public-Sector Change?

CHAPTER II: Tracking The Effects of Confounding Constraints: Experience With Planned Change in Public-Sector Settings, I

CHAPTER III: Estimating The Success Ratio of OD Efforts: Experience With Planned Change in Public-Sector Settings, II

CHAPTER IV: Evaluating Applications of Flexible Workhours: Experience With Planned Change in Public-Sector Settings, III

CHAPTER II

TRACKING THE EFFECTS OF COMPLICATING CONSTRAINTS: EXPERIENCE WITH PLANNED CHANGE IN PUBLIC-SECTOR SETTINGS, I

Over the last decade or two, observers have suggested that Organization Development could help business and public managers. Broadly, OD seeks to "improve an organization's problem-solving and renewal processes, particularly through a more effective and collaborative management of organization culture—with the assistance of a change agent or catalyst, and the use of . . .applied behavioral science."[1] OD is "a long range effort to consciously introduce planned change into an organization," as Golembiewski describes. That effort involves the organization's members, "both in diagnosis of problems and prescriptions of change."[2] More specifically, OD is a value-loaded technology oriented toward creating an open and problem-solving climate, supplementing the authority of role and status with the authority of knowledge and competence, building trust between individuals and groups, and so on.[3]

What can be said of OD penetration into the public sector? The prevailing opinion does not rest on very firm foundations. Boosterism exists, of course. But no comprehensive survey of practice exists, and hence prevailing opinion is suspect.

This chapter and the two that follow begin filling a critical void. This chapter inquires as to the overall impact of 13 common constraints on a batch of OD applications. A following chapter will assess the relative success or failure of several classes of OD applications in the public-sector. In these two chapters, the analytic microscope will operate at two different powers-of-resolution, as it were. Attention will be directed at 44 urban OD interventions. Later attention will be given to an array of 270 cross-sectional public-sector interventions. This cross-checks a coarse analysis with a finer-grained one. A third chapter looks at the public-sector success rate of a single OD design—flexible workhours or Flexi-Time—in a number of public settings.

Cumulatively, this cluster of three chapters provides reasonable perspective on the general ability to cope with the kind of constraints introduced in the initial chapter. There is no need to feign suspense. So we get on with the details by noting that success rates are appreciable.

I. COMMON WISDOM ABOUT OD APPLICATIONS[4]

Despite having to run faster to stand still, overall, public managers have been far less likely to employ OD designs than their business counterparts. Or at least so goes the common wisdom. Watchers of governments today largely see reactive public organizations, responding to environmental pressures through adjustment—a kind of unplanned change. Consider the urban arena only. More cops are put on the beat due to an increase in muggings; the treatment plant is enlarged because of unacceptable water quality; or an improved pay plan is designed to mollify an employee union. And still most urban systems seem to go on hurting, especially in human terms, as their efforts to adapt seem too little, or too late. Some would even argue that diverting scarce discretionary finances to technological invention is tantamount to keeping the patient alive by artificial means.

This record has numerous explanations, no doubt. Among them is this curious one. For some reason, even where public-sector applications have been vigorous—as in seven years of experience in La Jolla, California, city government[5]—documentation has been sparse. Little of the promotional hype that so often accompanied OD in the business sector has occurred in the public sector.

How can we explain this curious combination of obvious need to change and government-as-usual? No doubt two basic and related reasons account for much of this record:

- the common wisdom has long proposed that features more or less unique to the public sector serve as major constraints on OD applications

- the common wisdom maintains that few OD applications have been attempted, and hence that wisdom implies one or both of two points: little experience is available for dealing with the unique constraints ham-stringing public OD applications; or the unique constraints are so formidable that they essentially defy successful OD applications.

To test these two pieces of contra-OD wisdom, the available literature was scoured for OD interventions in urban governments and then in all public agencies, and all published efforts were retained that provide some modicum of detail about designs and their effects. The selected items seldom qualify as rigorous experimental designs; but they contain no purely-anecdotal boosterism.

II. TESTING FOR PUBLIC-SECTOR CONSTRAINTS

We begin with an extreme statement of public-sector refractoriness to OD. One observer concludes flatly that: "the unique constraints imposed on public organizations appear to render them almost immune from conventional OD interventions."[6] Nor is this alleged immunity a mere artifact of the paucity of public-sector experience, the observer adds. Indeed, as more OD applications get attempted in the public sector, that greater activity will only more forcefully demonstrate the need for a separate body of OD theory and approach.

This section tests this common argument in the urban area, basically via a two-step response. *First,* 13 alleged constraints on OD applications in the public sector will be introduced. *Second,* 44 urban OD applications will be reviewed to assess the actual impact of these constraints.

A. 13 Speculative Constraints

At a specific level, numerous authors have dealt with public-sector characteristics that differ from the private sector and that complicate OD applications. The following 13 constraints constitute a consensus-listing from major sources in the literature,[7] and obviously draw substantial inspiration from the previous chapter.

1) *Legal restrictions.* The public sector implies powerful constraints on OD applications that derive from common procedures, legislative restrictions, and separation of powers. For example, cities and urban counties are creatures of the state and have no powers of government

except those granted by the state. Although "home rule" is intended to loosen those restrictions and share power with municipalities and counties, many states require either a constitutional amendment or state statute to alter drastically the structure of government. These legal restrictions limit OD interventions.

2) *Lack of economic incentives and market indicators.* Many public organizations do not have clear-cut outputs—such as profits or productivity—which lend themselves to measurement. Evaluating the worth of an OD program may prove to be difficult, as a consequence. Some also argue that public-sector motivation to change and improve is reduced because of the lack of incentives and indicators.

3) *Multiple access.* Urban decision-makers are exposed to diverse constituencies which are plurally-needful. Specifically, managers and change-agents promoting OD interventions often must "sell" council members, chief administrative officers, special interests, and even the media. Any or all of these may withdraw support unilaterally, and thereby weaken or cancel the OD program. Life typically is simpler in business organizations.

4) *Quasi-governmental action.* Much local action occurs outside traditional organizational structures. Decentralized neighborhood centers, citizen-agency coalitions, and political parties or machines exemplify quasi-governmental actors and action. Their vitality frequently depends on the dedication of key citizens aggregated in loosely-linked and temporary networks, rather than in routinized operations. This provides a changeable and perhaps a somewhat-shaky base for OD applications.

5) *Public scrutiny and suspicion.* Urban decisions often are far more visible than in the private sector. A climate of distrust also may derive from public suspicion, whether based on sad experience or on a generally-jaundiced view of government power.

6) *Volatile political/administrative interfaces.* Constitutions separate powers, and yet social purposes often require relating or integrating those powers. As a result, uneasy interfaces develop between those separated by institutions or traditions—linkages between legislative and administrative units, between political and career officials, and so on. Objectives often clash, providing a political fault-line along which OD programs must operate. No comparable fault-line exists in the private sector, although most firms more or less distinguish "politics" from "administration," or policy-making from its implementation.

7) *Drawing boundaries.* One prime OD objective involves an open climate, which blends poorly with common public-sector difficulties related to "drawing boundaries." The point holds in at least two senses. Secrecy may be required or encouraged in some public work. In a more general sense, restricting the scope of public-sector interventions may be more difficult than in business, given sunshine laws, the media, and so on. Participants may not "open up" if they fear political reprisal, or because they do not wish their managerially-related and spontaneous reactions reported in the media.

8) *Diverse interests, values, incentives.* Public-sector features complicate or preclude agreement on a common set of goals, while OD interventions seek an environment in which individuals can meet their needs while meeting organizational needs. The greater the diversity of those needs, obviously, the greater the challenge. The point holds most dramatically for "rogues"—individuals with independent power-bases who have veto or initiating roles in the public sector. Thus a rogue could come from a safe district and chair a major legislative committee monitoring a public agency. Rogues in the private sector—who might have power-bases such as that of stockholders with very large holdings—are quite rare.

9) *Procedural regularity and rigidity.* Public policies and systems represent definite obstacles to change which, of course, is often precisely what they are intended to do. Adjustments may be more difficult to make because of general civil service rules which cannot be broached except by system-wide change, for example. Existing laws also may hinder developing a variable reward system, which takes away a major management tool. Public managers tend to depend on past practices, moreover, which tendency works against the OD objective of helping managers manage according to relevant objectives.

10) *Short time-frame.* Roadblocks such as the yearly budget process and one-year program elements make long-range planning very tenuous. Many full-blown OD programs take three to five years. The typical government time-frame seldom allows such latitude, given changing legislative coalitions, among many other factors.

11) *Weak chains-of-command and delegation.* Change in top leadership in the public sector can be more drastic, far-reaching, and frequent. Linkages between relatively indefinite-term politicians and administrative careerists can be generally weak, and top elected and appointed officials often give far more attention to fragmenting than integrative forces. Thus various urban agencies will ally with specific

interests, Federal agencies, local council-persons, and so on. Similarly, superiors tend to minimize the control exercised by subordinates, e.g., by keeping "short chains-of-command."

12) *Lack of professionalism.* The concept and practice of professional management is less developed in the public sector, although city managers constitute a long-standing exception. This anti-career and populist tradition works against several OD goals—including employee ownership of objectives, as well as a sense of close identification with, and commitment to, the goals of a public agency or government.

13) *Complexity of objectives.* Urban governments face a large number of complex and often-competing goals. Meeting them frequently requires the coordinated effort of several departments, each with its own incompletely overlapping or even antagonistic agendas. OD programs seek inter-unit collaboration, but the multiplicity of goals can complicate achieving that intent. Private-sector complexity can be substantial, but it generally pales in comparison.

B. Practical Impact of Constraints on Urban Interventions

Do these 13 constraints actually affect OD interventions? Table 1 implies a relatively clear answer: Yes, in general.

For urban interventions, Table 1 indicates that the 13 constraints can have a strong but variable impact. The "methodology" was simple. Two researchers read each OD report and almost always agreed as to the impact of a specific constraint. No effort was made to weigh the intensity of the constraints; and the approach patently cannot improve on the observational and reportorial skills of the several authors represented.

Caveats aside, what does the panel of highly-condensed summary of OD applications in Table 1 suggest to the prepared mind? Six highlights deserve attention here.

1. *Accelerating Rate of Diffusion*

What time-frame does Table 1 cover, and what distribution of OD applications in urban settings does it reflect? Several of the urban OD applications go back a substantial time, but most clearly cluster in the last five years or so of the research covered by Table 1. Approximately, Table 1 tracks the urban literature into 1979 but not through it. This clearly suggests an accelerating rate of diffusion of OD designs into urban settings, and implies a growing expertise for coping with public-sector constraints. Note also that a more-than-casual search of the literature before 1969 and after 1979 does not encourage any revision of the analysis below.

Key to Public Sector Constraints

1 – Legal restrictions

2 – Lack of economic incentives and market indicators

3 – Multiple access

4 – Quasi-governmental action

5 – Public scrutiny and suspicion

6 – Volatile political/administrative interface

7 – Drawing boundaries

8 – Diverse interests, values and incentives

9 – Procedural regularity and rigidity

10 – Short time-frame

11 – Weak chains-of-command

12 – Lack of Professionalism

13 – Complexity of objectives

● = Identifiable Operating Constraint

o = Explicitly-recognized Case in which Operating Constraint Becomes Facilitator

TABLE 1. Constraints on Specific Urban OD Interventions

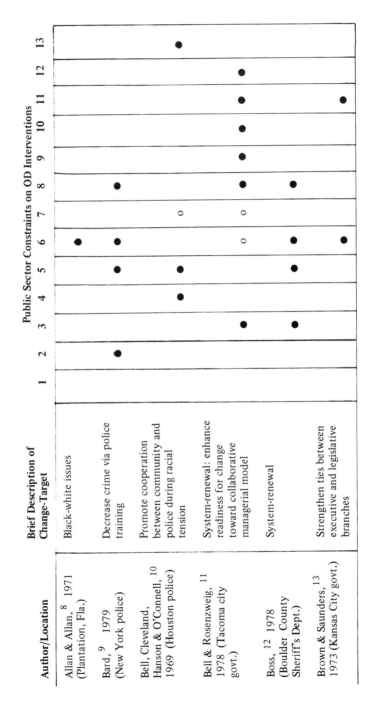

Author/Location	Brief Description of Change-Target	Public Sector Constraints on OD Interventions												
		1	2	3	4	5	6	7	8	9	10	11	12	13
Allan & Allan,[8] 1971 (Plantation, Fla.)	Black-white issues						●							
Bard,[9] 1979 (New York police)	Decrease crime via police training		●			●	●		●					
Bell, Cleveland, Hanson & O'Connell,[10] 1969 (Houston police)	Promote cooperation between community and police during racial tension				●	●		○						●
Bell & Rosenzweig,[11] 1978 (Tacoma city govt.)	System-renewal: enhance readiness for change toward collaborative managerial model			●			○	○	●	●	●	●	●	
Boss,[12] 1978 (Boulder County Sheriff's Dept.)	System-renewal			●		●	●		●					
Brown & Saunders,[13] 1973 (Kansas City govt.)	Strengthen ties between executive and legislative branches						●					●		

TABLE 1. Constraints on Specific Urban OD Interventions (Continued)

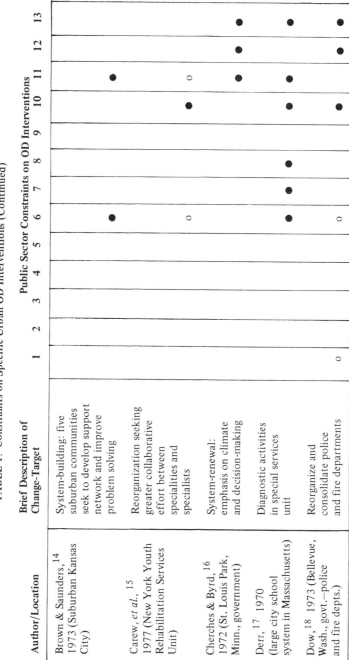

Author/Location	Brief Description of Change-Target	Public Sector Constraints on OD Interventions												
		1	2	3	4	5	6	7	8	9	10	11	12	13
Brown & Saunders,[14] 1973 (Suburban Kansas City)	System-building: five suburban communities seek to develop support network and improve problem solving						●					●		
Carew, et al.,[15] 1977 (New York Youth Rehabilitation Services Unit)	Reorganization seeking greater collaborative effort between specialities and specialists						○				●	○		
Cherches & Byrd,[16] 1972 (St. Louis Park, Minn., government)	System-renewal: emphasis on climate and decision-making						●	●	●		●	●	●	●
Derr,[17] 1970 (large city school system in Massachusetts)	Diagnostic activities in special services unit										●	●		
Dow,[18] 1973 (Bellevue, Wash., govt.–police and fire depts.)	Reorganize and consolidate police and fire departments	○					○				●		●	●

TABLE 1. Constraints on Specific Urban OD Interventions (Continued)

Author/Location	Brief Description of Change-Target	1	2	3	4	5	6	7	8	9	10	11	12	13
Driscoll, Meyer & Schamie,[19] 1973 (Louisville police)	Develop police skills in family crisis intervention					●				○		●		
Flynn,[20] 1976 (Eugene, Oregon high school)	Skill and team-building to improve staff decision-making	●				○				●		●		
Gentry and Watkins,[21] 1974 (medium-sized Alabama city)	Process-analysis activities during school desegregation					○				●		●		
Giblin,[22] 1976 (local Employment Service office)	Improve performance in local office of Dept. of Labor's Employment Service							●		●		●		●
Giegold & Dunsing,[23] 1978 (Virginia county and city)	Reduce stereotyping, increase communication flow and improve decision-making					●		○						
Gluckstein & Packard,[24] 1977 (Berkshire County, Mass. jail)	System renewal: develop new program for rehabilitation	●				○	○							

TABLE 1. Constraints on Specific Urban OD Interventions (Continued)

Author/Location	Brief Description of Change-Target	Public Sector Constraints on OD Interventions												
		1	2	3	4	5	6	7	8	9	10	11	12	13
Golembiewski, 25 1977 (Atlanta—MARTA)	System-renewal: modify consequences of existing functional departmentalization, with emphasis on executive appraisal						●	○	●			●		●
Golembiewski & Kiepper, 26 1978 (Atlanta—MARTA)	System-building: develop management team and create desired climate at start-up						●	○	●			●		●
Golembiewski and Perkins, 27 1978 (Atlanta—MARTA)	System-renewal: reorganize general manager's office, involving both staff and board of directors					●		●	○	○		●		●
Goodstein & Boyer, 28 1972 (Cincinnati health dept.)	Internal crisis and poor relationships with community			●		○	●	○	○			●	●	●
Klein, 29 1965 (one-industry New England town)	Community development program—Sensitivity-training					●						●	●	●

TABLE 1. Constraints on Specific Urban OD Interventions (Continued)

Author/Location	Brief Description of Change-Target	Public Sector Constraints on OD Interventions												
		1	2	3	4	5	6	7	8	9	10	11	12	13
Klein, Thomas & Bellis,[30] 1971 (Large city)	Explosive situation in police-minority relations			●		●			●			●	●	●
Krocker, Forsyth & Haase,[31] 1974 (Rochester police)	Tensions between police and youth							●	●	●	●	●		●
LeBaron,[32] 1978 (Southern California city councils)	Greater awareness among elected local officials of relevance of trust vs. power								●				●	
Levin & Stein,[33] 1970 (New York City School strike)	Forum for channeling conflicts in school-community relations	●						●			●		●	
Maiben & Schwabe,[34] 1973 (Barrington, Ill., govt.)	Organization improvement to keep pace with growing community demands		●			●					○		●	
Mohrmam, Mohrman, Cooke & Duncan,[35] 1977 (medium-sized midwestern U.S. city school system)	Develop professional decision-making capability					●	●			●	○	●		●

TABLE 1. Constraints on Specific Urban OD Interventions (Continued)

Author/Location	Brief Description of Change-Target	Public Sector Constraints on OD Interventions												
		1	2	3	4	5	6	7	8	9	10	11	12	13
Olmosk & Graverson,[36] 1972 (Northern England city of half-million population—school system)	Multi-racial tension in schools													
Parker,[37] 1974 (Syracuse police)	Improve police-community relations			●		●	●				●			
Perkins, et al.,[38] 1973 (Richmond government)	Improve delivery of services to neighborhood residents				●	●				●	●			●
Ready & Faison,[39] 1973 (Pensacola, Fla. government)	System-renewal: government leaders anxious to improve human input and problems-solving	●				●	●							
Reddy & Lansky,[40] 1975 (large municipal police division)	Value, norm and power conflicts					●		●	●	●	●	●		

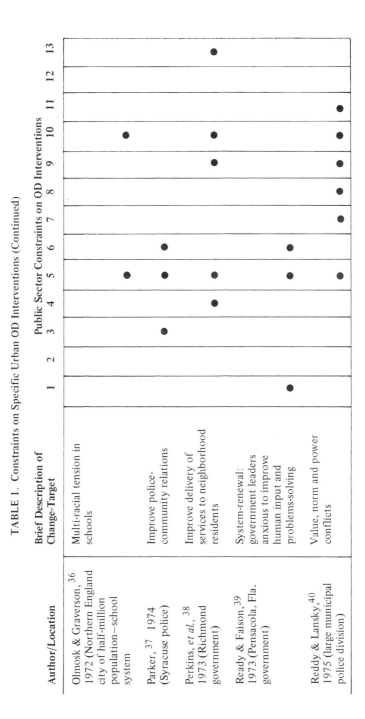

TABLE 1. Constraints on Specific Urban OD Interventions (Continued)

Author/Location	Brief Description of Change-Target	Public Sector Constraints on OD Interventions												
		1	2	3	4	5	6	7	8	9	10	11	12	13
Reppucci & Saunders, 41 1978 (Connecticut School for Boys)	Ease leadership change, introduce reorganization, and increase staff involvement	●					●			●		●	●	
Ross & Hare, 42 1973 (three California cities' general government)	System-renewal: aid cities' planning process and create climate of effectiveness		●							●	●			
Sata & Pfister, 44 1975 (Seattle Police Department)	Atmosphere of increased police-community conflict			●				●		●				
Schmuck, 45 1974 (West-coast U.S. urban school district)	Parent-teacher communications and collaboration					●					●			●
Sebring & Duffee, 46 1977 (Pennsylvania regional correctional institution)	Considerable conflict in win-lose situation	●	●			●		●	●			●	●	●

TABLE 1. Constraints on Specific Urban OD Interventions (Continued)

Author/Location	Brief Description of Change-Target	1	2	3	4	5	6	7	8	9	10	11	12	13
Shellow,[47] 1965 (Washington, D.C. suburban Maryland county police force)	Prepare police officers for mediating racial conflict					●			●					
Singer,[48] 1972 (Binghamton, N.Y. police force)	Help city deal with human problems resulting from urban renewal			●		●				●				
Tanner & Shakoor,[49] 1978 (large city)	Team organization and decision-making for housing project staff									●		●	●	●
Teahan,[50] 1975 (Detroit police)	Intradepartmental conflict and lack of understanding among white and black officers						●							
Thompson & Giegold,[51] 1977 (Lynchburg, Va., city government)	System-renewal					○						○		
Weisbord, Lamb & Drexler,[52] 1974 (Eastern U.S. city police department)	Reorganization into collateral police organization					○			●			○		●

Public Sector Constraints on OD Interventions

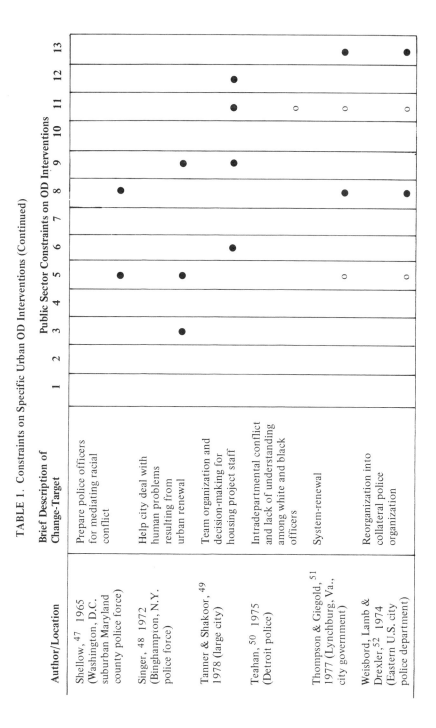

2. Clusters of Common Constraints

In addition to bunching-up in time, Table 1 also implies that urban OD applications tend to face clusters of constraints. Specifically, eight of the constraints—#5, 6, 8, 9, 10, 11, 12 and 13—are particularly common. These eight constraints fall nicely into two clusters: external to the specific locus of application; and internal to it.

The prominence of the external constraints—#5, 6, 8, and 9—does not surprise. As might be expected, constraint #5—Public scrutiny and expectations—seems most widespread. In 18 of the 44 cases, in fact, the demands and watchfulness of their constituencies were explicitly mentioned as impacting directly on OD applications. Of course, there is no telling how many potential OD applications were *not* attempted because of concern over public scrutiny.

Three other external constraints also reflect the impact of the public legal/procedural network on OD interventions. One constraint—(6) Volatile political/administrative interface—could be powerful. For example, a city council grew so impatient with a manager and an OD program that it cut off support for both. The two other common external constraints—(8) Great variety of interests, values, and incentives; and (9) Procedural regularity and rigidity—suggest more of the same kind of trouble for public-sector OD applications. In an extreme example of constraint (8), for example, the community as a whole became the client of an OD intervention,[53] after it became apparent to the consultants that diagnosis and consultation limited to one particular government agency would not deal adequately with the problem.

A cluster of four other constraints got about equally-prominent mention—(10) Short-time frame, (11) Weak chains-of-command, (12) Lack of professionalism, and (13) Complexity of objectives—and they seem more internally-oriented while still being affected by the degree of public scrutiny and legal restrictions. For example, a strong OD effort in Tacoma, WA,[54] slowed when the city manager moved on to a larger city after a typically-brief tenure. Relatedly, several departments involved in an OD effort may agree in principle that communications need improving or that intergroup cooperation should be enhanced, but they may still have difficulty cooperating because their priorities differ. Consider the reorganization of the general manager's office of a transit authority.[55] Virtually all major actors agreed that change was appropriate, even vital. But one coalition wanted to run its own shops with minimal interference; several assistant managers insisted on continuing to report directly to the general manager; and still others were set on maintaining or increasing black influence in the decision-making structure.

What does a careful reading of the impact of such constraints imply? The constraints really exist, patently, and must be anticipated in the design of OD applications. Let the public-sector designer of OD interventions beware, then. Relatedly, the constraints may impact expectations about outcomes. Crudely, the constraints may imply a "lower batting average"—more difficult change-targets, less pervasive and persisting change, and so on. Is this "lower" average "so low" as to contraindicate public-sector OD applications? That question defies a categoric answer, but the companion chapters conclude that the "lower batting average" is still "pretty high." Moreover, an answer clearly will depend on public-sector need—the greater it is, the more reasonable the resort to OD designs even if they fare less favorably and require greater resources than comparable private-sector efforts.

3. A Constraint-Free Class of Application?

As a kind of mirror image of the clustering of constraints, Table 1 also suggests a curious regularity. Those OD interventions aimed at a particular government agency (e.g., schools) or in response to a crisis (e.g., a confrontation between police and ghetto residents) seem to experience a greater number of constraints than those OD programs introduced government-wide. Why is this? We provide only two speculations. An intervention initiated during a crisis, particularly involving police, rests in an explosive environment among highly-opinionated participants with extremely-different agendas and perspectives, as well as with common and easy access to the media. To provide a second perspective, organization-wide interventions usually are endorsed by top management, with at least the tacit support of department heads and a general agreement on the objectives.

4. De-fanging Some Constraints

Constraints do not constitute inevitably-negative givens, Table 1 also suggests. In fact, in 16 cases an expected constraint not only failed to materialize, but actually was negated by circumstances or conscious action. Consider constraint (7), Drawing boundaries. In one case, a team-building session between council and administrators was televised with positive consequences, on very definite balance. The fourth estate seemed to love this "media-event" in prospect, but counted it as dry and boring both during and after-the-fact. In several other cases, the boundary issue was handled in a contrary way. Although the agency was subject to a sunshine law in one case, personnel matters are specifically excluded. The OD effort was announced in the media, but media presence was not permitted because personnel issues were the basic topics.

The lesson seems clear enough. It is possible to neutralize some common restraints, or even to turn them to the advantage of an OD program.

Table 1 also suggests that the constraints can be overcome or minimized in two ways. Thus situations may provide substantial wriggle-room for public managers, as when politicos choose to "look the other way" because of happenstance or general policy. For example, in a massive reorganization in a state division, top management was committed to change,[56] and no evidence exists concerning legislative interest except to get things running more efficiently. In this case, the absence of one constraint—(6) Volatile political/administrative interface—in effect helped avoid constraint (11)—Weak chains-of-command.

Moreover, constraints can be overcome or minimized when parties usually on opposite sides of the fence join forces, by serendipity or because of explicit design. To illustrate, in Pensacola, FL, elected and appointed officials both promoted an OD intervention.[57] Similarly, the City Council of Bellevue, Washington, actually removed major legal restrictions (constraint 1) by hurriedly passing an ordinance consolidating the police and fire departments, thereby facilitating the city manager's change-effort.[58] In several cases, the linking of (for example) legislative and administrative interests was an explicit OD design feature, and success/failure on that crucial element constituted a go/no-go decision for subsequent design phases.[59]

5. Constraint/Trauma Break-Even Point

Speculatively but credibly, Table 1 implies that even formidable constraints can be over-ridden because of the substantial trauma involved in not doing so. That is to say, to consider only constraints must be misleading. Since the "other side of the equation" needs equal attention, the literature's fixation on constraints seems critically biased. Illustratively, public-sector pressures—e.g., due to a need for greater productivity because tax burdens are widely seen as onerous—may build so high as to overcome even formidable constraints. Felt-need can overcome constraint, in short; and "problems" may be "opportunities."

But let us resist going too far beyond Table 1. At a minimum, the table suggests that many of the OD applications in Table 1 rest on substantial pain, tension, and failure. That may explain why they got attempted, constraints on public-sector OD notwithstanding. The traumas were substantial enough to encourage overcoming the constraints, in short.

6. Constraints Can Convert Into Motivators

Finally, some of the constraints on public OD programs can also be facilitative under certain conditions. Consider constraint (5) Public scrutiny and suspicion. The usual view is that this constraint impedes administrative action, and evidence for that point of view is not hard to marshal, especially when non-traditional technologies like OD are at issue. Given sufficient pain, tension, or failure, pretty clearly constraint (5) can also serve to motivate ameliorative action. Table 1 provides some evidence of this conversion of a constraint into its opposite.

III. TESTING FOR CONSTRAINTS ON ALL GOVERNMENT OD APPLICATIONS

Does the deliberate restriction above of focus to urban applications bias the results? Will a larger collection of OD applications yield a different pattern?

These are serious questions, but fortunately ones *now* testable. Using the same set of constraints as does Table 1, Table 2 summarizes the record for constraints in a batch of 270 public-sector OD applications[60] drawn from all areas and levels of government. Roughly, Table 2 tracks the OD literature from approximately 1950 through early 1980, using a detailed search-process that sought written reports of applications from these several sources:

- seven specialized bibliographies

- searches of the several computerized listings (e.g., ERIC) of publications in social science journals

- a review of 88 non-listed journals, including 10 from overseas

- over 100 books

- personal letters sent to 50 well-known OD change-agents, especially soliciting unpublished materials such as internal memos, unpublished dissertations or theses, and so on.

Table 2 implies two major conclusions. *First,* public-sector constraints do not obviously differ when general governmental applications are compared with urban-only efforts. Thus the same two clusters of constraints again have the highest observed incidences. In sum:

"External" Constraints, Incidence of	"Internal" Constraints, Incidence of
# 5 Public scrutiny — 87	#10 Short time-frame — 52
# 6 Volatile interface — 62	#11 Weak chains of command — 70
# 8 Diverse interest, values — 111	#12 Lack of professionalism — 78
# 9 Procedural rigidity — 124	#13 complexity of objectives — 61

This distribution mirrors Table 1 closely, in sum.

Second, Table 2 should not be taken to mean that the constraints always inhibit OD efforts. In a number of cases, as Table 3 makes explicit, constraints can become facilitators. This is particularly so in two cases—constraints #9 and #12, which refer to Procedural regularity and rigidity as well as to Lack of professionalism, respectively. There seem to be two classes of such transformations. Interpretively, for example, Procedural regularity and rigidity can become so bad as to be good, in the sense that the constraint becomes a motivator to do something about blunting the constraint's effects.

TABLE 2. Incidence of Common Constraints on OD Applications

Level of Government	Total Applications	Observed Incidence of Individual Constraints†												
		1	2	3	4	5	6	7	8	9	10	11	12	13
I. Local Government (e.g., schools, community organizations, police, general government, etc.)	158	15	24	21	15	79	47	25	85	74	39	42	51	41
II. State Government (e.g., departments or agencies, executive offices, universities)	49	6	10	1	1	3	7	4	4	17	1	11	14	4
III. Federal Government (e.g., departments or agencies, military units, etc.)	63	7	9	3	9	5	8	10	22	33	12	17	13	16
	270	28	43	25	25	87	62	39	111	124	52	70	78	61

†More than one constraint can be coded for any individual application. Hence, observed constraints >270.

Based on Carl W. Proehl, Jr., *Planned Organizational Change.* Unpublished doctoral dissertation, University of Georgia, 1980.

TABLE 3. Common Constraints Mentioned as Factors

Level of Government	Total Applications	Observed Incidence of Individual Constratins Mentioned as Facilitators												
		1	2	3	4	5	6	7	8	9	10	11	12	13
I. Local Government	158	1	2	1	3	6	6	5	4	20	0	3	7	0
II. State Government	49	0	1	0	0	0	1	0	0	1	0	0	6	4
III. Federal Government	63	0	0	0	0	1	1	1	0	4	0	1	3	0
	270	1	3	1	3	6	8	6	4	25	0	4	16	4

Based on Carl W. Proehl, Jr., *Planned Organizational Change.* Unpublished doctoral dissertation, University of Georgia, 1980.

Less common is a second case of how constraints can become motivators by conscious action. For example, if legislative and executive interests can be mobilized to support an OD effort, that provides a powerful push and motivation for participants. In a few cases—e.g., the Spokane interventions in municipal government—such a coalition was an explicit feature of early stages of the design. In the usual case, different legislative and executive interests can whip-saw OD efforts. In a few cases—e.g., Project ACORD in the U.S. Department of State—planners even neglected this major source of mischief, only to be blind-sided by it at later stages of the OD effort.

How common are such constraint→motivator effects? Common enough so they should not be neglected, in gross terms. More specifically, one can calculate a kind of *jiu-jitsu effect*. The 270 cases were coded as containing 1,445 incidences of constraints, and 80 incidences of constraints that had become motivators. Conveniently, one can calculate a transformation effect of some 5.5%. Specifically, $1445/80 = .0554$.

IV. SIX CONCLUSIONS ABOUT THE COMMON WISDOM

Tables 1-3 summarize the impact of constraints—initially for urban OD applications and then for all available OD reports in the public sector. This exploratory exercise concerning constraints on public-sector OD applications easily supports six conclusions.

First, public-sector OD does seem to face a unique set of constraints—different sometimes in degree, sometimes in kind. Thus there is a politics/administration interface in all organizations, such as the "seam" between boards of directors and management in business firms. But the public-sector interface is far more volatile, due to institutional factors such as the separation of powers and many other elements besides.

Second, the three tables also imply that the character and interplay of constraints on public-sector OD applications is such that unreflective transfer of private-sector approaches and perspectives is ill-advised. It may even be that a separate body of theory, research, and practice will be appropriate. In the interim, several reinforcing OD values—e.g., involvement and ownership by the client in the design as well as in its consequences—can be very helpful in avoiding too-facile transfer, given sophisticated clients and non-hucksterish change-agents.

Third, the incidence of constraints does not seem to vary between urban applications and those in all governmental contexts. That is to say, Tables 1 and 2 do not differ in any obvious ways in this central regard.

Fourth, several trends suggest that the pressures on public administration will grow more onerous, if anything. Consider only increased participation in government by the public and by unions, possible austerity of the Proposition 13-type, and continuing attention to merit principles as well as to affirmative action. Such factors may intensify public-sector constraints on OD interventions, although the vectors-of-effects do not all point in a consistent direction.

Note that one cannot say conclusively whether this perceived trend is more dark cloud or more silver lining. These growing pressures often may be expressed as a need for greater productivity per dollar spent, for example. And this need may become great enough to overcome what seem formidable constraints against OD efforts.

Fifth, the number and range of OD applications may be surprising to some, especially because a hundred or perhaps even a thousand unpublished applications probably have been held for every one intervention which gets transformed into printer's ink. Illustratively, the U.S. Army alone recently trained hundreds of OD intervenors for field duty, mostly relying on a survey/feedback design.

Sixth, Tables 1-3 imply a conclusion and suggest a question. The conclusion: the constraints may be tougher in the public sector, but they are not *that* tough. The constraints are clearly not immobilizing, given the number and coverage of available studies. Indeed, in a notable percentage of cases, a constraint can become—or can be made to become—a facilitator of an OD effort. Such an effect was estimated as occurring about 5 percent of the time in the batch of 270 governmental applications.

This conclusion is impressionistic, of course, and motivates a bottom-line question. How can we estimate the more specific success or failure of published OD applications? A working answer, obviously, would go far toward permitting a confident judgment about the magnitude of the constraints inhibiting public-sector OD applications. Two companion chapters will seek to provide such an answer to *the* bottom-line question, in the public sector.

FOOTNOTES

[1]Wendell L. French and Cecil H. Bell, Jr., *Organization Development* (Englewood Cliffs, NJ: Prentice-Hall, 1982), 4.

[2]Robert T. Golembiewski, *Approaches to Planned Change, Vol. 1* (New York: Marcel Dekker, 1979), 10-11.

[3]NTL Institute for Applied Behavioral Science, "What is OD?," *News and Reports* 2 (June 1968): 1.

[4]Sections A and B appeared in an earlier form in Robert T. Golembiewski and David Sink, "OD Interventions in Urban Settings, I: Public-Sector Constraints on Planned Change," *International Journal of Public Administration* 1 (No. 1, 1979): 1-30.

[5]George A. Shipel, Juanita Brown, and M. Frances Kaufman, "The Management of Planned Change in Local Government: An Empirical Example," *Southern Review of Public Administration* 4 (September 1980): 176-189.

[6]Edwin J. Giblin, "Organization Development: Public Sector Theory and Practice," *Public Personnel Management* 5 (March 1976): 108-118.

[7]The sources include: Robert T. Golembiewski, "Organization Development in Public Agencies," *Public Administration Review* 29 (July 1969): 367-377; William B. Eddy, "Beyond Behavioralism?," *Public Personnel Review* 31 (July 1970): 169-175, Timothy W. Costello, "Change in Municipal Government," *Journal of Applied Behavioral Science* 7 (March 1971): 131-145; William B. Eddy and Robert J. Saunders, "Applied Behavioral Science in Urban Administration," *Public Administration Review* 32 (January 1972): 11-16; Neely Gardner, "Power Diffusion in the Public Sector," *Journal of Applied Behavioral Science* 10 (July 1974): 367-372; Giblin, 108-118; and William B. Eddy and Thomas P. Murphy, "Applying Behavioral Science to Urban Management," in Charles H. Levine, ed., *Managing Human Resources* (Beverly Hills, CA: Sage Publications, 1977), 201-224.

[8]Thomas K. Allan and Kathryn H. Allan, "Sensitivity Training for Community Leaders," in *Proceedings 1971*, 79th Annual Convention of the American Psychological Association, 577-578.

[9]Morton Bard, *Training Police as Specialists in Family Crisis Intervention* (Washington, DC: U.S. Dept. of Justice, Law Enforcement Assistance Administration, National Institute of Law Enforcement and Criminal Justice, U.S. Government Printing Office, 1970).

[10]Robert L. Bell, Sidney E. Cleveland, Philip G. Hanson, and Walter E. O'Connell, "Small Group Dialogue and Discussion: An Approach to Police-Community Relationships," *The Journal of Criminal Law, Criminology and Police Science* 60 (June 1969): 242-246.

[11]Cecil H. Bell, Jr. and James E. Rozenzweig, "OD in the City: A Potpourri of Pluses and Minuses," *Southern Review of Public Administration* 2 (March 1978): 433-47.

[12]Wayne Boss, "The Not-So-Peaceful Incident at Peaceful Valley: A Case History of an OD Effort in Criminal Justice," in Golembiewski, *Approaches to Planned Change, Vol. 1*, 315-336.

[13]F. Gerald Brown with Robert J. Saunders, "Organization Development in Kansas City, KCOD and SIGN: Six Cases of Organization Development in Municipal Governments," in *First Tango in Boston* (Washington, DC: National Training and Development Service, 1973), 287-348.

[14]*Ibid.*

[15]Donald K. Carew, Sylvia I. Carter, Janice M. Gamache, Rita Hardiman, Bailey W. Jackson, III, and Eunice M. Parisi, "New York State Division of Youth: A Collaborative Approach to the Implementation of Structural Change in Public Bureaucracy," *Journal of Applied Behavioral Science* 13 (July 1977): 327-339.

[16]Chris E. Cherches and Richard E. Byrd, "Shared Management: An Innovation," *Public Management* 54 (May 1972): 11-13.

[17]C. Brooklyn Derr, "Organization Development in One Large Urban School System," *Education and Urban Society* 2 (April 1970): 403-419.

[18]Cabot J. Dow, "Organization Change and Development—The Bellevue Experiment with Emergency and Safety Services," in *First Tango in Boston* (Washington, DC: National Training and Development Service, 1973), 265-286.

[19]James M. Driscoll, Robert G. Meyer, and Charles F. Schamie, "Training Police in Family Crisis Intervention," *Journal of Applied Behavioral Science* 9 (January 1973): 62-82.

[20]Wayne C. Flynn, "Collaborative Decision-Making in a Secondary School," *Education and Urban Society* 8 (February 1976): 172-182.

[21]Joe E. Gentry and J. Foster Watkins, "Organizational Training for Improving Race Relations," *Education and Urban Society* 6 (March 1974): 269-283.

[22]Giblin, 108-118.

[23]William C. Giegold and Richard J. Dunsing, "Team-Building in Local Jurisdiction," *Public Administration Review* 38 (January 1978): 59-63.

[24]Norma B. Gluckstein and Ralph W. Packard, "The Internal-External Change-Agent Team: Bringing Change to a 'Closed Institution,' " *Journal of Applied Behavioral Science* 13 (January 1977): 41-52.

[25]Robert T. Golembiewski, "You Seem to Have Given Up on Us. . ., You Don't Seem to Care for the Authority," *UMTA Case Study Project on MARTA Management* (1977), 1-29.

[26]Robert T. Golembiewski and Alan Kiepper, "MARTA: Toward an Effective Open Giant," *Public Administration Review* 36 (January 1976): 46-60.

[27]Robert T. Golembiewski and Richard F. Perkins, "Reorganizing the General Manager's Office," *UMTA Case Study Project on MARTA Management* (1978), 1-35.

[28]Leonard D. Goodstein and Ronald K. Boyer, "Crisis Intervention in a Municipal Agency: A Conceptual Case History," *Journal of Applied Behavioral Science* 8 (May 1972): 318-340.

[29]Donald C. Klein, "Sensitivity Training and Community Development," in Edgar H. Schein and Warren G. Bennis, *Personal and Organizational Change Through Group Methods* (New York: John Wiley & Sons, 1965): 184-200.

[30]Edward B. Klein, Claudewell S. Thomas, and Elizabeth G. Bellis, "When

Warring Groups Meet: The Use of A Group Approach in Policy-Community Relations," *Social Psychiatry* 6 (No. 2, 1971): 93-99.

[31]Larry L. Krocker, Douglas R. Forsyth, and Richard F. Haase, "Evaluation of a Police-Youth Human Relations Program," *Professional Psychiatry* 5 (1974): 140-154.

[32]Melvin J. LeBaron, "New Perspectives Toward More Effective Local Elected Councils and Boards," in Robert T. Golembiewski and William B. Eddy, eds., *Organization Development in Public Administration, Vol. 2* (New York: Marcel Dekker, 1978), 235-253.

[33]Gilbert Levin and David D. Stein, "System Intervention in a School-Community Conflict," *Journal of Applied Behavioral Science* 6 (September 1970): 337-352.

[34]Dean H. Maiben and Charles J. Schwabe, "Management By Objectives," in *First Tango in Boston* (Washington, DC: National Training and Development Service, 1973), 83-129.

[35]Susan A. Mohrman, *et al.*, "A Survey Feedback and Problem-Solving Intervention in a School District—'We'll Take the Survey but You Can Keep the Feedback,' "in Philip H. Mirvis and David N. Berg, *Failures in Organization Development and Change* (New York: John Wiley & Sons, 1977), 149-189.

[36]K. Olmosk and G. Graversen, "Group Training for Community Relations," *Interpersonal Development* 3 (1974): 100-114.

[37]Glenn M. Parker, "Human Relations Training: Improving Police/Community Relations," *Training and Development Journal* 23 (October 1974): 7-12.

[38]Richard E. Perkins, *et al.*, "A Developmental Approach to Community Change: A Collaborative Approach for Solving City Agency Service Delivery Problems," in *First Tango in Boston* (Washington, DC: National Training and Development Service, 1973), 1-47.

[39]R.K. Ready and Frank A. Faison, "Who Pitched That Inning?," in *First Tango in Boston*, (Washington, DC: National Training and Development Service, 1973), 143-169.

[40]W. Brendan Reddy and Leonard M. Lansky, "Nothing But the Facts—and Some Observations on Norms and Values: The History of a Consultation with a Metropolitan Police Division," *Journal of Social Issues* 31 (1975): 123-38.

[41]N. Dickson Reppucci and J. Terry Saunders, "Innovation and Implementation in a State Training School for Adjudicated Delinquents," in Richard R. Nelson and Douglas Yates, eds., *Innovation and Implementation in Public Organizations* (Lexington, MA: Lexington Books, 1978), 97-116.

[42]Joyce D. Ross and Garry Hare, "Organization Development in Local Government: Results of an IPA Grant," in *First Tango in Boston* (Washington, DC: National Training Development Service, 1973), 253-264.

[43]Lindberg S. Sata, "Laboratory Training for Police Officers," *Journal of Social Issues* 31 (1975), 107-114.

[44]Gordon Pfister, "Outcomes of Laboratory Training for Police Officers," *Journal of Social Issues* 31 (1975): 115-121.

[45]Richard A. Schmuck, "Bringing Parents and Students into School Management," *Education and Urban Society* 6 (February 1974): 205-221.

[46]Robert H. Sebring and David Duffee, "Who Are the Real Prisoners? A Case of Win-Lose Conflict in a State Correctional Institution," *Journal of Applied Behavioral Science* 13 (January 1977): 23-40.

[47]Robert Shellow, "Reinforcing Police Neutrality in Civil Rights Confrontations," *Journal of Applied Behavioral Science* 1 (July 1965): 243-254.

[48]Henry A. Singer, "Training a City in Sensitivity," *Training and Development Journal* 26 (May 1972): 20-23.

[49]W. Lynn Tanner and Muhyia A. Shakoor, "OD at the Grass Roots—First-Line Management Team-Building in a Public Housing Project," in Golembiewski and Eddy, *Vol. 2*, 297-312.

[50]John E. Teahan, "Role Playing and Group Experience to Facilitate Attitude and Value Changes Among Black and White Officers," *Journal of Social Issues* 31 (1975): 35-45.

[51]John T. Thompson and William C. Giegold, "How to Facilitate Organizational Change," *The Virginia Polytechnic Institute and State University Quarterly Magazine* 11 (No. 3, 1977): 23-25.

[52]Marvin R. Weisbord, Howard Lamb and Allan Drexler, *Improving Police Department Management Through Problem-Solving Task Forces* (Reading, MA: Addison-Wesley, 1974).

[53]Goodstein and Boyer, 318-340.

[54]Bell and Rosenzweig, 242-246.

[55]Golembiewski and Perkins, 1-35.

[56]Carew, *et al.*, 327-339.

[57]Ready and Faison, 143-169.

[58]Dow, 265-286.

[59]Golembiewski and Kiepper, 46-60.

[60]The full bibliography may be found in Carl W. Proehl, Jr., "Planned Organizational Change: Assessing Impacts Using Comparative Analysis" (Ph.D. diss., University of Georgia, 1980), 1-164. David W. Sink aided Proehl in treating the 270 cases to permit their use for present purposes.

CHAPTER III

ESTIMATING THE SUCCESS RATIO OF OD EFFORTS: EXPERIENCE WITH PLANNED CHANGE IN PUBLIC-SECTOR SETTINGS, II

This chapter and its companions provide multiple perspective on the efficacy of Organization Development in public settings. The preceding chapter emphasized that public-sector applications face major constraints—greater in degree, at least, and perhaps different in kind, from experience in the private sector. But the public administrationist needs to be more aware than immobilized, for that earlier chapter implies that the constraints signal "caution" far more than "stop."

This chapter and the one following seek to add to that general awareness by asking *the* key question: Given the several constraints, how well does a panel of different public-sector applications work in practice?

Three emphases will dominate the working answer to the key question. As in the previous chapter, the batch of 44 urban studies will be utilized as a first-cut at estimating success rates. Similarly, also, the success ratio will be determined in a large population of 270 governmental OD reports. OD's impact on "hard criteria" will be assessed—on productivity, turnover, and so on. This will be done even though most of the data come from business settings.

I. TOWARD INFORMED SUPPORT/OPPOSITION

The available literature provides a starting point. Several comparative studies[1] suggest an appreciable success rate for various OD applications, but such work has two major limitations for present purposes. The data-bases for such summary studies tend to be small, on the order of tens or scores of cases. For example, the admirable study by Porras deals with 35 cases.[2] And Morrison's useful methodological overview involves 26 cases.[3] In addition, only a small fraction of such data-bases refer to public-sector applications. Perhaps 1:10 represents the usual proportion of public/business applications, and one-tenth of a small data-base does not provide a very solid foundation for generalizations.

Two conclusions seems appropriate. The available literature does not suffice to inform enthusiasts fully, although it encourages them. And the literature's limitations certainly do not silence critics. Drawing on his experience as a student of OD interventions, to illustrate, Giblin concludes that "the unique constraints imposed on public organizations appear to render them almost immune from conventional OD interventions."[4] Others conclude that public-sector OD—if defined as something more than "tinkering with the system"—will be very difficult, if not palpably impossible, for a broad range of reasons. Illustratively, Burke concludes that:[5]

> Most OD consultants find working with bureaucracies, especially public ones, to be difficult at best . . . Apparently, most OD consultants either become more pragmatic and realistic or they have given up when it comes to working with large, bureaucratic organizations.

II. A SIMPLIFIED REVIEW OF OD TECHNOLOGY

Hence this chapter provides needed direction for both enthusiasts and critics. Relying on a large panel of OD applications, it differentiates several classes of interventions and then estimates their effects.

A. Some Specific Classes of Designs

Each OD application will be *sui generis* to an extent, and typically will combine several basic designs. As a first-cut, however, these alternative designs can be classified in terms of eight classes of activities. These eight classes are listed here in order of their complexity and subtlety:[6]

- *process analysis activities*, or applications of behavioral science perspectives to understand complex and dynamic situations. These perspectives can be very simple—e.g., as in routine retrospection among task-group members who ask: How do we feel about what we just did? The perspectives also can be complex, as in seeking to understand interpersonal conflict in terms of differing predispositions of actors via administration of psychological measures and their analysis in terms of applicable theory.[7]

- *skill-building activities*, or various designs for gaining facility with behaviors consistent with OD values, as in giving/receiving feedback, listening, resolving conflict, etc.

- *coaching/counselling activities*, which seek to apply OD values in intimate situations, as between a pair-in-conflict via "third-party consultation."

- *diagnostic activities*, which often include process analysis, but which also may employ interviews, psychological instruments, or opinion surveys to generate data from and for members of some social system. These data get fed-back into that system, to serve as the raw material for action-research sequences: diagnosis, prescription of changes, implementation, and evaluation.

- *team-building activities*, or efforts to increase the efficiency and effectiveness of intact task-groups. Variants may use T-Group or sensitivity training modes,[8] as well as one or more of the activities listed here. Whatever the learning design, the foci are dual: on team processes, as well as on the task and its socio-technical context.

- *inter-group activities*, which seek to build effective satisfying linkages between two or more task groups, such as departments in a large organization.[9]

- *technostructural activities*, which seek to build need-satisfying roles, jobs, and structures. Typically, these activities rest on a "growth psychology" such as that of Maslow, Argyris, or Herzberg. These structural or policy approaches—job enlargement, Flexi-Time, and so on—often are coupled with other OD activities.

- *system-building or system-renewal activities*, which seek comprehensive changes in a large organization's climate and values, using complex combinations of the activities sketched above, and having time-spans in the 3-5 year range.

These eight activities fit with varying precision into the three basic OD modes: interaction-centered; structure; and policies/procedures. Process analysis, skill-building, and coaching/counselling are basically interaction-centered. Technostructural and system-building will emphasize structure, although obviously not to the exclusion of the other two modes. Team-building and inter-group activities often will have dominant interaction emphases, but also often deal with structure and, especially, policies/procedures.

III. TESTING A PANEL OF URBAN OD APPLICATIONS

This introductory vocabulary will be used to differentiate 44 urban OD applications, as well as to suggest the range of such efforts and also to give some sense of their consequences.[10] The analysis will not be reproduced here in detail; but four summary points highlight the main findings.

A. Covers Substantial Number and Broad Range

The panel of urban OD applications presents no analog of the 97-pound weakling, to begin with perhaps the most obvious feature of the accumulated urban OD research. Indeed, the number and the range of this sampler of OD applications may surprise. The common-wisdom typically assumes the rarity of OD in the public sector. That element in the common wisdom must now be tempered substantially, given that the present batch of applications probably represents a tiny fraction of actual applications. And although 44 cases may qualify as "rare," 440 or 4400 certainly do not. Most observers are surprised, indeed, that 44 published reports of urban applications existed when the research summarized here was completed.

B. Responds to Major Challenges

The size of the panel of studies does not seem to have been gained at the expense of avoiding the tough cases, moreover. Urban OD applications clearly do not specialize in easy pieces. Even the brief descriptions of change-targets should establish that point, with plenty to spare. Witness: "explosive situation in police/minority relations;" "reorganization of general manager's office;" "total structural change;" "internal crisis;" and so on. Even more to the point, over one-quarter of the studies undertake comprehensive system-building or system-renewal activities, with longish time-frames. Often, these system-oriented OD efforts also involve basic structural change.

C. Emphasizes Some Designs, Neglects Others

The panel of urban OD applications has an uneven quality. And that unevenness implies significant room for improvement in future applications and research.

The unevenness can be expressed along several dimensions. For example, urban public-sector applications tend to favor some kinds of designs, and to underutilize others. Thus team-building designs definitely are favored, as are skill-training activities. Over 68 percent of the cases use one or the other, or both. These designs may be classified as interaction-centered, in general. Less favored are techno-structural activities, of which the urban batch contains five cases. Private-sector experience is comparable, if not identical, incidentally.

D. Has Attractive Success/Failure Ratio

Finally, the success/failure ratio in the urban applications will not embarrass OD intervenors, granted that reckoning impact can be chancy business. For the quality of the research designs underlying the 44 studies covers a broad range—from casual and short-lived research designs to determined efforts to gather a range of data over a period of years. Moreover, it seems probable that "negative" results will not be reported as frequently as "positive" effects. Finally, observers may differ in interpreting effects in the urban applications, despite safeguards to moderate the grosser interpretive problems. Two independent observers reviewed each of the 44 studies, and assigned each to one of four categories:

1. *highly positive effects* on the efficiency and effectiveness of some relatively-discrete system

2. *definite balance of positive effects*, defined interms of mixed but generally favorable effects: e.g., mostly but not all intended

effects occur on a number of variables; or positive effects occur in one system while negative but not counterbalancing ones affect another

3. *no appreciable effect*

4. *negative effects*, that is those which reduce the efficiency or effectiveness of some sub-system or a broader system of which it constitutes a part

The results of this laborious cross-checking? Observers' individual ratings correlate .73, which indicates substantial agreement.

So what can be said of the success rate, given these qualifications? *Approximately 90 percent* of the ratings indicate at least a "definite balance of positive effects" in the 44 separate studies. Specifically, the 44 applications generate this distribution of effects, in the eyes of two independent observers:

Highly positive effects	12	27.3%
Definite balance of positive effects	27	61.4
No appreciable effect	3	6.8
Negative effects	1	2.3
Not ascertainable	1	2.3
		100.1 (due to rounding)

IV. THREE MORE TIMES —
SAY WHAT ABOUT A FAVORABLE SUCCESS RATIO?

The direct if qualified conclusion above may surprise, if not shock, given the emphasis in previous chapters on the constraints with which public-sector OD must cope.

Can the 90 percent ratio of positive effects be credibly attributed to the probable biases in the population of 44 cases? To be sure, the success ratio derives from published studies, and that may induce a bias in that failures may not get publicized since editors may resist giving space to negative results.[11] Or it might be that the OD intervenors were crafty. Perhaps they picked only the "easy pieces," and hence had a high batting average. Or some might even argue that the OD intervenors simply let their enthusiasm get the better of them, either because of simple overexuberance or blatant self-interest. And 44 cases constitute a thin data-base.

One cannot credibly argue that such possible biases account for the bulk of the 90 percent success rate. But that leaves open the issue of the firmness of the 90 per cent estimate.

Aggressive testing constitutes the basic strategy here. Three other alternative approaches to estimating success rates are summarized here. These three tests do not quiet all doubts, but they do help substantially.

A. A Replication Via Four Levels of Detailed Variables

A dissertation by Carl W. Proehl, Jr., analyzed 574 OD applications, among which were the 270 public-sector cases introduced in Chapter II. Two tables provide summary data about this large population of cases. Thus Table 4 details the frequencies of such OD efforts, classified by the year in which results were reported as well as by level of government at which the interventions occurred. The cases clearly cover a broad range of time, and represent all levels of government. In addition, Table 5 indicates that the 270 cases involve substantial proportions of all classes of OD designs. The 270 cases, in sum, did not concentrate on the simpler designs. Indeed, nearly a third of the cases involved the two most demanding approaches.

TABLE 4. Public-Sector OD Applications, 1950-79, N = 270

	1950-54	1955-59	1960-64	1956-69	1070-74	1975-79	Totals
Federal	0	0	3	11	28	21	63
State	0	0	0	11	21	17	49
Local	1	1	1	18	100	37	158
							270

Based on Carl W. Proehl, Jr., *Planned Organizational Change*. Unpublished Ph.D. dissertation, University of Georgia, 1980.

TABLE 5. Incidence of Eight Classes of OD Activities in Public-Sector OD

Class of OD Design	Individual Applications Classified by Dominant Design	
	N	Percent
Process Analysis	10	4%
Skill-building	65	24
Coaching/Counselling	19	7
Diagnostic	14	7
Team-building	51	19
Inter-group	38	14
Technostructural	44	16
System-building or system-renewal	29	11
	270	100%

Based on Carl W. Proehl, Jr., *Planned Organizational Change.* Unpublished doctoral dissertation, University of Georgia, 1980.

What estimate to place on the success associated with the 270 public-sector reports summarized in Tables 4 and 5? Proehl considered change-targets at four levels of analysis—individual, leader, group, and organization. More or less, *7 out of every 10 change-targets responded positively to OD interventions in the 270 separate studies.* This seems a pretty-fair batting average, confirming the order of magnitude of the differently-calculated success rate for the 44 urban applications.

Now for selected details. The procedure in the Proehl study was quite elaborate, and applied to a broad range of OD interventions—human-processual as well as technostructural approaches—following on the model of a smaller-scale study by Porras. Details would be onerous here, but we can simplify meaningfully in the service of brevity. Proehl observes:[12]

> In order to replicate the Porras study,[13] each of the . . . studies in this research's data-base was searched for the 308 variables developed by Porras and Berg.[14] When one of the variables was found, it was coded according to whether it had improved ("0") or not improved ("1") during the course of the change project. Once all of the variables present in each study were identified and coded, the "percentage of positive reported change" was calculated for each organizational level (individual, leader, group, or organization) or study. This was accomplished by dividing the number of positive variables by the

total number of variables in which chance was desired in each organizational level of each study. For example, a change effort which sought to change five individual-level variables and reported three of them as having changed positively was given a score of 60%. Scores ranged from 0% in a change effort which failed to produce any positive change in process and outcome variables to 100% for a case in which positive change got reported in all variables for which change was desired.

I repeat: using this complex scoring process, Proehl found that change-targets at four levels of abstraction changed as expected, on the average, in about 7 of 10 cases in 270 public-sector applications when all relevant variables in the set of 308 were coded for each application. The specific percentages of positive reported change are:

• Individual level: 78.1 per cent

• Leader level: 68.1 per cent

• Group level: 77.9 per cent

• Organization level: 72.4 per cent

B. A Replication Via An Overall Evaluation

Proehl's 270 cases also were evaluated in a less detailed way. Specifically, how successful were the 270 cases in terms of the four evaluative categories applied to the 44 urban cases? Those categories include:

• highly-positive effects
• definite balance of positive effects
• no appreciable effects
• negative effects

In sum, this kind of evaluation provides overall or global counterpoint to the more detailed evaluation attempted by Proehl in his replication of Porras.

What do the data show? Table 6 provides a summary of the results. Somewhat over 8 of each 10 cases (84 per cent), in sum, were considered by two independent observers to have at least a definite balance of positive effects. The correlation between the two sets of ratings was .78, which suggests substantial agreement between the observers. In addition, almost all cases of disagreement involved the first two evaluative categories: highly-positive effects and definite balance of positive effects. So the agreement was even greater if the reader will settle for a definite balance of positive effects *or better* as the relevant choice-point in differentiating the OD efforts.

Significantly, also, the success estimates in Table 3 are very much like those for private-sector applications. Despite public-sector constraints, then, OD intervenors seem to have learned how to make tolerably-precise adaptations to government of their values-cum-technology.

TABLE 6. Degree of Success of 270 Public-Sector OD Applications

Rating Categories	Individual Applications Classified by Degree of Effects	
	Number	Percent
Highly Positive Effects	110	41%
Definite Balance of Positive Effects	116	43
No Appreciable Effect	18	7
Negative Effects	26	9
	N=270	100%

Based on Carl W. Proehl, Jr., *Planned Organizational Change.* Unpublished doctoral dissertation, University of Georgia, 1980.

C. A Replication Dealing With "Hard Criteria" Only

A recent study by Nicholas[15] provides yet a third perspective on OD success rates, this time with an exclusive focus on "hard criteria"—turnover, absenteeism, costs, objective productivity data, and so on. Nicholas focused on three broad categories of OD interventions:[16]

- Human Processual Approaches

    1. training experiences that focus on interpersonal behavior and group processes, as in "structured laboratory training"

2. team building

3. survey/feedback

- Technostructural Approaches

    1. job design and enlargement, or consolidating "horizontal" work functions to provide greater variety

    2. job enrichment, or "vertical" consolidation of functions to provide greater task identity and significance

    3. sociotechnical systems design to produce self-maintaining and relatively autonomous work groups

- Multifaceted approaches that include both human processual and technostructural designs

Nicholas focused on 65 empirical studies, and found 168 outcome variables on which "hard data" had been gathered, which he classified into four classes: work force behavior, monetary or financial performance, productivity, and output quality.

As Table 7 shows in the column "Overall," somewhat over 50 per cent of the interventions in Nicholas' batch has "significant positive effects."

There is no one obvious way to interpret such success rates. Basically, how "high" is 50 per cent? From one point of view, that rate implies that chances of major success are only one out of two. From another perspective, the chances are 100% or nearly so that conditions in the organizational targets would not have changed for the better in the short-run if just left alone; indeed, conditions may well have worsened. Depending upon which of these two perspectives one adopts, evaluations of the 50 per cent success rate will differ.

But at least three points seem clear enough. First, the success rates for "hard criteria" are lower than the rates reported above, which often deal with self-reports about satisfaction, or productivity, or whatever. These may be called "soft data;" and/or they may be viewed as attitudes that are easier to change, and possibly as requiring change before improvements will occur in measures like turnover, absenteeism, grievance rates, and so on.

TABLE 7. Summary of Impact of OD Interventions on "Hard Criteria"

Percentages of Significant Positive Change by Major Classes of Variables, by Components of Classes, and Overall

OD Approaches	Work Force				Monetary or Financial				Productivity					Overall	Total Number of Studies
	Turnover	Absenteeism	Grievance	Total	Costs	Profits	Sales	Total	Efficiency	Effectiveness	Quantity	Total	Quality		
o Human processual	71%	57%	0%	60%a	0%	100%	100%	60%	50%	33%	50%	45%	50%	54%	15
o Techno-structural	43%	62%	0%	52%	42%	100%	NR	43%	45%	67%	40%	48%	67%	53%	36
o Multifaceted	NR	NR	NR	50%	NR	NR	NR	57%	NR	NR	NR	38%	60%	47%	14
															65

NR = Not reported
a = Each percentage reported is a short-hand for such a formulation: of 15 variables measured in 11 studies, 60 (9) showed significant positive change.

Derived from John M. Nicholas, "The Comparative Impact of Organization Development Interventions on Hard Criteria Measures," *Academy of Management Review*, Vol. 7 (October 1982), pp. 531-542.

Second, Nicnolas seems to set a high standard for "significant positive change." He defines it in one of two ways: as a "statistically significant" difference on a measure before vs. after an intervention, where statistical tests have been applied; or as a 20 per cent change, or better, where statistical techniques have not been used.[17] Needless to say, a 20 per cent increase in productivity, or a 20 per cent reduction in absenteeism, is extremely attractive. Were such changes to occur quite broadly, in fact, profound dynamics would be unleashed. So here Nicholas' standard of "significant change" is high indeed. On the other hand, a "statistically significant" difference can be quite "small" in absolute or percentage terms. Scientists will be impressed, of course; but practical folks may be underwhelmed by confident assertions that changes are "non-random," even if "small."

Third, Nicholas' findings rest on the character and comprehensiveness of his batch of 65 studies and, if anything, a complex of factors suggests that his success rates are understatements because of studies included in his batch and those not included.

Consider only two points that suggest a bias toward the low side. Thus Nicholas notes that "job enrichment with worker participation" has the greatest positive impact on "hard measures"—70 per cent.[18] But most of the studies in Nicholas' category of "Technostructural approaches"—9 of 17 studies—relate to job enlargement or enrichment *without worker participation*, and these have a success rate approximating 42 per cent. This inclusion reduces the "significant positive" impact of Technostructural approaches to 53 per cent, overall. But one could reasonably argue that the latter applications violate rather than respect OD norms associated with participation, involvement and ownership, and hence should *not* be in the Technostructural batch of studies. To be sure, as Nicholas notes, "traditional enrichment programs include participation of middle management and first line supervisors . . ."[19]

To a similar point, Nicholas reports that multifaceted approaches have the lowest success rate—47 per cent, based on 14 studies. This may be correct, but the results may be artifactual. Thus Nicholas notes that the Multifaceted category covers a range of applications, "including but not restricted to changes in policies and procedures (e.g., use of 'flex-time')."[20]

Here Nicholas' results do not square with the approach in this book. Indeed, the following chapter reports on applications at 74 sites of Flexi-Time alone, drawn *only* from the public sector, which in the aggregate impact very favorably on a range of "hard criteria."[21] The success rate reported there approximates 80-90 per cent. Note also that large numbers of Flexi-Time applications also have been made in businesses, with high success rates on both "hard"[22] and "soft"[23] measures.

In sum, on this third point, one can reasonably challenge Nicholas' sample of 65 applications, on grounds of both inclusion and exclusion. In both cases, the most probable effect is that Nicholas' batch of applications would *not* have a bias toward the high side of estimating success rates.

V. A FEW GUIDES FOR ENHANCING PUBLIC-SECTOR OD APPLICATIONS

Although tests of two different populations of OD efforts in the public sector yield generally-substantial estimates of success rates, at least two different classes of factors encourage restraint. Consider that the success rates above may be artifactual in the sense that the methological rigor of available research varies substantially. Some have even proposed that the studies with the weakest research designs generate the most positive results.[24] The evidence based on the largest batch of cases that tested for such effect, however, does *not* find major differences in results when various classes of the rigor of research designs are distinguished.[25]

Another factor encouraging restraint is the interpretation that one puts on the success rates above. The data imply only that *whatever* unique constraints exist in the public sector usually can be accommodated to by the kinds of OD intervenors who write up their experiences.

This is no cute conclusion, and suggests that we know quite a bit about how·to develop such accommodations to the characteristics of the public sector. Let me illustrate here, briefly, some of the guidelines which experience suggests enhance the efficacy of public-sector OD applications, given the real constraints that loom significantly there. Only summary attention will be given here to five guidelines, but two later chapters of this volume will augment the treatment in major ways.

First, pick strategic spots for OD applications. Given the serious public-sector constraints, that is, probably better no application than a low-probability one. What defines high-probability situations? Acute pain is a good enough general indicator—pain great enough so as to put normal constraints into less formidable perspective.

And what about specific indicators of high-probability opportunities for public-sector OD applications? Each case will have unique features, but consider North Carolina, which hosted a robust set of OD activities.[26] An incoming governor wishes to distinguish his administration—as a "real team" that is open and responsive—from its predecessor. That predecessor represents a very different set of interests and alliances; is characterized as a set of more or less conflictful departmental baronies, some legally independent; and follows the "old ways." Moreover, success in this differentiation will increase the probability that the new administration will gain a unique prize. For the first time in modern history, forces are brewing that will legally permit a sitting governor to succeed self. The premium in North Carolina obviously was the quick development of an executive team, agreement about policies and objectives, and so on. Such conditions raise the probability of successful OD applications in the public sector.

Second, public-sector OD interventions must be sensitive to herky-jerky and uneven time-pressures. Hurry up, then wait: this often characterizes the public sector. The prudent OD intervention thus carefully builds designs having several stages, even with specific go/no go choice points. This is good advice for all OD, but its relevance is greatest in the public sector. Alternatively, public-sector interventions initially should tend toward limited-purpose designs, as contrasted with comprehensive social contracts pointed toward broad cultural change in organizations. Skill-training and coaching/counselling activities best represent limited-purpose designs. Team-building is intermediate in its demands in time, energy and commitment. System-building or system-renewal activities have the longest time-frames and greatest energy requirements, but they also promise the greatest pay-outs.

Third, public-sector applications should emphasize policy and structural interventions far more than is presently the case. Not that interaction-centered designs deserve neglect, but they sometimes can be seriously counterproductive. Thus interaction-centered designs can reveal a "new and satisfying way" for relating to others, a revelation that may merely aggravate dissatisfaction about how things "have to be" because of the legal-procedural features of the public sector that often defy modification or change. For example, these unattractive features may derive from centralized rules applicable throughout a jurisdiction, promulgated by a centralized personnel agency, and enacted by a distant legislature intent as much (or more!) on preserving its own avenues of access as on enhancing the efficiency/effectiveness of administrative units. In effect, technostructural activities can provide valuable reinforcement for behaviors and attitudes consistent with OD approaches. Moreover, technostructural rigidities may contraindicate a range of interaction-centered OD designs, except as explicit band-aids or as cooling-out for policies, structures, and procedures that cannot be changed and will continue to produce negative effects in system members.

Fourth, the OD intervenor in the public sector very often must accept a political and limited rather than a technical and comprehensive definition of success. This necessity is fraught with peril, of course, for OD intervenors easily could become mere tools for purposes they neither divine nor accept.

An illustration may provide some guidance on this treacherous point. This author once held an OD design for an unlikely combination—local police, Black Panthers, and a White Citizens' Council. Technically, the design had few of the usual desired objectives or effects: the three groups were not somehow brought closer together, did not empathize more with each other, did not develop collaborative norms, etc. However, the design was right-on for the limited political purpose in question: to have the parties mutually convince one another of their preparedness and resolution to wage urban war, to more accurately estimate the costs/benefits to each of such an outcome, and to discuss the conditions that would or could lead to that consequence. The hope was that each of the three groups would see the virtues of detente, however narrowly-based, as well as the value of a temporary forum to check-out uncertainties or ambiguities. And a frustrating realization suffused the whole experience: "success" would be defined in terms of something dreadful *not* happening and, of course, many factors other than an OD intervention can explain a non-event. So even a great success could be marked down as only reflecting an unrealistic fear about an improbable event which did not occur.

Fifth, OD intervenors must be cautious about simply applying designs to the public sector because of consistently good private-sector results. Basically, this admonition urges that careful diagnosis should proceed *any* OD application, *wherever*. This basic position also encompasses the possibility that private/public differences may be very pronounced and common.

The primacy of diagnosis over disputation concerning public/ private differences can be illustrated briefly. For example, classic OD designs are available to deal with crises of conflict or disagreement, and those designs have quite predictable effects. Unreflective public-sector use of such designs may be ill-advised, however. For "crises of agreement" seem to me endemic there, or at least far more common than in the private sector. Details would be burdensome, but here note only that the two types of crises require different approaches. Illustratively, crises of conflict often require only new data, while crises of agreement must primarily overcome despair and fear of exclusion. Consider these two responses to the same information:

- "Oh, so that's what's wrong, I didn't know that. What can we do to solve that problem?"

- "Sure, I knew that. Nobody talks about it much, because there's nothing that can be done. That's just the way things are around here."

Although the second response seems more characteristic of the public sector, many similar private-sector cases will be encountered.[27] Careful prior diagnosis is required in both cases before selecting a design.

FOOTNOTES

[1]E.g., Peggy Morrison, "Evaluation in OD: A Review and An Assessment," *Group and Organization Studies*, Vol. 3 (March, 1978), pp. 42-70; and Jerry Porras, "The Comparative Impact of Different OD Techniques and Intervention Intensities," *Journal of Applied Behavioral Science*, Vol. 15 (April 1979), pp. 156-178.

[2]Porras, *op. cit.*

[3]Morrison, *op. cit.*

[4]Edward J. Giblin, "Organization Development: Public Sector Theory and Practice," *Public Personnel Management*, Vol. 5 (March 1976), p. 108.

[5]W. Warner Burke, "Organization Development and Bureaucracies in the 1980s," *Journal of Applied Behavioral Science*, Vol. 16 (July 1980), p. 429.

[6]Sections B and C are adapted from Robert T. Golembiewski and David Sink, "OD Interventions in Urban Settings, II: Public Sector Success with Planned Change," *International Journal of Public Administration*, Vol. 1 (No. 2, 1979), pp. 115-141.

[7]Arthur Blumberg and Robert T. Golembiewski, *Learning and Change in Groups* (London: Penguin, 1976), pp. 22-35.

[8]*Ibid.*, esp. pp. 57-61.

[9]For one example, consult Robert T. Golembiewski, "Transitioning Between the Several MARTAs," *UMTA Case Studies on MARTA Management*, 1978.

[10]The references for the individual studies in Table 1 may be found in the preceding chapter.

[11]Much can be learned from failures, a crucial point often neglected in the behavioral sciences and in OD. On both aspects, see Philip H. Mirvis and David N. Berg, *Failures in Organization Development and Change* (New York: John Wiley & Sons, 1977).

[12]Carl W. Proehl, Jr., *Planned Organizational Change: Assessing Impacts Using Comparative Analysis*. Unpublished doctoral dissertation, University of Georgia, 1980.

[13]Porras, "The Comparative Impact of Different OD Techniques and Intervention Intensities."

[14]Jerry I. Porras and Per Olaf Berg, "Evaluation Methodology in Organization Development," *Journal of Applied Behavioral Science*, Vol. 14 (April 1978), pp. 151-173.

[15]John M. Nicholas, "The Comparative Impact on Organization Development Interventions on Hard Criteria Measures," *Academy of Management Review*, Vol. 7 (October 1982), pp. 531-542.

[16]*Ibid.*, p. 532.

[17]*Ibid.*, p. 533.

[18]*Ibid.*, p. 534.

[19]*Ibid.*, p. 535.

[20]*Ibid.*, p. 534.

[21]For the original sources, consult Robert T. Golembiewski and Carl W. Proehl, Jr., "Public-Sector Applications of Flexible Workhours: A Review of Available Experience," *Public Administration Review*, Vol. 40 (January, 1980), pp. 72-85; and Golembiewski, "Public-Sector Productivity and Flexible Workhours," *Southern Review of Public Adminstration*, Vol. 4 (December 1980), pp. 324-339.

[22]E.G., Stanley D. Nollen, "Does Flexitime Improve Productivity?," *Harvard Business Review*, Vol. 57 (September 1979), pp. 16-18, 76, and 80.

[23]E.g., Robert T. Golembiewski and Carl W. Proehl, Jr., "A Survey of the Empirical Literature on Flexible Workhours," *Academy of Management Review*, Vol. 3 (October 1978), pp. 837-853.

[24]D.E. Terpstra, "Evaluating Selected Organization Development Interventions," *Journal of Applied Psychology*, Vol. 66 (1981), pp. 541-543.

[25]R.J. Bullock and Dan Svyantek, "Positive-Findings Bias in Positive-Findings Bias Research: An Unsuccessful Replication." Unpublished MS., 1983.

[26]For an interpretive overview, see David H. Kiel, *Impact of the First Three Years of the North Carolina Governor's Program for Executive and Organizational Development, 1979: A Summary and Analysis of Results*. Mimeod., September 1980. See also Kiel's "An OD Strategy for Public Implementation," *Public Administration Review*, Vol. 42 (July 1982), pp. 375-383.

[27]E.g., Robert T. Golembiewski and Ronald Fox, "Something Awkward Happened on the Way to Breaching the Barriers to Creativity." Paper prepared for delivery at the Fall Meeting of the Organization Development Network, San Francisco, October 10, 1980.

CHAPTER IV

EVALUATING APPLICATIONS OF FLEXIBLE WORKHOURS: EXPERIENCE WITH PLANNED CHANGE IN PUBLIC-SECTOR SETTINGS, III

This chapter implies a biblical theme: The last shall be first, or at least damn convenient and impactful.

OD innovations concerning policies and procedures were historically the last to receive detailed attention, and yet this chapter assigns an important place to such interventions consistent with OD values. Indeed, in some senses, experience with one such intervention puts it in a class by itself—considering simplicity of concept, a high degree of apparent goof-proofness, minimum demands on the development of appropriate attitudes and skills, as well as a burgeoning record for broad-ranging and positive impact.

This may seem an overblown introduction to flexible workhours— henceforth, Flexi-Time or F-T—but the available experience justifies it, even given a tentativeness appropriate to major methodological inelegancies in the research. Broadly, F-T programs in the last decade or so have proliferated around the world, and most observers associate them with a broad range of positive effects for organizations as well as their members, in personal life as well as at work. F-T may rightly be said to be a major managerial innovation, simple though it seems.

Basically, this special status inheres in F-T's responsiveness to individual differences and situational variations. For example, within general guidelines and policies, the individual determines what daily hours of work are "too early" or "too late," "too much" or "too little." This capacity for self-equilibration makes F-T a prototypic OD effort, which basically seeks ways of increasing responsible freedom at work. Moreover, F-T applications also encourage a variety of other adaptations at work consistent with OD values. Thus supervisors must trust employees in reasonable ways, which means defining a "reasonable day's work" and minimizing supervisory obtrusiveness.

The innovation initially permeated business organizations, and is getting much more public-sector notice.[1] Paradoxically, the diffusion of this innovation has proceeded apace, in both arenas, without two crucial kinds of knowledge: a comprehensive review of the available F-T literature; and a sophisticated understanding of why, when, and how F-T "works."

Perhaps the apparent simplicity of the F-T concept explains this neglect. The basic F-T model provides for two kinds of daily hours: a band of "fixed hours" of variable duration, often 3-5 hours; and some "variable hours," often two periods of 2-3 hours that come earlier and later than normal workhours. Employees must be present during the fixed hours. And they may otherwise so arrange their arrival/departure times during some accounting period that they work enough variable hours to meet their conditions of employment. Typically, this means 35-40 hours per week. Many variations exist in specific F-T plans concerning how many hours can be "banked" to reduce workhours, what conditions constrain employee choice, and so on. Time-recording devices also often are used, but not always. These differentiating details get no further attention here.

I. HOW GOES IT WITH F-T IN THE PRIVATE SECTOR?[2]

The major available reviews of the literature imply that the common wisdom seems quite justified in terms of global outcomes, especially in business-sector applications,[3] even though we lack an understanding of the specifics of why and how F-T "works." Conveniently, consider a 1978 review, which covered 20 studies involving 79 separate applications, with all but 5 coming from private-sector experience. Overall, F-T seems to generate positive effects under a broad range of conditions. The reviewers conclude in that summary effort:[4]

> Despite real limitations in available studies, both behavioral and attitudinal data encourage F-T applications. "Hard" data indicate that F-T is at least low-cost and may indeed imply handsome dividends on several critical organization measures. "Soft" data strongly reinforce such a bias toward F-T applications, as seen from three organizational perspectives—that of employees, first-line supervisors, and managers.

These conclusions derive from a panel of studies which make a serious effort to track F-T effects, and which report them in sufficient detail to permit some confidence about interpretations. This panel was selected from a mass of bibliographic citations—dominantly boosterish in tone, and anecdotal and impressionistic when describing effects—which now run into the hundreds. The citations come from published sources, in the main, but also include in-house studies, dissertations, and studies by external consultants. Our definition of what constitutes a "serious effort to track F-T effects" would not satisfy rigorous canons of empirical research, but it does exclude the most casual efforts.

The optimistic findings of the initial review have survived additional search. Data concerning an additional 130 applications, again dominantly from business, were found in the next 18 months or so that meet our general criteria. They require no substantive changes in the interpretations of the original review.[5] More casual search extends the tone of findings to the present time.

II. SKETCHING THIS APPROACH TO PUBLIC-SECTOR F-T APPLICATIONS

What may be said of F-T applications in the public-sector? Globally, the literature reflects two themes: hurry up, and wait. The "hurry up" theme is well-represented by Rubin's recent article (see footnote 1), which deftly describes the F-T notion, summarizes its anticipated advantages, suggests that now is the time to get on with more public-sector applications, but only gently reviews the available public-sector experience. The "wait" theme gets profound expression in the on-going research plans of the U.S. Office of Personnel Management, which completed a three-year program of research on F-T even as applications burgeoned.

This article proposes to slip between these two common public-sector emphases. How? Our evolving panel of "serious" F-T studies contains 32 public-sector bibliographic items which will be analyzed below basically via interpretation of five tabular summaries. In order, the tables:

- present an overview of major characteristics of the literature;

- summarize F-T's major effects on employee attitudes;

- provide perspective on the major supervisory attitudes related to F-T;

- review behavioral effects of F-T applications observed in public agencies; and

- provide a separate and special overview of F-T's effects on productivity, via a test of three prominent aspects of the common wisdom.

Generally, the model for analysis in the original review will be followed below.

Two major notes are in order here. First, the first four emphases above will be approached via 32 separate F-T studies, which refer to applications at 74 sites. These 32 cases are described in the first four tables below. Thirty citations deal with applications at one site or within one unit of government, applications for which we have been able to secure specific evaluation reports, either from published or internal sources. Two summary studies—each reviewing 22 applications—also are listed below the broken line toward the bottom of the several tables below. Of the latter 44 applications, 14 are described individually above the broken line. Original evaluations concerning the remaining cases in the two summary studies were not available to us.

Second, the fifth table below (Table 12) tests three aspects of the common wisdom about the public sector. It relies on a batch of 16 F-T studies that deal with "measured productivity," as variously defined.

III. MAJOR CHARACTERISTICS OF PUBLIC-SECTOR F-T APPLICATIONS

The panel of public-sector studies has at least seven major characteristics, as Table 8 helps establish. First, as an important preliminary note, F-T applications can differ significantly, as in the degree of employee discretion they permit. Many versions allow employees to change their hours of work without notice, day by day; but a few require prior clearance with supervisors and no subsequent change without notice. Similarly, some versions permit "banking" of excess hours worked one day, to be used to reduce hours worked during another day, or week, or even month. Other plans permit no banking, in contrast, so starting time determines quitting time.

Table 8 does not distinguish these and other program variants, given the small number of cases. Possibly, perhaps even probably, such distinctions may isolate significantly-different clusters of effects in larger data batches or in research comparing alternative ways in which individuals can influence their workhours. [6]

Second, public-sector studies provide little specific insight about a desirable model of implementation. Hence Table 8 stands moot on this critical point. This deficiency also characterizes the private-sector literature, albeit in lesser degree. Some may even argue that it does not make much difference, in that we have been able to unearth only two F-T applications that "did not work," and those in organizations which saw F-T autocratically and foolishly imposed.

While holding out the possibility that even autocratic and top-down implementation may succeed, more often than not, we encourage building into F-T applications numerous opportunities for involvement, participation, and even broadly-based veto. Illustratively, in a major business application, the full implementation cycle had these major features *from the outset*:[39]

- all line managers in a large R & D operation were presented several options for increasing employee freedom and discretion at work, including the F-T concept;

- possible advantages/disadvantages of the several options were discussed in terms of how each option "would work here;"

- all managers committed to try a lengthy pilot study with one F-T variant within a part of R & D, which variant they helped design;

- all managers helped develop an evaluation effort whose data they agreed would permit them to determine the success or failure of the pilot *in their eyes*;

- several of the managers volunteered their units as experimental and comparison groups for the duration of the pilot study, after checking with their subordinates; and

- at the conclusion of the pilot study, and utilizing both attitudinal and performance measures, managers decided about continuation and further diffusion of the F-T variant.

TABLE 8. Overview of Panel of Public-Sector Studies Reporting Specific Flexi-Time Effects

Study	Setting	Union Involved?	Study Design	Comparison Group (s)?	Hard/ Soft Data?	Statistical Treatment?
Air University Maxwell A.F.B. Alabama (1975) [7]	100 employees	?	Post only	No	S	None
Atlanta Regional Commission (1979) [8]	All employees (approx. 60) in metro planning agency	No	Post/Long Post	No	S	None
Crawford (1979) [9]	Four departments, Prince George, Maryland County Government	Yes	Post only	No	S	None
District of Columbia (1975) [10]	400 employees in Department of Human Resources	?	Generally Post only; some Pre/Post comparisons	No	H/S	None
Environmental Protection Agency (1977 & 1978) [11]	Headquarters, Environmental Protection Agency	?	Generally Post only; some Pre/Post comparisons	No	H/S	None
Finegan (1977); Bureau of Government Financial Operations (1975 & 1976) [12]	1450 employees, U.S. Treasury Department	?	Generally Post only; some Pre/Post comparisons	No	H/S	None

TABLE 8. Overview of Panel of Public-Sector Studies Reporting Specific Flexi-Time Effects (Continued)

Study	Setting	Union Involved?	Study Design	Comparison Group (s)?	Hard/ Soft Data	Statistical Treatment?
Finkle (1979) [13]	950 employees in five New Jersey State Agencies	?	Pre/Post	No	H/S	None
General Services Administration (1977) [14]	100 employees of National Personnel Records Center; 26 employees of Central Reference Division of Office of National Archives	?	Pre/Post	No	H/S	None
Giammo (1977); Social Security Administration (1974) [15]	Eight offices and bureaus of the Social Security Administration	Yes	Pre/Post	Yes	H/S	None
Harvey & Luthans (1979) [16]	27 employees in a human services agency	?	Pre/Post	Yes	H/S	Analysis of Variance
Mueller & Cole (1977); U.S. Geological Survey (1977) [17]	2700 employees; Washington, DC offices of a Federal agency	Yes	Generally Post only; some Pre/Post comparisons	No	H/S	None

TABLE 8. Overview of Panel of Public-Sector Studies Reporting Specific Flexi-Time Effects (Continued)

Study	Setting	Union Involved?	Study Design	Comparison Group(s)?	Hard/ Soft Data?	Statistical Treatment?
Naval Ship Engineering Systems Command, Port Hueneme, Calif. (1975)[18]	1700 employees	?	Generally Post only; some Pre/Post comparisons	?	H/S	None
Office of Accounting, Department of Labor (1977)[19]	All 112 employees in the office	Yes	Pre/Post/Long Post	No	H/S	None
Osteen (1979)[20]	46 offices of the Library of Congress	Yes	Pre/Post	No	H/S	None
Port Authority (1975)[21]	850 non-unionized employees	No	Pre/Post	No	H/S	None
Reutter (1973)[22]	250 employees in three agencies of Baltimore City government	Yes	Post only	No	S	None
Salvatore (1974)[23]	110 employees in a Canadian Federal agency	Yes	Generally Post only; some Pre/Post comparisons	No	H/S	None
Santa Clara (1975)[24]	Juvenile-Adult Probation Dept.	Yes	Pre/Post/Long Post	No	S	None

TABLE 8. Overview of Panel of Public-Sector Studies Reporting Specific Flexi-Time Effects (Continued)

Study	Setting	Union Involved?	Study Design	Comparison Group (s)?	Hard/ Soft Data?	Statistical Treatment?
Seattle Civil Service Commission (1975) [25]	167 employees	?	Post only	No	S	None
Shulman (1979) [26]	Federal Home Loan Bank; 20 departments with 225 employees	No	Post only	No	S	None
Stevens & Elsworth (1979) [27]	90 clerical workers in three Australian government departments	?	Pre/Post	No	S	F-Test; Multiple Discriminant Analysis Procedure
Swart (1974) [28]	33 employees in Inglewood, Calif. all but police & fire personnel	?	Post only	No	S	None
Thornton (1973) [29]	50 members of Personnel Department in a Canadian Federal agency	?	Pre/Post	No	H/S	None

TABLE 8. Overview of Panel of Public-Sector Studies Reporting Specific Flexi-Time Effects (Continued)

Study	Setting	Union Involved?	Study Design	Comparison Group (s)?	Hard/ Soft Data?	Statistical Treatment?
Transportation Systems Center (1979)[30]	Employees at Transportation Systems Center of the Department of Transportation's Research & Special Programs Admin.	?	Pre/Post	No	H/S	None
Uhlmann (1977)[31]	Denver regional office, HEW	?	Pre/Post	No	H/S	None
U.S. Army Natick Laboratories (1974)[32]	1200 laboratory employees	?	Generally Post only; some Pre/Post comparisons	No	H/S	None
U.S. Information Agency (1975)[34]	33 employees	?	Pre/Post	No	H/S	None
Vieth (1977)[35]	1335 civiliam administrative employees, Tinker A.F.B.	?	Post only	No	H/S	None

TABLE 8. Overview of Panel of Public-Sector Studies Reporting Specific Flexi-Time Effects (Continued)

Study	Setting	Union Involved?	Study Design	Comparison Group (s)?	Hard/ Soft Data?	Statistical Treatment?
Walker, Fletcher & McCleod (1975) [36]	125 employees in two British Civil Service offices	?	Post only	No	S	None
Ronen Primps & Cloonan (1978) [37]	Summary of 22 U.S. Federal applications	Yes	Pre/Post	?	H/S	?
U.S. Army (1977) [38]	22 flexitime experiments in various army units	?	Pre/Post	No	H/S	None

When word about the experiment and its subsequent diffusion to all of R & D spread, corporate officials at first wanted to extend *the* F-T variant throughout headquarters' operations, in one fell-swoop. Consistent with the design above, however, they were urged alternatively to specify only the maximum F-T properties to which they were willing to commit. With the help of corporate personnel, major cost-centers then could variously decide on specific F-T variants—to suit different kinds of work, employee preferences, and so on. Almost all cost-centers decided to implement F-T, using basically four variant designs, which variously approached the maxima authorized by corporate officials.[40]

Third, existing F-T applicatons in the public sector clearly cluster in a narrow range: they often relate to professional and clerical jobs in white-collar settings, and they usually involve small numbers of employees. Both factors may simplify socialization and informal controls, making such applications an easier piece. One can reasonably raise the question of the generalizability of F-T effects to thing-processing or production settings, consequently, and perhaps also to worksites with large numbers of employees.

Fourth, some of the available studies detailed in Table 8 exclude various categories of employees. Thus the Port Authority application excludes all union employees, and Inglewood's application does not cover fire or police services.

We lack knowledge about what effects such exclusions generate, but we can be certain that—as in the case of teaching, fire and police personnel—there will be numerous public jobs to which only restricted F-T variants may be appropriate, or none at all. Morale problems may inhere in such exclusions, whether they are necessary or merely convenient.

Fifth, available studies deal with an important source of variability in that they occur in both union and non-union settings. But the research is all-but-moot concerning the specific characteristics of appropriate hosts, whether management or union. Of course, willingness to experiment with F-T implies a definite preference for influence-sharing vs. authoritarian systems. And F-T applications clearly do not require the range of skills associated with many other approaches to participative management, such as team-building. Plainly, however, we cannot specify the characteristics of a "culturally prepared" host organization from the available research.

Sixth, about half of the sources in Table 8 give attention to behavioral as well as attitudinal measures, to "hard" as well as "soft" data. Much organizational research justly gets criticized for its basic reliance on "soft" data; and bottom-line effects often are neglected in idealistic visions of a new humanism. So both hard and soft data are desirable in F-T studies.

Seventh, and most prominently, F-T research may be criticized on technical grounds as deficient in several obvious particulars. For example, only two studies in Table 8 utilize control or comparison groups. Despite the great problems of providing real "controls" or "comparisons," especially in the field, they do help eliminate hypothetical explanations for observed effects alternative to the treatment.

Moreover, about half of the 32 studies in the panel use a post-test-only design, and they permit only such weak conclusions: X percent of respondents after Z months of experience with F-T report that they are satisfied with effects. More robust interpretations would be supported by observations made just before and some time after an F-T installation, in contrast. Such Pre/Post designs were used in about half of the individual studies reported in Table 8. Longitudinal studies are rare. These report observations at several points surrounding an F-T treatment, and permit substantial confidence about F-T effects. Table 8 contains two such cases—Pre-test vs. Short Post-test vs. Long Post-test—which convention means that three or more observations were made, at least one before an F-T intervention, another shortly thereafter, and one or more additional observations over an extended period of time.

Finally, at best, virtually all public-sector F-T studies use only straightforward data-arrays, without any statistical treatment. Statistical methods only serve to aid choice-processes, of course. But they can usefully help distinguish mere randomness in data from noteworthy variations. Only two of the present panel of public sector studies utilize statistical methods for comparing data.

These technical criticisms do not reflect mere methodological fussiness. Not all managerially-useful research need follow the natural-science model. Indeed, following Porras and Roberts, we need to distinguish at least four kinds of useful and legitimate "research:"[41]

- *implementation research*, as in the use of diagnostic interviews or surveys to permit choice of appropriate interventions;

- *evaluation research*, which tests for global outcomes to assess the potency of interventions;

- *assessment research*, which focuses on global outcomes as well as on the processes inducing them; and

- *theory-building research*, which is oriented toward discovering fundamental relationships; as by testing hypotheses.

F-T studies basically provide examples of only the first and second types; and quite weak examples at that. More assessment and theory-building research are much needed, given that implementation and evaluation research will predominate for most practical purposes.

IV. MAJOR ATTITUDINAL EFFECTS: EMPLOYEES

The sketch above of F-T's behavioral effects has a special salience, given that the common wisdom has always seen F-T's most powerful effects acting on employee attitudes. Note that critics have been restrained when it comes to predicting awkward "soft" outcomes of F-T—on employee satisfaction, morale, and so on—even when they aggressively deny any positive effects on output, costs, or other "hard" indicators. To be sure, critics do worry that with F-T co-workers may be less available, that communication may become more difficult, etc.

The total F-T literature—again, predominantly business-oriented—provides very strong support for the rosy view. Indeed, the reported attitudinal effects are all-but-unanimously positive.[42]

But what of public-sector F-T effects on employee attitudes or feelings? Five points seem most relevant concerning Table 9, which summarizes governmental experience with F-T. Where possible, actual percentages are cited. Where such magnitudes are not provided by researchers who nonetheless report a consequence, Table 9 uses such conventions as "effect cited."

First, public-sector F-T studies give major attention to "soft" effects, as is suggested by the substantial number of columns in Table 9. These columns, moreover, refer only to the most common attitudinal effects attributed to F-T.

Second, the positive effects have it, on overwhelming balance. The negative effects seem tolerable—as in the percentage reporting abuse of

TABLE 9. Summary of Attitudinal Effects Reported by Employees in All Available Public-Sector Studies

Study	% Urging F-T Be Continued	% Reporting Productivity Increased	% Reporting Morale Improved	% Reporting Greater Control of Work & Personal Life	% Reporting Decreased Availability of Others, Less Communications Efficiency	% Reporting Resentment of Time-Keeping System	% Reporting Abuse of F-T	% Reporting Favorable Effects on Commuting
	$\bar{x} = 96.1\%$ in 12 studies	$\bar{x} = 38.1\%$ in 9 studies; effect cited in 8 other studies; $\bar{x} = 5.2\%$ in 6 studies report decreases	$\bar{x} = 69.8\%$ in 9 studies; effect cited in 9 other studies	$\bar{x} = 74.0\%$ in 6 studies; effect cited in 14 other studies	$\bar{x} = 10\%$ in 3 studies; effect cited in 3 other studies; 15% in 1 study report increases	$\bar{x} = 23.5\%$ in 4 studies; effect cited in 5 other studies	10% in 1 study	$\bar{x} = 60.9\%$ in 8 studies; effect cited in 11 other studies
Ronen, Primps & Cloonan (1978)	100% of 6 reporting agencies	Effect cited	Effect cited	8 of 8 reporting agencies	Opposite effect cited in one agency	Both positive and negative attitudes cited		12 of 12 agencies reporting
U.S. Army (1977)	85%	85%	100%	100%				77%

F-T, which probably approximates the level of abuse under other systems of workhours. Note one exception—the whopping 80% of respondents who report resentment with the time-keeping system adopted at the Atlanta Regional Commission. Even there, 95% of all employees want F-T to continue, including all of the supervisors.

Third, the panel of public-sector studies deals only with individual attitudinal items, as is true of the full F-T literature, with only one exception.[43] The psychometric properties of the data—whether they constitute scales, or generate independent factors, and so on—do not get explored. This leaves the findings summarized in Table 9 open to criticism. Specifically, the eight attitudinal items reported there are the most frequently referred to. But those eight items might tap eight orthogonal dimensions, or some smaller number. Those eight items might even measure only the same phenomenal domain eight different ways. It makes a great difference, on technical and substantive grounds.

Fourth, public-sector F-T studies resemble the broader family in an important and related regard. As we concluded elsewhere, F-T studies do not utilize available scales or instruments—tapping involvement, tension at work, satisfaction, and so on—that would provide insight concerning why and how F-T applications "work." This conclusion seems appropriate, then:[44]

> Such scales or instruments often constitute relatively-known quantities in terms of their dimensionality, reliability, validity, and so on . . . Altogether, the failure to use conventional effects reflects the primitive state of the available F-T literature.

Fifth, the overall thrust of the data trends cannot be reasonably doubted, whatever the lack of elegance in design and methods. Table 9 implies profound and positive shifts in attitudes following F-T applications, which provide major motivation for F-T applications.

V. MAJOR ATTITUDINAL EFFECTS: SUPERVISORS

In the speculation about F-T effects, both proponent and critic emphasize the first-line supervisory role. The issues related to this critical linking role are significant ones. Does F-T deprive the immediate supervisor of a significant control-point? Does it complicate the scheduling and monitoring of work? Does it make communications more difficult?

Such questions relate to both organizational traditionalists as well as humanists. The former often see F-T as implying a loss of leverage for keeping employees in-line; and organizational humanists are mindful of the literature which stresses the first-line supervisor's central role in influencing the quality of workinglife, which role they have no desire to complicate.

What does the record show? For the full array of F-T studies, optimism seems definitely appropriate. The balance of effects clearly favors positive outcomes. As we summarized the available evidence:[45]

> Overall, no more than a fifth of the direct supervisors surveyed ever report that F-T complicated their job—in scheduling employee work, in communicating, etc. Typically, the percentages of first-line supervisors reporting such negative effects are substantially lower than 20 percent—more like 5 to 10 percent.
>
> ...first-line supervisors imply that F-T has desirable effects that seem to more-than-counterbalance any negative effects. For example, at least 70 percent of each population of first-line supervisors wanted their F-T programs to continue, with the average being closer to 90 percent ... Forty percent or more see a lessening of commuting problems under their F-T programs.

And what of the public-sector experience, as summarized in Table 10? Note that the nine effects referred to there are the most frequently cited ones in the panel of studies.

We highlight only four points implied in Table 10. First, actual research attention belies the avowed criticality of the first-line supervisors. About a third of the public-sector panel of studies fail to provide any data about impacts on the first-line supervisory role; and most studies deal with only one or a few issues of relevance, typically in generalized terms rather than specific magnitudes.

Second, the weight of the available data clearly supports the view the direct supervisors, at worst, report only modest negative effects of F-T. The paucity of entries in columns 4-8 of Table 10 suggests the point. And even in the case of the Atlanta Regional Commission—which reports the highest proportion of negative effects—the full description of the application does not generate alarm.

Third, reports from first-line supervisors also imply that F-T's desirable effects more-than-counterbalance any negative effects. For example, even in the Atlanta Regional Commission—the exceptional

TABLE 10. Summary of Attitudinal Effects Reported by Employees in All Available Public-Sector Studies

Study	% Urging F-T Be Continued	% Reporting Productivity Increased	% Reporting Morale Increased	% Reporting Increased Problems Scheduling Employee Work	% Reporting Increased Problems Scheduling Personal Time	% Reporting Increased Problems in Communicating with Colleagues	% Reporting Increased Problems Accounting for Employee Time	% Reporting Abuse of F-T	% Reporting Favorable Effects Commuting
	$\bar{x}$ = 99% in 6 studies	$\bar{x}$ = 35.1% in 4 studies	$\bar{x}$ = 75.8% in 4 studies	1.5% report major problems, 21.5% minor problems in 1 study	$\bar{x}$ = 22.5% in 2 studies	$\bar{x}$ = 17.5% in 2 studies		10% in 1 study	61% in 1 study
		effect cited in 9 other studies	effect cited in 4 other studies	effect cited in 7 other studies	effect cited in 4 other studies	effect cited in 3 other studies decreases reported in 2 other studies	effect cited in 3 other studies	effect cited in 2 other studies	effect cited in 5 other studies
Ronen, Primps, & Cloonan (1978)	Effect cited	Effect cited	3 of 3 agencies reporting	Opposite effect cited in 1 agency	Opposite effect cited in 1 agency	Opposite effect cited in 1 agency	Effect cited		2 of 2 agencies reporting

case where approximately 20-40 percent of first-line supervisors report greater problems in scheduling and in communicating with colleagues—all supervisors urged the continuance of F-T beyond a trial period. Consistently, substantial majorities report increases in morale: the crude average approximates 55 percent, even including one case of an agency reporting no overall increase which was entered in the calculation as 0 percent. This seems a positive effect, whatever the individual meanings attributed to "morale" by respondents. Finally, many supervisors report a lessening of commuting problems under their F-T programs.

Fourth, although the panel of public-sector applications does not reflect the point, longitudinal research implies that first-line supervisory attitudes about F-T might lag behind those of employees. In one case, for example, supervisors remained initially cautious about F-T. In contrast, employees were highly positive about F-T from the start. After 6 months, however, the supervisors had climbed on the band-wagon, while employees maintained or even raised their enthusiasm for F-T.[46]

The supervisory lag has a credible explanation. F-T implies some changes in supervisory behaviors/attitudes that require time for working through.[47] Sooner rather than later, however—the slim data imply—almost all supervisors have or gain the skills and patience to develop any changes appropriate for F-T. And then supervisory caution or suspicion dissipates. This adaptive process is encouraged and reinforced, one suspects, by the employee's positive response to F-T.

Note that, if a learning-lag does exist for first-line supervisors, Table 10 understates the favorableness of supervisory reactions to F-T. As Table 8 implies, longitudinal studies are rare. Almost all studies use Pre/Post or Post-only designs—the former compared observations before a F-T applications with observations at a later time, usually a matter of no more than a few months; and the latter design makes observations only after a F-T application, as when respondents are asked how satisfied they are with F-T.

VI. MAJOR BEHAVIORAL EFFECTS

Along with F-T's obvious effects on heightened employee discretion and enhanced attitudes, as Tables 8 through 10 imply, proponents typically argue that F-T applications will induce a number of organizationally-attractive behavioral outcomes. Two approaches below seek to test such optimistic predictions about "hard" outcomes, in contrast to "soft" outcomes like those on attitudinal change just reviewed.

The review has two stages. F-T effects on five common behavioral indicators will be sketched, to begin. Then the focus will shift to a test of three aspects related to a significant behavioral indicator—measured productivity.

A. Five Behavioral Indicators Impacted by F-T

Five behavioral indicators—sick leave or absenteeism, tardiness, turnover, overtime, and general trends in costs—often become focal in discussions of F-T effects. Illustratively, most propose that F-T tends to reduce tardiness, as well as absenteeism and sick leave, especially those of the one-day variety. What rationale supports such a view? An employee under conventional workhours who oversleeps, or who succumbs to an urge to take advantage of a sale, might "call in sick" even if only an hour or so of lateness is contemplated. Such white lies would not be necessary under F-T. F-T also is often thought to reduce turnover, by making conditions at work more attractive. Many also argue that overtime will be reduced, with the flexible hours permitting longer (or shorter) workdays when the situation requires. Relatedly, flexing employees could provide longer service-days for users, without overtime, a consideration of some magnitude in the public sector.

Critics doubt these sunny prospects. For example, they maintain that F-T will only increase costs. Thus more employees might be necessary to provide coverage, costs of supervision might increase, and overtime charges might rise, particularly as hourly workers remain to provide support services to salaried employees who are flexing a workday longer than normal.

The ayes have it, quite decisively, when the total F-T literature is surveyed.[48] Favorable behavioral effects dominate in these studies, which basically reflect business-sector experience.

What does the slimmer public-sector literature reveal about the behavioral effects of F-T applications? Table 11 summarizes the available data, reported as specific magnitudes whenever possible. General terms also are used—for example, "no appreciable effect" or "reduced"—to provide the most suitable summary of results.

TABLE 11. Summary of Five Behavioral Effects Reported in All Available Public-Sector Studies.

Study	Sick Leave	Absenteeism	Tardiness	Turnover	Overtime	Trends in Costs
	reduced x̄ = 26% in 5 studies	reduced x̄ = 63% in 3 studies	reduced or eliminated in 9 studies	reduced in 3 studies	39% of offices in 1 study report a small decrease and 23% a substantial decrease; 15% report a small increase	3 studies report no net change
	reductions in both noted in 12 other studies				reductions in 4 other studies	2 other studies report minor increases
	no appreciable effect in 1 study				no appreciable effect in 1 study	3 studies report decreases
Ronen, Primps, and Cloonan (1978)	Decrease in 12 agencies; no change in 2 agencies; increase in 1 agency		Decrease in 10 agencies			Decrease in 2 agencies; no change in 2 agencies; mixed results in 6 agencies
U.S. Army (1977)	Both reduced		Reduced	No change	Reduced	Some net savings

What do the public-sector data suggest? Three conclusions seem appropriate, relying basically but not exclusively on Table 11.

First, the literature may surprise many when it comes to reporting behavioral or "hard" effects. Thus about 70 percent of the studies report such data, and Table 11 has about one entry of an effect for each empty cell. That is to say, the definite majority of studies reporting behavioral or "hard" data each utilized several indicators, on the average.

Second, Table 11 implies that the benefits of F-T applications outweigh their costs, as determined by behavioral measures. For sick leave, absenteeism, tardiness, and turnover, the record implies almost universal improvement, with a few notices of "no appreciable effect" or "no change" adding only a little variety to the results. Trends in overtime and other costs, moreover, seem at least unchanged. Indeed, they trend downward in almost all cases.

This strong trend attracts attention, especially since it coincides with trends in the full family of F-T studies. At the very least, then, the data imply that F-T does not worsen major features of the worksite, as critics warn. Of course, one might argue that this feature of the F-T literature reveals that "negative findings" do not get published. Even if true, this does not account for the substantial number of unpublished sources included in our evolving F-T panel that unanimously report similar effects.

Third, F-T can have important bottom-line effects external to the employing organization, which effects Table 11 does not cover. Consider the effects on an urban transit property when 51,000 public employees in one Canadian city went on F-T. To simplify, F-T had several positive effects, at "marginal cost" to the transit property. Illustratively:[49]

- peak demand for service was significantly "flattened" and demand was distributed more broadly on both sides of the previous peak;

- bus operating speeds in the downtown area were improved; and

- improvements occurred in the efficiency of the utilization of both operators and vehicles.

B. Public-Sector Productivity and F-T

Attention to F-T will now do triple-duty. Effects of F-T on measured productivity constitute the prime target, this time utilizing a separate batch of 16 public-sector studies providing "hard" data about output. And the analysis also will shed some light on two general concerns about OD applications. Specifically, OD applications in the public sector often have been seen as constrained by three factors:

- confusion has been expressed concerning how the behavioral theories underlying OD apply in government, given that their development has been rooted largely in business or industrial contexts

- unique or at least especially intense institutional and historical constraints make OD interventions more difficult in the public sector, if not impossible

- the effects of public-sector OD interventions are more difficult to judge, since "hard data" are seldom available and because "soft data" relating to attitudes and opinions pose problems of reliability and validity

The three sections below, in turn, will show how these three factors apply only in diminished senses, if at all, to the OD intervention called F-T.

Some general observations usefully precede the detail to follow. To begin, perhaps curiously, public-sector F-T studies pay more common attention to productivity than do their private-sector counterparts. Does this herald a new day a-coming?

Moreover, productivity measurement often is difficult, and especially so in many public agencies. In addition, the results can be questionable even when measurement is attempted. Witness the various ways of emphasizing what reporting systems seek—as by "balloon-squeezing," inflated estimates, and neglect of major "intangibles." Perhaps paramountly, many see F-T as a low-cost fringe benefit—as improving the quality of work and as impacting on employee attitudes and turnover—but as not especially relevant to productivity.

Although public-sector studies can be faulted on grounds of research design, finally, the trends below are consistent with the best available private-sector study.[50] Details would be burdensome here, and their interpretation cannot be certain. In capsule, however, five work units in a financial firm were studied for specific effects of F-T applications on productivity. The results? Two of the 5 units reflected significantly productivity increases; and three units showed no major change. The authors conclude:

> Given the differing outcomes of the experimental groups, as well as experimental design limitations, no clear-cut conclusions with regard to the impact of flexible working hours on productivity can be made. The results based on five units are mixed.

This conclusion probably understates the case. For many F-T proponents would emphasize that productivity did not *significantly decrease* in any of the five cases. Since F-T is no-cost or low-cost, and given a stable level of productivity, positive effects on employee attitudes often will be sufficient to encourage F-T applications. The attitudinal impacts of F-T—as the sections above demonstrate—are overwhelmingly positive.

F-T and "Growth Psychology"

Basically, F-T may be viewed as a way of increasing employee freedom and discretion at work. The 6 differences between applications can be critical.[51] But the general F-T model clearly is consistent with the "growth psychology" which underlies OD.

Eschewing details, F-T plans provide for two kinds of daily hours: a band of "fixed hours" of variable duration, often 3-5 hours; and some "variable hours," often two periods of 2-3 hours that come earlier and later than normal workhours. Employees must be present during the fixed hours, and they need only arrange their arrival/departure times during some accounting period that they work enough hours—typically, 35-40 hours per week. Many variations exist in specific F-T plans concerning what conditions constrain employee choice, and so on, but *the* constant involves increasing employee freedom and choice, consistent with the several versions of "growth psychology" prominent in the management literatures.

The reader can easily develop the numerous senses in which F-T fits with various prominent behavioral models: Maslow's pyramid of needs;

McGregor's Theory Y vs. X; Argyris' dimensions for self-actualization; and Herzberg's distinction between motivators and hygiene factors, among many other possible and variously-precise variations on substantially-common conceptual themes. For example, F-T permits movement from dependence to growing independence, in Argyris' terms. And F-T similarly enhances the work itself and the employee's sense of personal responsibility, which the reader will recognize as Herzbergian motivators.

From a related angle, F-T can be viewed in frustration/aggression terms.[52] By increasing an employee's control over environment—as by sleeping late on some days, responding to individual diurnal rhythms,[53] by being more able to make arrangements for a suddenly-sick child unable to attend school, and so on—F-T can be said to decrease frustration, with possible effects on work. To develop the point somewhat, in the general case it is unlikely that some frustrating stimulus will (for example) increase productivity. Rather, at least five cases need to be distinguished:

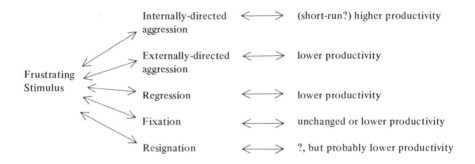

The odds on frustration leading to increased productivity do not seem great, then. And even internally-directed aggression—as when one aggresses against self by "working harder"—can have a range of consequences. Many successful football coaches, for example, seek to channel frustration in two ways: towards this week's "enemy"; and towards their own players, with the intent of energizing greater effort. Both approaches can back-fire, as in fights with one's teammates, or in guilt when a "target opponent" gets seriously hurt.

F-T and Constraints on OD Applications

There has been an appreciable time-lag in public-sector adoptions of the F-T model, and this may suggest some general public-sector constraints at work. This lag could be established in many ways. But here consider only that F-T applications had spread quite widely in Europe by the late 1960s; the first major longitudinal research study in American business had appeared in the early 1970s;[54] but it was not until the late 1970s that the major public administration journal carried any extensive mention[55] of what many consider a major managerial innovation.

Beyond this general time-lag, however, F-T appears not to have encountered any special constraints in public-sector applications. The results in business[56] seem quite comparable to the public-sector experience.[57] Moreover, applications in both sectors have similar failure-rates—very, very low. Finally, prevailing institutions and practices in public personnel institutions do not present anywhere near the obstacles to F-T that they pose for several other classes of OD designs. Interaction-centered OD has experienced some resistance, sometimes of a political character,[58] and sometimes because of concerns that democratic administration may undercut popular control over administration.[59] OD focusing on structure has had a far more difficult time, largely because (I judge) autocratic bureaucracy is so deeply-entrenched in the ideation and practice of public personnel administration—in structure, position classification, job design, and related manifestations that were originally intended to safeguard Administration from Politics.

F-T and Measured Productivity

Surprisingly, as noted, public-sector studies of F-T are (if anything) more concerned about *measured productivity* than studies in the private sector. Most private-sector studies of F-T report few "hard data,"[60] and the prevailing opinion there generally inclines to satisfaction with F-T as a low-cost program that has overwhelmingly-positive reflections in "soft-data" as in self-reports about productivity, cooperation, an enhanced worksite, greater control over one's work, and so on.

Table 12 summarizes a variety of information about 16 public-sector studies of F-T applications that have reported "hard data" about variations in productivity.[61] The table permits two broad classes of summary conclusions—the first urges a variety of cautions about interpreting Table 12; and the second class presents several nonetheless-probable conclusions about F-T applications in the public sector.

1. *Six Cautions About Table 12.* At least six cautions about the studies summarized in Table 12 require up-front emphasis. First, despite major efforts, the original reports of 7 of the studies were not available for present review. These studies were available in summarized form only.[78]

Second, most F-T applications involved units of small size doing clerical or professional work. So questions about the generalizability of results to larger contexts are appropriate.

Third, individual studies usually measured one or a few aspects of the quantity or quality of production. This implies the possibility that the data reflect "balloon-squeezing"—looking good on some measures of the job, but only by neglecting others.

Fourth, the studies typically use only pre vs. post comparisons, often with short observational intervals of less than 6 months, without comparison groups. Longitudinal studies covering a year or longer—referred to as Long-Post in Table 8—would be more helpful in eliminating alternative explanations of observed effects. Use of comparison groups would serve a similar purpose. For example, an apparent change on a Short-Post observation might constitute only a temporary outlier in a data-set covering a broader span of time. Without comparison groups, similarly, one might miss the fact that an apparent increase might only reflect a general trend rather than the F-T application. Experience also implies that some F-T effects take several months to develop, especially with respect to supervisory behaviors and attitudes.[79]

Fifth, only one of the 16 studies in Table 12 uses any statistical treatment beyond simple arrays of data. Patently, this implies questions as to whether observed "changes" were only random variations in the data-set rather than noteworthy shifts due to F-T applications. One cannot answer this key question by eyeball examination: When is a change "big enough" to be considered non-random?

Sixth, despite a few exceptions that seek to get at underlying processes,[80] almost all F-T studies have a simple "outcome bias."

TABLE 12. Summary of Public-Sector F-T Studies Reporting on Measured Productivity

Setting	Union Involved?	Study Design	Comparison Group(s)?	Statistical Treatment?	Hard/ Soft Data?	Effects on "Hard" Productivity Indicators
Air University, Maxwell Air Force Base (1978)[62]	N = 100	?	Post only	No	None	H/S	Increase of 10% in "successful contracts made on first call from outside"
Bureau of Policy Standards (1978)[63]	N = 200	?	Pre/Post	No	?	H/S	"Inconclusive results"
Bureau of Recruiting and Examining (1978)[64]	N = 240	?	Pre/Post	No	?	H/S	Measured (but unspecified) increase "in hours of morning service"
Civil Service Commission, Seattle Region (1978)[65]	N = 129	?	Pre/Post	No	?	H/S	Increase in indicator of "communication with other offices in Washington and Alaska"
Department of Labor (1977)[66]	All 112 employees in 3 units of Office of Accounting	Yes	Pre/Post/ Long-Post	No	None	H/S	Increase of 3% per net staff hour"
Library of Congress (1978)[67]	N = 150	?	Pre/Post	No	?	H/S	Increase of 6.9% "over first quarter"; increase of 14.0% "over second quarter"

TABLE 12. Summary of Public-Sector F-T Studies Reporting on Measured Productivity (Continued)

Setting	Union Involved?	Study Design	Comparison Group(s)?	Statistical Treatment?	Hard/ Soft Data	Effects on "Hard" Productivity Indicators
Social Security Administration (1974)[68]	N = 120 in Bureau of Data Processing	Yes	Pre/Post	No	?	H/S	Increase of 11.6% in "office productivity" measured in terms of "median productivity per hour per clerk"
Social Security	?	Yes	Pre/Post	No	?	H/?	Increase of 40% in "work units per hour"
Social Security Administration (1979)[70]	N = 353 in 3 work units	Yes	Pre/Post	No	?	H/?	Increase of 21% in "work units per hour", comparing "3-month post-test average vs. same period prior year"
Social Security Administration, Bureau of Disability Insurance[71]	100 benefit organizers	Yes	Pre/Post	Yes	None	H/S	No difference in quality or quantity in experimental vs. comparison unit, although productivity increased in both
U.S. Army (1977)[72]	Detroit Engineer District	?	Pre/Post	No	None		Increase of 5%: hours per standard work-unit decreased from 2.93 to 2.79 hours
U.S. Army (1977)[73]	Regional Dental Activity, Alameda, Calif.	?	Pre/Post	No	None	H/S	Increase of 10.7% for technicians: average monthly weighted work units per hour increased from 7.82 to 8.66

TABLE 12. Summary of Public-Sector F-T Studies Reporting on Measured Productivity (Continued)

Setting	Union Involved?	Study Design	Comparison Group(s)?	Statistical Treatment?	Hard/ Soft Data	Effects on "Hard" Productivity Indicators
U.S. Army, Automotive Command (1975)[74]	?	Pre/Post	No	None	H/S	Increase of 2%
U.S. Geological Survey (1977)[75]	Yes	Pre/Post	No	None	H/S	Decrease of 3.6% in Map Production in 1 area; and increase of 14.3% in another area
U.S. Information Agency (1975)[76]	?	Pre/Post	No	None	H/S	Increase of 4.5% in vouchers processed by Accounts Payable and Claims Section; and reduction of 16% in backlog
U.S. Navy, Finance Office (1975, 1976)[77]	?	Pre/Post/ Long-Post	Yes	Wilcoxon test	H/S	No change in quantity of work of experimental group as compared to control group: "expected increase" did not occur. Significant decrease in error rate of experimental vs. control group

Informed speculation abounds as to the specific processes energized by F-T applications, but data concerning them are in short supply.

2. *Four Encouragers of A Robust Interpretation.* Given such cautions, other factors encourage a relatively robust interpretation of the studies reflected in Table 12. Thus the available studies do encompass a broad range of relevant conditions that imply some generalizability. For example, at least 6 of the 16 applications—and no doubt several others—occurred in union settings. Some of the literature implies that unions imply generally-unexplored complications for OD efforts.[81] Hence F-T's successful application in union contexts encourages some optimism about the usefulness of the intervention.

Moreover, the general thrust of Table 12 suggests a definite balance of positive effects on measured productivity. Specifically, 18 of the total of 23 reported measures imply increased productivity, and markedly so in a number of cases. Only 2 of the 23 measures reflect any drop in productivity.

In addition, the overall thrust of the data is quite powerful when coupled with other trends in effects associated with F-T applications. Specifically, almost all F-T studies include "soft" or attitudinal data as well as "hard" data, which may be considered more objective or non-reactive. This often permits multiple cross-comparisons to confirm or deny what "hard" or "soft" data alone imply.

Extensive cross-comparisons clearly reinforce the overall thrust of Table 12. Thus attitudinal data very affirmatively attribute a broad range of favorable effects of F-T on aspects of productivity.[82] Moreover, a range of "hard" data—on absenteeism, overtime, various costs, and so on—provide similar reinforcement for the positive effects implied by Table 9.[83]

Finally, the trend in Table 12 gains added attractiveness from the low cost of F-T applications. Available data, for example, indicate that F-T requires changes in the behaviors of supervisors. But these changes involve competences that almost all supervisors have or can come to develop in brief time-frames; they involve little training and other overhead support; and those new supervisory behaviors or attitudes tend to be ones that employees prefer and respond positively to.[84]

These low costs for F-T applications and relevant training contrast sharply with the high costs often associated with other OD interventions, especially interaction-centered designs. These often imply costly training in attitudes and behavioral skills, as in group decision-making or intact work units undergoing T-Group or team-building experiences.[85]

VII. SOME EBULLIENT TENTATIVENESS

Overall, then, public-sector F-T applications have the same pattern of positive vs. negative effects as business applications. Both "hard" and "soft" data, relating to both employees and supervisors, strongly support such a conclusion.

Despite real questions about the number and quality of public-sector studies, the data provide adequate support for two conclusions. Based on what we know, further diffusion of the F-T concept seems appropriate. At the same time, much remains to be learned about F-T effects, as well as about the conditions of application that especially encourage positive effects. For example, questions have been raised about the long-run effects of F-T programs. Given their positive short-run effects, do these decay over time?[86] The available data are not conclusive,[87] but they suggest the need for longitudinal research, and also for reinforcement or booster-shots concerning the mutual obligations and benefits implied by F-T programs.

Despite the welter of details establishing F-T effects, moreover, this analysis of F-T is more important for what it illustrates—the possibility of increasing responsible freedom in public organizations, without great costs and with major opportunities for increasing individual initiative and choice. Numerous other OD designs can have similar effects, focusing on personal interaction or structure, as well as policies and procedures like F-T. The other designs serve similar values, even as they vary widely in details of applications, required training, and costs.

FOOTNOTES

[1]As in Richard S. Rubin, "Flexitime: Its Implementation in the Public Sector," *Public Adminstration Review*, Vol. 39 (May 1979), pp. 277-282.

[2]The material through Table 3 is reprinted essentially from Robert Golembiewski and Carl W. Proehl, Jr., "Public-Sector Applications of Flexible Workhours: A Review of Available Experience," *Public Adminstration Review*, Vol. 40 (January/February 1980), pp. 72-85.

[3]Robert T. Golembiewski and Carl W. Proehl, Jr., "A Survey of the Empirical Literature on Flexible Workhours: Character and Consequences of a Major Innovation," *Academy of Management Review*, Vol. 3 (October 1978), pp. 837-853. See also William F. Glueck,"Changing Hours at Work," *Personnel Administrator*, Vol. 24 (March 1979), 62-67; and Stanely D. Nollen, "Does Flexitime Improve Productivity?," *Harvard Business Review*, Vol. 57 (October 1979), pp. 16-18, 76, and 80.

[4]Golembiewski and Proehl, "A Survey of the Empirical Literature on Flexible Workhours," p. 852.

[5]Robert T. Golembiewski and Carl W. Proehl, Jr., "A Survey of the Empirical Literature on Flexible Workhours: An Update." A paper prepared for delivery at the Annual Meeting of the American Psychological Association. New York City, New York, September 4, 1979.

[6]Such differentiating effects are attributed by Harvey and Luthans to "staggered hours" vs. "flexible hours" as the term is used here. See Barron H. Harvey and Fred Luthans, "Flexitime: An Empirical Analysis of its Real Meaning and Impact," *MSU Business Topics*, Vol. 27 (Summer 1979), pp. 31-36.

[7]Air University, Maxwell Air Force Base, Alabama, "Summary Report of Flexitime Program in the Federal Government," Bureau of Policies and Standards, U.S. Civil Service Commission, December 5, 1975.

[8]Atlanta (Ga.) Regional Commission, "Proposed Flexible Hours Plan," internal memo, July 1978; and "Flexible Hours Program: Evaluation Survey Results." Internal memo, January 1979.

[9]Robert Bruce Crawford, Untitled draft report. Prepared by the Office of Personnel, The Prince George's County Government, 1979.

[10]District of Columbia Department of Human Resources, Washington, D.C. "Summary Report of Flexitime Program in the Federal Government," Bureau of Policies and Standards, U.S. Civil Service Commission, December 5, 1975.

[11]Environmental Protection Agency, "Flexitime in EPA Headquarters," internal memo, October 1976; "Semi-Annual Headquarters Flexitime Evaluation," internal memo, August 1977; and "Final Headquarters Flexitime Evaluation," internal memo, July 1978.

[12]James R. Finegan, Testimony before Subcommittee on Employee Ethics and Utilization of the Committee on Post Office and Civil Service on H. R. 2732, Party-Time Employment and Flexible Working Hours, October 4, 1977, pp. 155-165; Bureau of Government Financial Operations, "Summary Report of Flexitime Program in the Federal Government," Bureau of Policies and Standards, U.S. Civil Service Commission, December 5, 1975; and "Evaluation of Experimental Flexitime Program," internal memo, September 1976.

[13]Arthur L. Finkle, "Flexitime in Government," *Public Personnel Management*, Vol. 8 (May 1979), pp. 152-155.

[14]General Services Administration, "Flexitime Report," internal memo, April 21, 1977.

[15]Thomas Giammo, Testimony before Subcommittee on Employee Ethics and Utilization of the Committee on Post Office and Civil Service on H. R. 2732, Part-Time

Employment and Flexible Work Hours, Octboer 4, 1977, pp. 150-152; and Social Security Administration, "Federal Offices Try Flexible Hours," *The Office* (December 1974), p. 70.

[16]Harvey and Luthans, *op. cit.*

[17]Oscar Mueller and Muriel Cole, "Concept Wins Converts at Federal Agency," *Monthly Labor Review*, Vol. 100 (Feberuary 1977), pp. 71-74.

[18]Naval Ship Engineering Systems Command, Port Hueneme, California, "Summary Report of Flexitime Program in the Federal Government," Bureau of Policies and Standards, U.S. Civil Service Commission, December 16, 1975.

[19]Office of Accounting, Department of Labor, "Pilot Flexi-time Project in the Office of Accounting," internal memo, October 1977.

[20]Cicily P. Osteen, "Library of Congress Managers Assess Their Experiences With Flexitime," internal memo, August 30, 1979.

[21]Port Authority of New York and New Jersey, Planning and Development Department, "Flexible Workhours Experiment at the Port Authority of New York and New Jersey," December 1977.

[22]Mark Reutter, "Baltimore's Changing Work Styles: Employees Determine Own Working Schedule Under Innovative Program Begun in City by Insurance Company," *The Sunday Sun*, Baltimore, Maryland, November 25, 1973, p. 1d.

[23]P. Salvatore, "Flexible Working Hours: The Experiment and its Evaluation," Personnel Branch, The Department of Communications of the Government of Canada, internal memo, January 1974.

[24]Santa Clara County, California, Juvenile and Adult Probation Departments, "Flexitime Summary Report," internal memo, 1975.

[25]Seattle Civil Service Commission, "Summary Report of Flexitime Program in the Federal Government," Bureau of Policies and Standards, U.S. Civil Service Commission, December 5, 1975.

[26]Jill E. Shulman, "Flexitime as an OD Intervention," *OD Practitioner*, Vol. 11 (October 1979), pp. 11-15.

[27]Errol D. Stevens and Rod Elsworth, "Flexitime in the Australian Public Service: Its Effect on Non-Work Activities," *Public Personnel Management*, Vol. 8 (May 1979), pp. 196-205.

[28]J. Carroll Swart, "What Time Shall I Go to Work Today?," *Business Horizons*, Vol. 17 (October 1974), pp. 19-26.

[29]L. V. Thornton, "Report on Flexible Hours Experiment in the Personnel Branch," Ottawa, Canada: Personnel Branch, Department of Consumer and Corporate Affairs, April 1973.

[30]Transportation Systems Center, "Evaluation of Flexitime Model at TSC," internal memo, August 1979.

[31]Gary J. Uhlmann, Testimony before Subcommittee on Employee Ethics and Utilization of the Committee on Post Office and Civil Service on H. R. 2732, Part-Time Employment and Flexible Work Hours, July 8, 1977, pp. 87-95.

[32]U.S. Army Natick Laboratories (Massachusetts), "Summary Report of Flexitime Program on the Federal Government," Bureau of Policies and Standards, U.S. Civil

Service Commission, December 1974.

[33]U.S. Army Tank Automotive Command (Michigan), "Summary Report of Flexitime Program in the Federal Government," Bureau of Policies and Standards, U.S. Civil Service Commission, December 1975.

[34]U.S. Information Agency, "Summary of Flexitime Program in the Federal Government," Bureau of Policies and Standards, U.S. Civil Service Commission, December 1975.

[35]Warren Vieth, "Tinker Employees Drift into Flexitime," *Oklahoma City Times*, August 29, 1977, p. 5.

[36]James Walker, Clive Fletcher, and Donald McLeod, "Flexible Working Hours in Two British Government Offices," *Public Personnel Management*, Vol. 4 (1975), pp. 216-222.

[37]Simcha Ronen, Sophia Primps, and John Cloonan, Testimony before the Senate Committee on Governmental Affairs on S517, Flexitime and Part-Time Legislation, June 29, 1978.

[38]U.S. Army, "Flexitime Experience in the Department of the Army," internal memo, September 1977.

[39]Robert T. Golembiewski, Rick Hilles, and Munro Kagno, "A Longitudinal Study of Flexi-Time Effects," *Journal of Applied Behavioral Science*, Vol. 10 (July 1974), pp. 503-532; and Robert T. Golembiewski, Samuel Yeager, and Rick Hilles, "Factor Analysis of Some Flexitime Effects," *Academy of Management Journal*, Vol. 18 (September 1975), pp. 500-509.

[40]For details, consult Golembiewski, Hilles, and Kagno, *op. cit*. See also Robert T. Golembiewski, *Approaches to Planned Change* (New York: Marcel Dekker, 1979), Vol. 2, esp. pp. 215-253.

[41]Jerry I. Porras and Nancy Roberts, "Toward A Typology of Organization Development Research," Research Paper No. 470, Stanford University, Graduate School of Business, 1978.

[42]Golembiewski and Proehl, "A Survey of the Empirical Literature on Flexible Workhours," pp. 845-847.

[43]Virginia E. Schein, Elizabeth H. Mauer, and Jan F. Novak, "Impact of Flexible Working Hours on Productivity," *Journal of Applied Psychology*, Vol. 62 (No. 4, 1977), pp. 463-465.

[44]John Bonsall, "Flexible Hours: Progress Report No. 1." Internal memo, OC Ottawa-Carleton TRANSPO. April 2, 1974, p. 15.

[45]Golembiewski and Proehl, "A Survey of the Empirical Literature on Flexible Workhours," pp. 847-849.

[46]Golembiewski, Yeager, and Hilles, *op. cit.*

[47]Golembiewski and Proehl, "A Survey of the Empirical Literature on Flexible Workhours," p. 849.

[48]*Ibid.*, pp. 850-851.

[49]Golembiewski, Hilles, and Kagno, *op. cit.*, esp. pp. 519-526.

[50]E.g., see Lee A. Graf, *An Analysis of the Effect of Flexible Working Hours on the Management Function of the First-Line Supervisor*. Unpublished doctoral dissertation,

Mississippi State University, 1976; and Robert T. Golembiewski, Ronald G. Fox, and Carl W. Proehl, Jr., "Is Flexi-Time for Employees 'Hard Time' for Supervisors: Two Sources of Data Rejecting the Proposition," *Journal of Management* (No. 2, 1979), pp. 241-259.

[51]Harvey and Luthans, *op. cit.*

[52]Robert T. Golembiewski, *Behavior and Organization*. (Chicago: Rand McNally, 1962), pp. 127-148.

[53]Paula Patkai, Kerstin Pettersson, and Torbjorn Akerstedt, "Flexible Working Hours and Individual Diurnal Rhythms," *Reports from the Psychological Laboratories*, University of Stockholm, Vol. 406 (December 1973).

[54]Golembiewski, Hilles, and Kagno, *op. cit.*

[55]Rubin, *op. cit.*, and Golembiewski and Proehl, "Public-Sector Applications of Flexible Workhours: A Review of Available Experience."

[56]Golembiewski and Proehl, "A Survey of the Empirical LIterature on Flexible Workhours"; Glueck, *op. cit.*; and Nollen, *op. cit.*

[57]Golembiewski and Proehl, "Public-Sector Applications of Flexible Workhours: A Review of Available Experience."

[58]Donald P. Warwick, *A Theory of Public Bureaucracy* (Cambridge, Mass.: Harvard University Press, 1975), pp. 59-83.

[59]Frederick Mosher, *Democracy and Public Service* (New York: Oxford University Press, 1968), p. 374.

[60]Golembiewski and Proehl, "A Survey of the Empirical Literature on Flexible Workhours," pp. 845-847.

[61]See Robert T. Golembiewski, "Public-Sector Productivity and Flexible Workhours: Testing Three Points of the Common Wisdom re OD," *Southern Review of Public Administration*, Vol. 4 (October 1980), pp. 269-302.

[62]Ronan, Primps, and Cloonan, *op. cit.*

[63]*Ibid.*

[64]*Ibid.*

[65]*Ibid.*

[66]U.S. Department of Labor, Office of Accounting, "Pilot Flexitime Project." Internal memo, October 1977.

[67]Ronan, Primps, and Cloonan, *op. cit.*

[68]Nollen, *op. cit.*

[69]*Ibid.*

[70]*Ibid.*

[71]J. Carroll Swart, *A Flexible Approach to Working Hours*. (New York: AMACOM, 1978).

[72]U.S. Army, "Flexitime Experience in the Department of the Army. Internal memo, September 1977.

[73]*Ibid.*

[74]U.S. Army, Tank Automotive Command, *op. cit.* See footnote 33.

[75]Nollen, *op. cit.*

[76]See footnote 34.

[77]Charles M. Lampman, "Flexitime, Organizational Change, and the Traditional Hierarchical Organization: A Follow-Up Report," Unpublished report. San Diego, Cal.: Navy Finance Office, December 1975a; and U.S. Navy Sea Support Center, "Continuation of Flexi-Time," Internal memo. San Diego, Cal., December 1976.

[78]Ronan, Primps, and Cloonan, *op. cit.*; and Nolan, *op. cit.*

[79]Golembiewski, Fox, and Proehl, *op. cit.*, pp. 248-250.

[80]Robert T. Golembiewski, Keith Billingsley, and Samuel Yeager, "Measuring Change and Persistence in Human Affairs," *Journal of Applied Behavioral Science*, Vol. 12 (December 1976), pp. 133-137; and Graf, *op. cit.*

[81]P.S. Goodman, *Assessing Organizational Change* (New York: Wiley-Interscience, 1979).

[82]Golembiewski and Proehl, "Public-Sector Applications of Flexible Workhours," *op. cit.*; Nollen, *op. cit.*; Ronen, Primps, and Cloonan, *op. cit.*; and Swart, *op. cit.*

[83]Golembiewski and Proehl, "Public-Sector Applications of Flexible Workhours;" Roonan, Primps, and Cloonan, *op. cit.*

[84]Graf, *op. cit.*; and Golembiewski, Fox, and Proehl, *op. cit.*

[85]See Robert T. Golembiewski, *Approaches to Planned Change*, esp. pp. 85-132.

[86]Glenn Rainey and Lawrence Wolf, "Flexi-time: Short-Term Benefits, Long Term . . . ?", *Public Administration Review*, Vol. 41 (January 1981), pp. 52-63.

[87]Robert T. Golembiewski, "Do Flexible Workhour Effects Decay Over Time?," *Public Productivity Review*, Vol. 6 (March 1982), pp. 35-46.

PART C

Why Does Public-Sector OD Need to Do Better-than-Average?

CHAPTER V: Toward a Political Theory for OD, I:
The Ideational Poverty of Democracy/
Administration Couplings

CHAPTER VI: Toward a Political Theory for OD, II:
Administration that Reinforces
Democratic Ideals

CHAPTER V

TOWARD A POLITICAL THEORY FOR OD, I: THE IDEATIONAL POVERTY OF DEMOCRACY/ADMINISTRATION COUPLINGS

This chapter and the one following it tread on significant ground, and they also risk exacerbating an already-bad situation. What follows constitutes a primer toward expanding the commons, if you will, between political philosophy and that applied science usually called Organization Development, or OD. This significant mutuality gets approached via analysis of several conceptual pairings that embody the essence of the matter by simplifying it, and this is risky. Specifically, this chapter seeks to develop three major points:

- that Democracy *and* Administration proved an unreachable goal, however attractive in concept

- that Democracy *vs.* Administration has come to characterize dominant thoughtways, but only with some increasingly serious costs

- that greater attention should be given to Democracy *within* Administration, and perhaps even to Democracy *through* Administration

I use the capitalized form consciously, and self-consciously. For these emphasized pairings are so convenient, and yet the first two sets of them are so much a part of the present difficulty that I hesitate using the last pairing even in this preliminary effort to transcend the conceptual limitations of the two other pairs. I hesitate, as I say; but I do not desist.

I. DEMOCRACY *AND* ADMINISTRATION: TWO COMMON AND RECURRING SIMPLICISMS

Ideologs have at once simplified and obfuscated what might be called the political theory of how the public work is to be done in a representative polity. The theme "Democracy *and* Administration" characterizes much of the early literature. Moreover, numerous contemporary examples of the same breed are easy to find, including the New Public Administration, Ostrom's "democratic administration," as well as the several "power to the people" movements of recent memory, among numerous others.[1]

What basic agreements unite such ideologies, early and late? In common, they propose or assume that popular democracy and practical administration can be made easily compatible. Two themes suffice to highlight this definitional artistry—one deals with a common interpretation of the "classical theory of democracy"; and the second reflects a congenial view of how the state's work is administered.

A. A/The Interpretation of "Classical Democratic Theory"

A common interpretation—indeed, observers like Marini consider it *the* interpretation—of our basic political heritage plays a major role in this resolution-by-definition. Call it Democracy I. Looking back at those thinkers and activists who contributed to the "classical theory of democracy," to approach the point, many observers conjure-up a tidy image of our political heritage as it comes down to us from our posterity. For example, many commentators attribute such content to the prevailing interpretation of the classical theory, or Democracy I:

- humans are "rational, active, interested citizens" blessed with major "liberty," "freedom," and "rights"[2]

- the characteristic citizen's mode emphasizes self-determination[3] and broad participation in public choice-making processes

- citizens either perceive "the common good," or can come to do so with pleasing frequency and certainty

- for many purposes, as a major convenience for all, citizens chose delegates or representatives to "enact the popular will into law"

- various forces—internal ones such as conscience or public spiritness, as well as external ones such as an informed and watchful electorate—reinforce this faithfulness to the "popular will" or "political will," necessarily so because of human imperfections, capacity for self-deception, and variable ability to transcend self-interests

- commonly prominent among these devices for multiple, mutual control are numerous sets of potentially-counterbalancing interests, often expressed as majorities of the electorate—in Congressional districts, states, legislative committees, and so on.

Democracy I rests on a specific morality, of which Redford isolates three major component ideals.[4] The first is the ideal of individual realization, which proposes that: "Man is, for man, the ultimate measure of all human values." A second ideal—that all persons "have worth deserving social recognition"—provides an equalitarian component of democratic morality. The third ideal, Redford notes, prescribes universal participation as the best way of protecting social worth on "all matters where social action is substituted for individual action." Individual liberty will exist only where persons participate in some meaningful ways—participate in decisions or in controlling those who do make them.

So much, then, for the sketch of this common view of Democracy I. Where could one expect to find such an interpretation? Practically anywhere and at any time, proposes Marini.[5] And he marshals a large bulk of supporting evidence, certainly sufficient evidence to document that this is *a* widely-held interpretation. It may even be *the* dominant interpretation, as Marini argues.

One source suffices to suggest the range of such an interpretation, the issue of *a* or *the* interpretation aside. Consider the approach of Riker, who accepts propositions like those above as a moral imperative and then seeks to determine how reality can approach that ought. He signals his intent directly in a section titled: "How Shall Is Become What Ought to Be?" Riker is thus more careful than many, while still operating within their tradition. Riker notes his basic concern with "a picture of the ideal form of democracy," and acknowledges that his ideal assumes "too many 'unprovables' for it to pass unchallenged by philosophers." These assumptions include:[6]

> . . . a relativistic and pragmatic epistemology, which places "truth" (not ultimate truth, with which it is not concerned, but truth as man can know) in

the hands of the majority or a series of majorities. It assumes also a rationalist axiology, i.e., the belief that men are able to know their own interests and act to achieve them. It assumes the psychological theory that men have both social and anti-social propensities or, in theological terms, that men are fashioned in the image of God as well as endowed with original sin. In ethics, it assumes a particular goal of conduct (universal self-respect).

Riker will not debate whether these assumptions are correct or true. Rather, he accepts those assumptions because others have. But he accepts them in a sense that many others have neglected: to get on with determining how the ideal can be approached in practice. Thus Riker notes of the assumptions that "[it] is enough to know that they have been accepted into the democratic heritage and that many men have chosen them with democracy to guide their lives." Riker proposes to get on with the heavy work. "The concern here is with the more pressing questions: How can the democratic method be made to work? It is, of course, foolish to expect a millennium; but, since democrats are sure that democracy can mean a better life for all, it is worth while to consider this less exalted, less philosophical question. How can democracy be?" [7]

B. A Congenial View of Administration

A nicely-compatible view of practical administration complements this uncomplicated view of our classical political heritage. Eschewing details, the congenial view—let us call it Administration I—has such major features:

- expressions of the popular or political will are clear and unambiguous, or are capable of being made so enough of the time, in large part because of the sharp limits on government activity

- much public work requires skills in ample if not abundant supply among the citizenry, at least after a tolerable period of preparation

- a few experts and specialists are necessary for practical administration, to be sure

- but not to worry—whether the state's work is done by those with native or highly-cultivated skills—because those to whom operational delegations are made will not only accurately perceive the public will but also can be counted on to labor "faithfully to see that the will of the people governed" gets implemented

This view of Administration did not always come as straight-vanilla, of course, but its ubiquity cannot be doubted. True enough, the concept came in diverse varieties, strengths, and blends: the view was variously shaded as "is," "ought," and "if," in multiple combinations, for example. Some proposed that Administration I applies nicely to what exists; perhaps most others have seen it as a prescription of some ideal condition, as does Ostrom, which *could* exist in far larger measure if some easy steps were taken. Ostrom argues essentially that small governmental units will permit popular control over administration. A few have taken even more radical views, as in the argument that administrative weakness if not incompetence provides a good—perhaps even the very best—protection for individual liberties. Consider the case of a past-president of the U.S. Chamber of Commerce who observed: "Efficient government is dangerous. It eats holes in our liberties."[8]

In sum, the essentials of Administration I have been accepted by many—by some wildly-improbable bed-fellows, and across broad reaches of time. Adherents include Jacksonians and other American nativists, for example, as well as doctrinaire Marxists.

Let us illustrate the genre. Many seem to believe that almost anyone could (or should be able to) faithfully execute the public will. Witness the doctrine of "happy versatility" associated with President Andrew Jackson.[9] He rejected the "gentlemanly qualities" required for office in the Washington and Jefferson administrations, and was concerned their corrosive elitism might produce a bureaucratic aristocracy, possibly even a hereditary one. Hence in his first annual message to Congress, Jackson argued that only good results when the "public benefits" require the removal of some office-holder, or even the periodic flushing-out of large numbers. This would "give healthy action to the system," at the very least. This justified "spoils politics." And no great loss would occur in any case, since the public duties were so "plain and simple" that large numbers of persons could perform them.

Far more complex was the related vision of the good society held out by Marx. His Democracy *and* Administration basically rested on an *if*, far more than on an *is* or a *should*. Since managers and technocrats exploited the masses, in the Marxian view, true freedom could exist only if all (or sufficient) people were poly-specialized and/or if the level of specialization were somehow radically reduced. As I concluded elsewhere: [10]

> Marx was so touchy about the specialization of work that he promised a return in his utopia to a harmonious state of nature in which everyone performs every economic function whenever he gets the urge. Thus would the injustice born of specialization be eliminated. Other Marxists were at once more realistic and more incredible. They realized that Marx's harking back was effective propaganda, at best. Yet they also realized the significant advantage that Marx's state of nature provided so cheaply. Consequently, Marx's evasion became so exaggerated that some conceived the job of administering the Communist state as requiring no talents greater than those of the ordinary clerk, which any comrade could provide as he willed.

II. DEMOCRACY SUFFERS AND SUBORDINATES ADMINISTRATION: DEMOCRACY VS. ADMINISTRATION BECOMES DOMINANT

Despite its numerous incarnations as a major thoughtway for influencing action, Democracy *and* Administration flounders as an ideal in the turbulence of its own consequences. These consequences have varied, but prominent among them have been spoils politics, the abuses of power reflected in the revelations of the muckrakers of several ages, and the serious dysjunctions in The Great Society between preachment and practice.

Demonstrating why and how Democracy *and* Administration could not win for losing preoccupies this section. Dating from the early 1900s, the conceptual focus shifted to what will be called Democracy *vs.* Administration, which will be conveniently labeled Democracy II and Administration II. The analysis here will emphasize four related themes:

- the inadequacies of Democracy *and* Administration

- the development of a more sophisticated concept of Democracy than informed Democracy *and* Administration

- the pairing of this upgraded Democracy II with a simple and autocratic concept of Administration II, whose vitals constitute the "theory of bureaucracy"

- the permeation of the common wisdom by an uncomplicated rationale for this pairing, which rationale is often potent even though usually implicit.

A. Demonstrating That Democracy *and* Administration Limps Badly

The multiple inadequacies of Democracy *and* Administration can be established easily, and yet the demonstration has not stuck. Over historic time, the demonstration has been accomplished time and again, only to have the basic notion appear in other guises but nonetheless essentially so.

We shall later ponder this paradoxical consequence, but for now we focus on how the pairing of Democracy I and Administration I does not satisfy. Critics win easy victories over Democracy *and* Administration in the same basic way. To simplify, critics demonstrate that the "facts of American government" seriously conflict with the "classical theory," and also that bureaucrats are much more than faithful servants of a clear common will.[11] Marini provides one example of a successful attack on Democracy *and* Administration via a debunking of the common interpretation of the "classical theory of democracy." He vigorously seeks to ascertain whether that interpretation is justified, based on a textual analysis of major sources in the democratic tradition. He is underwhelmed, in sum, by the fidelity with which common interpretations capture the essence of the political tradition.

Time and again—focusing on Locks, the *Federalist Papers*, John Stuart Mill, and so on—Marini shows how the dominant interpretation often caricatures, in two senses. First, the usual interpretation plays fast-and-loose with major political thinkers. In contrast to the purportedly-prevailing view, for example, Marini notes:[12]

... "classical theorists" assumed a leader/led or ruler/ruled dichotomy in modern societies, each assumed a hierarchy of unequal governmental power, and none assumed that each man was able or could be expected to conduct governmental affairs as well as every other man. None of the theorists anticipated that the future would produce omnicompetent, politically alert, interested and active self-governors

. . .

Moreover the notions about bureaucracy ... do not at all resemble the supposedly classical theory that bureaucrats are few and simply carry out the will of the people. None of the theorists assume such a radical equality among men as to be so devoid of leadership recognition as classical theory was supposed to have been.

In sum, Marini rejects any implication that a textual basis exists for Democracy *and* Administration, in the sense in which that pairing is used here.

Second, Marini insists, not only does the common view misinterpret the classical tradition, but that error also ages poorly. That is, the prevailing misinterpretation becomes an even "more impressive delusion as it persists among theorists living in increasingly complex industrial societies." In sum, complex modernities undercut both aspects of Democracy *and* Administration. To illustrate, getting data to a modern citizenry sufficient for reasonable decision-making poses greater challenges than those envisioned either in the political tradition or its often-simplified interpretations. Relatedly, Jackson's "happy versatility" has a radically-lower apparent truth-value under conditions of computerization, programmatic complexity, and extensive public services than it did in his day, when it was tenuous enough.

To make a long story very short, for purposes of introduction, the succeeding leitmotifs often became: Democracy *vs.* Administration. How that came to be, and why, get attention in the following three sections.

B. Upgrading the Concept "Democracy"

Despite the now-and-again potent allure of Democracy *and* Administration, criticisms like that of Marini convinced many of the need for major conceptual reconstruction of that hardy pair. We can label one emerging central core of meaning Democracy II without implying that all such variants are identical. Rather, the label intends to highlight that their common driving motive involved bringing Democracy I more into accord with contemporary life, to make it more realistic. Exhibit 1 provides one such upgraded view of Democracy II, which can be labeled "pluralist," "polyarchical," or some such. Commonly, pluralist models propose that—depending in part on the scale of things—one can envision several kinds of "democracy," each of which (if you will) may be considered "less democratic" than the preceding variety.

EXHIBIT 1. Varieties of Democratic Forms or Levels in Complex
Systems

---

o *committee democracy,* in which all members have a more or less
   equal say while in face-to-face contact

o *referendum democracy,* in which all viewpoints on an issue get
   represented; although all members seldom will express themselves, the basic trust exists that they could speak if they found
   it necessary or desirable to do so

o *representative democracy,* in which some large group selects or
   elects a smaller set to speak and decide in the collective name

o *polyarchical democracy,* or "representative democracy as we know
   it," which includes all of the above forms while additionally
   providing roles for

   — "big government" and "big business"

   — interest groups of diverse varieties, sizes, and memberships

   — political parties

   — delegated authority, such as that granted by a legislature to
      administrative agencies, or that variously distributed
      throughout the presidency, and so on

Based on Robert A. Dahl, *After the Revolution? Authority In A Good Society,* (New Haven,
Conn: Yale University Press, 1975), pp. 67-81.

Each of these forms has two aspects—to permit a substantial degree of popular control, and to curb the power of top authorities—and in the case of polyarchy these aspects get approached via an elaborate set of what Lindblom calls "authoritative rules."[13] Directly and indirectly, certain patterns of political behavior become associated with these rules and "guarantee the following familiar rights and prerogatives:"[14]

- freedom to form and join organizations, social, political, and economic

- freedom of expression

- right to vote

- eligibility to seek public office

- competition for support by political leaders

- multiple and alternative sources of information

- free and fair elections which determine those who will wield major authority in political roles

- the making of government policies is responsive to votes and other expressions of preference

These rules are only imperfectly approached in all polyarchical systems, of course, and some have been operative only in quite recent years.[15]

Especially severe conceptual problems inhere in polyarchy, which is the "least democratic" of all forms, such rules notwithstanding. Let us consider here only two senses in which polyarchical systems and their rules are imperfect in permitting popular control as well as in curbing the power of top authorities. First, consider the problems in a polyarchy which derive from the burgeoning of delegated authority which, in turn, is exercised by officials who "once appointed, are protected from removal on political grounds." The difficulties of democratic control of officials thus insulated in this "least democratic" of forms gets forceful expression by Mosher: "It is now of course clear that in every developed country in the world the vast majority of public officers and employees are in this category; that many of them command specialized knowledges and skills which give them unique competence in some subject-matter fields—competence that neither the people nor their elected or appointed political officers possess."[16]

Second, similar imperfections characterize the business sector of polyarchical systems. As Lindblom concludes:" . . . the imperfections of polyarchical controls are gross, all the more so perhaps in the largest polyarchies . . . . All the imperfections . . . . arising out of the underlying struggle for authority, or out of the impossibility of achieving a precise control over the bureaucracy, or out of its inadequate mechanisms for rational choice, especially economic choice, will frequently prevent a response of government to popular volitions or cause government policy to move in directions opposed to popular volition."[17] Specifically, Lindblom dwells on several sources of corporate or business discretion, which cumulatively lead to imperfect popular control in polyarchical systems:[18]

- consumers seldom have the competence to make or influence the multitudinous technical decisions related to product character and mix

- especially in large corporations, the timing and degree of response to even specific and apt consumer demands can be substantially influenced or even determined by officials

- corporate elites can often determine important aspects of product decisions: the timing and character of financing new investments, the degree to which production will be concentrated in one firm or dispersed among many, and so on.

- corporate elites can influence popular attitudes through public relations and advertising

- etc., etc.

This list of sources of imperfect popular control could be extended, of course. But we can be parsimonious here, especially if one point gets appropriate emphasis. Such imperfections in polyarchical or pluralist systems patently make imperfect *direct* attempts at popular control by consumers. Much the same imperfections apply, perhaps even in added measure, when *indirect* popular control is at issue—as when governmental bureaucracies seek to act in behalf of consumers. If such bureaucracies grow powerful enough to control business decisions, to paraphrase Lincoln, who then would be able to control the controllers?

The conceptual burden for polyarchical or pluralist systems seems clear. Both in theory and practice, democratic morality has to be infused into levels and structurings of governance whose complexity far exceeds that built into Democracy *and* Administration. Relatedly, polyarchical or pluralist models provide for a drastically-changed role for individual citizens, even as individual dignity remains the core value. The key pluralist assumption is that huge concentrations of wealth and power will be characteristic of contemporary society—industrialized, urbanized, and organized—from which assumption it follows that the individual so central in democratic philosophy cannot really hold his own. But the pluralist still has high hopes. As Dye and Zeigler explain:[19]

> ...[the pluralist] hopes that "countervailing" centers of power will balance each other and thereby protect the individual from abuse. Groups become the means by which individuals gain access to the political system. The government is held responsible not by individuals but by organized groups and coalitions of groups (parties). The essential value becomes participation in, and competition among, organized groups. Pluralism asserts that the dispersed pattern of power among many groups safeguards both individuals and groups against arbitrary and capricious actions of a dominant group. Pluralism contends that the American system is open and accessible to the extent that any interest held by a significant portion of the populace can find expression through one or more groups.

Redford neatly expresses the changed role for individuals. He notes, with particular regard to the now vastly-significant role of administration, that "... the attainment of the democratic ideal in the world of administration depends much less on majority votes than on the inclusiveness of the representation of interests in the interaction process among decision makers."[20] The basic reason was clear enough to Redford, as he notes in articulating the "first characteristic of the great body of men subject to the administrative state." To wit: almost all people, almost all of the time, "are dormant regarding most of the decisions being made with respect to them. Their participation cannot in any manner equal their subjection. Subjection comes from too many directions for man's span of attention, much less his active participation, to extend to all that affects him."[21] As a more or less direct consequence, then, Democracy II takes essential shape for Redford: "I propose that the system is more or less democratic in the degree to which the multiple strategic centers of interaction in decision making are, in their totality, responsive to the total variety of interests affected by the decisions." [22]

Four elements highlight major features of such an updated concept of Democracy II. First, such a concept did not emerge full-blown. It proved possible to enrich the common interpretation of the classical theory of democracy only in fits and starts, that is to say. The staying-power of the simpler ideas is suggested, for example, by the several waves of discovery of "pressure groups" extending well over half a century.[23] Why was this repetitious insistence necessary? By hypothesis, Democracy *and* Administration did not provide a hospitable conceptual home for such potent supra-individual actors as pressure groups. Hence the need for periodic rediscoveries to motivate conceptual change, and to make it stick.

Second, upgraded concepts of Democracy II did not sweep all before them. Strong ideological cross-currents still exist. One need only recall recent rallying cries—e.g., "Power to the people!"—to provide sufficient evidence about this uneven penetration of Democracy II and the incomplete conversion to it in real-life-settings. No less intense has been some academic reaction, as in the case of the "neoelitists" who propose that all organizations tend to be governed by small fractions of their membership and also that these elites have very similar backgrounds and values. So great do the similarities seem to Dye and Zeigler, in fact, that they postulate the existence of an "American socio-political elite." The two scholars extend these two assumptions in ways that fundamentally clash with pluralist approaches: [24]

> The members of this elite articulate the values of society and exercise control of society's resources. They are bound as much—if not more—by their elite identities as they are by their special group attachments. Thus, instead of constituting a balance of power systems within American society, organized interest groups are seen as platforms of power from which a relatively homogeneous group—an elite—effectively governs the nation. These leaders are more accommodating toward each other than they are competitive. They share a basic consensus about preserving the system essentially as it is. They are really held accountable by members of their group. Members have little or nothing to say about policy decisions. In fact, leaders influence followers far more than followers influence leaders.

Third, even given definite eddies within tides, Democracy II definitely shifted in significant ways. To simplify, prior interpretations were firmly rooted in the active and informed individual citizen, whose basic political home was in the "more democratic" of Dahl's four forms. Enriched concepts retained that preference but—whether joyfully or kicking and screaming—later-day ideologs emphasized the demands of polyarchy. How to choose which blend of the several varieties of democracy? Dahl systematically observes that blends in specific cases will depend on many factors: personal choice; the number and character of affected interests; the competences required and those available to various sets of actors; and the economies of using scarce resources—time, effort, dollars, and so on.[25] All that having been said, the proportion of realistic blends will definitely emphasize large collective actors prancing on polyarchical stages; and those blends must recognize the burgeoning salience of professionalization—of what Redford [26] describes as "the attitudes growing out of concentrations of training, interest, and function that affect the behavior of men within their positions in the public service." The drift is clear to Dahl: "A representative body . . . may itself be viewed as delegated authority, but in order to be effective representative bodies need to delegate authority still further to administrative bodies."[27] Neither Democracy I nor Adminstration I can credibly be seen as channelling that flood tide.

Fourth, refurbished Democracy II did not solve all relevant problems. Indeed, its development exacerbated the severity of theoretical problems while also relocating them in less-accessible and recalcitrant conceptual and practical loci. Consider two popular thoughtways—"interest group liberalism" and "the theory of countervailing power"—each of which in their own way generated great problems while promising to resolve or reconcile forces-in-tension.

Interest group liberalism proposed a hopeful and facile thesis. Given that individuals often have to aggregate to impact on public policy, and given that some interests are effectively organized and represented (e.g., economic interests) and others in only episodic and/or puny form (e.g., consumers), *the* solution required creating the conditions for a "fair fight." Public policies should encourage the robust and fair representation of all interests, with government playing the roles of balancer and referee.

Not bad for openers, perhaps, but analysis and experience soon indicated the sharp limits of the approach,[28] even if one neglects the macro-issue of how the individual survives among massive group forces.

We can illustrate only here, but at least these five problems sucked the life juices from interest group liberalism:

- the notion might apply well enough when there were plentiful resources, but it applies far less effectively or at least less obviously under conditions of scarcity

- relatedly, if a few interests want incremental amelioration of their conditions over time, that was one thing; but many interests demanding simultaneous, right-now, and major improvement pose a very different and more critical problem, especially as resources are scarce

- which is to say that scarcity and sharply-increased demand exposed *the* major attraction/deficiency in interest group liberalism's emphasis on process rather than on goals. That emphasis in effect finesses the specification of values and preferences that alone could temper scarcity-cum-demand

- practically, moreover, developing and maintaining some just balance of forces is no easy task

- and "government" could be foe or nebish to some underorganized interests, even as it was friend to others

The "theory of countervailing powers" also disappointed even as it attracted, and for somewhat the same reasons. Galbraith directs forceful attention to countervailing powers as a restraint on private economic power that compensates for "the widespread disappearance of competition in its classical form." Forcefulness was appropriate. Not only had competition all but disappeared, Galbraith notes, but it had usually been replaced by a small group of firms in tacit or open collusion. Hence it was easy to assume that no real restraints on private power exist. Galbraith disagrees: [29]

> Indeed this conclusion was all but inevitable if no search was made for other restraints and so complete was the preoccupation with competition that none was made.
>
> In fact, new restraints on private power did appear to replace competition. They were nurtured by the same process of concentration which impaired or

destroyed competition. But they appeared not on the same side of the market but on the opposite side, not with competitors but with customers or suppliers.

The obvious weakness? Galbraith warns that the model will apply less forcefully during periods of inflation, for example.[30] Moreover, potential countervailers—unions, management, and government— might find attractive reasons to collude to violate the needs or preferences of even their own members.

All such ameliorative approaches to Democracy II exacerbated the classic problem of governance, that is to say, as the level of conceptual resolution of issues got placed into the higher orbit of large collectivities. Who controls the controllers? That question had only one clear answer. That control would far outstrip the simplifications associated with Democracy *and* Administration. For example, "the individual" at least did not stand front-and-center in such revisionist thought. Witness the new type-questions. How could individuals impact upon such goliaths? Or put otherwise, how could major elements of human-scale be built into such solutions-that-were problems?

C. Pairing Autocratic Bureaucracy with, and Subordinating It to, Refurbished Democracy

To put the profound need simply, an Administration II was needed to complement Democracy II. In fact, that need was filled quickly—indeed, mercurially—in gross concept if not in reality. Compared to the frequent firestorms concerning the conceptual enhancement of Democracy, the agreement about what constitutes Administration II came both swiftly and softly. Administration II ineluctably but with awesome tenacity became associated with the "theory of bureaucracy." This seemed to simplify analytical and practical tasks, and it certainly demotivated effective criticism.

The preceding paragraph oversimplifies in the service of convenient generalization, and that simplification can be improved on. Roughly, two aspects must be distinguished in the historical coupling of a constrained concept of Administration II with an enriched Democracy II. These aspects relate to: a general mind-set; and the specific properties of bureaucracy.

The Matrix Mind-Set Gets Lambasted

Somewhere in the early decades of the 1900s, a kind of matrix mind-set came increasingly to condition thought about Administration II. Some call this mind-set an "orthodoxy." However labelled, the cluster of ideas was quite pervasive and influential. Briefly, the cluster includes such more-or-less related components: a belief in "principles" of administration associated with a simple-minded concept of "science;" a neglect of values, if not an absolute preference for being value-free and value-neutral; a related and variably-radical separation of "politics" from "administration;" an emphasis on thoroughgoing centrism with authoritarian if not totalitarian tendencies; and so on. This cluster of ideas requires only evocation here, given that numerous sources provide highly-convergent detail for interested readers.[31]

Whether orthodoxy or not, the cluster defined a conceptual domain that attracted episodic attack even as its basic essence rolled on. Especially after World War II, that is to say, that orthodoxy got convincingly clobbered in multiple ways: methodologically, as well as practically and prescriptively. Methodologically, for example, Dahl convincingly demonstrated that values could hardly be excluded from a "science of administration," for at least three basic reasons. That is: "science" cannot "construct a bridge across the great gap from 'is' to 'ought';" administration involves in part a study of aspects of human behavior, which is inherently valuing and valued; and all administration occurs in social settings, which are value-loaded.[32] Relatedly, observers like Appleby argued that the sharp separation of "politics" from "administration" was ill-advised, especially as a description of what exists,[33] but also as a prescription of what should exist in a well-ordered democratic state.[34]

The conceptual opponent did not wilt, however. Even contemporary commentators like Thayer[35] and Ostrom[36] still feel it necessary to attack the matrix mind-set. These scholars offer a similar prescription: we need not only modify common meanings of Administration, but especially how we practice it. Ostrom takes the less extreme position. As Marini explains:[37]

> . . . while he thinks that obsessive devotion to an unmitigated single hierarchy in our polity is a danger and reprehensible, he seems to think that the mitigation of hierarchy involved in federalism, republicanism, checks and balances, rule of positive law, overlapping jurisdictions, and the like may be

sufficient (that is, he does not call for absolute abolition of all hierarchical arrangements or inequalities of influence).

In contrast, Marini emphasizes,[38] Thayer goes all the way. He argues for ". . . the absence of any inequalities and he assumes that hierarchy easily can and must be eliminated." Both men reflect a high confidence that their prescriptions will do the job, in kaleidoscopic senses. Indeed, Marini notes uncharitably of Thayer's optimism that the elimination of hierarchy and competition is an all-purpose remedy as well as being both necessary and possible. "Indeed, all aspects of life from International Affairs to office sexual affairs will be changed or improved" as hierarchy is eliminated.

The Theory of Bureaucracy Survives

If the conceptual combat resulted in proponents of the matrix mind-set losing most of the battles, they remained in firm control of the significant battleground. Given the easy vulnerability of the orthodoxy, in sum, its compatible guidelines for the practical structuring of work tended to survive. These compatible guidelines—the "theory of bureaucracy"—have a familiar form:

- a well-defined chain of command that vertically channels formal interaction

- a division of labor based upon specialization by major function or process that vertically fragments a flow of work

- a system or procedures and rules for dealing with contingencies at work that reinforces the reporting insularity of each unit

- promotion and selection based on technical competence, which is defined consistently with the first three items

- impersonality in relations between organization members and between them and their clients

The theory of bureaucracy could not lose for winning, in effect. Its foundations had been sorely tested, and found wanting, without doubt.

Thus the theory's logical inconsistencies have been clearly portrayed;[39] the awkward and counter-productive practical consequences of the theory have been urged;[40] and its incompatibility with democracy has been persuasively set forth.[41] Yet it basically survives, in many guises in most organizations and most markedly in the public sector.

D. Rationalizing A Conceptual Odd Couple

The basic pairing—of Democracy II with autocratic bureaucracy—should have excited major conceptual attention. Simply, however, it did not. Democracy *vs.* Administration reigned supreme, with only a few discordant observations over the years that fell far short of carrying the day, even as they were convincing.[42]

This curious situation implies two questions for immediate analysis. What rationale generally carried the day, almost by default? And why that intriguing and crucial lack of attention?

What Rationale Carried the Day?

Despite variable criticism of its basic aspects, Adminstration II became subordinated to, if suffered by, an enriched concept of Democracy II, in almost a knee-jerk sense. Directly, as Democracy II tore loose from the simplistic tethers of common interpretations of the classical theory of democracy, Administration had to be conceptually restricted in very strict ways. It was as if ideologs could tolerate only so much complexity, and had to balance it with simplicism. If Democracy II came to mean far more than control by an alert and informed citizenry, Adminstration II came to be conceptually viewed as a simplified stimulus/response linkage.

What rationale underlays Democracy *vs.* Administration? Consider a simple component of that rationale, but a potent one. That conceptual pairing rests on—or perhaps, permits—what Redford calls "a simple model of overhead democracy." He explains:[43]

> It asserted that democratic control should run through a single line from the representatives of the people to all those who exercised power in the name of government. The line ran from the people to their representatives in the Presidency and the Congress, and from there to the President as chief

executive, then to departments, then to bureaus, then to lesser units, and so on to the fingertips of administation. Exceptions to the single line were acceptable only for the judiciary, and perhaps also for certain quasi-judicial and quasi-legislative functions and the auditing function.

But Redford is concerned as well as certain. "Few if any, would deny that the overhead route is an essential means of implementing democratic morality in the administered society," he observes. But on the other hand, Redford worries: "The traditional model is simplistic." It does not adequately define administration as it operates; nor does it convincingly prescribe efficient and effective administration.

Certainty definitely carried the 20th century, concerns notwithstanding. Hence the "simple model of overhead democracy," in numerous variants, is seen as central in the rationale supporting this age's emphasis on Democracy *vs.* Administration. For example, Dunsire expresses well the dominant sense of how—and perhaps also the desperation about why—Administration II conceptually linked citizenry, elected leaders/representatives, and administrators. Dunsire observes: ". . . both the theory and the practice of administration rest on the premise that leaders of organization know what their subordinates are doing. If this is not true, or less true than it is generally assumed, then one of the axioms of democratic government ceases to apply."[44] In this context, Dunsire approvingly quotes Kaufman and Couzens: "In general terms, democracy in the modern state presupposes that changing a handful of officials in high places will ultimately change the actions of thousands of employees throughout the system. Subordinate compliance is thus a pillar of democratic governance."[45]

The deep need to subordinate Administration to Democracy gets reflected even more clearly by Dahl, whose work was used above to model the conceptual developments in Democracy II. Dahl was acutely aware of developments on one side of the Democracy/Administration duality. Basically, he paid for the enrichment of Democracy II by seeking to bound Administration II all the more tightly. That is, Democracy II requires complex delegations of authority; delegation requires numerous hierarchical sub-divisions; and the more extensive that delegation—which is to say, the more open it becomes to abuse—"the stronger we may want the controls within the hierarchy to be."[46] Otherwise, the probability of popular control becomes so tenuous as to call into question the conceptual changes Dahl prescribes for Democracy II.

Whatever may be said of others, Dahl did not just stumble into Democracy vs. Administration. He made the journey, step by step. He was clear about where his argument started—". . . if you want to maximize the effectiveness of the people in achieving your purposes. . . " And Dahl also was clear about where his argumentation took him—". . . you will need some stages of government you may consider less 'democratic' than others."[47] In the modern state, Dahl notes this "paradox of democracy" cannot be avoided. Referring to the forms or levels of Democracy distinguished in Exhibit 1, he explains:[48]

> If you think that polyarchy is less 'democratic' than primary democracy, you will nonetheless need to prescribe several stages of polyarchy. What is more, you will need adminstration, and administration will need hierarchy. Otherwise, "the people" who rule may turn out not to be the people but the bureaucrats. I do not see how we can stretch the meaning of "democratic" authority to include the hierarchy of administration. *Consequently, . . . rule by the people requires not only democratic forms but also nondemocratic forms of delegated authority.*

Other ideational developments in Dahl also indicate the explicitness and comprehensiveness of what he intends. The "delegated authority" which he would sharply constrain is *not* restricted to "government agencies." Thus he notes that ". . . nothing could be less appropriate than to consider the giant firm a *private enterprise.*" The notion, in fact, represents "an absurdity."[49] Indeed, *all* economic enterprise ought to be thought of as "a public service." From this perspective, Dahl concludes, "a private economy is a contradiction in terms."[50] By direct implication, then, Democracy vs. Administration should apply to all organizations.

One need not force a conclusion about Dahl, nor about the dominant opinion he represents even as he differs from it in nuance and shading. For Dahl, in sum, dealing with either Democracy or Adminstration implies a profound paradox that rests in operating realities, not in misinterpretations of historical ideas. Administration II must be subordinated to Democracy II, he proposes, and the two must be played by very different rules. In this elemental sense, Democracy *and* Administration implies a pairing of incompatibles. Democracy *vs.* Administration becomes the core prescription for Dahl.

Why The Lack of Attention?

If obviously convenient in its variable strengths, explicitnesses, and extensivenesses, Democracy *vs.* Administration still astounds, as does the meager explicit attention that has been devoted to its gross features, never mind its ramifications. Given Dahl's enormous ranges of delegated authority whose hierarchical controls are to be constrained in the service of Democracy II, for example, the "paradox of democracy" would seem to be very painful, if not crippling. One can reasonably wonder if the conceptual bargain has given away the essence of Democracy in seeking to protect it. Relatedly, one wonders about the general failure to pursue another line of attack. Would it have been possible to conceptually enrich Administration, as opposed to defining its properties as the mirror image of enhanced Democracy? Generally, albeit with some noteworthy exceptions, that was not done in this country.[51]

The inattention to this fundamental conceptual change requires some substantial explanation. Certainly convenience alone does not explain the general, persisting, and unreflective adoption of Democracy *vs.* Administration. Seven interacting factors highlight the convenience of the concept.

1. *Saving Democracy from Itself.* Perhaps central in the gestation of Democracy *vs.* Administration were certain political problems associated with the "imperfections" of American popular sovereignty around the turn of the century. Corruption, bossism, alliances of political machines with crime, and tragically-loose standards in the production of foods and medicines: the muckraking literature gave these and similar targets a high priority.[52] Not very far below the surface—and often stage front-and-center—was the related and reinforcing fear of the hordes of immigrants who arrived in urban centers around the turn of the century.[53] At the very least, they often were unskilled, easy to manipulate politically, and were the raw material out of which new and basic coalitions were forming. Also close to the surface were concerns about the "native migration"—those numerous and often-sad millions who in the 1900s began drifting off the land, clustering in urban areas, to join the high-fertility immigrants already there. These two streams of people became the raw materials for new and revolutionary coalitions—in politics, in unions, and so on.[54]

Many observers got stiff-necked about what popular sovereignty had wrought, but one could argue that the hurly-burly was profoundly functional for the survival of representative democracy. Thus Thompson notes that "in the Civil War . . . massive immigration into newly forming cities, both from within and from abroad, created low-consensus, heterogeneous political communities with great problem-solving needs. A workable level of consensus was created through 'corrupt political machines', which traded administrative resources for political support (consensus). Thus were the cities built, and in just a few decades." Thompson wisely concludes that, under such conditions: "Maintaining the consensual basis of a political community looms as a larger problem, in the eyes of the political elite, than efficient administrative problem-solving. Administrative resources are used for reasons of political maintenance."[55]

However one evaluates such a position today, at that time many influentials despaired that popular sovereignty could do the required job, unless aided in major ways. The total sense of it got represented in various ways, none of them clearer than this passage from Woodrow Wilson:[56]

> Even if we . . . could form out of perfectly instructed heads a few steady, infallible, placidly wise maxims of government . . . would the country act on them? That is the question. The bulk of mankind is rigidly unphilosophical, and nowadays the bulk of mankind votes. A truth must become not only plain but also commonplace before it will be seen by the people who go to their work very early in the morning . . .
>
> And where is this unphilosophical bulk of mankind more multifarious in its composition than in the United States? To know the public mind of this country, one must know the mind, not of Americans of the older stocks only, but also of Irishmen, of Germans, of Negroes.

As the political focus shifted from "acreage to population," in Raymond Moley's telling phrase, no wonder that for many ideologs administratively-relevant approaches to "coping with the political problems of their polity"[57] took on an elitist and antiseptic quality. Conveniently, the "business" and "science" of that day provided a ready model for improvement. As Marini notes:[58]

> The political theory of public administration concentrated on considerations mainly of "how to get the job done" [and] its basic assumptions were that

well-meaning and understanding individuals would come to similar conclusions about goals, and the people could be prevented from being "meddlesome," and that the "best men" could use technology to engineer the good life for the lesser folk . . . to discover the principles of operation of government [to restructure it] so that it worked better, cleaner, and quieter.

Many discordant and ironic ideological emphases get bundled together in Marini's faithful summary of common strains in rhetoric around the turn of the century. The forces-in-tension often trend in not-obviously-compatible ways. Administration II gets subordinated to Democracy II, and thus is freed to save popular democracy by serving it with technical and professional skills that are in some sense above commonly-conceived political processes and insulated from them. But the basic thrust seems clear enough. Administration II gets buoyed by unreflective emphasis on "business" and "science" to counteract some awkward aspects of popular sovereignty. One god is diseased, dying; long live the new god. Representative democracy would at once be served, saved from its own excesses, and yet remain secure. A major political foundation of Democracy *vs.* Administration, in effect, involved protecting the republic from politics and some of its effects, hopefully temporary effects.

2. *"Sam, You Made the Pants Too Long."* This simple rhetoric had a reasonable-enough stimulus, but the ideation often became master rather than slave. For some people, the rhetoric was designed only to get the political rascals out—as well as to get the technocratic elite in, and to keep them there. For them, the patchwork of ideas constituted only a way of holding-the-line during unprecedented political, social, and economic turmoil. For most others, the core concepts relating Administration and Democracy slipped such convenient moorings. The ideology soon became much more of a tether on the future than holding-the-line.

Overall, let us characterize the sense of how an incautious ideational blend got exaggerated. Politics was, well, dirty and corrupt, and its actual practice had the general effect on many of critically threatening the ideal of popular democracy. Administration was competent, scientific, and—er—tidy and neat. *The* problem thus seemed to have three major components:

- to remove much content and people from the realm of Politics, and to locate them in Adminstration

- to make sure that the right people—an appropriately-restrained and protected technological elite—ran Adminstration

- to save Democracy from itself by limiting popular sovereignty which—now less encumbered—could retain its supremacy over the major issues in the interval during which a more sophisticated electorate might somehow evolve

This constitutes a very full ideological plate, and requires much twisting and turning to avoid two very real ogres—fascism on one hand, and communism on the other—each sharing the feature of being a major alternative to regimes that somehow prove incompetent to maintain popular support while doing the jobs required for tolerable governance.

The ideological agenda got worked in multiple ways, whose fullness is quite beyond this treatment. But some sense of developmental extensions-out-of-control can be suggested by three major points, each of which requires at least passing mention. First, the emphasis on "science"—meant quite generally—soon got embroiled in very-specific arguments about the role of "facts" and "values." In part, the debate had scholarly roots, as in disputes centering around "logical positivism" and other philosophic schools. In part, also, the debate was fueled by exuberant claims that the facts would set us free, that explicit programs for action would leap from collections of data, suitably assembled.[59]

In a rough sense, then, a basically-political rationale got extended-in-extremis by intellectual and practical forces. The results were often quite untidy—value and empirical issues got twisted and transmuted, for example, as ideologs sought to provide verbal rationalizations for what had come to exist. But the results have been no less profound for their incautious extension, as in the case of why and how various historically-overlapping developments—such as civil service reform—were both reinforced by and provided reinforcement for the only-then-increasing bureaucratization that came to be *the* legitimate model for structuring organizations. As Meyer notes: "It may be that the causes of bureaucratization lie as much in historical as in contemporary events . . . a series of developments . . . around the turn of the century [that] have affected organizations existing since."[60] These developments include: the reform movement in local government; the civil service movement; and the hegemony of scientific management. Such developments were nestled in a calculus of efficiency, but Meyer has his doubts about such a direct motivation of forces that gave rise to a "basic transformation of organizations" around the turn of the present century. Meyer cannot be certain, but his analytical antennae tell him that we need a major research effort concerned with the "social, political, and economic changes that give rise to bureaucratic structures in the first place." Meyer poses some reasonable questions for such research. For example, "one wonders whether 'merit' principles were, in part, a response to alliances between machine politicians and immigrant groups that threatened WASP elites."[61] Useful wondering, that.[62]

However innocent and even useful value-free positions may have been up to a point, that is to say, they often got extended far beyond that point and raised merry hell for ideologs as well as practicioners. For example, the fact/value separation encouraged the development of specialized areas of inquiry, as in "wisdom" and "fact" or "philosophy" and "science." This simple extrapolation caused much profound mischief, even though it provides tidy reinforcement for Democracy *vs.* Administration and for the subordination/separateness of the latter to/from the former. However appropriate such an approach is for certain kinds of inquiry, it very poorly suits people-oriented inquiry and especially the applied sciences, which inherently involve values and valuing. Failure to provide a reasonable place for values and goals does not mean that such efforts will stop. Day-to-day pressures will be too compelling; and ways will be found to deal practically with that which got conceptually finessed. In the absence of specification of values or goals, as Marini argues, technical conventions will come to dominate. As he notes concerning one case:[63]

> The theory of public administration came eventually to utilize manipulative social technology and "machine man" imagery, and these were reconcilable with notions of "democracy" and the good life only because the operational notion of "democracy" was at basis ... elitist in operation even during radicalization of the myths.

Second, a sharp separation of Politics from Administration was one of the most extreme extensions of the fact/value distinction. Basically, the position distinguished two types of truth-tests, or guides for action. The first relates to political processes which are inherently value-loaded and value-generating; and the second pertains to scientific or technical knowledge embodied in "canons of good practice."

Again, reasonably bounded, the distinction was unexceptional; but reasonableness did not constitute the order-of-the-day. Illustratively, one can easily maintain an *analytic* distinction between willing or choosing, and acting on that will or choice. This distinction might even be helpful.[64] Common usage far exceeded these modest bounds, however. Thus the analytical distinction often became transmuted into a distinction between real loci and real actors—as between lower-level public administrators on the one hand and, on the other, legislators and elected or high-level appointed officials. This proved troublesome. Hence it became necessary for a generation of scholars to prove and reprove that the analytic distinction did not correspond with reality. Practically, however, such sloppy extensions of thought did provide ideological support for major developments in public administration, e.g., the protected and allegedly-neutral civil service, especially at the federal level. So the awkward idea gave birth to major institutions which provided powerful reinforcement for that idea.

Third, the realm of administration expanded enormously. Not only did governments grow in size. And not only were large proportions of public employees put in protected status as civil servants who were "out of politics" and thus were often carelessly viewed as dealing with facts rather than values, with technical execution or implementation rather than with policy-making. In addition, vast public realms were depoliticized in intent, if not always in fact. Diverse manifestations of this strong tendency come to mind: the rise of professional hegemony, as in the city manager movement or in educator-run school systems; the proliferation of specialized authorities or single-purpose taxing districts; the technical direction of vast areas of the economy and life, as by so-called independent regulatory commissions; professional control of mental and health care; and so on and on.[65]

3. *A Little Help from your Friends, and Practically Everyone Else.* Support for the ideological fragments sketched above came from many sectors, and often strange ones. This broad range of support, by hypothesis, explains the incredible vitality and persistence of thought-fragments that were imprecise and often conflictful, at best. The ideation could not make it on its own, in short.

Two illustrations suggest the diversity of this support. Thus the administrative orthodoxy could appeal to both friends of the technocrats as well as to their opponents. That is, neutral civil servant and sharp separation of politics/administration could be seen as independence for Administration or as subordination to Democracy, or both. This constitutes a powerful combination because—even though it dissolves with the acid of even gentle critical analysis—analysis was no match for stereophonic convenience.

That the bureaucratic principles came to be seen as the bulwark supporting popular democracy by enforcing the subordinacy of administrative activities poses no problem of proof. Consider an extreme example. Bureaucratic principles are *the* major deterrent to the unauthorized and unauthorizable robbery from its "owners"—the general public—of the "tool" of administration. The principles inhibit public officials from such theft, in short; and any less-autocratic or less-restrictive guides would only encourage this fateful robbery.[66]

As for the administrative orthodoxy being seen as granting independence to Administration, many saw such ideological features as implying improvement on, and insulation from, the awkward effects of popular government and local controls. One may speak of the nationalization of adminstration—in government, in the military, and the economy.[67] In this view, professionals in effect agreed to a major trade-off to do better what they saw as necessary to run the emerging state: freedom from local pressures was to be paid for by possibly-greater central control, balanced by the professionals' advantages in initiating and sustaining agendas. No doubt existed in many quarters concerning what was at stake, in any case, or what would save the day. As Charles Beard noted: "The future of civilized government, and even, I think of civilization itself, rests upon our ability to develop a science and a philosophy and a practice of administration competent to discharge the public functions of civilized society."[68] For people like Beard, the orthodoxy permitted getting the right people in, and keeping them there.

The same ideological features—when catalyzed by a robust sense of Democracy II—also could attract those concerned about controlling the "administrative state." The unity of command prescribed by the "simple model of overhead democracy" promised safety from exploitation by the professional managers for whom great potential power inhered in the positions they occupied.

In addition, the orthodoxy had elements congenial to both the ideological left and right. Thus many observers appreciate how the themes of that orthodoxy—the preeminence of business methods, a stress on science and expertise, a distaste for politics of the immigrant-centered and urban type, and so on—would appeal to the Chamber of Commerce and to the National Association of

Manufacturers. The point has been remarked numerous times, often disparagingly as yet another evidence of the cogency of the economic interpretation of history and politics.

However, few appreciate that much the same rationale suited (for example) the Marxist, whose ideology usually stood at such extreme odds with the view that good business equals good government, and vice versa. That is, Marx and Engels proposed that the private ownership of the means of production led to the domination of person over person. In contrast, public ownership under socialism or communism would lead to and require only the "administration of things." Consequently, one could envision a "withering away of the state," conceived in its historical meaning as a system of force. Ebenstein in this regard draws useful attention to some central features of Marxist doctrine, which bear a close resemblance to the distinction between Politics and Administration in America. He notes of that doctrine that: [69]

> The *administration of things* is a matter of technical *knowledge* and not of political *will*. Government as an agency of settling disputes between men by force would be replaced in the classless society by administration as a scientific method of using resources in the best way in accordance with verifiable procedures of science and technology. Locke was the first modern writer to define property as a relationship of man to things, inasmuch as he saw the origin of property in the admixture of human effort to natural resources. Marx's concept of *publicly owned property as a relationship between man and things* closely follows Locke's concept of private property.

Beyond this crucial commonality, moreover, Ebenstein goes on to identify a similar utopianism in the ideology of Marxism/Leninism and classical liberalism—the perfectability of human nature via institutions so arranged that government as a vehicle of force becomes unnecessary and anachronistic. Ebenstein concludes:

> In the classical doctrine of liberal democracy, the equitable distribution of private property seemed to point to such a state of harmony; in the classical doctrine of Marx-Engels, the . . . collective ownership of the means of production would assure a basic equality of men that would make government in the traditional sense unnecessary. Both classical democracy and classical Marxism suffer from an excessive optimism with regard to the perfectability of man, and both wrongly assume that any system of society can be devised that can achieve perfect harmony of interests.

4. *Holding the Technocrats At Bay*. Consider an extension of an important theme introduced above. Looked at from an important perspective, much of the ideational ferment just reviewed relates to the rapid emergence of the professional manager, technocrat, or knowledge-worker. From this point of view, for example, the sharp separation of Politics from Administration can be seen as an effort to at least hold-the-line while social controls were developed sufficient to prevent unchecked power from ineluctably accruing to the specialized managerial and scientific elites.[70] But a substantial sense of dynamic tension had to be retained, for over-control was as perilous as under-control. Hence such devices as the "protected civil service" can be seen as a *quid pro quo* for providing what all modern societies need to survive.

Evaluations differ as to how effectively the technocrats have been controlled, but their new presence and significance seem indisputable. Perhaps the modal popular opinion variously recognizes that our technocrats can create monsters as well as solutions, as dramatized in the persona of a Dr. Frankenstein or of a Jekyll/Hyde. Others warn that our managerial society induces mindless and self-defeating service to an "organizational imperative" that jeopardizes any real sense of individual freedom. Few would disagree with Drucker's description of the current situation, however:[71]

> The emergence of management as an essential, a distinct and a leading institution is a pivotal event in a social history. Rarely, if ever, has a new basic institution, a new leading group, emerged as fast as has management since the turn of the century. Rarely in human history has a new institution proven so indispensable so quickly; and even less often has a new institution arrived with so little opposition, so little disturbance, so little controversy . . . .
>
> Management, which is the organ of society specifically charged with making resources productive, that is, with the responsibility for organized economic advance, therefore reflects the basic spirit of the modern age. It is in fact indispensable—and this explains why once begotten, it grew so fast, and with so little opposition.

Why emphasize this theme here? Simple enough. If anything, these several related developments—of managers, of professionals, and of the sciences—had a more profound impact on government than on business. Concerning the "scientific revolution," for example, Price concludes that it ". . . seems certain to have a more radical effect on our political institutions than did the industrial revolution, for a good many reasons," of which Price emphasizes three.[72] First, the scientific revolution has momentously succeeded in upsetting the previous government/business equilibrium, in "moving the public and private sectors closer together." In what senses? For openers, much modern enterprise will follow technological developments that respond to public policy and are financed by government. Moreover, government will be a major customer, and many firms will be significantly dependent on their public business, to risk a play-on-words.

Second, relatedly, a new order of complexity in the administration of public affairs resulted from the scientific revolution. This impact takes protean forms, as in the basic issues of control and responsibility. Consider a contrast, simplified but suggestive. The industrial revolution rested on new forms of expertise and brought a widening range of complexities but, as Price emphasizes, it left undisturbed the essential questions of managerial or owner control. The scientific revolution, in contrast, raises far more serious problems of comprehension and control, not only for the business manager but especially for our newly-active government in its executive, legislative, and judicial manifestations.

Third, that is to say, the "scientific revolution is upsetting our system of checks and balances," not only in a constitutional but also in broader senses as well. Perhaps the dominant (and simple) response to the problems of the industrial revolution was government as balance wheel or regulator. "Everyone admitted that it was possible for economic interests to control politics," Price explains, "but the remedy seemed to be clear: regulate business to prevent abuses, and keep selfish business interests out of the political process." What Price calls "independent sources of moral judgment"—basically coming from theological and university sources—contributed to that balance. Today, however, these safeguards have been variously diluted. Thus universities—and especially their science—are deeply involved with both government and business; the universities also helped diminish the impact of theological authorities; and government could only with growing incredibility even pretend to an arm's-length relationship with business over a broad range of activities.

Even if the implied conclusion seems crystal-clear, it has such profound import as to justify emphasizing the obvious. The special salience for governance of scientific and technocratic developments may help explain why Administration II has persisted with greater tenacity in the public sector. Relatedly, that special salience may also help explain why business research and practice were more early and energetically occupied with separating the wheat from the chaff of that concept, especially with reference to the theory of bureaucracy.[73]

5. *Keeping Up With Two Incomparable Joneses.* The four tendencies above, in interaction, had their momentum increased by two important historical tendencies of the natal days of public administration. The first feature emphasized the burgeoning sense of administration as a science, with the all-but-universal emphasis on business. The second historical feature was the European preeminence in administration during the 19th Century. As Waldo notes:[74]

> In his landmark essay of 1887, "The Study of Administration," Woodrow Wilson, after premising that it is becoming "more difficult to run a constitution than to frame one" urged America to learn the "science" of public administration from Europe, free it of the spirit of autocracy, and put it to the service of democracy. To civicly aware Americans of the post-Civil War years Europe seemed a model of public administration competence, honesty and efficiency.

In complex ways, these two historical features facilitated the curious grafting of Administration II to Democracy II. To simplify, the general thrust amounted to keeping up with the best administrative practices of two kinds of Joneses, those overseas and those in business. Directly, the general admiration implied a too-hopeful view of how differences between cultures or values could be accommodated, of how Wilson's dictum re freeing the European science of administration from its autocratic spirit could be realized. Wilson himself did not help much, as in his optimistic but too-facile example: we could borrow a murderer's knife-sharpening technique without also adopting his intent.[75] This was true as far as it went, but it did not go very far. Thus many routinely failed to make the crucial distinction on which Wilson insisted: "Our own politics must be the touchstone for all theories. The principles on which to base a science of administration for America must be principles which have democratic policy much at heart."[76] Even Wilson was not very effective at respecting his own counsel, however, in large part because it was very, very general. Despite the value-respecting stance just quoted, for example, his position trended toward "how-to-do-it" (in his words) as contrasted with "what-to-do," with "tested practices" or techniques from business or overseas that had worked in other normative contexts. Moreover, Wilson provided little useful guidance for separating technique from its underlying norms. "We have only to filter [the science of administration] through our constitutions," he prescribed, "only to put it over a slow fire of criticism and distil away its foreign gases."[77] However, managerial orientations or techniques often could not be separated from intent: they were built upon and reflected specific cultural or value choices. As Waldo notes:[78] ". . . for the most part the admired European administrative technology was deeply embedded in culture and institutions and could not be simply extricated and transferred."

This inextricability of technique and values characterized the bureaucratic principles, for example, which were rooted in autocratic cultural norms. Adopt the principles, in short, and you buy into those norms—whether you are aware of it or not. This value incompatibility was less a problem for American business in those days, where the image of the authoritarian owner-entrepreneur loomed very large indeed.[79] But the principles poorly suited our general views of political democracy, and even more poorly the broad ethical and religious notions that may be labelled Judaeo-Christian.[80] However, this point often got overwhelmed by the general admiration of business as well as of European administrative efficiency and honesty. In extreme cases, in fact—as in rhetoric about universal principles of administration—the recognition of differences in values or cultures all but disappeared.

6. *"But It's our Bastard."* There is no telling how many people were influenced by such currents in the ideological air but—on *a priori* grounds—we can expect a more down-to-earth issue to have had an impact on the general acceptance of the pairing of Democracy II and Administration II. They tell a story about Stalin, whom most Russians considered a bastard. But German eagerness during World War II to rid Russians of Stalin found few takers. The rationale: to Russians, Stalin was at least *their* bastard, with known if generally unadmired characteristics. The German successor might very well also be a bastard, with perhaps even worse features; and in any case, that bastard would be someone else's.

So it was with Democracy *vs.* Administration, that odd conceptual pairing of Democracy II with Administration II. Some clearly perceived the conflict or contradiction of coercive bureaucracy and representative democracy. But they believed a choice had to be made, and in that choice political democracy dominated, in largest part because the alternative to a coercive bureaucracy was vaguely defined. For example, Mosher sees some virtue in collegial decision-making as a partial antidote to coercive hierarchy; and he notes that a substantial degree of this development has occurred in many public agencies, "particularly those controlled by single professional groups." But Mosher had reservations about allowing Administration too long a leash, and not only in the senses that corruption, collusion, or rule by a technological elite might result. Mosher adds a reasonable caution:[81]

> . . . I would point out that democracy within adminstration, if carried to the full, raises a logical dilemma in its relation to political democracy. All public organizations are presumed to have been established and to operate for public purposes—i.e. . . . ., purposes of the people . . . It is entirely possible that internal administrative democracy might run counter to the principles and objectives of political democracy in which the organizations of government are viewed as instruments of public purpose.

Although Democracy *vs.* Administration might well be considered a bastardized pairing, then, it at least had known features that seemed to fit prevailing notions about popular sovereignty even in the very violation of those notions. Two more or less distinct variants characterize most of the reactions. Thus the late Hans Kelsen put the profound point in simple terms: "The democracy of the part can be contrary to the democracy of the whole."[82] A common maxim of past generations put the point in a more specific and comprehensive perspective: "Autocracy during [workhours] is the price of democracy after hours."[83] Both variants no doubt shared the concern that a less-coercive concept of Administration might unexpectedly have even worse features than its predecessor, flawed and simplistic though Administration II most definitely was.

7. *Nature and Its Kind Abhor a Vacuum.* Stereophonically, also, the pairing of Democracy II and Administration II may also reflect a very basic human tendency. "Our heads are never empty," Heaton expresses the point with power, "because it is our nature to imagine when we do not know."[84] Relying in part on the work with sensory deprivation,[85] which does not seem to deter one's sensory nerves from firing, Heaton draws this broad generalization:[86]

> We fill our heads, from childhood on, with fantasies or assumptions about the physical and social structures around us and then these mental models shape our perceptions. Matching our environmental models, we develop self-images and then these images shape and control our self-perceptions, hope, actions, and reactions.

Given the range of vital issues associated with replacing Democracy *and* Administration, *in a hurry*, no wonder that all of the pieces did not fit. Conceptually, Democracy II posed serious issues of controlling and motivating public employees. Intellectual, political, and practical urgencies coerced responses; the kaleidoscopic and far-from-congruent adaptations remained, often long after their complex stimuli had been variously warped, or changed, or even dissipated; and those responses, once reasonable enough, often persisted even after theory and experience had evolved better-suited ways of doing what needed to be done.

We can only illustrate here the curious pastiche of ideational fragments whose aggregation was encouraged—perhaps even forced—by major intellectual, political, and social forces. Three points must suffice here to suggest the broader point: ideas—often conceptually opposite or irreconcilable—were incautiously blended; and new approaches and techniques were nested gently in strange normative contexts, some newly-formed but most solidly rooted in a vision of a simple past.

First, Adminstration II was initially nested in a set of notions about a *merit system* that are dominantly ethical in their designations and connotations. When Mosher writes about the ideational parents of the merit system, to illustrate, he emphasizes the chief role of the Protestant Ethic which prescribes "respect for, even worship of, work not merely as a practical necessity but as a high moral imperative."[87] Other ethically-loaded contributors to the merit idea include:[88]

- individualism, or the heavy emphasis on the person evaluated with respect to one's "merit" in comparison and competition with all others

- egalitarianism, or the primacy of equal treatment for all—albeit within unstated limits that have proved flexible over time—regardless of individuating factors such as race, sex, income, formal education, and political affiliation

- separatism, or the prescription that the merit system should be "removed from the rest of government and conducted disinterestedly, scientifically, and independently"

- unilateralism, which views "government as sovereign, and its decisions, when reached through proper procedures, final"

Second, the basic merit notion not only saw approaches to personnel administration in moralistic terms—as "good" or "bad"—but it also was negative in its basic orientation. Thus merit reformers knew that they wished to avoid the spoils approach to personnel administration, to stamp-out an evil that was a "disgrace to republican institutions."[89] But where to go from there? "There was not very much original thought about the best kind of substitute for spoils," Mosher concludes; "beyond competitive entrance examinations and security of tenure."[90]

This moral orientation and negative emphasis proved an awkward combination, however understandable in the context of pressures abuilding. Tough practical questions tended to inspire answers whose primary test was superficial consistency with often-opposed ideals, for example, rather than answers that were probable or practical. Consider one tough question. How do you assure the responsiveness of a public service which is politically neutral and protected, but which exists in a context which heavily relies on elections and political parties?

Beyond neglect, the temptation seems to have been dual. Thus I see a tendency to seek solutions to one problem at a time, with little concern that one solution might cause other and more virulent problems. Consider Woodrow Wilson, who saw civil-service reform "as but a prelude to a fuller administrative reform." Creating distance from "politics" certainly made it easier to implement merit reforms.[91] But one could also argue that a protected service made it practically harder to bring-off the fuller reform at a later time, once that neutral and protected service had been put in place, as firmly as that was typically done.[92]

Relatedly, I see a reliance on resolution-by-verbal-inventions, often having self-fulfilling features. How to assure responsiveness of a politically-insulated and professionalized public service? "A possible intellectual escape from this dilemma resided in the doctrine of the separation of politics and policy from administration," Mosher notes. He adds: "I call it an 'intellectual escape' because I doubt that it had any more empirical basis in the 1880's than it has today, if as much."[93]

Was this improbable intellectual escape worth the costs? Real doubts about that can be entertained, at least. For example, the separation requires major conceptual support, as via the prescription of a bureaucratic model. This common prescription complements the differentiation of the two realms—Politics and Administration—which is a johnny-come-lately idea in political and intellectual history; and the prescription no doubt gained major support because of its convenient fit with the simple notion of a merit system and the special problems it poses. But those conveniences at best finesse major developmental issues. The point will get fuller attention later. Here note only that bureaucratic prescriptions deal tangentially at best with such issues as the professionalization of so much of the public service. As the early debate between Finer[94] and Friedrich[95] highlights, the tidiest approach to dealing with administrative responsibility involves a direct responsiveness to popular mandates which Finer calls "objective responsibility" and equates with representative democratic processes. With widespread professionalization, however, the tidiest approach does not inspire great confidence. As Friedrich notes, popular sentiment *and* technical knowledge must be subtly blended. The latter must come from a sense of professional responsibility, which may be influenced by popular mandates but resides more specifically in individual consciences, as well as in the training and ethics that (for good or ill) get day-to-day reinforcement from professional peers. Bureaucratic prescriptions do not help resolve such subtleties. As Mosher concludes: "Our dependence upon professionals is now so great that the orientations, value systems, and ethics which they bring to their work and which they enforce on one another are a matter of prime concern to those who would strengthen the democratic system."[96]

Third, ample evidence suggests that ideologs were their own worst enemies in seeking to mate incompatible ideas. Consider that in the rationale supporting merit reform, efficiency was definitely not the primary consideration, "and not [even] a very close second . . ."[97] But inexorably along came the later faith in science and scientific method applied to practical affairs—the cult of efficiency. Mosher notes: "It may be noted that the new 'good' of efficiency did not, so far as the public service was concerned, displace the older one of a politically neutral merit system. The deities complemented and supported each other."[98]

But that convenient support had to be very temporary. For example, the positivist mental pathways often associated with "science" were fundamentally corrosive of the very ethical bases of public service reform, such as the Protestant Ethic. Moreover, even casual observation raises serious questions about major verities. "The developments in recent decades in the 'real world' of government have brought to the policy-administration dichotomy," Mosher notes by way of illustration, "strains which have grown almost beyond the point of toleration. In fact, on the theoretical plane, the finding of a viable substitute may well be the number one problem of public administration today."[99]

III. DEMOCRACY *VS.* ADMINISTRATION AS NAIVE: ITS DESCRIPTIVE AND PRESCRIPTIVE INADEQUACIES

Despite its ubiquity, Democracy *vs.* Administration can be regarded as naive. Consider only three approaches to this significant conclusion. In common, those approaches propose that Administration II either does not satisfactorily describe what commonly exists, or that when the concept does govern what exists, major negative consequences can be expected.

To introduce this section with a summary conclusion—Democracy *vs.* Administration needs to be evaluated explicitly in terms of its descriptive and prescriptive inadequacies, whatever its ideological attractions or other conveniences. Three points support this conclusion. Thus the diminished influence of spoils politics and partisan politics in staffing and managing public bureaucracies was to a substantial degree merely replaced by a new and more subtle set of allegiances and loyalties, which may be called administrative or program politics. Moreover, Democracy *vs.* Adminstration does not facilitate the cyclic character of American governance. Finally, respect of the bureaucratic model implies major individual and organizational costs.

A. Encouraging and Not Containing "Program Politics"

Part of the agenda associated with Democracy *vs.* Administration involves limiting the role of spoils politics as well as of partisan politics. At the Federal level, both were substantially accomplished. Indeed, the practical limits might even have been surpassed in the zeal for a wall-to-wall protected service. As both stimulus for such efforts, as well as ideological apologia therefor, Democracy *vs.* Adminstration must be awarded very high marks.[100]

This victory had its untoward consequences, however, and two will be emphasized here. First, most observers agree that the approaches defending against spoils politics often had the effect of complicating public management. That is, competence to do the job represented *the* goal, but protectionism often became the operating result.

Protectionism came in diverse costumes: as a desire for fair pay, which often had the perverse effect of equally rewarding unequal work; of commendable efforts to protect employees against arbitrary removal, which could get transmuted into jungles of policies and procedures that in mythology, and often in practice,[101] provided shelter even for the catastrophically incompetent or ill-placed; and of a passion for equal treatment that sired technical trappings that could drive out essence and substance. Of early public personnel administration, consequently, Sayre noted with fire that they represent the triumph of mechanics and technique. He emphasized the substantial perversion of all three purposes subsidiary to competence which underlay our public personnel systems:[102]

- the guarantee of equal treatment of all employees and all applicants for employment;

- the application of the logic or theory and methods of Scientific Management; and

- the development of a public career service.

How did these laudable goals fare, specifically? Poorly. With special reference to the third subsidiary goal, for example, Sayre concludes:[103]

> Stated in its most positive terms, the objective represents an effort to provide the conditions of work which will attract and hold a public service of optimum talents. In its negative aspects, the goal has been translated into an elaborate system of protectionism. In the area of methodology the negative connotations have slowly but surely won the dominant position . . . .

And Sayre wrote before the days of affirmative action, employee due-process, and widespread public unionization.

Other observers were even less restrained. One old Washington-watcher, for example, considered World War II in retrospect. Our biggest obstacles to the successful pursuit of the war were not provided by the Germans or Japanese, he opined. Rather, that dubious distinction should go to the U.S. Civil Service Commission, now the Office of Personnel Management.[104]

Second, the emphasis on prescription in Democracy *vs.* Administration implies a critical conceptual short-fall—in sum, Administration II does not describe administration as it is. Basically,

Adminstration II presumes its province is "scientific" or "technical." In sharp contrast, that domain also seems pervasively if variably "political." As Rourke notes: ". . . in many ways policy-making within the executive agencies is indistinguishable from the process which takes place within legislative assemblies . . . bargaining or the adjustment of conflicting interests is as constant a feature of administrative politics as it is of relations among legislators and legislative committees."[105]

This conceptual deficit, or mis-orientation, has profound implications for both description and prescription. Consider in this regard only program and professional loyalties, which gave rise to a new kind of politics, different from party politics but still impactful. Program and professional loyalties, or administrative politics, curiously heighten the stress on competence and yet urge a loosening of traditional personnel protections. Operating or line managers play the crucial role. They typically agree about the need for expert staff and, if anything, may surpass in that regard the most ardent reformers of years past. But these managers also urge that they can hardly do that expert job without greater control over their own personnel. As Kaufman observes, in words that age well: "Top management . . . of the line agencies, their organizations now protected against the raids of the spoilsmen, have begun to pray for deliverance from their guardians."[106]

Why did the conceptual simplicity of the reformist era come undone so quickly in this regard? At least two clusters of contributors come to mind. One cluster may be labeled "growth." This includes, but does not refer only to, massive increases in the number of civil servants. More centrally, the emphasis here is on an expanding and diversified line of products and services, requiring an unparalleled blend of specialists or professionals, with escalating pressures to change or adapt within shortening time-frames. The second cluster of contributors relates to a growing sense of self-identity of these specialists or professionals, along with a dawning sense of their own potency or (some might say) even arrogance. Kaufman observes: [107]

> . . . the component elements of the civil service, developing a continuity (as a result of the merit system) and a sense of the importance and difficulty of their work (as a result of specialization), began to display an awareness of themselves as identifiable bodies in society and a deep interest in expanding and perfecting the programs they administered; in a word, they gradually came to exhibit the characteristics of a series of sizable bureaucracies.

The general trend was clear to Kaufman, writing in the mid-1950s: "Party loyalty of the patronage days gave way to program and professional loyalty." [108]

The prescriptive thrust of Democracy *vs.* Administration also encourages a related kind of descriptive myopia. This concerns the possibility of keeping Administration II responsive to the central direction and control that many hoped Democracy II would provide. Reality has proved recalcitrant. Overall, our representative institutions are so structured as to deliberately inhibit just such central direction and control. All three major governmental powers—legislative, executive, and judicial—are more likely to be at semi-cross-purposes, due to differing constituencies and priorities as well as shared powers. Exacerbated by the burgeoning size and complexity of the public services, then, Democracy *vs.* Administration often had the curious effect of complicating what it sought to resolve, of solving one set of problems by inducing another and more intractable set of difficulties.

We can only dramatize the point here, and from a limited perspective at that. Bluntly put, the Solitary Organization implied by the bureaucratic model—one "head," with units closely articulated by unambiguous and unconflicted lines of authority—falls short in two distinct senses. Thus it fails to characterize general practice; and even when it does, mischief often results. Three points give some perspective on this curious duality.

To begin, the Solitary Organization does not dominate practice the way it dominated—indeed, almost monopolized—thought. At the Federal level, in contrast, Kaufman draws attention to numerous "self-directing bureaucracies" in these terms: [109]

> . . . [some] agencies began to function almost autonomously, behaving less like parts of a large team than individual, independent establishments. With the end of the spoils system, the civil service has been growing steadily into a corps of specialists who outlast political officers. The politicians come and go; the civil servants remain. The transients are amateurs, laymen; the permanent body is expert. In the relations between the two groups, it was often the political officers who felt themselves at a disadvantage, psychologically, factually, technically. Political control declined somewhat in force; some agencies went into virtual free-wheeling and others partially so.

The names of such free-wheeling agencies may change from era to era, and legislative or executive efforts to tether them have had varying degrees of success—witness recent efforts directed at the FBI and the CIA. But the general point remains.

Moreover, to extend analysis of the Solitary Organization, the dynamics described above seem to reflect necessity far more than bureaucratic intransigence. As Redford concludes: ". . . administrative relations are multi-directional: they flow upward and downward and laterally in varied channels. The model gives the lie to the monistic theory of public administration—the theory that authority moves down a single line." [110] And most observers use some "clustering" metaphor—"policy-making subsystems," [111] "little groups of policy neighbors," [112] a "triangle," [113] and so on—to suggest more or less stable confluences of responsibility and interest, of "separated institutions sharing powers." [114] These clusters typically involve an executive agency or bureau, Congressional subcommittees, and affected interest groups; and they seem generally necessary to provide sufficient focus for aspects of the public work, with two significant qualifications. Thus the characterization is meant in a dynamic rather than a static sense. In the general case, considerable slack exists within such sub-systems, in largest part because the several major aggregates of actors will incompletely agree—if not heatedly disagree—in various issue-areas, within aggregates as well as between them. [115] In more or less exceptional cases, moreover, the common quasi-equilibrium will be decisively changed, typically by the intrusion or involvement of actors in some broader arena. As Dodd and Schott explain: [116]

> These subsystems . . . are often in substantial agreement on the basic policy issues confronting them—an agreement that may not coincide with the majority views of the larger institutions of which they are a part. These subsystems tend to develop a momentum of their own, proceeding along policy lines that are mutually advantageous to the members of the subsystem until some outside crisis or force challenges their existing consensus (or threatens the balance of power among them). When this happens, the traditional triangle is broken, and the arena in which policy decisions are made shifts to other competing subsystems or into the larger institutions of which the subsystem members are a part—the Congress, the presidency, the bureaucratic departments, and the public.

Finally, the costs of even a single agency approximating the Solitary Organization can be substantial. All too often, these internal "tight bureaucracies" stifle dissent, invade privacy, inhibit creativity by pervasive routinization, tap phones, cover-up cost overruns, and so on. Hence President Carter's support of whistle-blowing, which is a double-edged strategy apparently urged by the desperateness of common consequences of too-successfully following the bureaucratic model.[117] Hence also the commonality of bureaucratic "initiative" that deliberately seeks to short-circuit the chain-of-command—to help trigger some action, to assure that some point-of-view gets more adequate expression, and so on. These by-passes often involve the Presidency,[118] both going up the hierarchy as well as down; and leaks to the media or Congressional sources are also used.

B. In Inhibiting Systemic Responsiveness

Democracy *vs.* Administration also has major prescriptive and descriptive limitations in connection with the kind of flexibility, even cyclicality, that has in the past characterized American governance and no doubt will (and probably should) do so in the future. The preceding section, in part, emphasized the internal or managerial inflexibilities associated with Democracy *vs.* Adminstration. In effect, this section provides macroscopic counterpoint concerning the concept's incongruence with systemic needs or tendencies.

Consider Kaufman's approach. He believes it necessary at a minimum to distinguish three major emphases in our public administrative history; representativeness; politically neutral competence; and executive leadership.[119] These three emphases appear in complicated mixtures, but with definite central tendencies over time. "None of these values was ever totally neglected in any of our past modifications of governmental design," Kaufman notes, "but each enjoyed greater emphasis than the others in different periods." The dynamics of change are uncomplicated. As Kaufman explains: [120] "At different points in time, enough people (not necessarily a numerical majority) will be persuaded by one or another of these discontents to support remedial action—increased representativeness, better and politically neutral bureaucracies, or stronger chief executives, as the case may be." The condition is far from static. Indeed, an emphasis on one of the classes of discontent in effect allows the other classes of discontent to accumulate and—sooner or later—this motivates a change in emphasis. As Kaufman concludes: ". . . no totally stable solution has yet been devised. So the constant shift in emphasis goes on."

Democracy *vs.* Administration does rather poorly in even relating to this cyclicality, let alone in facilitating it. If anything, that notion seems best attuned to only one of Kaufman's major emphases, and would seem to complicate efforts to give greater attention to others. For example, representativeness in its several senses has with justification received much recent attention. That is, civil servants were overwhelmingly white and male, and especially so at middle and upper levels. Except via rapid growth in total public employment, any substantial redistribution of employment/promotion by race or sex would be complicated by many of those features which (in part) protected public employees from spoils and partisan politics. Similarly, as many presidents came to learn, the "civil servant" could on occasion be downright uncivil when it came to neglecting an executive program without sufficient administrative allegiance and support.

C. In Incurring Individual and Organizational Costs

As many sources make plain, the traditional approach to structuring work following the "principles" detailed above has a substantial potential for mischief. Indeed, it implies significant individual and organizational costs, under a wide variety of circumstances.[121]

Two points here add some perspective on this macro-point. Basically, that model jeopardizes identification with and psychological ownership of work by employees. The effects have received most attention recently at low levels or organization, where the incidence and virulence of the "blue-collar blues" has been widely remarked.[122] Some highly-publicized remedial work has begun at these levels, typically in the form of QWL (or quality of working life) improvements.[123] These personally and organizationally-debilitating effects of bureaucratic structures were highlighted a half-century ago in the radical reorganizations begun by several industrial and commercial giants,[124] and received more recent public-sector counterpoint in such agencies as NASA.[125]

How to express this loss of identification with and ownership of work risked by the conventional model? In gross terms, the French have a saying that graphically portrays the effects: they refer to going about work "with one buttock." In more theoretical terms, the common insistence on Democracy *vs.* Administration has the general effect of forcing reliance on a narrow range of means of influencing behavior, a narrowed range that also has a high pain-to-gain ratio. To suggest the broad point in a convenient but narrow way, Kelman distinguishes three behavior-influencing modes or processes: [126]

- *compliance*, in which case the influence is accepted to receive some reward or avoid some punishment controlled by the influencing agent

- *identification*, in which case the influence is accepted so as to maintain or develop a satisfying relationship with the influencing agent

- *internalization*, in which case the influence is accepted because it is congruent with the learner's own value system

Interpretively, bureaucracy emphasizes the compliance mode, which has its very-mixed virtues. And bureaucracy often will complicate, if it does not preclude, a major reliance on internalization. The traditional structure is so need-depriving, by hypothesis, that it encourages psychological avoidance if not rejection of work. This is multiply awkward, especially in the sense that internalization implies the greatest potential for self-starting and self-controlling behaviors, kinds of behaviors that not only simplify life in organizations but also vivify and energize it.

In addition, still-scarce evidence suggests that the summary conclusions above about the effects of the bureaucratic model apply with special force in the public sector, where they are leavened by various related reinforcing features such as civil service systems which have as their ostensible goal the safeguarding of Administration from Politics. [127] In a recent study, for example, Rainey highlights the lack of relevant study and provides some intriguing comparisons of middle-level managers in public vs. business organizations. With appropriate reservations, Rainey reports data relevant to an often-asserted serious problem among public personnel—"the harmful impact of civil service systems upon incentives and motivation." He emphasizes these significant differences: [128]

- public middle-managers report a weaker connection between their performance and such personal incentives as pay, promotion, and recognition for work done

- public managers score lower on several facets of satisfaction with work

- public middle managers report that formal personnel procedures constrain the ability to recognize and reward superior performance

Such comparisons are consistent with, but obviously do not establish, a greater public-sector overdose of Administration II.

Several caveats are in order about such public-sector tendencies. Thus the available research can hardly be considered adequate, although several studies point toward similar conclusions.[129] Moreover, some (but not many) observers would flatly deny that the differences sketched above apply generally.[130] And the available results, however one evaluates them, "do not necessarily indicate that government managers are lower in motivation or performance," as Rainey notes.[131] Indeed, given differences in the kind of work, compensation packages, and so on, that demonstration would be very difficult to bring off in a credible manner.

IV: DEMOCRACY VS. ADMINISTRATION
AS SERIOUSLY COUNTERPRODUCTIVE:
BUREAUCRATIC EFFECTS UNDERCUT DEMOCRATIC IDEALS

Accumulating evidence implies that the conventional model can be seriously counterproductive as well as naive in the several senses detailed above. That is, Democracy *vs.* Adminstration undercuts in significant ways what it purports to support, in normative and pervasive senses as well as in the descriptively-oriented and narrower senses detailed in the preceding section. Klein well-phrased the present point that Administration II poorly serves both work and the broad democratic process. She notes:[132]

> . . . the manner in which employees participate in . . . work life . . . is critical for the use they make of formal mechanisms for representation and consultation and also for their attitudes of constructive interest, of satisfaction and dissatisfaction. [She adds: the] bulk of the scientific evidence suggests that the more the individual is enabled to exercise control over his task and to relate his efforts to those of his fellows the more likely is he to accept a

positive commitment. The positive commitment shows in a number of ways not the least of which is the release of that personal initiative and creativity which constitutes the basis of a democratic climate [which has relevance not only to work but extends far beyond it].

This represents a very serious indictment, and by far transcends the relative quibbles raised in the preceding section. Hence the argument moves deliberately—from Administration II's general inadequacy at work, and then moving on to how it can impact on political praxis. The long and short of it implies a tragedy: a concept of administration offered in the service of democracy can undercut the very ideals it was intended to serve.

A. The General Case of Political Socialization

We have no trouble today acknowledging and even appreciating how life-experiences can condition our political behavior and preferences, and neither did ancient political philosophers like Plato. So the point is not new, although history implies that the point does get forgotten and has to be periodically rediscovered.

Of late, "political socialization" has received substantial attention in the research literature, and a number of major pathways have been explored. Consider, for example, the research concerning how a person's experiences in groups variously condition political practice and belief in later life. Verba summarizes well the sense and significance of such work. He notes of political acts—voting, avoiding political activities or relishing them, obeying constituted authorities or not, and so on—that they get substantially determined by a person's primary groups—the family, play groups, and so on, early in life and in many ways. Verba explains: [133]

In such groups individuals develop nonpolitical personality traits and general expectations from interpersonal relations. These traits and interpersonal expectations first receive specifically political content when the individual faces a particular political situation. Or the influence of the primary group can be more directly and manifestly political. Within the primary group, individuals may learn generalized attitudes toward government and the state. These general attitudes include trust and confidence in government, respect for the state and its symbols, respect for law, and the like. On the other hand, the political attitudes learned in the primary group may be quite specific. These may be support for a particular party or issue.

Verba then goes on to review the literature supporting his basic contention.[134] He suggests the influence of personality traits on political behavior, shows how individuals are trained for political participation in such settings as the family, and illustrates how people gain experience for broader political roles, among other major features of his argument.

B. The Specific Case of Political Socialization at the Worksite

Granting as we do the general impact of life experiences on political performance, the several relevant American literatures have been generally loathe to acknowledge the relevance of a particular case of that general rule. How does the worksite influence political behavior and preferences? That constitutes a neglected question, with only a handful of exceptions saving the literature from coming-up completely blank in this regard.[135]

This section somewhat remedies neglect, by posing one question. If Administration II exists, what reasonably-probable political consequences can be expected? The senses in which one's experiences at work influence or even determine the character and quality of an individual's linkages to political systems still constitute major agenda-items for the future, but some promising beginnings have been made. Perhaps the most promising research seeks to relate experiences at work to political attitudes and performance.[136]

Many commentators note a central paradox in the western experience: representative government exists in various forms in the political arena; but our basic organizational forms have been and steadfastly remain authoritarian if not autocratic, in both public and business sectors. In relatively recent years—here and there, especially in the Scandinavian countries, and in some socialist countries—ideology and some practice seek a closer balance between work and governance. Illustratively, these general values underlay one American effort to improve the quality of working life (QWL):[137]

- *Increased security.* The first area of security involves health and safety, which we intend to improve by creating the best possible environment, with a minimum of hazards. Security against loss of job is more difficult to achieve, as the Harman Automotive Division is part of a market which is subject to fluctuations that are beyond our control. No one can promise that a worker will never be laid off. In the *overall* sense, security from loss of job depends on effectively operating the plant to assure recovering the major portion of the available business, so the plant continues in business and continues employing workers.

- *Increased equity.* By making the distribution of work, the organization of work, the rewards of work, and the rules under which we work as fair and as reasonable as they can be.

- *Increased individuation.* By recognizing that all people are not the same, but have different interests and needs, and by increasing the opportunities for people to develop in their own ways.

- *Increased democracy.* By giving each worker more opportunities to have a say in the decisions that affect his life, including his work life.

Of special moment, such efforts reverse the usual formulation, or at least add an opposing vector to it. Political democracy $\rightarrow$ reasonable control over the worksite takes on aspects of this formulation: control over the worksite $\rightarrow$ political democracy. In QWL efforts with values like those above, democratic forms of political governance do not suffice. The emphasis shifts to creating authority structures at work (and later, elsewhere) that will permit people to develop resources for participative politics. This, Elden notes, "inverts the popular radical cry." 138

Let us call this yearning-cum-direction industrial or organizational democracy, allowing for loose usage of the last term. Basically, its various forms commonly seek to avoid some such self-fulfilling cycle, drawing on Elden: 139

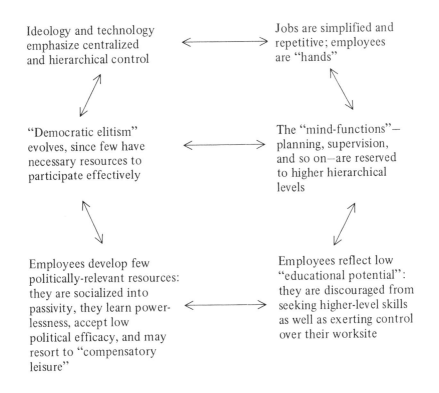

A cycle compatible with bureaucracy, in sum, poorly suits the requirements of political democracy.

Alternatives to the common approach to organizing work have been sought with increasing vigor, especially over the last two decades, for two basic reasons. Increasing numbers of influentials have become concerned with the incongruence between political and work arenas. Moreover, probably the primary impetus derives from accumulating evidence [140] that associates major motivational and economic deficits with the traditional approach to organizing work, at least beyond early stages of development. Some of this research has been reviewed in the preceding section, and the awkward economic and emotional effects of the bureaucratic model of organizing work include: low satisfaction, low output, high absenteeism, and so on through a dour litany.

Averting the bureaucratic cycle has a growing priority. Beginning with early work with supervisory styles [141] and group decision-making, [142] aspects of an applied organizational science have been evolving unevenly. For example, several alternatives for organizing work have been developed—job enrichment, [143] autonomous teams, [144] socio-technical variants, [145] organizing around flows-of-work vs. functions [146]—and they all tend toward a definite ideal-type. Relying on Elden, this ideal-type would have such properties, among others too numerous to mention here, that contrast sharply with properties of the bureaucratic model for organizing work: [147]

Contrasting Authority Structures

	Hierarchical/Elitist	Self-Managed/Democratic
Basic unit for organizing work	one man, one job	a group which aggregates related tasks necessary for a flow of work
Flow of control and relevant information	basically vertical	up, down, or across the organization, as the situation requires
Work routines	fragmented and simplified; little learning possible	integrated into "whole" tasks with variety, learning possibilities, and intrinsic rewards
Locus for handling variances	next highest organizational level above level where variance occurs	within a group or a team as a whole: little variance is "exported" upward in the hierarchy

Basically, the alternative model rests on two fundamental tenets. It implies that individuals have a kind of internal gyroscope—some set of basic needs or preferences toward which people tend, at least when they have a reasonable opportunity for doing so, and sometimes even when the opportunity is limited or hazardous. Generally, the gyroscope is oriented toward moving toward greater competence and comprehensiveness, toward growth. Moreover, the alternative model implies the powerful effects of small groups—in meeting individual needs for intimacy, acceptance, and security as well as for setting and maintaining norms that legitimate certain ranges of behavior while proscribing others. Specifically, the bureaucratic model emphasizes one-to-one, leader-to led relationships. The alternative model focuses on groups as well as on one-to-many supervisory relationships.

Mountains of research have been devoted to the mixed effects of the traditional model for organizing work, which on balance denies the two fundamentals of the alternative models. Thus the traditional model tends to neglect individual predispositions toward growth and comprehensiveness, the model being especially neglectful at lower organization levels. By hypothesis, this need-deprivation is frustrating and results in low satisfaction and/or productivity, which seem common abreactions to frustation. In some few cases, to sketch an interesting deviant outcome, frustrated individuals can direct their aggression inward and work harder. In addition, the traditional model at least neglects groups, and even seeks to undercut them so as to (one supposes) make individuals more dependent on authority figures by denying them opportunities for social comparison and control. For example, that model emphasizes vertical and one-to-one relationships. By hypothesis, one of two effects will occur. The formation of groups may be inhibited, in which case most individuals will suffer need-deprivation under most circumstances, and low satisfaction and/or productivity often will result. Note that highly-dependent employees or high-authoritarians may prefer this vertical, one-to-one pattern, but they usually constitute a minority of employees. Alternatively, underground groups may develop and persist, despite the contrary thrust of the traditional model and its underlying philosophy. In such cases, which probably constitute a distinct minority, groups often will be highly-cohesive and have contra-management norms. There satisfaction may be high—because, for example, such groups control their worksite and can successfully hassle management—but productivity typically will be low.

The key questions concerning the broader political effects of such alternative approaches to organizing work have seldom been embodied in conscious research designs, but the available evidence provides ample motivation for additional work. Consider one case, [148] which asked one of the key questions: If a worksite were set up to reflect the self-managed/democratic alternative for organizing work, would favorable consequences on broader political attitudes and behavior result? The research focused on three sets of consequences: those affecting the work unit, those impacting on work, and those affecting political outcomes beyond the worksite. As for the latter, questionnaire items focused on

- *personal potency*, or the degree to which one feels powerless and controlled by fate or luck

- *political efficacy*, which measures one's attitude to being able to influence government and seems to co-vary with the degree of political participation by individuals

- *social participation*, which relates to the degree that individuals involve themselves in various discretionary-time organizations— i.e., those oriented to community, service, and so on

What were the major co-variants of the self-managed/democratic alternative for organizing work? A complete answer to this question would overwhelm the present review, involving as it does complex statistical [149] and interpretive [150] issues. So we satisfice here, perhaps barely so, by referring only to Elden's summary conclusion: [151]

> . . . democratized authority structures are likely to benefit individual workers (more work satisfaction, personal development and skills acquisition); their organization (increased identification and contribution as reflected for example in better quality, less absenteeism and turnover); and their social class or society as a whole (increased political resources more widely diffused, and decreased alienation) . . . .

Elden drives home his basic conclusion in italics. "In other words," he notes, having "some power over one's work co-varies with one's attitudes toward taking up participative opportunities . . . Empirically there appears to be a *political dimension to everyday worklife*." [152]

Such conclusions still should be couched in tentative terms, but they have encouraged further work which, if anything, only adds further attractiveness and urgency to this line of research. Convenient summaries of such related work exist; [153] and the more specialized reader can usefully consult some of the specific research. [154]

V. DEMOCRACY VS. ADMINISTRATION AS THE IRONY OF IRONIES: TOWARD AN IDEAL AND PRACTICAL REPLACEMENT

In another place,[155] Nelson has engagingly argued that the history of the American national bureaucracy can be seen as a set of ironies. Using his metaphor, the discussion above may be said to reflect the irony of ironies: the attempt to put administrative autocracy in the service of political democracy was powerfully motivated by the best of intentions but, increasingly, the manifest incongruence has clear and present costs.

Is there some alternative coupling of Democracy and Adminstration that promises normative relief and is yet practical? The next chapter answers this question affirmatively, if tentatively.

FOOTNOTES

[1]For an analysis of several of these bodies of thought, see Robert T. Golembiewski, *Public Administration as A Developing Discipline* (New York: Marcel Dekker, 1977), Part 1, pp. 117-201.

[2]Frank Marini, *The Political Crisis In American Public Administration*. MS., 1979. Unpublished lectures presented at University of Missouri, Columbia, 1978.

[3]William H. Riker, *Democracy In the United States* (New York: Macmillan, 1953), esp. pp. 14-17.

[4]Emmette S. Redford, *Democracy in the Administrative State* (New York: Oxford University Press, 1969), p. 6.

[5]Marini, *The Political Crisis In American Public Administration*.

[6]Riker, *op. cit.*, p. 35.

[7]*Ibid.*, p. 35.

[8]Quoted in Dwight Waldo, *The Enterprise of Public Administration* (Novato, Cal.: Chandler and Sharp Publishers, 1980), p. 29.

[9]Robert H. Simmons and Eugene P. Dvorin, *Public Administration* (Port Washington, N.Y.: Alfred Publishing Co., 1977), pp. 128-131.

[10]Robert T. Golembiewski, *Men, Management, and Morality* (New York: McGraw-Hill, 1965), p. 14.

[11]For two rounds of such discovery, see James Burnham, *The Managerial Revolution* (New York: John Day, 1941); and Milovan Djilas, *The New Class* (New York: Praeger, 1957).

[12]Marini, *op. cit.*, pp. II-41 and 42.

[13]Charles E. Lindblom, *Politics and Markets* (New York: Basic Books, 1977) p. 133.

[14]*Ibid.*, p. 133.

[15]As Lindblom, *ibid.*, p. 133, notes: ". . . only as late as 1929 did the United Kingdom sanction universal adult suffrage; France not until 1945; and Switzerland not until 1971."

[16]Frederick C. Mosher, *Democracy and the Public Service* (New York: Oxford University Press, 1969), p. 3.

[17]Lindblom, *op. cit.*, pp. 150-151.

[18]*Ibid.*, pp. 152-155.

[19]Thomas R. Dye and Harmon L. Zeigler, *The Irony of Democracy* (Belmont, Cal.: Wadsworth, 1970), pp. V-VI.

[20]Redford, *op. cit.*, p. 44.

[21]*Ibid.*, p. 66.

[22]*Ibid.*, p. 57.

[23]Starting with Arthur F. Bentley's seminal *The Process of Government* (1908) at least four waves can be distinguished. Wave 2 focused on books such as Pendleton Herring's *Group Representation Before Congress* (Baltimore: Johns Hopkins University Press, 1929); Wave 3 got prime impetus from David Truman's *Governmental Process* (New York: Knopf, 1951); and Wave 4 gets major expression in David G. Garson's revisionist *Group Theories of Politics* (Beverly Hills, Cal.: Sage Library of Social Research, 1978).

[24]Dye and Zeigler, *op. cit.*, p. vi.

[25]Robert A. Dahl, *After the Revolution?* (New Haven, Conn.: Yale University Press, 1975).

[26]Redford, *op. cit.*, p. 52.

[27]Dahl, *After the Revolution?*", pp. 93-94.

[28]Basically, see Theodore Lowi, *The End of Liberalism* (New York: Norton, 1969); and also his "The Public Philosophy: Interest Group Liberalism," *American Political Science Review*, Vol. 61, (March 1967), pp. 52-24.

[29]John Kenneth Galbraith, *American Capitalism: The Concept of Countervailing Power* (Boston: Houghton Mifflin, 1952), pp. 118-119.

[30]*Ibid.*, p. 143.

[31]The classic analysis may be found in Dwight Waldo, *The Administrative State* (New York: Ronald Press, 1948) focuses on the turn of the present century and that undervalues much earlier developments toward our present pattern of administrative organization that appear in clear form in Jackson's presidency about a century earlier. For an overview, see Robert T. Golembiewski, "Organizing Public Work, Round Three," pp. 237-270, in Golembiewski and Aaron Wildavsky, editors, *The Costs of Federalism* (New Brunswick, NJ: Transaction, 1984).

[32]Robert A. Dahl, "The Science of Public Adminstration," *Public Adminstration Review*, Vol. 7 (Winter 1947), pp. 1-11.

[33]Norton E. Long led the charge in this respect, as in many others. He left no doubt what his world looked like. "However attractive an administration receiving its values from political policy-makers may be, it has one fatal flow. It does not accord with the

facts of administrative life." See his "Public Policy and Administration: The Goals of Rationality and Responsibility," *Public Administration Review*, Vol. 14 (No. 1, 1954), p. 23.

[34]Paul Appleby, *Policy and Administration* (University, Ala.: University of Alabama Press, 1949).

[35]Frederick C. Thayer, *An End to Hierarchy! And End to Competition!* (New York: New Viewpoints, 1973).

[36]Vincent Ostrom, *The Intellectual Crisis in American Public Adminstration* (University, Ala.: University of Alabama Press, 1973).

[37]Marini, *op. cit.*, p. VI-51.

[38]*Ibid.*, pp. VI-51, VI-34.

[39]Herbert A. Simon, "The Proverbs of Administration," *Public Administration Review*, Vol. 6 (Winter 1946), pp. 53-67.

[40]As in Golembiewski's *Men, Management, and Morality*.

[41]Perhaps the most impactful demonstration of this kind was provided by Philip E. Slater and Warren G. Bennis, "Democracy Is Inevitable," *Harvard Business Review*, Vol. 42 (March 1964), pp. 51-59.

[42]The critical tradition goes back to at least Francis W. Coker, "Dogmas of Administrative Reform," *American Political Science Review* 16 (August 1922), pp. 399-411.

[43]Redford, *op. cit.*, pp. 70-71.

[44]Andrew Dunsire, *Control in a Bureaucracy* (New York: St. Martins' Press, 1978), p. 73.

[45]Herbert Kaufman and Michael Couzens, *Administrative Feedback* (Washington, D.C.: The Brookings Institution, 1973), p. 4.

[46]Dahl, *After the Revolution?*, *op. cit.*, p. 94.

[47]*Ibid.*, p. 94.

[48]*Ibid.*, p. 94.

[49]*Ibid.*, p. 120.

[50]*Ibid.*, p. 120.

[51]Note, for example, the late and halting emphasis in this country on "industrial democracy" of the style characteristic of many European countries. See Ted Mills, "Leadership from Abroad: European Developments in Industrial Democracy," pp. 115-129, in W.J. Heisler and John W. Houck, editors, *A Matter of Dignity* (Notre Dame, Ind.: University of Notre Dame Press, 1977).

[52]Eric Goldman, *Rendezvous with Destiny* (New York: Knopf, 1952), esp. pp. 171-176.

[53]"Melting pot" ideology notwithstanding, fear of immigrants has been a very real if variable force in American Politics, both early and late. See *ibid.*, pp. 36 ff.

[54]See the telling analysis of Samuel Lubell, *The Future of American Politics* (New York: Doubleday Anchor Books, 1956).

[55]Victor A. Thompson, *Without Sympathy or Enthusiasm: The Problem of*

Administrative Compassion (University, Alabama: University of Alabama Press, 1975), p. 48.

[56]Woodrow Wilson, "The Study of Administration," *Political Science Quarterly*, Vol. 2 (June 1887), p. 201. His emphases.

[57]Marini, *op. cit.*, p. IV-2.

[58]*Ibid.*, p. IV-5.

[59]These claims were common and appeared, for example, in Frederick W. Taylor. See Waldo, *The Administrative State*, p. 178.

[60]Marshall W. Meyer and Associates, *Environments and Organizations* (San Francisco: Jossey-Bass, 1978), p. 12.

[61]*Ibid.*, pp. 12-13.

[62]For an example of how such research might be conducted, see Marshall W. Meyer and M. Craig Brown, "The Process of Bureaucratization," pp. 51, 77, in *ibid*.

[63]Marini, *op. cit.*, p. IV-6.

[64]As Andrew Dunsire argues at length in *Implementation in A Bureaucracy* (New York: St. Martin's Press, 1978); esp. pp. 1-15.

[65]Such concessions often become territory to be struggled over in the 1960's and the 1970's, of course, as in the matter of neighborhood control over schools.

[66]Victor Thompson, *Without Sympathy or Enthusiasm*. See also Waldo, *The Enterprise of Public Adminstration*, esp. pp. 110-112.

[67]See two important works: Matthew A. Crenson, *The Federal Machine: Beginnings of Bureaucracy in Jacksonian America* (Baltimore, Md.: Johns Hopkins University Press, 1975); and Stephen Skowronek, *Building A New American State* (New York: Cambridge University Press, 1982).

[68]Public Administration Service, *The Work Unit in Federal Administration* (Chicago: Public Adminstration Service, 1937), p. 3.

[69]William Ebenstein, *Great Political Thinkers* (New York: Rinehard and Co., 1956), pp. 657-658.

[70]For capitalist economies, Burnhan, *op. cit.*, voiced such a warning. Djilas, *op. cit.*, later noted that socialist countries faced a similar challenge from their managerial elite.

[71]William G. Scott and David K. Hart, *Organizational America* (Boston: Houghton Mifflin, 1979).

[72]Don K. Price, *The Scientific Estate* (Cambridge, Mass.: Harvard University Press, 1965), pp. 15-16.

[73]This summary paragraph helps understand why—from a position of pre-eminence in the study of administration and management through the 1940's or even later—public administrationists have of late lagged so badly. Consider the 1965 review by Francis Rourke and Robert Peabody, which still applies, more rather than less: "Public Bureaucracies," pp. 810, 813, 816, and 807, in James G. March, editor, *Handbook of Organizations* (Chicago: Rand McNally, 1965).
Looked at another way, fundamental dissatisfaction with the bureaucratic model in major businesses may be dated accurately enough in the 1920's, when a family of

related structural innovations led to organizational breakthroughs for many industrial and commercial goliaths. See Alfred D. Chandler, *Strategy and Structure* (Cambridge, Mass.: MIT Press, 1962). Public Administration is yet to experience such a pervasive set of changes.

[74]Dwight Waldo, "Public Management Research," p. 9. Paper delivered at the Public Management Research Conference, Brookings Institution, Washington, D.C., November 19-20, 1979.

[75]Wilson, "The Study of Administration," p. 220.

[76]*Ibid.*, p. 220.

[77]*Ibid.*, p. 219.

[78]Waldo, "Public Management Research," p. 9.

[79]The concept of private ownership has undergone massive changes since its high-water mark in what may be called Conservative Darwinism, which essentially urged the "survival of the fittest." The correlative challenge to religion and government was to make people equal in liberty satisfied with huge asymmetries in wealth. See Richard Hofstadter, *Social Darwinism in American Thought* (Philadelphia, Pa.: University of Pennsylvania Press, 1944).

[80]Golembiewski, *Men, Management and Morality*, develops the theme of this basic normative incompatibility.

[81]Mosher, *op. cit.*, pp. 18-19.

[82]Quoted in Waldo, *The Enterprise of Public Administration*, p. 91.

[83]Quoted in *ibid.*, p. 90.

[84]Herbert Heaton, *Productivity in Service Organizations* (New York: McGraw-Hill, 1977), p. 19.

[85]See, for example, John Rowan Wilson, *et al.*, editors, *The Mind* (New York: Life Science Library, 1969).

[86]Heaton, *op. cit.*, p. 19.

[87]Mosher, *op. cit.*, p. 203.

[88]*Ibid.*, pp. 204-205.

[89]See Waldo, *The Administrative State*, p. 192.

[90]Mosher, *op. cit.*, p. 65.

[91]Wilson's words hammer the point: ". . . administration lies outside the proper sphere of *politics* . . . Administrative questions are not political questions. Although politics sets the task for administration, it should not be suffered to manipulate its offices." "The Study of Administration," p. 210.

[92]In Wilson's words: "The field of adminstration is a field of business . . . It is a part of political life only as . . . machinery is part of the manufactured product." *Ibid.*, pp. 209-210.

[93]Mosher, *op. cit.*, p. 67.

[94]Herman Finer, "Administrative Responsibility in Democratic Government," *Public Adminstration Review*, Vol. 1 (Summer 1941), p. 335-351.

[95]Carl J. Friedrich, "Public Policy and the Nature of Administrative

Responsibility," *Public Policy,* 1940 (Cambridge, Mass.: Harvard University Press, 1940), pp. 3-24.

[96]Mosher, *op. cit.,* p. 10.

[97]Paul P. Van Riper, *History of the United States Civil Service* (Evanston, Ill.: Row, Peterson, 1958), p. 85.

[98]Mosher, *op. cit.,* p. 71.

[99]*Ibid.,* p. 6.

[100]Herbert Kaufman, "The Growth of the Federal Personnel System," pp. 41-42, in The American Assembly, *The Federal Government Service* (New York: Graduate School of Business, Columbia University, 1954).

[101]Removing a public employee is possible, of course, as Hugh Heclo demonstrates in *A Government of Strangers* (Washington, D.C.: Brookings Institution, 1977), p. 140.

[102]Wallace Sayre, "The Triumph of Technique Over Purpose," *Public Administration Review,* Vol. 8 (Spring 1948), pp. 134-135.

[103]*Ibid.,* pp. 134-135.

[104]John Fischer, "Let's Go Back to the Spoils System," *Harper's Magazine,* Vol. 191 (October 1945), pp. 360-361.

[105]Francis E. Rourke, *Bureaucracy, Politics and Public Policy* (Boston: Little, Brown, 1976), p. 127. See also Gordon Chase and Elizabeth Reveal, *How to Manage in the Public Sector* (Reading, Mass.: Addison-Wesley, 1983).

[106]Kaufman, "The Growth of the Federal Personnel System," p. 45.

[107]Corinne Lathrop Gibb, *Hidden Hierarchies: The Professions and Government* (New York: Harper & Row, 1966).

[108]Kaufman, "The Growth of the Federal Personnel System," p. 45.

[109]*Ibid.,* p. 47.

[110]Redford, *op. cit.,* pp. 80-81.

[111]J. Leiper Freeman, *The Political Process* (Garden City, N.Y.: Doubleday & Co., 1955), esp. pp. 14-15.

[112]Lawrence C. Dodd and Richard L. Schott, *Congress and the Administrative State* (New York: John Wiley & Sons, 1979), pp. 10-11.

[113]*Ibid.,* p. 11.

[114]Richard E. Neustadt, *Presidential Power* (New York: John Wiley & Sons, 1960), p. 33.

[115]Freeman, *op. cit.,* e.g., p. 51.

[116]Dodd and Schott, *op. cit.,* pp. 10-11.

[117]E.g., James S. Bowman, "Whistle-Blowing in the Public Sector," *Review of Public Personnel Administration,* Vol. 1 (Fall 1980), pp. 15-27.

[118]Morton Halperin, *Bureaucratic Politics and Foreign Policy* (Washington: Brookings Institution, 1974), p. 108.

[119]Herbert Kaufman, "Administrative Decentralization and Political Power," *Public Administration Review,* Vol. 29 (January 1969), p. 3.

[120]*Ibid.*

[121]For some of the technological features that· may be more compatible with traditional structures, consult Charles Perrow, *Complex Organizations* (Glenview, Ill.: Scott, Foresman, 1979), pp. 160-173. On the limits of such "contingency views," however, see John M. Jermier and Leslie J. Berkes, "Leader Behavior In A Police Command Bureaucracy," *Administrative Science Quarterly*, Vol. 25 (March 1979), pp. 1-23.

[122]The most influential statement of this kind was made in the HEW project, *Work In America*.

[123]For an evaluation of one such effort, consult Robert T. Golembiewski, *Approaches to Planned Change* (New York: Marcel Dekker, 1979), Part 2, pp. 300-330.

[124]Chandler, *op. cit.*

[125]Leonard R. Sayles and Margaret Chandler, *Managing Large Systems* (New York: Harper and Row, 1971).

[126]Herbert C. Kelman, "Processes of Opinion Change," *Public Opinion Quarterly*, Vol. 25 (Spring 1961), pp. 57-78.

[127]See Robert T. Golembiewski, "Civil Service and Managing Work," *American Political Science Review*, Vol. 56 (December 1962), pp. 961-973.

[128]Hal G. Rainey, "Perceptions of Incentives in Business and Government: Implications for Civil Service Reform," *Public Administration Review*, Vol. 39 (September 1979), pp. 443-445.

[129]E.g., Bruce Buchanan, "Government Managers, Business Executives, and Organizational Commitment," *Public Administration Review*, Vol. 34 (July 1979), pp. 339-347.

[130]Frederick Thayer, "The President's Management 'Reforms'," *Public Administration Review*, Vol. 38 (July 1978), pp. 309-314.

[131]Rainey, *op. cit.*, p. 445.

[132]Lisl Klein, *New Forms of Work Organization* (Cambridge, England: Cambridge University Press, 1976), p. 30.

[133]Sidney Verba, *Small Groups and Political Behavior* (Princeton, N.J.: Princeton University Press, 1961), p. 30.

[134]*Ibid.*, pp. 30-60.

[135]For relevant contrast, consult F.E. Emery and Einar Thorsrud, *Form and Content in Industrial Democracy* (London: Tavistock, 1969); and Klein, *op. cit.*

[136]This section draws heavily on Robert T. Golembiewski and Gerald Miller, "Small Groups in Political Science," esp. pp. 1-71, in Samuel Long, editor, *Handbook of Political Behavior* (New York: Plenum, 1980).

[137]Michael Maccoby, "Changing Work," *Working Papers*, Vol, 2 (1975), pp. 44.

[138]Max Elden, "Political Efficacy at Work." Paper presented for the Seminar on Social Change and Organization Development, Inter-University Center for Graduate Studies, Dubrovnik, Yugoslavia, 1977.

For useful inter-firm comparative research, see Donald V. Nightingale, *Workplace Democracy* (Toronto, Canada: University of Toronto Press, 1982).

[139]Elden, *op. cit.*, p. 3.

[140]E.g., Golembiewski, *Men, Management, and Morality.*

[141]Kurt Lewin, Ronald Lippitt and R.K. White,"Patterns of Aggressive Behavior in Experimentally Created 'Social Climates'," *Journal of Social Psychology*, Vol. 10 (1939), pp. 271-299.

[142]Donald W. Taylor, P.C. Berry and C.H. Block, "Does Group Participation When Using Brainstorming Facilitate or Inhibit Creative Thinking?," *Administrative Science Quarterly*, Vol. 3 (1958), pp. 23-47.

[143]E.g., Robert Ford, *Motivation in the Work Itself* (New York: American Management Association, 1969).

[144]Richard Walton, "Work Innovations at Topeka," *Journal of Applied Behavioral Science*, Vol. 13 (July 1977), pp. 422-433.

[145]Einar Thorsrud, *Model for Socio-Technical Systems* (Oslo, Norway: Work Research Institutes, 1976).

[146]Golembiewski, *Men, Management, and Morality.*

[147]Elden, "Political Efficacy at Work," p. 9.

[148]Max Elden, *Democracy at Work for More Participatory Politics*, Unpublished doctoral dissertation, University of California at Los Angeles, 1976.

[149]L.L. McQuitty, "Elementary Linkage Analysis for Isolating Orthogonal and Oblique Types and Typal Relevancies," *Educational and Psychological Measurement*, Vol. 17 (1957), pp. 207-229.

[150]Elden, *Democracy At Work For More Participative Politics*, especially Chapter 4.

[151]Elden, "Political Efficacy at Work," p. 18.

[152]*Ibid.*, p. 18.

[153]Elden, *Democracy At Work For More Participative Politics*, especially Chapter 6.

[154]P. Bernstein, *Workplace Democratization.* Unpublished doctoral dissertation, Stanford University, 1975. Bernstein's work was later published under the same title (New Brunswick, N.J.: Transaction Books, 1980).

[155]Michael Nelson, "A Short, Ironic History of the American National Bureaucracy," *Journal of Politics*, Vol. 44 (August 1982), pp. 747-778.

CHAPTER VI

TOWARD A POLITICAL THEORY FOR OD, II: ADMINISTRATION THAT REINFORCES DEMOCRATIC IDEALS

Collapsed to its essence, the analysis of Democracy/Administration couplings implies two robust conclusions: the two basic couplings of Democracy/Administration were easy ways out; and those conceptual conveniences imply serious, and growing costs. Let us put the matter in a direct way. Democracy *and* Administration implies an unattainable and unrealistic ideal under contemporary conditions, in general, which makes it an awkward general guide. Relatedly, Democracy *vs.* Administration seeks to meet reasonable concerns, but in ways that always were at cross-purposes and which now grow increasingly awkward.

How will analysis build beyond these two conclusions? Five emphases will dominate. In turn, attention will focus on:

- some reasonable concerns implied by Democracy *vs.* Administration which that pair met awkwardly

- a set of democratic values to guide the future development of organizations

- the sketch of a third evolutionary coupling—*Democracy within and through* Administration; or Democracy II *and* Administration III—which rests on basic complementarities with the democratic values referred to above

- a global description of one approach to Administration III—Organization Development, or OD—whose thrust emphasizes OD's value-loaded character in three central particulars

- illustrations of how specific OD designs can help make administration less coercive and more effective, at several levels of complexity

I. REFLECTING ON REASONABLE CONCERNS AWKWARDLY RESPONDED TO

The several major reasonable concerns underlying Democracy *vs.* Administration, awkwardly responded to, will profit from amplification. *First,* prudence encourages being encouraged about unchecked power, a concern which patently motivates the general acceptance of Administration II. But ample evidence implies that Democracy *vs.* Administration can overdo it in critical regards. On balance, Administration II often seems to exacerbate the problem of control, rather than simplify it. Certainly, that is the common message of the numerous cases in which bureaucratic controls can stifle and suppress a useful flow of information, at least as well as they can provide a kind of non-slip transmission belt from our broadly-political processes to the realization of their goals and objectives. Consider only this brief catalog implying how concerned (and correct!) administrative officials were neglected at first, and then later variously punished, by bureaucratic controls that subjugated rather than facilitated representativeness and responsiveness: C-5A cost overruns; CIA venturesomeness around the world; FBI inventiveness above, beyond, and in direct violation of the law of the land; numerous My Lai's; and so on. Protection of whistle-blowers provides puny counterbalance to costly self-sacrifice and perhaps a foolish encouragement of it.

Second, relatively non-coercive regimes cannot persist without pervasive popular support, a fact that clearly motivates pairing Democracy II and Administration II. Democracy II was widely seen as so vitiating popular support that extreme measures were called for in defining Administration II.

Even if understandable, this facile pairing undervalues the counter-case, whose attractions increase with time. In sum, popular support is not guaranteed or perhaps even encouraged by postulating Administration II—not as ideal and definitely not as purportedly-real. Even if this fiction constituted a reasonable simplification in the days of limited government and of small and self-effacing cadres of public servants—which I doubt—those days are long gone. Moreover, the analysis above attributes major costs to Administration II, both in terms of efficiency and of effectiveness, and those costs seem far more likely to erode popular support than to enhance it. Finally, Democracy *vs.* Administration proposes to serve systemic values by violating them.

That seldom will serve as a useful long-run strategy, granting its attractions when problems grew near-overwhelming and when knowledge concerning alternatives did not exist.

Third, Administration II emphasizes hierarchy—indeed fixates on it—as the basic safeguard against a technological elite seeking to govern.

Reasonably, a self-determinative Administration cannot be countenanced in a representative system, but the core overemphasis in the second coupling neglects major opportunities for democratic control. Appleby provides insight on the point by noting that administrative morality derives basically from two sources: from an open and multi-representational form of politics, which exposes administration to processes of review and evaluation; and from hierarchy, but hierarchy seen more as a vehicle for broadening the perspective applied to a decision than as a command-obey linkage.[1] It involves maximizing the former sense of hierarchy on the major issues; and it urges minimizing a sense of hierarchy that dominates and—one guesses—gets fullest expression in minor if not mickey-mouse issues. Administration II, in contrast, encourages a directive or autocratic supervision that best suits a command-obey sense of hierarchy.

Fourth, Administration II rightly implies that the needs of public employees are not primary. Granted. But the position here proposes that Administration II goes farther than it needs to, and certainly farther than it should.

To develop the point, consider the five variant ways in Exhibit 2 in which employee needs can be taken into account. The exhibit may be thought of as a scale running from most-to-least coercive, with the latter end of the scale being anchored in the bureaucratic principles. In sum, Administration II is anchored near the top of the list in Exhibit 2. In contrast, this argument focuses on organizational humanism, or on what Redford calls "moderate humanism."[2] Oppositely, much of the literature seems to view radical humanism as *the* alternative to Administration II.

II. PROJECTING VALUES TO GUIDE ORGANIZATIONAL DEVELOPMENT

What can be done to improve on these wrong-turns in response to reasonable concerns? At one level, no doubt can exist. Direction must come from specific values which, as it were, constitute the compass by which organizational designers will steer.

EXHIBIT 2. Five Ways to Respond to Employee Needs

- *managerial authoritarianism*, which is the simplest approach and the one most congenial to Administration II and its underlying bureaucratic principles

- *benevolent managerial authoritarianism*, in which the traditional organization of work is preserved but in which employee needs are responded to, as by

  — munificent wages and fringes to buy docility if not loyalty, on the "Generous Motors" model

  — various employee programs of a cultural or recreational nature

  — various counselling or educational programs that enhance employee performance, as in alcohol or drug rehabilitation, training or degree programs paid for in whole or part by the organization, and so on

  — various programs of the "cow sociology" type, whose goal is to keep employees contented and producing

- *traditional unionism*, of the kind which emphasizes the rights and responsibilities of the employment relationship and which typically

  — develops as an adversary response to managerial authoritarianism

  — encourages the evolution of a benevolent managerial authoritarianism as part of a new balance

  — in either case, focuses on wages and fringes, has a legalistic character, and does not affect the fundamental structuring of work and quality of working life

- *organizational humanism*, in which dual goals are maintained in a state of dynamic tension, sometimes by joint union/management efforts: organization demands, as reflected in production and quality standards; and employee needs, especially as they interact with structure and policies governing work which will be adjusted to employee needs as knowledge and other conditions permit

- *radical humanism*, in which individual needs dominate or reign supreme over organizational or union/guild interests, as in the prescriptions: An end to hierarchy! An end to competition![3]

When it comes to specific values plus ways-and-means of attaining them, more humility definitely should be the order-of-the-day. But humility does not require that we stand moot and immobile. Rather, a triune activism fits the bill: we need to be as specific as possible concerning our ideals; as certain as possible about what achievements constitute reasonable next-steps from where we are today; and as inventive as we can be in testing whether we are making reasonable progress toward our ideals, as contrasted with merely engaging in polysyllabic copping-out.

Broadly conceived, and closely following the wonderful book of Paul Bernstein,[4] this section provides some content for locating an organization on this crucial continuum: dehumanization $\longleftrightarrow$ democratization. Somewhat more specifically, an organization can be said to serve humanist or democratic values to the degree that it reflects six interacting components:[5]

- participation by all relevant organization members in decision-making, either directly or through representatives

- frequent feedback of the results of organizational performance, not only in terms of information but also in terms of variable rewards keyed to performance

- sharing of both management-level information and expertise throughout the organization

- guarantees of individual rights, which correspond essentially to the basic political liberties that are so commonly unavailable to individuals in both public and business organizations[6]

- the availability of appeal or recourse in cases of intractable disputes, decision-units of which will at least in part be composed of peers

- a set of supporting attitudes or values, which can be roughly described as a "democratic consciousness" for which enactment sufficient behavioral skills exist throughout the organization

Can one be more specific about these basic value-thrusts? I believe so, again relying on Goodman. Two major points get illustrative attention, in turn. These points relate to the patterns of control in organizations, as well as to the complex of attitudes/values/skills associated with enacting a democratic consciousness. Variations in such features, to make the implied point obvious, will locate different organizations at various points on the continuum:

dehumanization   ⟷   democratization

A. Democratization and Patterns of Control

The patterns of control that exist in an organization will go a long way toward determining its degree of dehumanization or democratization. The general point does not offend; indeed, it may seem obvious even though it is not.[7] In somewhat more detail, patterns of control may be related to three variable and related dimensions:[8]

- the *degree* of control exercised by various sets of organization actors, e.g., employees and the several levels of management

- the *ranges of issues* concerning which control is exercised by the several sets of actors

- the *hierarchical levels* at which specific degrees of control are exercised on sub-ranges of issues

Such distinctions can support quite-complex classifications of organizations, but present purposes permit only a brief suggestion of the fuller possible analysis. Emphasizing only the *degree of control* exercised by workers or employees, for example, Bernstein generates the useful distinctions reflected in Figure 3. The underlying hypothetical network takes some such form: under a broad range of conditions, enhanced employee control permits increasing the degree of psychological success possible for broad ranges of participants which,

FIGURE 3. Differences in Workplace Democratization and Degree of Control by Employees

ACTUAL FORMS AND PROCESSES		GENERAL LABELS
7 WORKERS council or Assembly SUPERIOR to managers (and if outside constituencies have representatives in this body, they must be approved by the workers)		FULL EMPLOYEE CONTROL or "SELF-MANAGEMENT"
6 Joint Power or PARTNERSHIP (workers and managers co-decide on joint board with many different voting proportions possible		
5 Workers wait till management has decided, then may VETO OR APPROVE: if veto, then management submits modifications	(collective bargaining)	JOINT MANAGEMENT or "CO-DETERMINATION"
4 MANAGER DELEGATES some decision generally to workers, reserving ultimate veto which is rarely used	(borderline form)	
3 Workers initiate CRITICISMS AND SUGGESTIONS and discuss them face-to-face with managers. Later still have sole power to decide, but usually adopt workers' proposals		CO-OPERATION or "CO-INFLUENCE"

Degree of Employee Control

- Threshold of Democratic Participation

2 Same as immediately above but managers usually reject workers' proposals		
1 Managers give PRIOR NOTICE of certain changes, workers have chance to voice their views and perhaps stimulate reconsideration		"CONSULTATION"

- Threshold of Regular Participation

0 Impersonal SUGGESTION BOX System. Managers accept or reject without giving reasons		

Published by permission of Paul Bernstein and Transaction, Inc. from Workplace Democratization by Paul Bernstein. Copyright ©1980 by Transaction, Inc. and Paul Bernstein, p. 48.

at least in the long run, will not only permit heightened participant satisfaction but also will tend to enhance system performance. Whence comes the effect on systemic performance? Certainly, we are still quite far removed from full knowledge about the crucial transformation. But one factor no doubt will play a major role in our evolving knowledge: enhanced employee control reduces the threat to and the consequent resistance by participants that can dissipate energies that might otherwise be devoted to performance.[9]

The point is *not* that ultimate control by everybody of everything will constitute the very best of things under all conditions. In some cultures, for example, enhanced control by some actors may be considered illegitimate, and hence positive consequences might not occur.[10] Or individuals might have deep personal needs for dependence or direction,[11] at least from time to time. Nonetheless, under quite general if incompletely-specified conditions, shared patterns of control have been quite regularly associated with positive outcomes for individuals and systems. This has been the case in experimental settings, such as the early field research in a pajama factory with participation in decision-making.[12] Perhaps the most dramatic, if generally unacknowledged, example comes from worker owned and managed plywood mills. Worker-ownership and management constitute a very high degree of employee control, obviously. Bernstein summarizes a range of comparisons which generally favor the worker-owned firms, despite some caveats about relying on output-per-manhour comparisons.[13] To merely illustrate here:

- in the 1950s, worker-owner firms averaged 115-120 square feet of plywood per man-hour while conventional firms generated 80-95 square feet[14]

- in the 1960s, the comparison favored worker-owned firms by 170 to 130 square feet[15]

- worker-owned firms paid wages higher than the industry level, which were justified to the satisfaction of the Internal Revenue Service in terms of greater productivity

- worker-owned firms have tended to maintain employment during economic slumps

B. Democratization and Enacted Consciousness

Such effects of enhanced employee control do not just happen, of course. These effects reflect an interaction between institutional ways of distributing control and what may be called "enacted consciousness"— the simultaneous occurrence of values, attitudes, and behavioral skills among participants such that the prevailing institutional features can come to operate as intended.

What can be said now concerning our knowledge of this "enacted consciousness" for the greater humanization of the worksite? In general, one is reminded of the partially-full glass of water. Our knowledge-reservoir is at once far from empty, yet remains substantially short of full. Given this in-betweenness,[16] Bernstein has done us the considerable favor of synthesizing two major sub-systems of traits which support an enacted democratic consciousness and also accord well with existing research and experience.[17] Basically, one sub-system relates to a variable resistance to being manipulated, i.e., to *outputs* of the processes of managing work; and the second sub-system he associates with *inputs* to the managing process, which sub-system encompasses traits relevant to creating and organizing policy. Hence the enacted consciousness in organizations may be defined in terms of two interacting continua:

- Compliance $\longleftrightarrow$ Resistance

- Passivity, abstention $\longleftrightarrow$ Activism

In Figure 4, further, Bernstein sketches a range of more or less specific behavioral skills associated with these two basic sub-systems. Some of the traits in Figure 4 are associated with only a single sub-system, as when servility and timidity are reasonably listed as indicators of proneness to being manipulated. In contrast, other traits—like "self-reliance, refusal to transfer responsibility"—are seen as useful in both sub-systems associated with what Bernstein calls "participatory-democratic consciousness." Note also that in many cases Bernstein lists opposed traits, indicated by $\longleftrightarrow$. Thus self-reliance is opposed by two basic sets of traits: servility and timidity in those prone to being manipulated; and dependence on authority figures in the case of those less able to create and organize policy.

FIGURE 4. Major Subsystems of Members' Traits in Organizations

	Relating to Outputs of the Managing Process		Relating to Inputs of the Managing Process	
		"Participatory-Democratic Consciousness"		
	I. More Prone to Being Manipulate	II. Less Prone to Being Manipulate	III. More Able to Create & Organize Policy	IV. Less Able to Create & Organize Policy
1.	Rigidity of thought		Receptivity to the new, flexibility	Overseriousness. dogmatism
2.	Servility, timidity	Self-reliance. refusal to transfer responsibility		Dependence
3.			Facility for compromise and receptivity to needs of others	Sectarian
4.	Indifferent, unquestioning	Inquisitive, interrogative		
5.	Extreme loyalty, deference, credulity	Critical thinking: —attempts to avoid distortions and preconceptions	—self-critical —carefully differentiates between means and ends —acknowledges inevitable limits	Defensive
6.	Simplistic thinking: black-and-white outlook		Expects multiple causation	
7.	Short time-sense	Seeks to analyze in depth Long time-sense		Superficial thinking Short time-sense
Rough Summation	Compliance	Resistance	Activism	Passivity, abstention

Published by permission of Paul Bernstein and Transaction, Inc. from Workplace Democratization by Paul Bernstein. Copyright © 1980 by Transaction, Inc. and Paul Bernstein, p. 97.

III. TOWARD DEMOCRACY $\leftrightarrows$ ADMINISTRATION VIA ACTION RESEARCH

The preceding two strands of analysis suggest three immediate directions for this chapter. *First*, Bernstein's conceptual work implies what values/attitudes/skills must be activated to develop an appropriate enacted consciousness in humanist organizations. In summary, Bernstein's conceptual distinctions can be thought of as generating four classes of organizations:

		Proness to Manipulation	
		Compliance	Resistance
Ability to Create and Organize Policy	Passivity, abstention	Traditional	Mock
	Activism	Litigious	Humanist

This simple typology implies many challenges and risks in organization change or development. Simple insistence to replace Traditional forms can be seriously counterproductive, for example, leading only to Mock or Litigious forms in the absence of an appropriate enacted consciousness.

Second, the preceding analysis adds perspective to earlier analysis of conceptual problems, and heightens the sense of urgency associated with working toward a resolution of those issues. Illustratively, I propose, Administration II often will encourage Litigious or Mock forms. Previous analysis should suggest Administration II's dual incapacity: it neither describes the organizational forms that lead to effective individual and system performance when they do exist; nor does Administration II prescribe those conditions congruent with the kinds of enacted consciousness sketched above. That constitutes a double-dose deficiency.

The challenge seems patent. Such considerations imply the virtue of a third coupling of the conceptual pair of central concern in this chapter and the preceding one—a coupling that avoids overemphasis and overcaution. The text will speak of Democracy II and Administration III or, in short-hand, Democracy $\leftrightarrows$ Administration.

This third convenient designation intends to represent Democracy *within* Administration, as well as Democracy resulting *through and from* Administration.

That is, the conceptual enhancement of Democracy II by scholars such as Dahl is retained; and the goal becomes one of seeking a compatible model of Administration III. Put otherwise, Administration II poorly suits Democracy II in numerous normative senses, not to mention the often-awkward empirical consequences it tends to generate. Relatedly, Democracy I and Administration I are seen as having only limited applicability in today's world, even though that applicability should be exploited wherever it exists or can be realistically approached.

Third, subsequent analysis must sketch an underlying methodology and technology that support Administration III. No mere ideological prophetic-call-from-the-wilderness will suffice. Basically, that methodology and technology must encompass two features. Thus they must be value-loaded in appropriate ways; and they must provide specific and workable ways-and-means for the effective involvement of organizational participants, as well as for the expression of their specific needs at particular points in time.

The following sub-section will sketch this methodology and technology, but one point already should be clear—normal or "straight science" is not up to the required task. Its strengths lie in the basic response only to the values of science—objectivity, neutrality as to outcomes, and so on.[18] Those operating biases are fine, but only for more-limited purposes than present ones.

A. A Sketch of Action Research

One step down the path toward Administration III involves distinguishing two kinds of endeavor—which we will here call "straight science" and "action research."[19] This analysis emphasizes the latter, which may be defined briefly as:

- ". . . an application of scientific methodology in the clarification and solution of practical problems. It is a process of planned personal and social change. In either view, it is a process of learning in which attention is given to the quality of collaboration in planning action and evaluating results."[20]

- as a process which ". . . aims to contribute both to the practical concerns of people in an immediate problematic situation and to the goals of social science by joint collaboration within a mutually acceptable ethical framework. Action research is a type of applied social research differing from other varieties in the immediacy of the researcher's involvement in the action process."[21]

Labels for the two kinds of work can vary: positivist[22] or expository[23] science as distinguished from action research; empirical theory as contrasted with goal-based empirical theory; and so on. Commonly, the failure to make the distinction, *and* to respect it, lies at the heart of much disagreement and substantial conflict in the management sciences generally, as well as in Public Administration specifically. The two kinds of endeavor can reinforce one another, but analysts cannot neglect the distinction. Analysts much choose, be faithful to their choice, and pay the associated price.

The target-phenomena and the conditions under which they are studied will determine the analysts's choice. Reliance on positivist science seems contra-indicated for designing organizations, for example.[24] Susman and Evered provide more general guidance about this critical choice. They advise:[25]

> . . . we suggest that the researcher ought to be skeptical of positivist science when the unit of analysis is, like the researcher, a self-reflecting subject, when relationships between subjects (actors) are influenced by definitions of the situation, or when the reason for undertaking the research is to solve a problem which the actors have helped to define.

Exhibit 3 usefully summarizes a number of major contrasts between positivist science and action research. This discussion only illustrates the multiple contrasts suggested by Exhibit 3, since the fuller job has been done elsewhere. Basically, the focus on action research helps reduce the argumentation that historically tended to become polarized into global extremes. Consider the issue of whether or not "principles of administration" exist or can be isolated. One camp proposed that "universal principles" could be found via a natural science approach—if only we had the wit, the will, and especially sufficient belief in their existence to motivate a search comprehensive and intense enough. One wing of this camp, indeed, believed that the "principles"

EXHIBIT 3. Some Contrasts of Positivist Science and Action Research

Points of Comparison	Positivist Science	Action Research
Value position	Methods are value-neutral	Methods develop social systems and release human potential
Time perspective	Observation of the present	Observation of the present plus interpretation of the present from knowledge of the past, conceptualization of more desirable futures
Relationship with units	Detached spectator, client system members are objects to study	Client system members are self-reflective subjects with whom to collaborate
Treatment of units studied	Cases are of interest only as representatives of populations	Cases can be sufficient sources of knowledge
Language for describing units	Denotative, observational	Connotative, metaphorical
Basis for assuming existence of units	Exist independently of human purposes	Human artifacts for human purposes
Epistemological aims	Prediction of events from propositions arranged hierarchically	Development of guides for taking action that produce desired outcomes
Strategy for growth of knowledge	Induction and deduction	Conjecturing, creating settings for learning and modeling of behavior
Criteria for confirmation	Logical consistency, prediction and control	Evaluating whether actions produce intended consequences
Basis for generalization	Broad, universal, and free of context	Narrow, situational, and bound by content

From Gerald I. Susman and Roger D. Evered, "An Assessment of the Scientific Merits of Action Research," *Administrative Science Quarterly*, Vol. 23 (December, 1978), p. 600.

had already been found, and critics could win some easy victories. For example, Dahl noted that cultural differences were sufficient to undercut the possibility of any *universal* principles of administration.[26] Such was the momentum of positivist science, however, that criticisms might stun but could not stop it. Commonly, proponents avoided defeat by shifting and enlarging the conceptual battleground, as in Scientific Management. Perhaps a critic cited an application that failed, or even a string of failures. No matter, at an ideational level. The contrary results constituted only a truism to true-believers, not a rejection: Scientific Management could exist nowhere until it existed everywhere.[27]

The notion of action research seeks to borrow from both camps, in effect, and thereby narrows the character of the debate by focusing on more manageable questions about which some tolerable precision is possible. Given that "universal principles" remain out of reach, for example, the narrower task still challenges. For example, can we develop approaches for dealing effectively with limited but still common problem-situations? Illustratively, we know that some natural-occurring social systems tend to generate more desirable consequences at work than others, and we can use such knowledge to help induce the planned development of similar norms and behaviors at other sites so as to increase the proportion of desired outcomes there. In this basic sense, action research is value-loaded from the outset, in sharp contrast to positivist science. And it seeks "principles" not in the universal abstract, but in association with specific desired outcomes. For example, the prototypic action-research question takes such a form: if you desire to heighten employee satisfaction at work, which specific style of supervision will contribute most to that goal *here* under specific conditions of member personality features, task characteristics, and so on? In addition, action research deals with the critical issue of how to help elicit the appropriate behaviors.

Put briefly, action research does not fixate on universal principles. Rather it focuses on what may be called "contingent regularities," with the preferences of immediate actors and their ownership of action-plans being among the major contingencies, along with whatever theoretical and practical knowledge/experience apply to the specific action-site. So action research implies a profoundity that can become a snare and a delusion if pushed too far. In brief, action research seeks to emphasize the role of what might be called "structures of consciousness" via the deliberate involvement of the "subjects of study," including the researcher. This contrasts sharply with positivist science, which posits sharp distinctions between "objective" and "subjective" reality. The ideal there prescribes arm's-length treatment of the objects of study. As Brown notes: [28]

> Organization realities are not external to human consciousness, out there waiting to be recorded. Instead, the world as humans know it is constituted intersubjectively. The faces (facta) of this world are things made. They are neither subjective nor objective in the usual sense. Instead, they are construed through a process of symbolic interaction. A revision of our symbolic structures, of our shared forms of perception and expression, is thus a revisioning of the world.

The view that social life can be in critical respects a conscious process of world-creation implies both great leverage over, and awesome responsibility for, our human condition. Action research often deals with "social reality," the ways and shapes in which "experience acquires significance," in Brown's revealing words; [29] and it highlights the basic hope-cum-terror that changes in structures of consciousness can generate changes in social structures, whether deliberately or by stagger-and-stumble. As Brown concludes about an emphasis on the world-creating aspects of action research, it

> . . . provides a bridge between theoretical and organizational praxes, as well as between what experts do and what workers do in their workday lives. We all create worlds. The more we are able to create worlds that are morally cogent and politically viable, the more we are able, as workers and as citizens, to manage or to resist. [30]

IV. PERSPECTIVES ON OD AS VALUE-LOADED

The bridge of action research having been blue-printed, as it were, two basic challenges require attending to. This section seeks to demonstrate that OD is appropriately value-loaded, "appropriately" defined in terms of the enacted consciousness suitable for humanizing or democratizing organizations. A following section will deal with a more pragmatic concern: specifically, does sufficient research and experience in OD indicate some reasonable next-steps for practical attempts to approach humanist ideals more closely?

The present approach to Adminstration III relies on organization development, or OD.[31] OD is value-loaded, as can be shown briefly from three perspectives:

- OD in broad concept

- OD as constituent designs

- OD in implementation

To put the same point in another way, these three perspectives can be said to reflect the senses in which OD is broadly political. If we accept Easton's definition of politics as involving the authoritative allocation of values in society, OD can be said to relate to that allocation process in significant ways—for systems, sub-systems, as well as individuals.

A. OD as Value-Loaded in Broad Concept

That OD is value-loaded in its broadest sweep can be established with no difficulty. From its earliest days, OD was seen as philosophy-cum-learning-designs for moving toward the creation of appropriate societies and cultures at the worksite.[32] More specifically, such values provide substantial shape and form for social and cultural reconstruction prescribed by OD:[33]

- full and free communication

- greater reliance on open confrontation in managing conflict, where participants psychologically own at least the causes of conflict and its consequences, as well as (hopefully) agree on approaches to managing the conflict. This contrasts with a reliance on coercion or compromise

- influence based on competence rather than on personal whim or formal power

- expression of emotional as well as task-oriented behavior

- acceptance of conflict between the individual and the organization to be coped with willingly, openly, and rationally

These few prescriptions give normative shape to Administration III, which has a clear affinity to the enacted participatory-democratic consciousness sketched in Figure 4, and which also rejects values/attitudes/skills appropriate for the bureaucratic principles for organizing work. This major point could be reinforced in multiple ways, but only two must suffice here. Note that the broad OD values above clearly dove-tail with the enacted consciousness suitable for a humanist organization. This enacted consciousness, recall, has two basic components: a reduced proneness to manipulation, and greater ability to create and organize policy. Specifically, Figure 4 advises that simple-and-sovereign causation suits well the enacted consciousness required for dehumanizing organizations. Oppositely, the OD values above call for admitting to analysis both emotional and rational-technical considerations, which implies multiple causality. The bureaucratic principles are more restrictive, seeking as they do to define emotional features as out-of-bounds. This precludes action research, in effect, and emphasizes a simple-and-sovereign approach to causality or co-variation.

Moreover, even sparse comments suffice to suggest that OD implies a far different social and cultural context for work than do bureaucratic principles. Consider full and free communication. In sharp contrast to OD values, the principles seek to compartmentalize knowledge and competence in the service of more facile organization control. Put another way, OD prescribes an organization whose broadly-defined political features more closely approach the democratic ideals than do the principles of bureaucracy.

The focus on OD as value-loaded is not lightly-chosen, in several senses. Indeed, the emphasis here seeks to learn from the past and also to transcend it in a significant particular. Thus action research should be nested in an explicit normative and ethical setting. Moreover, the awkwardness of Democracy *vs.* Administration inheres in substantial degree in its neglect of values, as well as derives from the casual assumption that managerial techniques could somehow be freed from underlying values or cultures.

B. OD as Value-Loaded in Constituent Designs

OD designs are often viewed in technical or helping terms, but they are nonetheless rooted in distinct values that are sharply distinguished from the values associated with bureaucratic principles. This crucial point can be approached from two perspectives—via narrowly-facilitative interventions, and also via broad interventions which especially imply value-preferences that can definitely be considered "in politics," specifically of the humanist variety.

To begin, even narrowly-facilitative interaction designs have a value-loaded character. For example, the simple sharing of information can have profound consequences on bargaining and control processes, and a central feature of OD designs involves the sharing of valid and reliable information. I am reminded of a hunting guide, whose behavior was being controlled by a wife who had convinced him that she would deliver him a boy-child only after he had sufficiently responded to her wishes. The couple already had three girl-children. Some simple information—that his wife had no such power and that, moreover, the male biologically determines the sex of any children—would change some personal bargaining processes and (perhaps) outcomes. Reasonably, then, Smith emphasizes the political character and the profound consequences of the apparently-simple and generally-appealing prescription for "open" interaction in organizations.[34]

Even these brief considerations should imply how OD designs rest on the traits that Figure 2 imputes to the participatory-democractic consciousness. For example, the basic bias of OD designs toward sharing valid and reliable information reinforces and requires many of the traits in Figure 4 associated with avoiding manipulation, as well as with a pro-active posture toward creating/organizing policy. Such sharing of information enhances flexibility and receptivity to the new, to illustrate; and such sharing also facilitates analysis-in-depth.

The value-loaded and political features of broader OD interventions are clearer still. Consider any structural change in an organization. Its inspiration may be rooted in what empirical research "tells us" about which structural arrangements are more likely to be associated with high productivity and satisfaction. And that empirical research, lacunae and all, has plenty to say! In that sense, structural change has a major technical component. However, the choice of any structural alternative and its implementation require a selection between values; and both that choice and its implementation activate processes that may be broadly called "political," and whose essential thrust is clearly "more democratic" than the principles. For example, structural change typically involves rewiring authoritative linkages, redesigning networks of who formally communicates to whom under which circumstances, and so on. These consequences definitely have a political component. As Schein observes:[35]

> Systemic change programs that impact a variety of organizational levels are most prey to political strategies designed to block the change effort. Supervisors, middle managers, the personnel department, and other staff groups, perceiving the change program as a threat to their power, employ a variety of tactics, both overt and covert. For example, middle managers can stall and de-energize in order to avoid loss of their power. The personnel department can discredit the change agent or block him by use of its expertise.

Similarly, radical restructuring in bureaucracies often implies a new concept of authority—as problem-solving vs. hierarchy-serving, or as based on a notion of influence shared up-and-down-and-across hierarchies vs. the trickle-down and tidy concept so central in the bureaucratic principles. Such major differences obviously involve significant choices between competing if not conflicting values, and broadly-political processes often will accompany those choices and efforts to implement them.

C. OD as Value-Loaded in Implementation

The value-loaded character of OD is nowhere clearer than in the processes of implementing choice or change. Implementation will of necessity be value-loaded and broadly political. The only questions involve the specific values that define and limit those choice-processes, and whether those guiding values get chosen consciously or by careless default.

The value-loadedness of OD implementation cannot be avoided, that is to say, but it can be diversely managed. As Schein notes,[36] the OD intervenor can take one of three basic stances with respect to implementation:

- The OD intervenor can conceptually "play down the politics of implementation and deny the pervasiveness of political behaviors in organizations," thus avoiding any direct confrontation with prevailing OD values as to openness and trust. The price may be ineffectiveness or failure, as the intervenor's ideology provides inadequate real-world guidance, especially with respect to systemic change.

- The OD intervenor can acknowledge the potential conflict of OD values and the politics of implementation and, by conscious choice, restrict self to interventions in which conflict is least likely. This may be reasonable, but it patently forfeits most opportunities for systemic change and it may relegate intervenor to Band Aid or cooling-out activities, which may be important but are self-limiting in crucial senses and (more significantly) can induce organization members to unwisely expose themselves when prudence calls for secrecy and deceit.

- The OD intervenor can conceptually acknowledge the potential conflict of OD values and the politics of implementation, all the better to consciously face the trade-offs that often will be required for effective implementation.

There should be little question about the bias advocated here, in the general case. Instead of pussy-footing on the issue of power, the OD consultant at the interface must resolutely help induce an *alternative system of power*, like that prescribed by OD values. That makes the OD intervenor an advocate, of course, and a probable-target for those with an interest in what exists. But little is lost thereby, because any significant intervention will by definition be "in politics," and no virtue inheres in neglecting that fact.

V. MOVING TOWARD ADMINISTRATION III VIA OD

More specifically, how should one move toward Administration III via OD? The most reasonable advice encourages caution, expects incremental advances as our knowledge and experience increase, and prescribes focusing on selected activities in those organizations that are experiencing sufficient trauma to motivate change and to heighten the probability of its successful implementation. That is, the action-research orientation of OD is not just another utopian ideology.[37]

To put this crucial point another way, one cannot expect that today's OD can "eat the whole thing." Oppositely, indeed, the reach and grasp of individual approaches toward Administration III will differ profoundly. Some OD interventions require "limited-purpose contracts"—e.g., flexible workhours applications often seem to do quite nicely with little prior development of appropriate attitudes, skills, and cultures. Other OD interventions may require substantial pre-work. For example, career planning implies major prerequisites—e.g., substantial flexibility in, if not actual change of, attitudes, skills, and structures in organizations. No career planning usually will be preferable to career planning without vital pre-work. That is, career planning requires not only a supportive socio-emotional culture, but also appropriate management practices and policies such as those related to the possibility that an individual might modify unsatisfying conditions related to a job, including the restructuring of work and its supervision.[38]

Beyond such introductory notions, two basic approaches for moving toward Administration III come to mind and, as it happens, considerable OD research and experience relevant to both have already been accumulated. *First*, ways and means have to be developed to directly energize multiple forms or levels of democracy within organizations. *Second*, complementary effort must go toward the development of what might be called "useful supports" for nonauthoritarian behavior in organizations. The basic challenge for Administration III, then, can be sketched in this way:

Energize Multiple Levels of Democracy ⟷ Provide Attitudinal and Behavioral Supports

Both aspects of this basic challenge get illustrative attention below, in turn. Note that the two foci here relate to Bernstein's distinction between inputs and outputs in organizations. Thus the present emphasis on how OD can energize multiple levels of democracy clearly relates to the patterns of control or influence in organizations, and may be associated with policy outcomes: who influences what range of issues at which levels of organization. Moreover, the emphasis on attitudinal and behavioral supports also corresponds to Bernstein's view of inputs—to the traits of participants that contribute to the specific enacted consciousness characteristic of an organization.

A. Energize Multiple Forms of Democracy

The *first* aspect of the challenge of moving toward Administration III involves energizing the several levels of Democracy II. It will not be necessary to start at ground-zero, fortunately. In effect, numerous available OD designs and research concerning their effects variously relate to these several levels. To illustrate, adding the individual level to Dahl's four forms of democracy:

	Applicable OD Designs
o Enhanced individual freedom and and responsibility	--flexible workhours --career planning --job enrichment --3rd party consultation --demotion experience --recognize and respond to personal life-transitions
o Committee Democracy, in which all members have a more or less equal say while in face-to-face contact	--team-building --sensitivity training with intact work teams --group decision-making
o Referendum Democracy, in which all viewpoints get represented although individuals do not necessarily speak out themselves	--interview/feedback --survey/feedback --group confrontations, as between units involved in a common flow of work, or customer and supplier
o Representative Democracy, in which some smaller selected group speaks out for a larger collectivity	--group decision-making by representatives --joint labor/management committee for quality of working life efforts --large agenda- and norm-setting meetings with diverse participants from various levels of one or more organizations
o Polyarchical Democracy, which includes the forms above and also provides roles for diverse interest groups and for complex delegations of authority	--collective bargaining and other forms of labor/management interaction that focus on quality of working life as well as pay-and-fringes [39]

Basically, the sketch above implies five significant points about how OD designs can energize the several forms or levels of democracy. *First,* much available OD practice can be cataloged in terms of the forms of democracy. Note that details about the several designs and their consequences are available in many places.[40]

Second, OD designs tend to cluster in the "more democratic" forms; that is, experience basically relates to the general enhancement of individual freedom and responsibility, as well as to organizational analogs of what Dahl calls Committee Democracy and Referendum Democracy. Consider team-building in small work units, which can be extended to large numbers of individuals in the same organization by arranging for numerous iterations of a similar design in many work teams at various levels, as well as by holding various interface or integrative meetings to test and reinforce learning. Hundreds or even thousands of individuals in work teams can be exposed—in parallel, as it were—to team-building designs intended to help induce appropriate norms, behaviors, and attitudes.[41] Typically, the focus is on improving the quality of communication processes—as by increasing trust, reducing risk, and increasing openness and owning—which in turn may later lead to technical and substantive improvements by work teams. These learnings in small groups then can be tested in interface experiences—as teams confront a common superior after having spent substantial time in developing appropriate attitudes or skills,[42] or as culturally-prepared teams seek to develop or enhance relations with other teams in a flow of work.[43]

Moreover, opinion-polling technology can be coupled with designs using face-to-face interaction—the combination is usually called survey/feedback—to encompass even tens of thousands of organization members. In effect, survey/feedback designs variously percolate up and trickle down. Results of opinion surveys from even very large populations, that is, can be variously disaggregated for in-depth analysis at various levels of organization, often through a "waterfall" or "cascade" design of action-planning meetings which consider data relevant to their own organizational level.[44] In a basic sense, survey/feedback may be thought of as a complex combination of Referendum Democracy followed by Committee Democracy. Employing a technology useful for large populations and employing statistical techniques that isolate comparative trends in various sub-groups, survey/feedback designs seek to improve both socio-emotional and task aspects of work. Basically, the survey captures the moods and attitudes of organization members about various aspects of the worksite; and hopefully the feedback energizes various sub-systems to begin doing something specific about those moods and attitudes in action-planning meetings at multiple levels of organization.[45] Since sampling methods can make periodic polling quite painless, finally, large systems can in effect maintain real-time programs of pulse-taking, which in turn can trigger periodic action-planning.

At the Representative Democracy level, OD experience and theory are thinner. Coch and French's classic experiment with alternative forms of decision-making, for example, implies the virtues of direct representation of employees in worksite decisions.[46] More recently, joint labor/management committees at the plant level have been used to help improve the quality of working life. And some experience exists with large agenda- and norm-setting meetings, simultaneously involving as many as 500 people from various sub-units of a large organization.[47] This experience implies that individual OD designs can impact on large numbers of individuals in short time-frames.

Third, at the Polyarchical level, it is perhaps best to say that the basic form and character of OD efforts have yet to be determined. In many European countries, codetermination by labor and management at macro-levels constitutes perhaps the most ambitious expression of interest at this level. Little American interest has been expressed in such macro-arrangements, until quite recently. For example, American unions have basically focused on wages-and-fringes, and with few exceptions have shown only episodic interest in the conditions of work and far less in the co-management or co-direction of work. In smaller systems, to be sure, experience with polyarchical approaches is growing. Schools provide perhaps the most fertile locus for such experimentation.[48] Efforts with similar spirit include various approaches to involving "underrepresenteds"—as via an ombudsman for consumers or clients of government services, various "public affairs" departments inside business corporations who are to serve as devil's advocates for consumer viewpoints that might otherwise not be given effective and regular voice, and so on.

Fourth, the several OD designs above clearly provide numerous opportunities to move toward the specific values/attitudes/behaviors associated earlier with the enacted consciousness appropriate for humanistic organizations. For example, career planning patently seeks to encourage (indeed, requires) organization participants who are less prone to being manipulated, as well as more able to create and organize the conditions of their organizational existence. See Figure 2 for numerous details. Moreover, career-planners need to cultivate a long time-sense, which Bernstein sees as a useful trait in both major subsystems that should characterize the "participatory-democratic consciousness." Similarly, career-planning rests on a growing self-reliance, and refusal to transfer responsibility. Oppositely, also, career-planning rejects what Bernstein describes in Figure 2 as "extreme loyalty, deference, credulity." This bundle of traits can be expressed in such dicta as: "The organization will take care of me."

Fifth, although much of the development of OD is bound-up with economic growth and burgeoning technological sophistication, OD designs have been employed with success under the cut-back conditions that have been encountered so often of late. For example, a demotion design pioneered an approach to meeting individual needs under difficult organizational conditions.[49] And related designs have been developed for humane responses to various aspects of reductions-in-force.[50]

B. Provide Useful Attitudinal and Behavioral Supports

Typically, energizing these several levels of democracy will depend upon building appropriate attitudinal and behavioral supports. Often, this will take place in such OD designs as those involving team-building, survey/feedback, and so on. At other times, such supports will derive from a variety of more-focused learning designs, as well as from changes in broad institutional and structural arrangements.

Exhibit 4 sketches four classes of such supports, along with a sampling of relevant OD designs, about which two general points can be made at the outset. *First*, the several designs all variously encourage the kinds of traits listed or implied in Figure 3 as central to an enacted participatory-democratic consciousness. Thus the several OD opportunities for individual choice—flexi-time, and so on—clearly serve to encourage such traits as self-reliance. Similarly, the several designs in Exhibit 4 identified as building or enhancing necessary attitudes and behavioral skills variously relate to Figure 3. Thus designs associated with giving or receiving feedback clearly seek to stimulate critical thinking. Further, OD designs that can induce appropriate atmospheres or styles seek to create an important edge for actors in their systems. Depending upon the system atmosphere or climate, the *same* behavior might be differently evaluated. Thus being inquisitive or

EXHIBIT 4. Arraying OD Designs by Four Major Classes of Attitudinal and Behavioral Supports

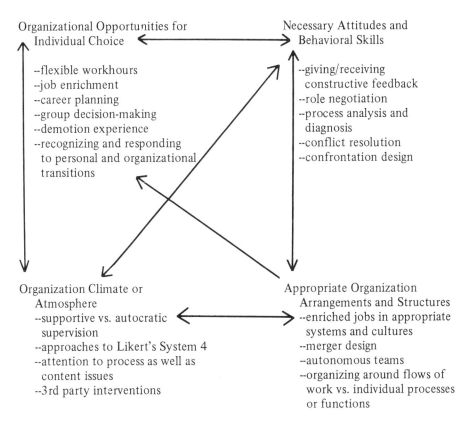

interrogative might in one system merely imply that the individual was "negative" or "difficult." In another system, precisely the same inquisitiveness could be interpreted as "constructive" or "positive" with respect to individuals and their systems.

Second, not all of these designs will be relevant in a specific organization at a particular time, of course; and some organizations might do well enough without any of them. Diagnosis is paramount, in short. Generally, however, such designs seem to have special attractions in certain kinds of organizations, e.g., those with multiple product-lines or programs, with a major technological component, under conditions of high turbulence and change, with a skilled and professionalized work force, and so on. But also note that many designs have proved generally useful in a wide range of organizations under diverse conditions.[51]

1. Organizational Opportunities for Individual Choice. Appropriate designs can cover a broad range. Some are conceptually simple, and can be implemented with modest skill and sparse commitment of resources under broad ranges of organizational conditions. Programs of flexible workhours illustrate this class of designs, as burgeoning research from both business and public sectors implies.[52] Other designs anchor the opposite end of a scale of resources/skills/commitments. Career planning typifies OD designs of this latter kind, and postulates that in the long run neither the individual nor the organization will profit from persons being in roles whose demands substantially outstrip an individual's skills and expectations. Working-through such subtle balancing requires substantial commitments from individuals and their organizations. One of the significant facets of career planning involves a recognition of stages of both individual and organization development, for example, as well as responses to them.[53]

2. Necessary Attitudes and Behavioral Skills. Opportunities for individual choice will not necessarily be taken advantage of, to be sure. Increasing the probability of such outcomes will depend substantially on the availability of appropriate skills and attitudes.

Appropriate designs here cover a broad range. Some attitudes and behavioral skills are quite generic—e.g., those associated with giving and receiving constructive feedback or with active listening—and will be more or less relevant at all stages of individual and organization development. Other designs will have more-specific targets, as in the case of role negotiation.[54]

3. Organization Climate or Atmosphere. Opportunities, plus appropriate attitudes and behavioral skills, constitute powerful motivation to make choices and to take the consequences. But experience indicates that organization climate or atmosphere will play a dominant role in influencing whether individuals with those attitudes and skills will take available opportunities, let alone capitalize on them. Even strong preferences and major opportunities can be thwarted by such prescriptions: "That just isn't done around here." To illustrate only, note the crucial significance to communication that derives from a crucial distinction: whether an atmosphere is "defensive" or not. Relying on Gibb's seminal work, consider this impactful contrast:[55]

Defensive Climates tend to be induced by, and to produce	Supportive Climates tend to be induced by, and to produce
• Evaluation	• Description
• Control	• Problem-orientation
• Strategy	• Spontaneity
• Neutrality	• Empathy
• Superiority	• Equality
• Certitude	• Provisionalism

These contrasts patently imply major differences in communication processes and outcomes.

Substantial OD experience exists concerning the induction of organization climate or atmosphere, experience relevant to both what should be done as well as to which pitfalls should be avoided.[56] Exhibit 4 lists a few relevant designs. These designs include discrete efforts to modify supervisory styles,[57] as well as to influence broad patterns of interpersonal and group relationships.[58] Generally, experience implies that simultaneous attacks from both directions work best. Indeed, attempts to modify supervisory styles without inducing an appropriate social or cultural context may not only fail, but they may prove seriously counterproductive.[59] Similarly, creating broad social expectations for individuals who lack appropriate behavioral skills also can be ill-advised.

4. Organization Arrangements and Structures. The final class of multiple reinforcers in this analysis—and often the most important reinforcers in practice—includes various organizational arrangements and structures for work. The point is often overlooked in OD. Indeed, by far the dominant interventions involve interaction-centered designs—those related to attitudes and behavioral skills as well as to climates or atmospheres. Such interventions can initially seem to succeed, and then suddenly fade out in the absence of appropriate changes in the way work is structured. For example, organizations departmentalized by functions will tend to encourage an authoritarian style of supervision. A careless superimposition on such structures of OD designs supporting non-authoritarian attitudes and behaviors can be traumatic, especially when the move is attempted in one big jump via interaction-centered design without corresponding changes in the organization of work or in its supporting culture.[60]

Some research and experience exists with appropriate structural forms, as is summarized in convenient sources.[61] Job enrichment is one such approach, for example. Care should be exercised to take a systemic view, however, especially because a Band-Aid approach tends to dominate. Specifically, job enlargement programs ill-suit organizations with a bureaucratic structure—e.g., departmentation of work by functions or processes. Numerous failures of job enlargement qua technique have been reported, specifically, and many of these failures can be attributed to an inappropriate systemic culture and structure for enlarged jobs. Most enrichment programs are applied as patches on a pre-existing structure and culture which poorly suits the approach. To illustrate:

Bureaucratic structures imply:	*Job enrichment implies:*
— authoritarian supervision	— supportive supervision
— monitoring of details of performance	— monitoring of overall performance
— limitation of an employee to a single or few operations in a total sequence	— control by an employee of a total sequence of operations
— separating worker from control of work	— integrating worker and control of work
— centralizing decision-making re operations	— decentralizing decision-making re operations
— etc.	— etc.

VI. CONCLUSION

The movement toward Administration III, then, can be viewed as the search for a useful middle-ground. The poles-of-argument seem clear enough. Thus Mosher[62] reasonably cautions that ". . . democracy within administration, *if carried to the full*, raises a logical dilemma in its relation to political democracy." This manuscript, in basic thrust, urges that bureaucracy within administration also raises logical and practical dilemmas in relation to political democracy as well as efficient and effective administration. In the present view, OD permits the exploration of the needed middle-ground for better meeting both individual needs and organizational demands.

FOOTNOTES

[1]Paul H. Appleby, *Morality and Administration In Democratic Government* (Baton Rouge, La.: Louisiana State University, 1952).

[2]Emmette S. Redford, *Democracy in the Administrative State* (New York: Oxford University Press, 1969), pp. 170-171.

[3]These prescriptions comprise the title of Frederick Thayer's *An End to Hierarchy! An End to Competition!* (New York: New Viewpoints, 1981).

[4]Paul Bernstein, *Workplace Democratization: Its Internal Dynamics* (New Brunswick, N.J.: Transaction Books, 1980).

[5]*Ibid.*, pp. 45-46.

[6]For a detailed demonstration of the extreme degrees to which normal political rights—e.g., those concerning freedom of speech—can atrophy in organizations, consult David W. Ewing, *Freedom Inside the Organization: Bringing Civil Liberties to the Workplace* (New York: E.P. Dutton, 1977), esp. pp. 5-11.

That the state of affairs has changed some in recent years, but not greatly, can be inferred from a comparison of Ewing's work with William G. Scott's *The Management of Conflict: Appeal Systems in Organizations* (Homewood, Ill.: Irwin-Dorsey Press, 1965).

[7]For an insightful and seminal view of some of the associated subtleties, see Arnold S. Tannenbaum, *Social Psychology of the Work Organization* (Belmont, Cal.: Wadsworth, 1966), esp. pp. 84-102.

[8]Bernstein, *Workplace Democratization*, p. 47, provides the inspiration here.

[9]Theoretic and empirical support for such networks can be generated by several sources, prominent among which is Chris Argyris, "Conditions for Competence Acquisition and Therapy," *Journal of Applied Behavioral Science*, Vol. 4 (March 1968), pp. 153-154.

[10]For an interpretation of the general point, see Robert T. Golembiewski, *Behavior and Organization* (Chicago: Rand McNally, 1962), pp. 114-148.

[11]The need to specify individual differences was manifest even in very early research with participation, as in the experimental studies of leadership and climate in children's groups. See Kurt Lewin, Ronald Lippitt, and Robert K. White, "Patterns of Aggressive Behavior in Experimentally Created 'Social Climates'," *Journal of Social Psychology*, Vol. 10 (1939), pp. 271-299.

[12]Lester Coch and John R.P. French, Jr., "Overcoming Resistance to Change," *Human Relations*, Vol. 1 (December 1948), esp. pp. 519-520.

[13]Bernstein, *Workplace Democratization*, pp. 18-19.

[14]Henry G. Dahl, *Worker-Owned Plywood Companies in the State of Washington* (Everett, Wash.: First National Bank of Everett, 1957); and Katrina V. Berman, *Worker-Owned Plywood Companies: An Economic Analysis* (Pullam, Wash.: Washington State University Press, 1967), p. 189.

[15]Berman, *op. cit.*, pp. 189-190.

[16]Thus Bernstein carefully warns in his *Workplace Democratization*, p. 96, that ". . . this representation is by no means intended to define fully or with great certainty the content of participatory/democratic consciousness. That alone would be the task of a book-length study, and there was no time for that in the present research. Secondly, empirical research in this area is still relatively sparse. Several of the terms utilized . . . are still quite broad and contain a great number of possibilities that need to be made explicit by further research. All that is intended here is to present some major probable components of the consciousness seemingly required to sustain democratization. It is merely a grounding for future research."

[17]Bernstein, *Workplace Democratization*, p. 97, acknowledges these sources underlying Figure 2: Chris Argyris, *Human Behavior In Organizations* (New York: Harper & Row, 1954); Paul Bernstein and Marjorie Young, "Democratic Mentality in the Czechoslovak Reform Movement," Mimeod., 1973; Paulo Friere, *Education for Critical Consciousness* (New York: Harper & Row, 1954); and Robert Theobald, *Alternative America II* (Chicago: Swallow Press, 1970).

[18]For an overview relevant to organization analysis, see Golembiewski's *Behavior and Organization*, pp. 47-86.

[19]Comprehensively, see Newton Margulies and Anthony P. Raia, *Conceptual Foundations of Organizational Development* (New York: McGraw-Hill, 1978), pp. 55-80.

[20]Kenneth Benne, Leland P. Bradford, and Ronald Lippitt, *T-Group Theory and Laboratory Method* (New York: John Wiley & Sons, 1964), p. 33.

[21]R.N. Rapport, quoted in Margulies and Raia, *op. cit.*, p. 63.

[22]Gerald I. Susman and Roger D. Evered, "An Assessment of the Scientific Merits of Action Research," *Administrative Science Quarterly*, Vol. 23 (December 1978), pp. 582-603.

[23]Peter B. Vaill, "The Expository Model of Science in Organization Design," pp. 73-88, in Ralph H. Kilmann, Louis R. Pondy, and Dennis P. Slevin, editors, *The Management of Organization Design* (New York: Elsevier North-Holland, 1976).

[24]Vaill, *op. cit.*

[25]Susman and Evered, *op. cit.*, p. 600.

[26]Dahl, "Three Problems In A Science of Public Administration."

[27]The point gets made at several places in, for example, Waldo, *The Administrative State.*

[28]Richard Harvey Brown, "Bureaucracy As Praxis: Toward A Political Phenomenology of Formal Organizations," *Administrative Science Quarterly*, Vol. 23 (September 1978), p. 378.

[29]*Ibid.*

[30]*Ibid.*

[31]Generally consult Golembiewski, *Approaches to Planned Change*, Parts 1 and 2.

[32]*Ibid.*, Part 1, pp. 1-190.

[33]Slater and Bennis, *op. cit.*, pp. 51-59.

[34]Ken K. Smith, "A Political Perspective on Openness," pp. 399-408, in Golembiewski, *Approaches to Planned Change*, Part 2.

[35]Virginia E. Schein, "Political Strategies for Implementing Organizational Change," *Group and Organization Studies*, Vol. 2 (March 1977), p. 43.

[36]*Ibid.*, pp. 46-47.

[37]For literature which positively evaluates the mix of costs/benefits of these two designs, consult Robert T. Golembiewski and Carl W. Proehl, Jr., "Public-Sector Applications of Flexible Workhours," *Public Administration Review*, Vol. 40 (January 1980), pp. 72-85; and Golembiewski, *Approaches to Planned Change*, Part 1, pp. 246-258.

[38]For example, a useful feature of career-planning design involves an analysis of the positive and negative aspects of a person's job. As one of the final tasks, individuals are instructed to choose as a change-target some undesirable aspects of their job, within general policy guidelines and with the help of peers and often a consultant. An individual chooses an aspect of work, plans to ameliorate it, seeks to implement that plan, and reports back to a group of co-career-planners. This design-element obviously requires careful pre-work at both policy and operating levels, but it has a powerful redeeming feature. The very possibility of attempting that change signals commitment to the significant proposition that—in the long run, at least—a high and growing congruence between individual needs and organization requirements constitutes a major goal.

More broadly, see Golembiewski, *Approaches to Planned Change*, Part 1, pp. 203-225.

[39]The major American expression of this approach is the labor-management collaboration relevant to improving the quality of workinglife. For an extended report on one such effort, see Paul G. Goodman, *Assessing Organizational Change* (New York: Wiley-Interscience, 1979).

[40]William G. Dyer, *Team-Building* (Reading, Mass.: Addison-Wesley, 1977).

[41]For an evaluation of one such large effort to implement a "parallel" design for many similar small work units in one organization, see Reuben T. Harris and Jerry L. Porras, "The Consequences of Large System Change in Practice," pp. 298-302, in Jeffrey C. Susbauer, editor, *Proceedings, 1978 Annual Meeting, Academy of Management.*

[42]The features and consequences of an early design of this kind were reported by Robert T. Golembiewski and Stokes B. Carrigan, "Planned Change in Organization Style Based on Laboratory Approach," *Administrative Science Quarterly*, Vol. 15 (September 1970), pp. 330-340.

[43]So-called "3-dimensional confrontation" designs were developed for this purpose. For features of the design and its typical effects, along with an explanatory model, see Golembiewski, *Approaches to Planned Change*, Part 2, pp. 138-152.

[44]For details, consult Robert T. Golembiewski and Richard Hilles, *Toward the Responsive Organization* (Salt Lake City, Utah: Brighton Publishing, 1979).

[45]For an inventive development of how and why survey/feedback designs can release and channel individual and group energies in organizations, see David A. Nadler, *Feedback and Organization Development* (Reading, Mass.: Addison-Wesley, 1977).

[46]Coch and French, Jr., "Overcoming Resistance to Change." See also the theoretical discussion of their results in Golembiewski, *Behavior and Organization*, pp. 123-148.

For details about the broad range of interventions applicable in organizations—especially concerning structure, policies and procedures—see Dennis T. Perkins, *et al.*, *Managing Creation* (New York: Wiley, 1983); and Robert Zager and Michael P. Rosow, editors, *The Innovative Organization* (New York: Pergamon Press, 1982).

[47]For some details, see Golembiewski, *Approaches to Planned Change*, Part 2, pp. 134-136.

[48]Richard A. Schmuck, *et al.*, *Consultation for Innovative Schools* (Eugene, Ore.: Center for Educational Policy and Management, 1974) provides broad perspective. For details about one effort, see Arthur Blumberg, William Wayson, and Welford Weber, "The Elementary School Cabinet: Report of An Experience in Participative Decision-Making," *Educational Administration Quarterly*, Vol. 5 (No. 3, 1979), pp. 39-52.

[49]Robert T. Golembiewski, *Public Administration As A Developing Discipline* (New York: Marcel Dekker, 1979), Part 2, pp. 99-122.

[50]Golembiewski, *Approaches to Planned Change*, Part 2, pp. 185-214); and Thomas D. Taber, Jeffrey T. Walsh, and R.A. Cooke, "Developing A Community-Based Program for Reducing the Social Impact of A Plant Closing," *Journal of Applied Behavioral Science*, Vol. 15 (April 1979), pp. 133-155.

[51]For an overview of these and other designs, see Golembiewski, *Approaches to Planned Change*, Parts 1 and 2.

[52]Robert T. Golembiewski, Ronald Fox, and Carl W. Proehl, Jr., "Is Flexi-Time 'Hard Time' for Supervisors?: Two Sources of Data Rejecting the Proposition," *Journal of Management*, Vol. 5 (Fall 1979), pp. 241-259; and Robert T. Golembiewski, Ronald Fox and Carl W. Proehl, Jr., "Flexitime: Supervisors' Verdict," *Wharton Magazine*, Vol. 4 (Summer 1980), pp. 43-47.

[53]Robert T. Golembiewski, "Mid-Life Transition and Mid-Career Crisis," *Public Administration Review*, Vol. 38 (May 1978), pp. 215-222.

[54]Roger Harrison, "Role Negotiation," pp. 178-190, in Robert T. Golembiewski

and William Eddy, editors, *Organization Development in Public Administration* (New York: Marcel Dekker, 1978).

[55]Ack R. Gibb, "Defensive Communication," *Journal of Communication*, Vol. 11 (September 1961), pp. 143-145.

[56]A classic case of what to avoid has been documented by Per-Olof Berg, *Emotional Structures in Organizations* (Lund, Sweden: Studentliteratur, 1979). Usefully, Berg focuses not only on an organization and the learning designs applied in it, but also on the firm's market environment as well as the broader social millieu.

[57]For a major effort, see Edward Fleishman, "Leadership Climate, Human Relations Training and Supervisory Behavior," *Personnel Psychology*, Vol. 6 (Summer 1953), pp. 205-222.

[58]E.g., Golembiewski and Carrigan, *op. cit.*

[59]As was the case in Fleischman's study, *op. cit.*, which relied on off-site training for supervisors. Neither back-home superiors nor subordinates had such training, and the work culture was left undisturbed. The results were not happy. The supervisors who had changed most during the off-site training, in fact, soon after returning to the worksite reported a regression not only to previous levels on several indicators, but even fell below their pre-training levels. The likely dynamics? The "big changers" returned home, and found themselves at greatest odds with back-home superiors and their culture. Frustration set in, perhaps because the big-changers were punished, which would account for their pattern of learning: two giant steps forward and three back.

[60]Berg, *op. cit.*, details a telling example of this kind, with the added touch that while learning designs were tending to democratize interaction, the structure and other practices were moving toward the bureaucratic model from a highly-personalized paternalism that had existed for generations.

[61]For an overview of structural forms and issues, see Robert T. Golembiewski, "Organizing Public Work, Round Three," in Golembiewski and Aaron Wildavsky, editors, *The Costs of Federalism* (New Brunswick, NJ: Transaction, 1984), pp. 237-270; and Golembiewski, "Public-Sector Organization: Why Theory and Practice Should Emphasize Purpose, and How To Do So," in Ralph Clark Chandler, editor, *A Centennial History of the American Administrative State* (New York: Wiley in press).

For a micro-view of experience with one structural form, as well as advice on how to do better, see Linda L. Frank and J. Richard Hackman, "A Failure of Job Enrichment," *Journal of Applied Behavioral Science*, Vol. 11 (October 1976), pp. 413-436.

[62]Frederick C. Mosher, *Democracy and the Public Service* (New York: Oxford University Press, 1969), p. 374.

PART D

How Can Public-Sector OD Do Better-than-Average?

CHAPTER VII: Seeking Guidance from Experience at the Interface, I: Intervention Guidelines Relating to Environmental Texture

CHAPTER VIII: Seeking Guidance from Experience at the Interface, II: Intervention Guidelines Focusing on Intervenor Behavior

CHAPTER VII

SEEKING GUIDANCE FROM EXPERIENCE AT THE INTERFACE, I: INTERVENTION GUIDELINES RELATING TO ENVIRONMENTAL TEXTURE

Not learning from history condemns us to repeat its failures. That elemental wisdom motivates this chapter and the one that concludes this volume. Simply, can we learn to do better-than-average in public-sector OD? This question preoccupies in the context of the previous two clusters of chapters. One cluster of four chapters suggests a pretty-fair batting average; and the other cluster urges that we do far better, not only to meet employee and organization needs but also to more closely approach the ideals of republic governance.

This chapter[1] and the one following propose a detailed and unequivocal answer to the question above: Yes.

The two chapters seek to learn from experience. The focus will be on a critical and ubiquitous interface—that between "politics" and "administration," at or near the top of public agencies. Examples suffice to pinpoint the target for analysis. That is, such an interface exists at the federal level between legislators, senior administrators who are political appointees, and the top-most levels of the career service, with boundaries defined by constitutions, laws, and traditions in ways that inhibit spanning. Indeed—as in the federal separation of powers—strong institutions and sentiments not only tend to complicate spanning those boundaries, but they also provide constitutional legitimacy for their fragmentation. Private-sector organizations may reflect aspects of the politics/administration interface but, for multiple reasons, do so in far less marked and persisting ways.

This focus on the interface will not permit doing all that is required, of course, but it should help. The interface patently represents a critical zone in public-sector OD applications, for one thing. And the interface has not received fulsome attention.

I. FIVE PERSPECTIVES ON AN OLD ISSUE

OD practice at the politics/administration interface is substantially ahead of the literature, and this chapter seeks to abstract the more essential features of my own experience that build on the long-noted differences between "private" and "public" spheres. Six OD applications at the interface get most attention, each of which

- involves a moderate- to high-technology mission

- is "in politics" in highly-visible ways

- is characterized by active and intense oversight of the managerial mission by legislative or political officials

- involves an OD consultant working both sides of the politics/ administration interface

The six applications will seldom be identified in specific ways, for numerous reasons besides those that will be obvious at many places in the text. Generally, however, the six OD applications include:

- a military program

- a legislative council involved in a program of municipal change

- policy-making bodies actively helping shape mass urban transportation systems

- a political appointee and his key executives supervising a large government jurisdiction bent on improving the quality of service for clients as well as on enhancing the quality of working life for employees

- a chief executive, newly-elected to office, and anxious to distinguish his regime from all predecessors

II. GUIDELINES EMPHASIZING TEXTURE AT THE INTERFACE

In what senses does the public sector have distinctive qualities and, derivatively, what tailor-making of interventions seems appropriate at the interface? This chapter will emphasize the former theme; and the succeeding chapter will focus more on how the OD intervenor can (and often should) respond to the specific texture of the interface. Over thirty guidelines derived from experience at the politics/administration interface hopefully provide both direction and counsel. These guidelines for intervenors seek to provide insight and to improve effectiveness within the context of typical OD values and goals.[2] These OD values and goals emphasize *openness, trust,* and *win-win interaction,* which many observers see as variously in conflict with political realities. What follows constitutes an effort to accommodate those values with common realities, while avoiding both purism and valueless opportunism.

Before detailing some guidelines responsive to the common features of the interface—to its texture, if you will—a few introductory comments should prove helpful.

The guidelines have a mini-history of their own—my evaluation of other available sets of guidelines for intervenors[3] has this bottom-line concerning their serviceability at the interface. In some senses, those guidelines are OK, they do not relate to some important themes; and in some cases what seems reasonable guidance in general can be seriously counter-productive at the interface. Hence the effort below, which began in much slimmer form.[4]

This version is not seen as an end-of-the-line. But it is more elaborate than its predecessors, and it also contains many more illustrative vignettes or war stories. The contrasts between this set of guidelines and others no doubt reflect differences in consulting style, to a degree. But my best guess is that most of the contrasts derive from the fact that the politics/administration interface differs from the contexts which others had in mind.

So, on to the specific task. The first two guidelines below seek to show how public-sector qualities imply great and probably unique challenges—one emotional, the other associated with the pervasive multi-leveledness of the interface. The first challenge requires developing *hope* that things can be different; and the second requires *competence* involving skills and theory about how to make a difference at so many levels, often simultaneously, when so many forces make it so hard to make a lasting difference.

Guideline 1. *Two qualities best describe the emotional tone at the interface—at least a gentle despondency, if not resignation or fatalism; and fear.*

1. *The Slough of Despond as Typical.* The modal emotional tone among those at the interface—in my experience, when they really let their hair down—ranges from despair that it is unredemptively "bigger than all of us,"[5] at the worst, to the resigned but ascerbic humor reflected in the public bureaucrat's pencil—erasers on both ends. Depending upon one's position at the interface, views of causality may differ. Politicals—both appointed and elective—tend to sputter and fume about the unresponsive and resistant bureaucracy, whose intransigence has been lately augmented by due process and unions; and career officials tend to disparage if not despair about passing political fads and personalities. But agreement tends to exist on one point: attempts at change at the interface often are likened to punching warm Jello—if you hit it hard and often enough, you can splatter some of it. But almost all of it remains; that remainder always takes the form of the bowl; and it congeals quickly.

The general emotional tone takes manifold forms, of course, some aggressively hostile but most definitely trending toward withdrawal or resignation. Perhaps the most poignant form of the latter adaptation I recall involved a grandmotherly (and hierarchically senior) envoy from an agency who—in part tactically but with basic sincerity—urged an OD team:

> "Please go home. You can't help us; nobody can help us. We're all stuck in this, and there's no way out, I sacrificed everything for the agency in my best years—my personal life and all. But it just rolls on and gets worse. Please go home to your families. You may be able to help them. Save your energies for where it may do some good.

> "Please leave us alone. Don't make the mistake we made. It doesn't pay."

She simply could not envision gearing-up for another disappointment. To a similar point was the editorial advice to the Project ACORD OD team: "Leave the Poor Old Foreign Service Alone,"[6] so that a number of critical actors could retire in peace. Or consider the recent headline: "Psychiatrist Cites Federal Workers' Woes."[7] A government psychiatrist in an experimental government program reported: "There's a sense of people feeling unproductive and caught in a bureaucracy. People have a sense of helplessness about their work," and especially so because Federal employees seem motivated and intelligent. Supervisors seem particularly troubled, we learn, because they despair about "how difficult it is to get people who should not be there out of the civil-service system." This supports the stereotype, of course.[8]

2. *The Pall of Fear as Typical.* I am also impressed with another quality of the emotional tone at the interface—the ubiquity of fear, of running scared, even for those relatively well-insulated from the more obvious forms of retribution. I refer here not to the general malaise of the existentialists—a kind of free-floating anxiety. The focus is on a Hobbesian variety of palpable fear rooted in the sense of political life as nasty, brutish, and short, a survival of the fittest in a basic tragedy where the rule-of-the-game is elemental: everybody takes care of Big Number 1.

This analysis gets little help from the literature, it is significant to note. Except for the redoubtable Hobbes and the wily old Machiavelli, the literature of politics all but disregards the roles of fear in governance, whether dysfunctional or functional. The OD literature improves on this neglect somewhat. There fear gets treated basically as a condition to be overcome, and especially so in the case of interaction-centered designs.

But so much the worse for the literature. For fear tends to be significant at the interface, even when fear cannot be reasonably said to dominate that locus, which it often does.

My dominant specific memory here involves *Cokus interruptus*, as it were. A longish meeting with an appointed executive had turned mellow and he—usually stiff, reserved, and distant—paid me the ultimate hospitality. He ordered us each a large bottle of Coca-Cola, which we proceeded to drink out of the bottle. His tie loosened, and his feet went to the desk top. We burped a lot, and enjoyed reflecting on a common triumph.

The phone rang. "He is?," my co-Coker responded after listening awhile. "When?," he asked, and then listened again.

A flurry of activity followed, in blurred speed: his feet came down, the phone got banged down, his and my half-full bottles were dumped in a waste basket, then covered with paper, his tie got straightened, and I was all-but-pushed out the door, with the observation that he was certain I understood.

The stimulus? An unannounced visit was being made by my contact's superior, I learned. Face-to-face interaction between the two was not an everyday thing, and occurred even more rarely on the subordinate's turf.

The superior would arrive in about 90 minutes.

Many analogs of this vignette checker my public-sector experience. What explains such evidences of fear, which are several magnitudes greater in general than in my private-sector experience? Let me try working toward an approximate answer, via eight points that more or less come to a common focus.

First, the strong motivation of many to be at the center-of-things no doubt contributes to the fear of being replaced and thus excluded. Some such notion has been advanced as explaining the special vulnerability of several Watergate feature-players: so young to be so highly-paid and so influential that they could easily persuade self to do marginal things, if not things clearly unacceptable to self.[9] I am also impressed with the importance of being "in" to individuals with no such obvious needs, with how quickly one can get "capital fever" and how long it lasts.

> A senior official, often a government appointee in the past and independently wealthy, was on a committee making significant recommendations about our southeast Asian adventures.
>
> He excused himself on the brink of a vote on a personally-repugnant recommendation. He went to the rest room, vomited, and cried.
>
> When composed, he rejoined his colleagues and voted for the recommendation, not wishing to jeopardize his standing on a committee where he saw himself as a solitary deviant, although he was among the actual majority.
>
> The vote was unanimous in support of the recommendation.

Janis has called the phenomenon "groupthink," and provides several cases of its occurrence at high government levels.[10]

Second, a paranoid quality often characterizes the interface, and fear not only contributes to that paranoia but also seems a reasonable product thereof. This quality often emphasizes that "politics is rough and dirty," and that there are so many different people or groups that can "get at you" from so many directions. Related symptoms appear often, and get very strong recent expression in Nixon's political philosophy. Thus the *Nixon Way* rested on such propositions: "Nobody is a friend of ours. Let's face it;" and "I believe in battle . . . continuing battle . . . That's my way."[11]

Third, "running scared" or a fear-response is not only reasonable in such a perceived-environment, but other purposes also may be served. Thus "running scared" can be a signal to others how much a person wants "it," which may suggest that a person will do enough of whatever is required to get and keep "it." Both features characterize one executive's behavior at the interface:

> A public executive and his immediate staff had offices leading off a large central reception area. The general informal rule was that all doors were to remain open and popping-in was an accepted practice.

> Occasionally, the executive would call in some but not all of his staff, and close his door. That door was visible to all his staff.

> The act was generally interpreted by those excluded as the executive's displeasure about something they had done, or did not do. The excluded never got any direct word, but they punished themselves with zeal. "I sit at my desk," one of the staff told me, "and I stare at that closed door. My guts churn. What's he telling to which of my competitors/colleagues? And why am I on the outside? What did I do? And how to avoid doing it in the future? That eats me up inside."

Fourth, fear often gets reflected in curious ways, as in ponderous caution. For example, consider the notable disinclination of many at the interface to confront a person who is to be dismissed, or should be dismissed. Even such a lusty soul as President Johnson shrank from this task. Better said, perhaps, Johnson was mightily disinclined to fire anyone, either obscure staff or prominent political appointee. Christian provides overall perspective:[12] "Dismissal was exceedingly rare . . . . The usual fate was to be assigned to . . . perform meaningless tasks or none at all . . . . A downtrodden outcast might ultimately resign, receiving a letter of acceptance from the President praising him for patriotic service." In specific cases, Johnson could be put into very deep predicaments by those who would neither resign nor obey his orders. Witness this curious dialog with Willard Wirtz, his Secretary of Labor, which no doubt has few private-sector counterparts:[13]

> "You cannot do what the President said not to do," Johnson said firmly.

> "I will not be able to take action . . . ."

> "Does that mean you resign?"

> "I will not make further comment."

"I want this done or your resignation."

"It will not be forthcoming." . . .

"You can't have a government where the President's orders are not carried out. I want them carried out or your resignation."

"You technically have it, don't you? Don't you have a letter of resignation I submitted when I came into office?"

"I don't know. If so, it is accepted. If not, I hope you will send me one."

"You have the right to remove me."

"I don't want to remove anyone. I just want my orders carried out. There are those who think you have been trying to put yourself in a position to be removed for some time."

Each such case has its own dynamics, but in common they seem to respect guiding rules at the interface. Don't make any enemies that you absolutely don't have to make. Moreover, even if you must risk making an enemy, as by dismissal, adopt the strategy that minimizes your personal risk, no matter what. Send someone else to do the deed, if absolutely necessary. Eisenhower sent Nixon; Nixon sent Haldemann or Erhlichman; Carter sent Jordan, and so on.

Fifth, the fear response often will be one way of showing some kind of responsiveness and, for good or ill, our institutions require substantial responsiveness from public officials. A general fearfulness may serve as a surrogate for such episodic stimulators of responsiveness as elections. In any case, versions of this view of representation are not hard to find. One columnist, for example, recently wrote what probably represents the thoughts of many:[14]

> I don't want Senator Talmadge to feel smug. I don't want him to take us for granted. I want him to sweat a little. I want him to hear footsteps.
>
> . . .
>
> I don't care who runs against Talmadge, but I do want to see him face a serious challenge, and I want him to know we aren't . . . political pushovers.

Sixth, the complex processes of establishing truth-value at the interface can generate fear, if not paranoia. Almost anything can seem to be "true," in sum, where the test of truth-value often is and/or can only be its acceptance by enough suitably-placed people. In an ultimate sense, of course, politics is defined as the art of the possible, and the "possible" gets defined in terms of sufficient acceptance. Hence by definition, politics is the realm of the *variably desired* rather than of the objectively-defined *true* or the *desirable*. So some substantial tension concerning the determination of truth-value is inescapably a part of the turf. Since interests and desires can and will differ profoundly, moreover, motivation aplenty often will exist to exacerbate this base-line tension in significant ways. For example, incautious puffery or just plain deceit can variously herniate political processes that are burdened enough under ideal circumstances. Thus:

- apparently fervent but spurious advocates of a specific desire can be marshalled to demonstrate "support/cause"

   I am reminded of the New York con man who made a good living representing the Fund for the Widow of the Unknown Soldier. More prosaically, many associations have misrepresented the desires of their members; or "associations" lobbying before legislatures have been *ad hoc* shells with few or even no members, albeit with definite interests and desires. Or "marchers" can be hired, at so much per head per day.

- pictures of overblown need can be imaginatively detailed

- estimates of costs can be creatively assembled

- variously-preposterous claims can be advanced

- real or fantasied inter-group competition can be mobilized into fearsome proportions, as in race relations

Generally, exacerbating the base-line tension in politics is disparaged as "just politics."

This subtle sense of how "appropriate truth" can be created, at least for a sufficient even if short time, can be variously illustrated. I recall noting to a local politico that: "Objectively, things looked pretty bad for your side." So much the worse for the facts, he implied. "In politics," he responded, "fear counts for a lot in creating what is true enough for one's purposes."

Organizational politics of both varieties sketched above can be found in both public and business sectors, of course, but the incidence and severity differ profoundly for many reasons. Every organization can more or less distinguish technical and political issues, for example. Public-sector organizations often involve a broader range of issues that can "go political," however; and broader ranges of their hierarchy are likely to perform in such a mode more of the time. Thus many observers cite "profit" as a greater discipliner in business; and so it can be, even though the criterion applies less broadly and specifically than is usually acknowledged. And others will stress that government is specially concerned with the "public interest," and hence should be more open to discussion, debate, protection of minority interests, sensitivity to the disadvantaged, and so on. And that is clearly the case, or should be. But too-definite lines ought not to be drawn in even this case. General Motors, for example, generously impacts on the "public interest."

Seventh, this sense of elastic possibilities concerning truth-value in politics gets powerful motivation from the kind of role-specialization common at the interface. More will be said on the point later, but here consider only the general distinction between "politico" and "expert." The two roles encourage different orientations to truth-value. For various reasons, in addition, in complex organizations it will often happen that different individuals and groups will specialize in one role or the other; and yet it becomes increasingly necessary to integrate the two perspectives as governments get into a burgeoning range of activities—activities having archane technical and scientific ramifications, activities whose consequences often ripple across broad domains, and activities which have to be performed to increasingly-exacting standards of cost, schedule, and sensitivity.[15]

What kinds of factors exacerbate this vital integration? In general, one can safely reply: Many factors will do so, almost all of the time. One observer, indeed, developed the several dysjunctions between "hierarchy" and "specialization" into a general theory of management which provides for a kind of perpetual coming-and-going at major cross-purposes.[16] As for the factors complicating the politico/expert integration, the reader will have to be content here with stark selectivity, which nonetheless establishes the great power of fragmenting forces. For example:

- Such integration implies substantial trust and confidence, which the interface often does not cultivate. Thus politicos have different power- and knowledge-bases, as well as often-shorter tenures, than the permanent bureaucracy in which many of the experts are located.

- For those at the interface, "life consists of watching the smallest details as well as the largest," while being on a fast-paced treadmill, as it were.[17] This can herniate schedules, induce frantic starts and awkward stops, and preclude attention to overall policy implications. This also implies substantial potential for tensions between politicos and the experts, who must gear implementation to this herky-jerky quality of the interface.

- Those with political responsibilities can be so burdened with responsibilities, interpersonal contacts, and frenetic pace as to be at once abjectly dependent on the expert and (perhaps, therefore) over-cautious about the expert. Illustratively, a detailed time-management study of U.S. representatives indicated that in their average 11-hour workdays they had 11 minutes of reading—beyond the 46 minutes daily spent answering mail and signing letters, and the 12 minutes spent in the office preparing legislation and speeches.[18]

- Although the research literature is sparse, the folklore and anecdotal evidence implies major sources of abrasion between politicos and experts. Thus the experts seem inclined toward jaundiced perceptions of the politicos: as uninformed, with short attention-spans, as satisfied with global and often-conflicting mandates that complicate implementation, and so on.[19] Such abrasions no doubt derive from the specialization of functions, and get reinforced by such institutional features as the separation of powers.

Eighth, and finally only for present purposes, the need to avoid inducing envy and jealousy by others can at once feed fear at the interface, and also draw nourishment from fear. Envy and jealousy get little attention in the literature on politics, but they seem important motivators of behavior. Schoeck has noted this neglect, and also attempted to build a general theory of behavior around envy. He sees many social controls and beliefs as based on the strong need to avoid inducing envy, as well as to manage its effects once induced. Schoeck explains:[20]

Envy is a drive which lies at the core of man's life as a social being, and which occurs as soon as two individuals become capable of mutual comparison. This urge to compare oneself invidiously with others can be found in some animals but in man it has acquired a special significance. Man is an envious being who, were it not for the social inhibitions aroused within the object of his envy, would have been incapable of developing the social systems to which we all belong today. If we were not constantly obliged to take account of other men's envy of the extra pleasure that accrues to us as we being to deviate from a social norm, 'social control' could not function.

Does some such effect explain the attraction of log-cabin presidents, the political long-livedness of the frugal Mayor Daley, and the special status of rags-to-riches persona who have not lost "the common touch?"

3. *Implications of Despair and Fear.* These two features of the emotional tone have profound implications for the behavior of intervenors at the interface, most of which will require far more groundwork in this chapter. The following chapter details a score of guidelines for intervenors, building on these implications.

But two related points can be made here. Paramountly, creating a sense of hope often will be the most necessary OD product at the interface. Most OD literature gives the primacy to inducing valid and reliable information, as well as to building processes and norms adequate to sustain the flow of high-quality data. This is all well-and-good, but often does not relate to the primary need at the interface.

Moreover, I certainly do not wish to disparage valid and reliable information, but *the* issues at the interface derive from outcomes common even when high-quality information is both available and shared: actors do not see how they can respond to what they know, *and* still maintain the support of a constituency sufficient to keep them in a valued spot. Or to say somewhat the same thing, the political *zeitgeist* often is so robust that politicos will respond to "it" even as they acknowledge the strangeness of doing so. Consider the case of Muskie's 1972 primary campaign in New Hampshire, which he "lost" even though he "won," because his margin was not "big enough" and he somehow developed a "loser" image while "winning." This was the case even though New Hampshire had perhaps only 100,000 Democratic voters, and Muskie shortly thereafter went on to win the Illinois primary, with 10 or 15 times the number of Democratic voters. One columnist concludes: "You can be perceived as the front-runner and wind up losing, even if you win. If that sounds like double talk, it is. It is also the strange double-think of political races given saturation coverage by the news media."[21]

This second point has two implications, one of which can be made generally clear here while the other will require substantial elaboration in the next chapter.

Implication I: Public-sector intervenors often will need to give as much or more attention to making available information "go down" in politically-acceptable ways as they will devote to generating that information. This often will occur *through the person* of the intervenor—as risk-taker or point-man, as well as through the intervenor as idea-generator or catalyst, e.g., as suggesting or being able to stimulate politically-acceptable ways of acting on available data. Both alternatives imply an active and broad role for the intervenor, that much seems clear even at this early point.

Implication II. Many OD designs are appropriate for inducing valid and reliable data under conditions of conflict or disagreement about information or preferences. This implies their inapplicability in those cases in which agreement exists but cannot be acted on because that jeopardizes valued memberships or risks the loss of support or client groups. Attention will be given below to the "crisis of agreement," which I find common at the interface. A design for such a case differs significantly from "crisis of disagreement."

Guideline 2. *Exacerbating these features of the emotional tone at the interface, and no doubt also contributing mightily to that tone, is a pervasive "multi-leveledness."* Life gets complicated fast, in short, what with everything at the interface at once being potentially-related to everything else, and yet so loosely-coupled with everything else.

Let us get somewhat more specific about what it means to say that the key words in a systemic perspective at the public interface are "multi-level," as well as more specific about what is meant by implying that the OD intervenor should discipline self to act consistently with this characterization. The demands in the public sector are sometimes similar to those in the private sector, again, but the former locus will likely pose unique or at least more intense problems. Four specifics about public-sector multi-leveledness must suffice here. In brief introduction, they describe major sources of multi-leveledness that inhere in: our republican form of government; the theoretic comprehensiveness required of intervenors at the interface; the need to apply broad ranges of OD interventions; and the diverse mixes of politicals and professionals.

1. And Republican Governance. Up-front, much of the multi-leveledness of the public-sector interface inheres in and derives from essential features of our republican form of government. Thus many—including this author—would propose that not only *does* multi-leveledness exist, but that it *should.* Thus OD intervenors not only cannot escape multi-leveledness; from this perspective, they should not even try to do so. Oppositely, indeed, intervenors should embrace multi-leveledness and nourish it.

Perhaps metaphors will help. Most organization students tend to work on hierarchical assumptions, and their metaphors show it: "Levels" of authority get connected by "lines" of authority and responsibility; and "superiors" monitor "subordinates," who aspire to "climb the ladder." This metaphor is troublesome even *within* a single business firm or public agency, because it grievously simplifies and rigidifies an enormously-more complex and dynamic reality. As a guiding metaphor for *the public sector,* the hierarchical metaphor is a far-greater bummer. Better but still inadequately one should think of government as did the late Morton Grodzins—for him, the separation of powers and checks-and-balances characteristic of our federal and state systems approximate a dynamic marble cake of multiple colors, as contrasted with a neat and stable hierarchy. Public-sector authority does not follow "lines," but oozes or darts, and twists or swirls; and responsibility may be hard or impossible to track. This complicates analysis but, as Churchill remarked of democracy, our system often may seem like the worst of all possible systems, except for all the others that have been tried.

To be sure, insight and consolation often do not satisfy. Witness that President Carter, under the stimulus of rising oil prices, switched from an advocate of less and smaller government, to a proponent of a thoroughgoing centralization of unparalleled peacetime power. And so also it was with a more sanguine issue, recreation. Recreation in 1962 was a "chaos of activity" to Morton Grodzins, who also saw it as "no less a chaos of private and public responsibilities."[22] Reformers did in this case what reformers often do. Grodzins described their position in this way:

> There is not neatness in the situation. Responsibilities overlap. Concern and effort are widely shared and appear to be poorly coordinated. It is difficult

even to describe who is accountable for what or to understand where one government's responsibility begins and another's ends . . . the observer is tempted to recommend that the system be made more simple and therefore more rational.

The critics see the "overabundance of concern" by agencies and interest groups and the "fragmentation of responsibility" as complicating "the outdoor recreation problem," and in some part even creating that problem.

Grodzins wisely urges that "neateners" be cautious, in a section engagingly entitled "The Virtues of Chaos." Rather than problems, he sees many advantages in "overabundance of concern" and "fragmentation of responsibility." The latter might not always be appropriate, but neither does it pose inevitable difficulty. Grodzins concludes: "Rather it is the desirable method by which American governments characteristically carry out almost all of their functional tasks."

And why is multi-leveledness, in short, "the desirable method?" Grodzins proposes four anti-neatness arguments:

- He urges that we as a nation "specialize in goals," rather than a single goal in a given field. The overlapping concern of many governments in a single issue-area enriches, then, and does not preclude some goals being established at central levels.

- Power is dispersed when many governments act in a single problem-area, and this preserves a desirable openness in our public institutions. No single standard exists, and no single set of decision-makers will dominate.

- The broad variety of expressed needs can be better responded to by many centers of power; or at least citizens will have multiple opportunities to influence public officials.

- You can never have too much public interest in recreation, so many governments can help in meeting the growing pressure on recreation resources, even if those governments all do more or less the same things.

An OD intervenor's irritations with the public sector, then, may derive from the only practical ways we know for preserving a generally-desirable system. The judgments seldom will be easy to make. Hence OD intervenors must tread warily, lest in their zeal to enhance a system they react only in knee-jerk fashion against some of its existing and desirable features.

2. *And Theoretical Comprehensiveness.* To articulate an obvious point only so that it will not be forgotten, OD intervenors at the interface have special need of a comprehensive theory of organizational reality as well as serviceable guides for their own practice. The interface is the institutional analog of a geologic faultline, the point-of-contact between massive and conflicting forces. Comparatively, the private sector is duck soup, although some narrowing of the difference has occurred recently. The intervenor at the interface must proceed with this awesome fact in mind. Given the nature of the public-sector territory, a theory or model of reality and serviceable guidelines for practice are so much more necessary than in most private-sector work. The intervenor at the public interface thus must deal with a critical deficit: the truth of the matter is that the gaps in available knowledge and experience are great.

This needed theoretical comprehensiveness encompasses two broad components—empirical and normative. The former will not long detain us here. Although many OD interventions downplay theoretic concerns in favor of the spontaneities of consultation, that seems to be their loss and, worse still, also their client's loss. Witness the emphasis of some on the "warm body" of the intervenor—on personal qualities and courage, as contrasted with theoretic knowledge. Personal qualities of sensitivity and courage can be very useful, but intervenors strong in those qualities alone can approximate unguided missiles in a china shop, to deliberately mix two metaphors. Intervenor insensitivity and pusillanimity will be a less dangerous combination. This is no place to detail the applicable theoretical knowledge and only the general case will be illustrated here. Sebring notes about one intervention that apparently succeeded, but in a way that troubled him. He emphasized intervenor's "failure to apply knowledge already developed in the behavioral science literature . . . ." More specifically, he notes:[23]

> [For example,] phase progression models of group development and developmental stage sequences in OD have been adequately described in the applied behavioral science literature and could have been applied in this case . . . [This way,] the authors could have predicted the shift in the nature of the client contract and planned for it in their intervention design.

The OD intervenor at the interface also is well-advised to brush-up on political theory—that is, on the appreciation of the values associated with governance which are not unique to the public-sector interface but which tend to appear there in particularly visible and impactful form. This is virtually terra incognita. Hence the preceding two chapters of this book devoted special attention to that theme.

3. And Range of Interventions. In addition to uneven concern about behavioral and especially political theory, most intervenors specialize in either interpersonal *or* rational/technical models. This bias need not be troublesome at many levels of organization; indeed, it often will simplify the consulting contract. The politics/administration interface seldom permits that kind of specialization, however, and failure to be sensitive to multi-level issues can have serious consequences. Reddin describes one case of his own myopia, which is probably widespread, although the locus of his experience is a private-sector interface.[24]

> I was once asked to plan a change program for a Montreal production subsidiary of a U.S. firm. Four of the subsidiary's general managers had been fired in six years for failure to show a profit. The trust level was low, and most managers had moved to a very low level of risk taking. After I had started to unfreeze, team build, develop candor, etc., an independent study by the parent company uncovered major errors in the transfer-price system within the subsidiary and from the subsidiary to the parent company. When changes in these prices were introduced, profits started to appear, and the current general manager stayed with the company for eight years. The company had really needed a cost accountant rather than a change agent.

Reddin illustrates better than he prescribed, in this case. The choice should not have been: change-agent or accountant? The situation called for a change-agent whose diagnosis took the system's reward-and-punishment practices into account.

This lesson applies in spades at the interface, and heightens the urgency of always-significant diagnosis. Hurtful and even bizarre behavior often makes sense as a reasonable adjustment to an eccentric reality, in sum. And it does no necessary good to seek to exorcise the hurtful/bizarre responses while the inducing reality remains unchanged. Paradoxically, in fact, a successful spotlighting of demons and bad vapors in interaction can be counterproductive. Consider one case:

> A certain public agency had great problems in effective interaction: trust was low, risk was high, and employees were (in their words) "constipated." Liberal

doses of "cousin T-groups" were applied in-house, with variable results which nonetheless tended to be seen as very punishing by most participants.

The likely cause? Openness was dangerous in this organization, which yearly removed the "bottom 10 per cent" of certain classes of employees based on appraisals, come rain or shine. A closed, low-profile adaptation was reasonable, given that a single supervisor could jeopardize or cut-short even a good career. Thus employees sought to avoid mistakes, did not "make waves," and so on.

The T-grouping, in effect, encouraged agency members in directions that native cunning reasonably proscribed because of constraints that most everyone believed "would take an act of God to change."

Moreover, the T-Grouping unfroze the wrong target-group, and may have hurt some of its members.

In sum, OD designs at the public-sector interface can easily become symptom-alleviating efforts, or worse, if they overlook the common overarching significance of structural and procedural interventions in the public sector. Let me state the implied underlying propositions:

• At levels both high *and* low, public-sector difficulties often will be caused or significantly mediated by broad structures or policies imposed by distal authorities, as in civil service regulations about pay or in legislative prescriptions that mandate a specific organization structure

• Private-sector difficulties toward the top of a hierarchy typically will have strong interaction components; structural and policy constraints will be most impactful at middle and especially lower levels

The implied conclusion? OD interventions should be specifically targeted and, in the public sector, this places a premium on designs oriented toward structures and policies. Interaction-oriented designs often will be only ameliorative there. Even though Band-Aid interventions often have their place, they must be carefully-bounded so as to leave no doubt about what is invariant and what might possibly change. Participants may only be encouraged to "open up" by interaction-centered designs, the likely later reaction to which may be to have their chains yanked, firmly and decisively. The probable consequence is one to be avoided, especially in the public sector: another confirmation that "nothing can be done," with a subsequent deepening of despair and, possibly, of fear.

The reader no doubt will recognize the often-posed dilemma. Given that "opening up" the interaction in a system can be dangerous if awkward structures and policies remain, to express the point, how can those structures/policies ever be changed unless many people can come to express themselves, and forcefully?

The dilemma admits of no easy resolution, and the public sector stands unparalleled in inducing such dilemmas. The public sector contains many cases of poor OD matches of technical/legal systems and preferred ways of inter/acting; and its technical systems are more difficult or impossible to change because they often apply government-wide, emanate from a legislature with other-than-management agendas, or both. Hence opportunities to intervene must be carefully assessed, and alternative modes of intervening must be weighed.

Moreover, even if the choice is to begin with interaction-centered designs, some weighty requirements must be simultaneously met. Basically, intervenors need good maps to determine whether any of the symptoms highlighted by interaction-centered designs can be traced to, or are aggravated by, procedural or structural features. Reasonable interventions must rest on solid diagnosis, in short, rooted in an increasingly-comprehensive theory of what-is-related-to-what, not only in terms of interaction but also (and perhaps, especially) in terms of procedure and structure. This does not disparage the topical relief of symptoms. Rather, it urges clear recognition of the possibility that topical relief can heighten problems and deepen despair, especially under conditions that commonly characterize the public sector.

4. And Encompassing Politicals and Professionals. OD interventions also must be multi-level in another ubiquitous and significant sense. Taking the systemic view typically means that the OD intervenor finds self working betwixt and between the *professionals* and the *politicals*—the *pros* and the *pols*. I italicize because by "professionals" I do not simply mean engineers, chemists, behavioral scientists, and the like; nor by "politicals" do I refer only to elected officials. Rather, I seek to focus on two generalized roles and—better still—I focus on two ways of thinking and relating. Following Mosher:[25]

- the "professional" role emphasizes "specialized knowledge, science, and rationality"

- the "political" role, in contrast, "focuses on negotiation, elections, votes, compromise"

Complex projects require both roles, often played by the same persons in a bewildering succession of switches. From time to time, an engineer might play a political role; and an elected official also might play a professional role. One of the major confounding characteristics of the public interface, in fact, is that the same individual often has to wear both hats, in lightning-like sequence or even simultaneously. That may understate the case, in fact. For example, the young head of a major public project summarized this basic transition in his first two years as CEO: "I came into the job recognizing that politics would be part of my new way of life, but believing that technical decisions would suffice in most cases. My new view? There is nothing in the whole project that isn't political, hasn't been, or might not be. The sooner you learn this, and can adapt to it without giving away the store, the better off you are."

The role specialization of politicals and professionals at the politics/administration interface is reinforced by many practices and traditions in this country, such as federal checks-and-balances, which can raise the tension between the two orientations which will appear in all organizations. Indeed, the interface may be defined as that uneven seam between politicals and professionals. Popularly-elected legislators seldom have administrative roles, for example, except in some commission forms of government; and constitutional and institutional provisions generally separate legislative and executive/administrative branches, each with different constituencies.

This multiply-reinforced specialization exacerbates the "built-in aversion between the professional and politics,"[26] an aversion that derives from the basic way each tends to test for truth-value. One seeks truth in stable technology or rational decision-making, and the other in volatile constituency-building. And professionals typically feel superior to the politicals, who often are viewed as a kind of articulate prostitute. In turn, the politicals often will be openly-scornful of the impracticality of the "big-domed people." Governor George Wallace caught the fulsome flavor of the point when he stressed the trained incapacity of one large professional group: "They can't," he noted, "park a bicycle straight." The twain may never meet, but the ideal case will be characterized by a mutual humility. Professionals will recognize that technology cannot make value-choices—that only humans can, and often only by utilizing processes that may be broadly characterized as "political." Politicals will recognize that no amount of negotiation or exchange can change some realities or quasi-realities. And both will seek to define with appropriate precision in diverse issue-areas what is "political" from what is intractable to its processes.

Of course, politicals also exist in the private sector, but with major differences. Primarily, private-sector politicals more often also have long-run operating responsibilities, which impose a powerful discipline. Moreover, private-sector politicals exist in nothing like the profusion nor with the multiplicity of independent power-bases characteristic of the public sector. And private-sector analogs of political institutions—such as the board of directors—tend to be weak replicas of popularly-elected legislatures, despite contemporary efforts to politicize those institutions, as by stockholder protests and by growing proportions of "outside directors."

Guideline 3. *Until explicitly proven otherwise, the intervenor should assume that a public agency is loosely-bounded or under-bounded, as contrasted with tightly-bounded or over-bounded.* The two types of systems can be generally distinguished, as in Exhibit 5.

Two points inhere in this emphasis on the boundedness of systems. Again, prior diagnosis gets definite primacy; and that diagnosis in an under-bounded system might well indicate a design-of-choice other than the usual interaction-centered design. An over-bounded system may respond well to interaction-centered designs, for example, since these can "free-up" individuals who had been constrained and repressed. The same prescription could be disingenuous in under-bounded systems, however, and might even be seriously counterproductive. Under-bounded systems might well profit from structural interventions to stiffen their "looseness." This might require complex changes in authority relationships and in work; or it can build on such simple notions as developing a matrix of who contributes what and when to which activities. This first-step can generate insight about why some things fall between the cracks and, hopefully, develop some ameliorative agreements that reduce this probability.

Role negotiation designs, for example, could well contribute to the latter end;[27] and basic structural revision might serve the former case.[28] Or if the system contains little of the attitudes/skills required

EXHIBIT 5. Features of Over-bounded and Under-bounded Systems

System Characteristics	Overbounded	Underbounded
Authority relations	Well-defined hierarchy and decision-making	Unclear authority sources, overlapping authority
Role definition	Overly specified and constraining roles; strict "job definition"	Uncertainty about limits of priorities or roles
Management of human energy	Difficult to release energy; dammed-up and blocked resources	Difficult to harness energy, physical and emotional dispersion
Communication	Easy to convene groups; problems with distortion and invalid information	Difficult to promote communication; absence of communication
Affect	Egocentric; ethnocentric; suppression of (strong) emotions	Negative internal and external emotions
Economic conditions	Stable and wealthy economic conditions	Uncertainty about sources of funding; "tight" money
Time frame	Relative long-term security; loss of responsiveness to change	Survival-oriented, crisis-oriented mentality

SOURCE: From Clayton P. Alderfer and David N. Berg, "Organization Development: The Profession and the Practitioner," p. 104, in Philip H. Mirvis and David N. Berg (eds.), *Failures in Organization Development and Change: Cases and Essays for Learning* (New York: John Wiley & Son, 1977).

by interaction-centered designs, intervenor might well start off with such gentler but often-impactful designs as flexible workhours[29] to develop confidence in the participative systems which are the goal of interaction-centered designs. Urging apt diagnosis and appropriate prescription are easier said than done, of course. But some things can never be repeated too often, so that no one will forget they are true, even if difficult.

Many intervenors have neglected the present points, with consequences that have sometimes been benign but which trend toward the dark or even the dismal. Generally, mindless applications of interaction-centered designs are the culprit—they with their generally-commendable goals of freeing-up people, opening people to new experience, and so on. In under-bounded systems, however, this "remedy" may simply compound the "disease."

Consider an overanxious new head of an agency that had a history of laissez-faire management. The new head wanted to change that, as well as to deal with other elements shaking the fragile agency.

The head was a young and attractive female who was unsure of her role, and acutely aware that she was the "new wave." She came into a previously all-male cluster of subordinates, older and on the stodgy side, and threatened by several recent appointments, including that of the new head. Several "mod squad" appointments had been made in the agency, with definite tensions resulting from contrasts of new vs. old—in language, clothes, work norms, etc.

The overkill intervention? Three week-ends of "encounter."

The results? Much non-work material was finally revealed, after great effort, that would have tested a more appropriately-bounded group. Both work and non-work suffered and intense cross-pressures developed around the theme: to meet the demands of work, peaking at the time, or to provide emotional support for several individuals?

I can do no better on this than our yard-man. He was always interested in what I did, and he caught me one mellow autumnal evening with my concerns showing. "Tough day, it appears," he noted. "Sure was," I said, quickly sketching a couple of days spent in undoing the intervention just detailed, and uncomfortable about some jargon I could not suppress: "role negotiation," "contacting," and probably more.

After several minutes, I stopped, convinced that I had said too much and too little. But the old man's eyes twinkled; he knew. "Some days you opens 'em up," his words fairly glistened in their clarity. "And then some days you zips 'em closed."

Enough said.

Guideline 4. *The public-sector interface is best conceived as a variously congruent set of multiple sub-systems or domains.* These several domains contribute very substantially to the multi-leveledness of the public sector and its general under- vs. over-boundedness; and these domains also constitute formidable obstacles that theory needs to encompass in order to permit effective diagnosis, prescription, and prognosis. This variable congruency of multiple domains also exacerbates the emotional tone at the interface—often "stuckness" reinforced by fear.

All organizations can be conceived in terms of a congruence of multiple domains or sub-systems but, again, the public sector tends to provide the most common, pervasive, and exotic examples of the general phenomena.

Some content can be provided for this notion, even as openness requires acknowledging that the last word on this topic will be a very long time in coming. Provisionally, then, this sketch will proceed at three levels. Attention will begin with a generic approach to multiple overlays; the focus will then be specifically targeted to the public sector; and finally some attention will be given to major implications for OD intervention in the public sector.

1. *Generic Overlays in All Organizations*. All organizations can be conceived as a congeries of variously-congruent overlays that must be integrated to get the necessary work done. For example, Pfiffner and Sherwood believe it necessary to distinguish at least five overlays of the traditional pyramidal structure of work:[30]

- the sociometric network, or who associates with whom

- the system of functional contacts, especially in contacts with and between specialists or in horizontal contacts with peers

- the centers of decision-making which may or may not coincide with the formal structure of work, due to accident, to the uniqueness of the decision, its issue area, or its arena, to special skills or interests of some actors in an organization, etc.

- the network of influence or power, which obviously will influence decision-making and which will derive at least in part from considerations other than formal status

- channels of communication that follow the "informal organization" which exists in all formal structures

As Golembiewski[31] and others have demonstrated, these generic distinctions support three powerful implications. First, all organizations can be characterized in terms of the variable congruence of such basic overlays with the formal structure of work. Second, various degrees of congruence will have quite specific consequences on significant outcomes—productivity, satisfaction, conflict, and so on. Third, to a substantial degree, control over the degree of congruence is possible via direct manipulation of policies and structures, as well as by the induction of appropriate attitudes and behaviors.

2. *Incongruencies More Specific to Public-Sector Organizations.* In the public sector, the congruence of domains or sub-systems demands another level of analysis in addition to the kind sketched above. For example, Weisbord argues that much of OD rests on an industrial model, where reality is less complex. At least in degree and perhaps in kind, Weisbord proposes, OD in medical centers must cope with the fragmenting tendencies of three basic sub-systems:[32]

- the task system, which is characterized by

  — abstract goals

  — diffuse authority

  — low interdependence between tasks

  — few valid and reliable measures of performance

- the governance system, which sets standards for performance

- the identity system, which undergirds the professional statuses of actors in the system and which (as in the case of doctors) results in difficulties in peer control and resistance to control by others

Conceptually, the degree of complexity can be suggested by a simple matrix. *Each* of the three systems involves its own set of the overlays described above, in this general form:

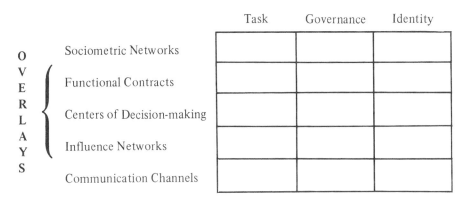

Systems

		Task	Governance	Identity
O V E R L A Y S	Sociometric Networks			
	Functional Contracts			
	Centers of Decision-making			
	Influence Networks			
	Communication Channels			

In contrast, Weisbord sees OD as having been built on an industrial model, which essentially requires dealing with only a uni-system, Task/Management, whose substantial congruence rests on:[33]

- concrete goals

- formal authority that is quite specific and focused

- high interdependence between tasks

- valid and reliable measures of performance

The several overlays above do induce some fragmenting tendencies within this Task/Management uni-system, but at lesser orders of magnitude than in the case of the public-sector matrix sketched above.

In sum, in Weisbord's concept, public-sector OD has to face a greater challenge: it has to integrate multiple sub-systems, which have very strong tendencies to go their separate ways. Weisbord's six-box model well-illustrates the point. Any OD intervenor, Weisbord advises, would do well to focus his diagnosis on the targets indicated in Figure 5. In the public sector, Weisbord argues, major slippages within and between the several boxes often exist, typically because of the cacaphonous array of "environmental impacts" on public systems. Thus public purposes are likely to be unclear and/or conflicting, since they often seek to please an enormous range of constituencies of legislative or judicial bodies whose interests are non-managerial or even anti-managerial. In any case, public sector rewards are not likely to support the needed activities. As an aberration inspired by the desire for "fairness" in the public sector, for example, equal pay for unequal contributions is likely to characterize wage and salary schedules. And so on and on, in general but not complete contrast to private-sector experience.

Converging evidence implies that Weisbord has a useful hold on significant aspects of public-sector reality. For example, Kouzens and Mico come to quite similar conclusions in contrasting Human Service Organizations (HSOs) with business/industry.[34] In general, as in Exhibit 6, they see major contrasts between the two broadly-defined classes of organizations. More specifically, Kouzens and Mico conceive of HSOs as involving the complex integration of the three separate

FIGURE 5. A Model of Management

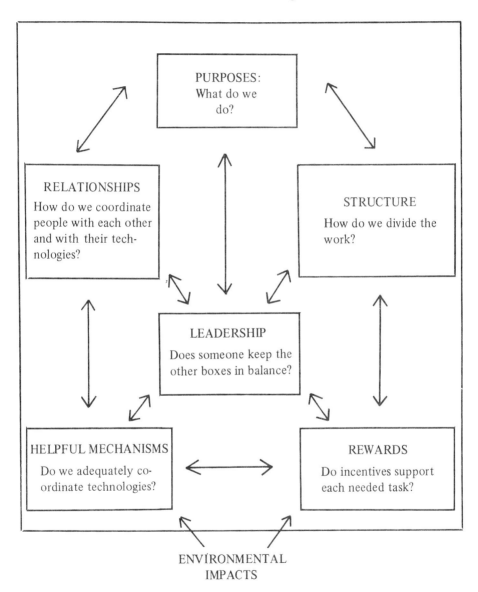

ENVÍRONMENTAL
IMPACTS

Adapted from: Marvin Weisbord, "Organizational Diagnosis: Six Places to Look for Trouble With or Without a Theory," *Group and Organization Studies*, Vol. 1 (December, 1976), p. 430.

EXHIBIT 6. Different Attributes of Human Service Organizations and Business/Industry

Dimension	Human Service Organizations	Business/Industrial Organizations
Primary motive	Service	Profit
Primary beneficiaries	Clients	Owners
Primary resource base	Public taxes	Private capital
Goals	Relatively ambiguous and problematic	Relatively clear and explicit
Psychosocial orientation of work force	Professional	Instrumental
Transformation processes	Staff-client interactions	Employee-product interactions
Connectedness of events and units	Loosely coupled	Tightly coupled
Means-ends relation	Relatively indeterminant	Relatively determinant
Outputs	Relatively unclear and intangible	Relatively visible and tangible
Measures of performance	Qualitative	Quantitative
Primary environmental	The political and professional communities	The industry and suppliers

Note: This chart was developed by the authors, but incorporates the thinking of [others]. Not all of these contrasts apply to all HSOs and industrial organizations. This table is meant to be illustrative, not definitive.

From James M. Kouzes and Paul R. Mico, "Domain Theory," *Journal of Applied Behavioral Science,* Vol. 15 (December, 1979), p. 454.

domains described in Figure 6, each of which has its distinctive features, clienteles, modes of operation, and so on.

In sum, Kouzens and Mico come to a conclusion identical to that of Weisbord. Public-sector OD efforts will tend to operate in multiple domains, and thus often are more subtle and complex than OD in business/industry.

3. *Implications for Public-Sector OD Interventions.* The elemental distinctions above have several prominent implications for OD intervenors, especially at the interface. First, the differences imply greater theoretical sophistication is required there. That is, if OD designs/experience rest basically on an "industrial model," public-sector applications have to be very sensitive to differences between hosts so that public organizations that approximate the

FIGURE 6. The Three Domains Encompassed by Human Service Organizations

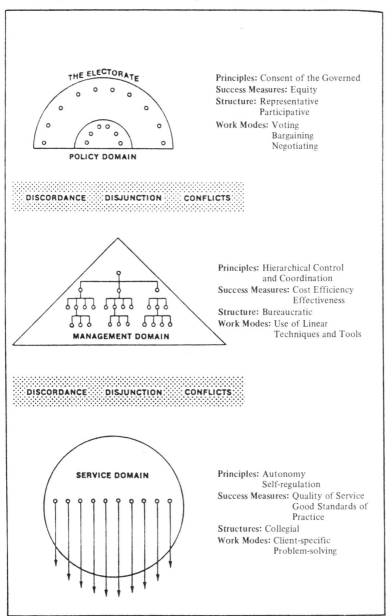

From James M. Kouzes and Paul M. Mico, "Domain Theory," *Journal of Applied Behavioral Science*, Vol. 15 (December, 1979), p. 458.

ideational base of current OD can be segregated from those which do not.

Second, the point above has short-run salience only. That is to say, all OD in the long-run should rest on a sophisticated taxonomy of groups and organizations, to whose diverse properties specific OD designs will apply quite well, poorly, or not at all. Developing evidence implies this basic conclusion,[35] but only early steps have been taken toward fitting specific OD designs to hosts of a particular class.[36] Hence vigilance about government/business differences is appropriate in the short-run, absent a taxonomy of types of organizations wherever they are found.

Third, the multiple domains or sub-systems of the public-sector make the intervenor's job a very difficult one. This applies both to action-skills, as well as to conceptual and theoretical sophistication. The intervenor's theoretical competence must encompass the behavioral sciences as well as the political theory on which our republican system rests. For example, the OD intervenor there must accommodate (in the terms of Kouzes and Mico) to the Policy domain as well as to the Management and Service domains. Such demands imply the common need for suitably-staffed OD teams. In any case, those demands pose major challenges for effective intervenor behavior, several guidelines for which get detailed in the next chapter.

Fourth, at a minimum, intervenors require the theoretical and practical skills to *confront and deal with the tensions* deriving from the multi-dimensionality of the public sector. The special trick here is to avoid the frustration of dealing only with symptoms even as the symptom-inducing forces often remain out-of-reach.

Fifth, public-sector intervenors often face ethical or moral choices resulting from this emphasis on symptomatic relief only. Essentially, should the intervenor opt not to "cool-out" participants? Rather, should one wait until the trauma is sufficiently great so as to force revolutionary change in symptom-inducing forces and institutions?[37] This provides an alternative to those who feel themselves only dupes to those in power, of course. But the choice always will be a hard one, and fraught with peril either way.

Sixth, convincing evidence implies that interaction-centered approaches are especially seductive in the public sector. The symptom-inducing forces there often derive from policies/procedures/structures imposed by distal authority figures. Improving interaction, in short, is more likely to be a contraceptive experience in the public sector, even a counter-productive one—unless changes in interaction affect distal authority figures, or unless managers have ample discretion and wriggle-room, both of which may be less probable in the public sector.

This implies that OD intervenors in the public sector, and especially at the interface, need more than interaction-only attitudes/skills. The good news is that major progress has been made in the last ten years or so in developing interventions that approach OD values via changes in structure and in policies/procedures;[38] and more progress can be expected.

Guideline 5. *The definition of "organization success" is very complex and unstable in the public sector, especially in two senses: the weighting of its numerous components may be highly volatile over time; and its more stable and heavily-weighted components often have little or nothing to do with effectiveness or efficiency, as conventionally understood. But such a definition often exists; and the intervenor is well-advised to learn about its component features, and especially about the changes in its features and their relative weightings over time.*

The overall sense of this guideline may seem unnerving for the OD intervenor. Thus it suggests the unavailability of a reliable compass by which to steer. Or perhaps better said, the guideline alludes to a compass that not only can simultaneously indicate several directions for the organization's course, but its directions also can be highly changeable and even mutually contradictory.

This phenomenon is neither news nor restricted to the public sector, of course. Especially during periods of turbulence, all organizations may be thought of as having "compass problems." And the intervenor is always well-advised to pay closer attention to OD values than to changeable organizational definitions of "success." In any case, the difficulties tend to be less extreme in the private sector for multiple reasons. Thus scale and multiple constituencies in the public sector certainly pose problems of different degree than in other organizations. Consider an Agriculture Department trying to move farmers off marginal land, or off small-scale operations, while the Rural Electrification minions were assiduously doing things to make farm life more attractive with the effect of discouraging the movement so ardently desired by other feds. Moreover, many businesses have a higher degree of control over what constituencies they will serve, and under which conditions.

1. *Amplifying on Public-Sector "Organization Success."* Establishing that this guideline is not a non-guideline will take some doing, with a modest first step being some greater definitional clarity. Most would agree a meaningful approach to "organization success" should provide for input/output comparisons—which include quantitative and qualitative costs of various levels of goods/services, some sense of the satisfaction of organization members or long-run morale, and some view of what service clients prefer and how much. Moreover, a useful approach would allow the tolerable prediction of likely sets of events under alternative decision-formats so that alternative "opportunity costs" could be compared. In the simplest cases, for example, the economic and other costs/benefits of various mixes of production would be calculable.

All in all, then, estimates of organization success will be critical in choice processes, but major difficulties complicate such estimates, in all organizations. For example, much has been written about the opportunities for such calculations and the enhanced managerial control they permit in the private sector, with a marketplace and "profit" or "loss." The reliance on "profit" is most meaningful at or toward the top of most organizations, however—that overwhelming majority organized in a centralized mode relating functionally-specialized departments. And typical "profit" calculations take into account only a narrow range of considerations—economic ones at that. Until recently, that is, "profit" calculations usually were made without considering the costs borne by the environment (as in pollution, hit-and-run mining or timber-cutting, and so on) or those costs borne by organization members (as in boredom, alienation, poor quality of working-life, and so on). So the adequacy of usual calculations of "profit" can be overstated easily. But the concept does provide some sense of a desirable and collective goal; it permits some measure of performance; and it does encourage some degree of self-control.

In the public sector, observers usually conclude, the problems of estimating "success" are more extreme if not absolutely intractable. If it desired to be contentious, this chapter might argue this is true only in superficial senses. More moderately, the point here definitely is not that "organization success" in the public sector is beyond estimate, as some have argued. Indeed, at any point in time, substantial consensus often will exist about many components of such success, and even about the weighting of its elements. For example, in post-Proposition 13 days, some aspects of "smaller and simpler are better" have begun to be dealt with, and here OD can be useful.[39] Not very long before, burgeoning growth and escalating complexity were *the* concerns, and OD's early development was buoyed by those concerns.[40]

To put the present position in a positive way, then, it has two central features: that many of the components of public-sector success can be highly variable over time, variable as to both number and weighting; and that the stable components often relate only or mostly to very broad considerations as to what is seen to be necessary/appropriate to preserve or enhance the perceived legitimacy of the regime. The basic challenge in the public-sector, remember, is on keeping the polity sufficiently together, to put it in crude terms, rather than on producing specific goods and services. The underlying criterion of "effectiveness" is a very broad one; and considerations of "efficiency" remain distinctly secondary. Consider the role of "spoils patronage." History shows it to have been wildly inefficient, but major claims can be made for its fundamental effectiveness at certain stages in the development of viable and relatively popular regimes in Great Britain and the United States, as through the nurturing of political parties which in turn have been significant in our representative political system.[41]

More broadly, the task of political statesmanship in representative systems focuses on the creation of a rolling readjustment, as it were—to preserve the essential consensus underlying any non-authoritarian regime, while moving toward systemic effectiveness *and* efficient use of material and human factors of production. Of course, there will be periods—of brief and sporadic reform movements, for example, or popular wars or causes—when public-sector "success" seems to take on substantial clarity and stability. But even such a definition will be narrow, will likely have no relation to efficiency as normally viewed, and it typically will be "politics as usual" before very long. That few regimes do well over any length of time in this rolling readjustment seems patent, as is evidenced by the fact that authoritarian regimes are the norm to which few lasting exceptions exist. Two temptations seem universal. Thus regimes can so narrowly define those who determine systemic effectiveness that regimes either tumble—as in the case of most aristocracies—or that regimes come to apply massive repression in seeking to keep the have-nots in check. Alternatively, regimes can profligately and suddenly expand expectations about who gets how much of what. Then prevailing supply/demand relationships usually get seriously out-of-phase, ballooning inflation may set in, and so on. In the latter case, of course, repression is often taken as the only apparent alternative to systemic disintegration.

So this chapter has a determinedly schizoid orientation to "organization success" in the public sector. In the broadest sense, humility seems appropriate for the OD intervenor estimating such success, in two senses. The basic judgment always will be political, not technical; and the intervenor must comprehend that that's the way it should be, except in deep extremis. At other times, many indicators of "success" will be firmly clear to most relevant actors. And here the intervenor must be bold, in three senses. Where these indicators are compatible with OD objectives, it can be full-speed-ahead even though organization members may have to be encouraged toward a fuller appreciation of which specific attitudes and behavioral skills have useful effects on systems. Where the degree of incompatibility is not great, or where the trauma-to-be-avoided is so great as to create special leverage for the OD intervenor, the intervenor might well launch an aggressive educational campaign among relevant actors concerning approaches consistent with OD values. Finally, where the incompatibility between indicators of "success" and OD values seems substantial, the intervenor must make a quick judgment call about the probability that the system can be influenced in desirable ways. No general injunctions apply here, since the relevant cases can cover an enormous range—from Albert Speer's use of advanced techniques to increase munitions production in Nazi Germany,[42] to such more mundane if still-troublesome cases as those in which a manager seems to want to use team-building to punish a subordinate in a roundabout way.

2. *Implications for Intervening.* What guidance do these considerations provide for practice? The following chapter will go into some detail concerning specific attitudes and behaviors that serve the intervenor at the interface.

Let us take a general approach here. The discussion above implies a kind of gestalt, or mind-set, which must blend forces-in-tension: heated activity with possibly-long periods of dormancy; boldness and then caution, as in a focus on specific efforts but with the flexibility to move across a broad range of issues with dispatch; and a commitment to goals that remains quite constant while their programmatic expressions can vary widely and can be halted at various stages of completion. The total sense of it is a kind of easy-rider orientation to constant goals while rocking-and-rolling to the inevitable quick-silveredness of definitions of "organizational success."

These general notions can be illustrated, but they hardly constitute firm decision-rules. Perhaps there is no one situation in which the intervenor can be more of a pain-in-the-lower-back, to illustrate, than in technically hounding a political issue. Moreover, despite the fact that it can be harsh medicine to take, the intervenor can in general take no sillier risk than to seek to make the political calls. Not only is that a role in which intervenor lacks expertise and legitimacy. But my experience is definitely that the political style at the interface tends to a dominant character—that is, it is non-confrontive, encourages people to talk themselves out, modulates even extreme messages from central figures, who tend to send unfavorable messages subtly and often via third-parties.[43] I expect this tendency has practical roots—in trying to avoid making an enemy, or not making more of an enemy than is absolutely necessary. And it may even imply that many politicals often will be more comfortable dealing with situations that permit arraying forces/masses against one another than in directly confronting (let us say) a Bella Abzug, a Sherman Adams, an Ehrlichman, a Haldeman, or a Midge Constanza. Hence the hounding intervenor will very likely only heighten the very behaviors and attitudes that OD values and philosophy proscribe. Consider:

> The issue concerns how certain groups should be composed. The CEO solicits the opinion of two intervenors. Both agree, generally, that groups composed of individuals of different status would be better for the learning purposes in question. "I can't risk that," says a CEO and notes he can't explain.

> One intervenor responds: "You call this shot different than we would. That's OK, as long as you understand we will lose something by homogeneous assignments. I prefer not to risk the loss of learning, but I can't judge your risk. I'm willing to go along with your judgment this time."

> The second intervenor persists in arguing from a technical perspective, and a face-saving compromise is finally reached that will have the CEO review three different rosters—two for heterogeneous groupings, and one for homogeneous grouping.

> After that is decided, intervenor #1 privately asks whether the lengthy decision was worthwhile. "I'll look at the three rosters," CEO observes, "but not much. I know how it will go—and you know where he can go."

> "He was a fool to agree to two heterogeneous groupings," CEO adds. "If you two do a reasonable job of setting them up, it'll split the vote; and it'll be easy for me to select the homogeneous grouping. If you do a lousy job, no doubt I'll be able to attack your professional competence."

Hence I prescribe fishing or cutting bait, as they say, as long as the trade-offs seem tolerable.

But such stories do not help much when it comes to the real crunches. For example, the most obvious implication for the intervenor—to accept a political and limited definition of success, and not fuss about the lack of technical and comprehensive definitions—also carries much potential for mischief. For example, the intervenor who lacks native cunning might thereby become a tool for purposes he neither divines nor accepts, becoming the rightly-feared technocrat. [44] Hence caution is the watchword, especially since a "system need" will not always be signally distinguished from a merely-convenient cooling-out of actors who—in the long-run view—should have been left to further heat up, and then explode. For the second time, consider an intervention for an unlikely combination—local police, Black Panthers, and a White Citizens' Council.

> The design had few of the usual desired objectives or effects: the three groups were not somehow brought closer together, did not empathize more with each other, did not develop collaborative norms, etc.

> However, the design was right-on for the limited political purpose in question: to have the parties mutually convince one another of their preparedness and resolution to wage urban war, to more accurately estimate the costs/benefits to each of such an outcome, and to discuss the conditions that would or could lead to that consequence. The hope was that each of the three groups would see the value of even a very-temporary forum to check-out ambiguities, at least until the crisis passed.

In addition to the severe ethical issues implied—which I convinced myself were overweighted by useful pay-offs—such cases have a quality that can also bedevil intervenors who reasonably value benchmarks for "success." A troubling realization/frustration suffused the whole experience: "success" would be defined in terms of something dreadful *not* happening and, of course, many factors other than the intervention can explain a non-event. So "great success" could be interpreted as "unrealistic fear", and the intervenor was in a no-win situation.

As the example above implies, intervenor will sometimes have to make the best estimate of probable effects, and then let 'er rip. For an intervenor cannot simply trust the political figures, suspending or finessing personal judgment in all cases.

Consider a critical situation in a long-standing consultative relation. The CEO must appoint a crucial task-force, but the person with by far the most-relevant technical skills for heading the unit presents a problem for the CEO. CEO has had a long-standing difficulty with the man—not trusting him; coming to the brink of removing him several times but being inhibited each time by circumstances or by another triumph of X's; and (quite possibly) seeing him as a competitor for the CEO's job.

The intervenor is aware of this history, and has linkages with both men. He outlines his position for the CEO first. "X should have the job, for obvious technical reasons. Moreover, politically, it also makes sense. Whatever happens, X will assume control when the task-force does its work. Not only that, but think of the possibilities if X is on the sidelines. He can simply reject the task-force's work, and that will put you [CEO] over a barrel. As head of the task-force, X can't do that. He also will be motivated to do a great job.

"And you, as CEO, can bask in whatever glory success brings X, if he succeeds, implying that you again have shown why you are CEO.

"And if X fails, you have got him where you always wanted him."

CEO supports with faint heart. "X is too smart to accept it, but you can test him out, if you really want to."

The intervenor contacts X, who is of a different mind. "As much as it exposes me," he notes in responding to the *same rationale* detailed above. "I have to take that task-force job, if it is offered. I can't risk anyone screwing it up, to make troubles for me later. And I really want the project to fly."

With light heart, intervenor returns to CEO.

CEO admits serious reservations, over a period of several weeks.

Intervenor and CEO meet for perhaps the tenth time on what will be done. "I just can't do it," CEO concludes.

"OK," says the intervenor. "I'm not again going to push you on why. This decision comes from your socks, and you haven't been able to convince me why you can't act.

"One thing *is* certain: this is the highest-priority item in our long relationship. If you don't give X the job, I don't have any confidence that I can ever impact meaningfully on you. And you would be a damn fool to trust me in the future, for we are on very different wave-lengths."

The CEO shook the intervenor's hand. "If that's how you need it to be," he said, "so be it."

From what sources did this impasse develop? I have long pondered the question, alone and with the CEO on occasion. We conclude we both did what we had to do, neither completely understanding why. In essence, our two orientations diverged radically. For me, the situation was straightforward; but not so for the CEO, perhaps because he saw more or different "politicized" issues than I did.

Guideline 6. *All organizational decisions rest on personal, technical, and political considerations, in diverse blends.* Some useful central tendencies in these blends can be distinguished, however, with significant implications for the intervenor. Note that, for present purposes only, "personal" here includes at least three realms: individual likes and preferences; ethical concerns, such as those reflected in OD values which get reinforcement from professional training and identifications; and moral standards which some derive from philosophic orientations to life (e.g., existentialism) and others see as emanating from a transcendental moral order.

These central tendencies can be simplified. In the private sector, the personal often comingles with the technical, but "the political" typically will be relatively distinct and stable. In the public sector, especially at the interface, not only will political considerations dominate, but almost any feature is politicized, has been politicized, or can quickly come to be politicized. Definitions of "the political" often will be volatile, but they need not be amorphous.

The core issue may be expressed simplistically in terms of three type-statements:

Type I: "My personal values and make-up incline me to . . ."

Type II: "Applicable technical or logical considerations require that . . ."

Type III: "In order to maintain a workable coalition or balance of interests, I
           must . . ."

Two approaches help illustrate these type-statements: interpretation of one live case of how where one sits determines what one sees; and a more general approach that distinguishes two modes for intervening.

1. *Toward Describing the Hetch Hetchy Episode.* In 1942, San Francisco Water Department head Nelson Eckart issued a Type I statement to his boss, Cahill: "Here's the key to the power house, here's the aspirin bottle, I quit." These apparently were the very first words Eckart spoke to Cahill on the latter's return from an unexpectedly-long trip to Washington. In the interim, Eckart not only had assumed Cahill's overall job as Utilities Manager, but also managed Hetch Hetchy Power Development as well as retained his own job as Water Department head. The combination proved too much for Eckart. To rely on a San Francisco gossip column:[45]

> . . . it was some days before Cahill discovered all the triple-personality kinks which had brought Eckart to the brink of madness. He discovered, in fact, a letter [ostensibly Type II] Waterman Eckart had written asking money for more water-works, another [again, I propose, Type II] letter Hetch Hetchy Eckart had written asking for more HH dough, and a final [and Type III?] letter Acting Utilities Manager Eckart had written denying both of his own requests. Naturally, Cahill asked what the devil.

> "From up here," Eckart explained [concerning what I take to be a Type III letter], "things don't look the same as they do down there."

2. *Advantage/Power vs. Truth/Love.* Looked at from another perspective, the three types of statements are differently amenable to two distinct models of intervening: what is usually called truth/love, as distinguished from advantage/power.

Truth/love interventions can be a tonic, in several senses. In various arenas—penultimately, in such loci as sensitivity training or T-Groups—they reign supreme. There the emphasis is on Type I statements. There love—or warmth, or support, or trust—becomes the engine for mutual exploration of the impact of self on others. As Schmuck and Miles explain:[46]

> Such a "tender" model states that shared expectations involving trust, warmth, and supportiveness are formed as the members of a working team gain confidence and skill in communicating clearly and openly. These norms and skills, in turn, support collaborative problem-solving and the rational use of information in making decisions. This model assumes . . . that the work . . . is carried on through interpersonal interactions and that heightening

abilities for problem-solving must commence with new norms for interpersonal openness and helpfulness.

In many cases, truth/love also can help reveal how Type II statements often can rest on Type I. Consider the pathologist at a murder trial, whose "technical" conclusions seem to have rested basically on his dislike of the defense attorney, who had belittled him in an earlier court appearance. In other cases, truth/love also might relate to Type II statements. As Le Baron notes about his work with city councilpersons:[47]

> As a result of experiencing, and reflecting upon, this process we have learned that local elected officials live within a dichotomy of power and trust; but they are more familiar with—and therefore, more capable of handling—power than trust. Power is inevitable to someone elected to a local office and its appearance cannot be avoided. Politics is the struggle for power. Therefore, power becomes the objective of an election as a means to an end, which is sought in order to further the political process. This power is dependent upon its recognition, and [upon] it being given to someone from someone. People elected to local councils and boards know their power does not exist in a vacuum. They know there is always a grantor-grantee relationship.
>
> As we look more carefully at both the power requirements, and power source of local elected officials we see a power base that is having some problems.

But truth/love interventions have their definite limits, especially in connection with Type III statements or situations, which characterize the interface. To be sure, Type III statements can sometimes—under truth-love impetus—be shown to be dressed-up rationalizations of statements of Types I or II. And intervenor aggressiveness concerning such transformations can be very helpful indeed.

But given a Type III statement or situation, the intervenor will be limited in major ways. At least five significant generalizations for the intervenor can be usefully associated with Type III cases.

First, when in doubt, public-sector intervenors should assume that political, or politicizable, considerations dominate.

Second, this assumption does not require abandonment of a truth/love mode, but rather urges its spritely and sensitive application. Intervenors may persistently test for any truth/love potential; they should assiduously seek to convince actors that at least some of what may appear to be advantage/power is usefully transformed into truth/love; and intervenors should be especially insistent about predicting the probable consequences of an extreme reliance on either mode.

Such aggressiveness by intervenors has its costs, of course. Some actors may feign truth/love while retaining an advantage/power mode. Here the intervenor can be an unwitting Judas goat; and hence the critical and conservative character of the first generalization.

Third, easy does it concerning insistence on truth/love applications, or self-delusions about their existence, even as the intervenor's commitment remains high. One may smile at crocodiles, in short; but one should not mistake them for love birds. Many OD intervenors have a critical trained incapacity in this regard, especially those intervenors with a dominant interaction-centered orientation. The present view urges no sell-out or cop-out, but rather respects the wisdom that an OD effort must begin from where a client-system is, while making sufficient progress to assuage an intervenor's concerns about a personal sell-out or cop-out.

Fourth, and a hard lesson to learn, rejections or postponements of truth/love do not necessarily disparage the mode or the intervenor. Typically, at the interface and in the public sector generally, it often will be the case that "it is nothing personal; it's just politics." Like politicals at their best, that is, intervenors best-suited to the interface will have "happy warrior" characteristics. Meg Greenfield caught just the right shading of these personal characteristics in describing the attributes of the politician who practices politics "in its very best sense; as a skill requiring generosity, compassion, sensitivity, a sense of fun and an ability to enjoy combat without getting uptight or nasty about it."[48]

Fifth, and perhaps paramountly, public-sector intervenors are well-advised to try to keep in mind what politics is about in principle, even as the trash and crudities swirl about them, as they certainly will. The Reverend Jesse Jackson strikes the balance referred to here, when he notes that:[49]

Politics—the art of the possible—is the highest art form available to man. It is the vehicle through which growth, national and international relations are expressed. It is also the mechanism through which goods and services produced by the economic system—whether capitalist, communist or socialist—are distributed, either fairly or unfairly.

Guideline 7. *The content of "the political" can be specified in ways that provide useful guidance for intervenors as well as for their choice of interventions.* Generally, intervenors and interventions are more impactful as they help to deal with "the political" in terms of OD values, in contrast to defining "the political" as off-limits.

Three components of "the political" provide specific perspective on the present point. Broadly, the three components can be said to characterize non-technical decision-making. Each of the points applies to both private and public sectors, albeit in variable degree. The degree of overlap merely testifies to the truism that all organizations have political aspects, but that some organizations have more of them, more commonly, and more intensely than others.

1. *Gaining/Retaining Power Is Primary.* Primacy in all organizations goes to building appropriate constituencies to gain power, but those constituencies have only some variable relationship to the efficiency or effectiveness with which some good or service is provided. For various reasons, constituency-building in the private sector is duck soup, relatively. Moreover, the solidity of these constituencies can have some substantial relationship to efficiency and to effectiveness.

Although there is for me no problem in helping gain/retain power in an OD mode, intervenors must tread warily. More or less grave ethical and moral issues may apply—a point that is at once patent and yet easy enough to neglect.[50] Specifically, a particular regime may utilize techniques and approaches that meet OD values at a micro-level—as in increasing employee control over the work environment—but only in the service of some evil macro-purpose, as was the case with some efficient and narrowly-satisfying operations in Hitler's Third Reich.[51] The OD intervenor's "ends" will likely be the politico's "means," and *vice versa*, a consideration that can be neglected only at great peril.

In the public sector, the associated moral and ethical dilemmas may seem obviously greater than in the business sector, but perhaps only apparently so. Specifically, the "profit motive" may seem to provide benchmark guidance for private-sector intervenors but, however "profit" is defined, even casual analysis demonstrates that the concept provides only very abstract guidance for the intervenor. Clearly, at least three critical questions get begged by the convenient assumption that the "profit motive" provides sufficient guidance for the OD intervenor: profit for whom, for what purposes, and how?[52]

In any case, the public-sector intervenor lacks even whatever comfort the "profit motive" may provide others. For good or ill, that is, our characteristic political institutions and traditions encourage much constituency-building that has at least the short-run effect of being more or less irrelevant to the effective or efficient provision of goods and services, if indeed that constituency-building does not severely complicate providing these goods and services. Given some verbal license, a contrast can be hazarded:

• Personal Decision: I like cohesive groups and the support they provide.

• Technical Decision: Does intervention X impact on the cohesiveness of work groups in ways that will increase output?

• Politicized Decision: Does intervention X contribute to maintaining a desired coalition, more or less regardless of its impact on output? And should that intervention be risked even if it does increase productivity, given its possible impact on the coalition? These questions relate to the private as well as the public sector. The crucial difference-in-degree: in the public sector, many more decisions can become "political," under a broader range of conditions, because so many more features are politicized or can quickly become so. Indeed, one might even define the "public sector" in terms of the degree of political or politicizable decisions, rather than as governmental vs. non-governmental.

This basic distinction may seem to provide an easy target, but profound dynamics are associated with it. Indeed, perhaps the most-widely accepted view of representative governance—the various forms of pluralism—fixate on the *process* of political choice-making and its rules, and tend to neglect outcomes expressed in terms of effectiveness or efficiency. Most "party platforms" provide ample evidence of the tendency, their goal being to attract a constituency that is big enough for the purpose at hand rather than to guarantee delivery of goods or services. Similarly, the specialization of the legislative role illustrates another of these public-sector features. At worst, this specialized role can induce painful tension between energetic narcissists who promise everything to everybody, and those administrative hewers of wood and carriers of water who have to deliver. At their best, of course, legislators provide an invaluable corrective for any corrupting tendencies that inhere in unchecked executive power, they help cement some sense of a collective consciousness with public agreements, they can help reconcile or even blend interests-at-odds, and they might even induce the more efficient and effective provision of goods and services.

Now it can be that the gaining/retaining of political power in the public sector is closely tied to efficiency and effectiveness, but that probability is not high. Directly, the available sub-constituencies have compound and confounded interests. Indeed, if anything, the growing prominence of single-issue politics suggests this long-standing tendency will become more extreme. Hence the gaining/retaining of power goes on in many arenas, involving sub-constituencies that overlap in wondrous ways, with interests that vary both within as well as between sub-constituencies, and involving elites that are variously (but, on the whole, not much) constrained by their several mass memberships.

2. *Goal/Performance Incongruencies.* A major derivative point is an old one, and does not require much more than stating. Public sector goal-setting is often complex and conflictful far beyond private-sector experience, both in the number of interests that can lay effective claim to having a voice but especially in the range and diversity of actually or potentially-conflicting goals. Moreover, the measurement of performance in the public sector is not only often difficult but may require the passage of long periods of time before any reasonable assessment of performance can even be attempted. Consequently, many public-sector organizations—especially at the interface—may not have meaningful real-time feedback relevant to their production, even if they want it.

The point can be put another way. Public-sector organizations are likely to be in close touch with the elites more or less representing their constituency-base. Most agencies will have very active and sensitive networks for this purpose, in fact. Indeed, *too much* of such feedback may be their basic problem, as when the components of performance salient to elites an agency associated with differ radically (as they often do) from the interests of agency service-providers and client service-recipients.[53] Hence this common complaint at the interface:

- we service-providers know what is wrong, and what our service-recipients want and need

- we know how to improve our performance and satisfy more clients

- but we can't act because of high-level agreements made by superordinates with other elites

OD intervenors can be variously helpful in dealing with such incongruities. Typically, for example, periodic team-building experiences can provide a kind of socio-emotional money in the bank, to help participants over the inevitable rough spots of interests-in-opposition. Or ventilation and emotional support induced by interaction-centered OD interventions can help people live with the incongruities without getting emotionally strung-out, or without perceiving them in personalized terms when they are "just politics."

3. *Timing Is Everything/The Mood Is All.* Severely complicating these issues related to the public-sector production function are the instabilities—even vagaries—of its major components. Politics is the art of the possible, that is, and the definition of the possible is written in quicksilver not in commandments carved in stone. "The possible" is the product of enormously complicated dynamics, including substantial admixtures of misinformation, puffery, and plain deceit. But that product can take on a great solidity, and often does. Hence actors at the interface will emphasize that "it's all timing," and *the* talent involves the quick-fix to fit the prevailing mood or time.

Although actors at the interface will speak concretely of "what's in the cards," their basic role is one of reacting, not dealing. "What will fly" has a phantasmagorical quality, often coming from where no one knows and heading toward where all seek to divine. The usual actor at the interface definitely is a counter-puncher, at best. Much discussion at the interface focuses on testing the precise boundaries of "the possible." Most there will empathize with the hoary adage that the wise captain sometimes can do no better than to keep his vessel afloat until the storms of political contention subside; few will willingly seek to "swim upstream" against the prevailing currents; and fewer still at the interface have any confidence that they can create or even significantly influence prevailing notions of "the possible." You catch the tide, if you are skillful and lucky enough; but you very seldom create it, and you often will be considered a fool for even trying.

Several points need to be made about "timing being everything." Paramountly, efficiency and effectiveness are only sporadically the big issues. "It's surely a crime," goes a common refrain, "but it's just not possible now to do anything about that because . . .;" and raconteurs at the interface can elaborate with intricate understanding about just what agreements make the system go, at any point in time. Moreover, "the possible" is subject to change, and indeed is not likely to be very lasting. So "full speed ahead" seems an appropriate signal, the better to take tactical advantage. On the other hand, "hurry up and wait" also often comes to characterize dynamics at the interface. That is to say, since feedback from multiple and not-always-accurate sources is involved, one can usually find new evidence for or against any definition of "the possible." And no one wants to be wrong in assessing a change, so the dynamics may at times have the character of either: a cautious incrementalism; or two giant steps forward, and then one and seven-eighths giant steps back. Typically, also, the definition of "the possible" can reflect exotic effects of the fact that all elements of the political system are not always salient, and many of them have different lead-times.

> There was a time of budget-consciousness when, as the saying of the time had it, "if someone brought up the 10 Commandments, efforts would be made to reduce them to 6 or 7."

> An agency sought to reflect its awareness of the times by bombarding its constituency with an elaborate campaign about how much the agency was doing to reduce budgets, etc.

> Schedules got so out of hand, however, that the agency was getting information about its cost-consciousness out to its various publics at just about the time that events known only to the agency elite patently required a "great leap forward" in program and spending.

> The agency was cautious about proposing that great leap, and in point of fact never did so. Agency elites basically fretted about the obtuseness of their support groups to obvious national needs, but with bittersweet awareness that they had helped develop the very definition of reality that now restricted response to a suddenly-changed situation.

OD interventions can variously service this aspect of "the political." Thus "keeping channels of communication open" often will be critical in taking advantage of opportunities that come and go. And the persona of the OD intervenor can be most important—as a kind of disinterested third party whose appearance can be taken by all to indicate another round of an alternative to the power/advantage mode. Despite moral and ethical traps, OD values will get acted on primarily as they bring home the bacon, as in facilitating timely responses to changing times and modes. No wonder in this.

Guideline 8. *Public-sector interventions characteristically pose greater difficulties of "drawing boundaries,"* at all levels, but especially at the politics/administration interface. This guideline says in another way that so much more at the interface is either political or can be politicized.

> A dramatic example comes to mind. In one design for police and community minorities, one of the earliest agreements required that all weapons be checked outside the meeting room.

> Very difficult meetings proceeded—with some progress, and remarkably with no leaks to the press which suggested a mixture of building trust and fear of alienating support groups.

> After several meetings, one participant notices a curious bulge in a pants leg—a bulge which proved to be a snub-nose pistol, loaded with bullets so prepared as to fragment on impact and cause nasty tissue damage.

> The processes leading to the discovery were intense, with the weapon-carrier claiming unsuccessfully that he just wanted to experience the sense of having "the ace in his boot."

> The violation of norms proved irreparable, especially after news of the incident leaked and was published. Self-serving leaks to the media quickly became the order-of-the-day. This accentuated polarization within the learning group, as a result (for example) of people posturing in group meetings for the purpose of later having their comments appear in the press to assuage their supporters. The group soon disbanded.

Several examples will illustrate how much more difficult it is to draw boundaries around a public-sector OD intervention, which lowers the probability that interventions will be attempted, and perhaps also reduces the likelihood that they will succeed. In a jurisdiction with a robust "sunshine law," to choose an extreme example, a team-building session might be open to the media, reflecting a motivation of "make public the management of the public's business." Awkward effects will be expected by most potential participants, and might even be probable. Thus participants might variously posture to client groups, rather than deal with one another and their relationships. And events that are reasonable enough, even innocuous, in some total process might if isolated by the media from their developmental web appear to be dramatic or portentous. Criticism of an elected official or a political appointee who is the administrative superior of a group of career employees, for example, might be administratively reasonble/necessary while also being potential dynamite were it to appear in the press.

Even with no "sunshine law" and without media presence, of course, such data at the interface might be leaked to the media, with some possible effect on programs or personalities.

Typically, the boundaries of OD interventions in the private sector are far narrower and easier to police. I know of not a single instance in which the media or an interest group demanded entrance to a private-sector OD intervention, for example. I know of many such demands in the public sector, and have personally been the resource person at several festivities with the media close-at-hand. In one case, the situation approximated revolving doors. The media were allowed in, except when (as state law provides) "personnel matters" are under discussion which—in a team-building session—was most of the time.

The literature contains numerous examples of the generic problem[54]—the difficulty of encapsulating or drawing boundaries for OD interventions in the public sector. What is true everywhere applies with special force at the politics/administration interface, where "leaks" are a common tactic in the complex higgling-and-piggling for position that goes on more or less continuously. This may dampen individual willingness to be open and to own ideas and feelings, for the varnished truth may seem far safer when one contemplates the various and well-entrenched enemies that any public agency or program is likely to have, each looking for a competitive edge. Problems are greatest with public designs such as group confrontations or mirroring efforts, for obvious reasons. Unfortunately, such designs also can be potent ones, as in making available multiple resources, in validating information, and in generating consensus and support for decisions, etc.

The ability to "draw boundaries" for OD experiences is convenient, but competing values do exist, and especially in the public sector. Thus "the public's right to know" is one such value competing with the drawing of boundaries for OD interventions. That tension between competing values cannot be resolved in any absolute sense but, if anything, cases of even minor doubt should be resolved in favor of the "right to know" rather than the convenience of an OD intervenor.

Despair is not necessarily in order, but some mind-expanding clearly will be necessary. For example, note that some urban team-building sessions—between managers and council members—have been televised in "sunshine law" jurisdictions, and without any major disruptive consequences.[55] Doubtless, however, today is not yet the time for any general adoption of such an approach to "doing the public's business in public."

Guideline 9. *The public-sector interface is often populated with a special kind of actor—the "rogue" or the "renegade."* The rogue has various names—many of them printable only by the standards of the new literature—but such a person is basically uncontrollable and thus is a fearsome beast at the interface, whose players by-and-large affect a superficial placidity even when powerful interests are intensely jostling one another. A Mafia-like code of public silence also tends to prevail; and "good losers" get as much approbation as "winners." Roguishness no doubt derives in part from deep psychological wellsprings, but an independent power-base certainly helps. Witness the now-and-again example of a congressman from a district with a homogeneous constituency who can run on a long national leash because the good folks back-home will return him to office, almost no matter what, as long as the narrow needs of the district get met.

Rogues can exist in the private sector, but I have seen few. This may be because executives in the private sector are less likely to have an independent power-base, except through such uncommon means as the ownership of very large blocks of stock.

The rogue can be some triumphantly-principled figure, but far more often than not he is a "gutter fighter"—a person careless with the truth, often Janus-faced, ambitious without discipline by even casual principle, a tattle-tale in his own interests, and so on. But he has a power-base. All this is to say that the rogue is distinguished mostly by degree from peers at the politics/administration interface. But that difference in degree is critical: it is the difference between "some" and "much too much."

OD designs typically have the effect of disciplining the rogue. Team-building designs can build effective corrals, for example. Indeed, virtually any public sharing of information probably will reduce the rogue's ability to have an impact. The rogue tends to be most influential, that is, when his peers do not "have their act together," as when two more-or-less equal factions stand in opposition to one another, are mutually suspicious, refuse to share information and so on. The rogue then can take the expedient side of the issue, or even all sides, given sufficient ingenuity and—ah—flexibility.

The disciplining of rogues is clearly no unalloyed good, for substantial reasons. First, rogues often are sinners, but they also might be saints. The engines of group forces could stamp out the one as well as the other. So the OD intervenor faces serious ethical issues in such cases, issues that are only-superficially finessed by pleading that one plays the role of "neutral group facilitator."

Second, the rogue may become a resourceful enemy, even if he can be a grudgingly-respectful one. I recall lunch with one rogue. He had tumbled from a position of major control over a significant public project, following several months of team-building. Basically, he fell victim to growing norms about trust and openness, which were reinforced by suddenly-strong ties of affection and friendship among his colleagues.

> "I never thought it would happen. Those pasty-faced jelly fishes [the rogue's colleagues] got together and tied one on me. As they got to really talking to one another, and thicker than fleas on a hound, they got me coming-and-going more times than I care to remember.
>
> "This team-building sure put a crimp in my style."
>
> "But nobody can call me dumb, Dr. Bob. I learned a big lesson. No more 'process facilitators' if I can stop it! And I'll bury you the first good chance I get, maybe even by using your own stuff from that egg-headed tome of yours. I'm wading through it now so I can better protect myself against your 'designs'."

Such directness can be disarming, even immobilizing, for few really enjoy being someone's target for today. But an opportunity exists even in such cases, for rogues can see virtue in OD once they get past the point of seeing the intervenor as a mere competitor for influence. In the case above, for example, I am relatively pleased that I responded:

> "You can try to get me if you want, Tom. In many circles, you're a good enemy to have.
>
> "And I'm sure glad that you bought the book and are reading it. Our kids can use the royalties.

"All I can say now is that I'll try hard to play by the same rules for all you guys. This time, your wings got clipped. Maybe next time, you'll come out ahead.

"In fact, 'next time' may be here already. I hear you have [some influentials] really out of joint [on a certain issue]. You want to take that through, so I can check out some things that disturb me and may bother you?"

Third, peers of the rogue tend to have bittersweet reactions to this disciplining aspect of many OD designs. One referred to a "next time it may be me" reaction. Even silver clouds have dark linings, as it were, and OD intervenors at the politics/administration interface must take note.

Fourth, the word gets around quickly at the interface, and this raises ethical issues for the intervenor. I have long since stopped counting the times when—in a burst of intense openness—some actor at the interface wished me well in general, and then noted specifically how happy he would be "to pull Joe's fangs," or "to put old Sam in his place," via a team-building design. Generally, I refuse to participate in an effort I come to believe is a kind of punitive expedition. But one can be fooled, for there are masters aplenty therein at the interface, and resourceful vigilance provides the only defense against being made a patsy.

Guideline 10. *The media have all the trump cards at the politics/administration interface, which massively distinguishes public sector OD applications from counterparts in business.* I know of no media firestorm in business, for example, like that induced by the OD application in the U.S. Department of State.[56] I refer to dominantly-useful features in our institutions and practices which may bedevil public OD applications. So this section does not in effect ask OSHA to proclaim that "the media may be harmful to the health of public-sector OD projects." But that is true.

A few points require making. First, the media tend to condense and simplify in ways that separate action from context, that focus on the dramatic moment in often-tedious lines of development. At its best, this saves the time of media-users and may dramatize some essential truth. At its worst, this tendency may distort reality and make grotesque what was beneficial or at least benign and even banal.

A number of change-agents were brought into a conservative city government to "unfreeze" public employees to help prepare them to face some upcoming challenges. Early resistance was so great that at one point several of the change-agents—all of them Ph.D.s—lashed out in profane ways. The episode was fueled by frustration that soon passed, and virtually all observers agreed that the mass sessions were definitely worthwhile, on balance.

But the story was too juicy to resist. Sample headline: "Tax $ Go for Postgrad Course in Cursing."

Second, the OD intervenor often will be limited in what can be reasonably shared with media personnel. I typically direct inquiring newspersons to responsible agency officials for responses to such questions: "So what did you do that was so great to earn your fee?" As for questions about OD techniques and philosophy, I will wax long and loud. But this makes lousy copy.

Third, the media can serve as variously-aware agents of rogues, for good or ill. The advantage is definitely with the rogue in such cases, especially one who has been a source of "good copy" in the past. Some preposterous and damaging things have been written about several of the public programs focal here, because "whatever X says is news," independent of its truth-value, or even because of its palpable falsity.

Fourth, even though discretion by the overwhelming bulk of media personnel can be counted on, useful backgrounders or off-the-record exchanges often are impeded by concerns over what a small minority might do with the information. Since there is no way to exclude the latter media persons, the former tend to get deprived as well. One public executive touched on an aspect of this issue in distinguishing media stars and non-stars: ". . . a star is interested in . . . looking very good. The way that he's going to look good is, usually, to make you look bad . . . . Other reporters, probably the vast majority, really seem to be interested in what is going on."[57]

Fifth, media representatives may have various personal and philosophical issues with OD at the politics/administration interface. Basically, these issues center around the efficacy of zesty conflict in connection with public matters. Truth to be told, successful OD interventions may over time reduce the gross amount of overt conflict, as individuals or groups order their priorities, reduce the interpersonal garbage in their interaction, cooperate, and so on. The elimination of conflict *per se* is no particular goal of the kind of OD interventions I prescribe at the politics/administration interface, however. Indeed, it is a juicy irony that, especially early in the game, the OD intervenor frequently will be accused of "creating conflict where none existed." The issues here certainly are matters of fine-tuning, and minor adjustments can have significant effects. I like the flavor of this exchange:

> An aggressive reporter was complaining to a political official: "Things are duller around here since Bob G. came around. We have fewer juicy fights.
>
> "How else can we get at the truth, except that people push against one another publicly? That's not only good copy, but it's good public policy. I fear lack of conflict."
>
> The public official responded in his courtly manner: "Maybe so. But remember, we aren't trying to learn to fight less, just more effectively."

FOOTNOTES

[1]The essence of this and the following chapter has had various developmental forms. The present form relates most closely to Robert T. Golembiewski, "Guidelines for Intervening at the Interface: Managing the Tension Between OD Principles and Political Power." Paper delivered at the Annual Meeting, American Society for Public Administration, Baltimore, Md., April 1979.

[2]For an extended discussion of these OD goals and values, see Robert T. Golembiewski, *Approaches to Planned Change* (New York: Marcel Dekker, 1979), Part 1, especially chapters 1-3.

[3]For examples of such guidelines, see: Herbert Shepard, "Rules of Thumb for Change Agents," *OD Practitioner*, Vol. 7 (November 1975), pp. 1-5; and Jerry Harvey, "Eight Myths OD Consultants Believe In . . . and Die by," *OD Practitioner*, Vol. 7 (February 1975), pp. 1-5.

[4]Robert T. Golembiewski, "Managing the Tension Between OD Principles and Political Dynamics," pp. 27-46, in W. Warner Burke, editor, *The Cutting Edge* (La Jolla, Cal.: University Associates, 1978).

[5]For a sense of the building literature—relevant to a "motivational deficit" about the ability to make a difference, about the lack of confidence that good (or bad) works will be rewarded (or punished), and so on—consult such sources: Frank T. Paine, Stephen J. Carroll, Jr., and Burt A. Leete, "Need Satisfactions of Managerial Level Personnel In A Government Agency," *Journal of Applied Psychology*, Vol. 50 (No. 3, 1966), pp. 247-249; Jesse B. Rhinehart, R.P. Barrell, A.S. De Wolfe, J.E. Griffin, and F.E. Spaner, "Comparative Study of Need Satisfactions in Governmental and Business Hierarchies," *Journal of Applied Psychology*, Vol. 53 (No. 3, 1969), pp. 230-235; Bruce

Buchanan III, "Government Managers, Business Executives, and Organizational Commitment," *Public Administration Review*, Vol. 39 (September 1979), pp. 440-447. For broad perspective on the motivational consequences of public employ, see also Lyman W. Porter and James L. Perry, "Motivation and Public Management." Paper presented at Public Management Research Conference, Brookings Institution, Washington, D.C., November 19-20, 1979.

Note also that such sources do not necessarily imply that public officials are somehow "different," but rather imply only responses by them sensitive to the public-sector environment. Generating these responses may be costly, in fact. Some recent research, indeed, implies that public-sector employees generally have needs and preferences that are poorly-served by their institutional and procedural contexts, even though that context is often taken mistakenly to reflect needs and preferences characteristic of public employees. Specifically, will public employees fear and reject or accept vigorous performance appraisal, which is rare in public agencies? The common wisdom suggests fear and rejection, but sparse empirical data do not support the common wisdom.See Nicholas P. Lovrich, Jr., Paul L. Shaffer, Ronald H. Hopkins, and Donald A. Yale, "Do Public Employees Welcome or Fear Merit Evaluation of their Performance?," *Public Administration Review*, Vol. 40 (May 1980), pp. 214-221.

[6]Stewart Alsop, *Saturday Evening Post*, June 1966, p. 14.

[7]*Atlanta Constitution*, October 1, 1979, p. 6A. See also Douglas La Bier, "Emotional Disturbances in the Federal Government," *Administration and Society*, Vol. 14 (February 1983), pp. 403-448.

[8]In such matters, public personnel policies often cannot win for losing. For example, the Civil Service Reform Act 19 1978 sought to improve policies that made the federal government, in the words of a Senate report, "a refuge for the incompetent." The Act thus provides that each agency develop a "performance appraisal system" by October 1981, so as to provide a basis for evaluating employees. The American Federation of Government Employees argued in mid-1978 that this Act prohibits any discipline of non-performing employees till such systems were in place in late 1981!

[9]John Dean, *Blind Ambition* (New York: Simon & Schuster, 1976).

[10]Irving L. Janis, *Victims of Groupthink* (Boston: Houghton Mifflin, 1972).

[11]For a broader related treatment, see Bertram H. Raven, "The Nixon Group," *Journal of Social Issues*, Vol. 30 (No. 4, 1974), pp. 297-320.

[12]George Christian, *The President Steps Down* (New York: Macmillan, 1970), p. 10.

[13]*Ibid.*, pp. 236-237.

[14]Lewis Grizzard, *The Atlanta Constitution*, July 23, 1979, p. 1-C.

[15]Allan W. Lerner, *Experts, Politicians, and Decision-Making in the Technological Society* (Morristown, New Jersey: General Learning Press, University Programs Modular Series, 1976), esp. pp. 7-8.

[16]Victor A. Thompson, *Modern Organization* (New York: Knopf, 1961).

[17]Bruce Adams, "The Limitations of Muddling Through: Does Anyone in Washington Really Think Anymore?," *Public Administration Review*, Vol. 39 (No. 6, 1979), p. 547.

[18]David Obey, chairman, *Commission on Administrative Review: Final Report* (Washington, D.C.: Government Printing Office, 1977), p. 632.

[19]For an unusually-detailed picture of these tensions at the Federal level, see James Burnham, "Some Administrators Unkindly View Congress," pp. 127-134, in Robert T. Golembiewski, Frank Gibson, and Geoffrey Y. Cornog, editors, *Public Administration* (Chicago: Rand McNally, 1976).

For a detailed comparison of state legislators and administrators, see also James M. McDuffie, *An Examination of the Reciprocal Perceptions of Legislators and Executives in Georgia State Government.* Unpublished doctoral dissertation, University of Georgia, 1980.

[20]Helmut Schoeck, *Envy: A Theory of Social Behavior* (New York: Barce & World, 1966), p. 1.

[21]Bill Shipp, "Is Florida Carter's New Hampshire?," *Atlanta Constitution*, October 10, 1979, p. 4A.

[22]Morton Grodzins, "The Many American Governments and Outdoor Recreation," esp. pp. 66-68, in *Trends in American Living and Outdoor Recreation* (Washington, D.C.: Government Printing Office, 1962).

[23]Robert H. Sebring, "Knowledge Utilization in Organization Development," *Journal of Applied Behavioral Science*, Vol. 15 (June 1979), pp. 194-196.

[24]W.J. Reddin, "Confessions of An Organizational Change Agent," *Group and Organization Studies*, Vol. 2 (March 1977), p. 38.

[25]Frederick Mosher, *Democracy and the Public Service* (New York: Oxford University Press, 1968), pp. 108-109.

[26]*Ibid.*, p. 109.

[27]Roger Harrison, "Role Negotiation," pp. 84-96, in W. Warner Burke and Harvey Hornstein, editors, *The Social Technology of Organization Development* (Washington, D.C.: NTL Learning Resources Corporation, 1972).

[28]Robert T. Golembiewski, "Infusing Organizations with OD Values: Public Sector Approaches to Structural Change," *Southern Review of Public Administration*, Vol. 4 (September 1980), pp. 269-302.

[29]Consult, especially, Robert T. Golembiewski and Carl W. Proehl, Jr., "Public Sector Applications of Flexible Work-hours," *Public Administration Review*, Vol. 40 (January 1980), pp. 72-85.

[30]John Pfiffner and Frank Sherwood, *Administrative Organization* (Englewood Cliffs, N.J.: Prentice-Hall, 1960), esp. pp. 18-27.

[31]Robert T. Golembiewski, "Authority As A Problem in Overlays," *Administrative Science Quarterly*, Vol. 9 (June 1964), pp. 23-49.

[32]Marvin Weisbord, "Why OD Hasn't Worked (So Far) In Medical Centers," *Health Care Management Review*, Vol. 1 (Spring 1976), esp. pp. 20-22.

[33]*Ibid.*, pp. 22-25.

[34]James M. Kouzes and Paul R. Mico, "Domain Theory," *Journal of Applied Behavioral Science*, Vol. 15 (December 1979), pp. 449-469.

[35]David G. Bowers and Doris L. Hausser, "Work Group Types and Intervention

Effects in Organizational Development," *Administrative Science Quarterly*, Vol. 22 (March 1977), pp. 76-94.

[36]As in the useful distinctions between the five type-conditions of team-building hosts made by William G. Dyer, *Team-Building* (Reading, Mass.: Addison-Wesley, 1977).

[37]This strategy was emphasized, for example by Saul D. Alinsky. See *His Reveille for Radicals* (Chicago: University of Chicago Press, 1946).

[38]See Golembiewski, *Approaches to Planned Change*, Part 2, pp. 33-348.

[39]*Ibid.*, Part 2, pp. 185-214.

[40]Lee Bolman, "Organization Development and Limits to Growth." Paper presented at the 1978 Annual Meeting, Academy of Management, San Francisco, Cal., August 9-12.

[41]Paul P. Van Riper, *A History of the United States Civil Service* (New York: Harper & Row, 1958).

[42]Ethan A. Singer and Leland M. Wooton, "The Triumph and Failure of Albert Speer's Administrative Genius," *Journal of Applied Behavioral Science*, Vol. 12 (January 1976), pp. 79-103.

[43]The characterization holds even under conditions of unusual fate-control, as in organized crime. See Martin A. Gosch and Richard Hammer, *The Last Testament of Lucky Luciano* (New York: Dell, 1976).

[44]Singer and Wooton, *op. cit.*

[45]Quoted in Herbert A. Simon, *Administrative Behavior*, 2nd edition (New York: Macmillan, 1957), p. 214n.

[46]Richard A. Schmuck and Matthew B. Miles, editors, *Organization Development in Schools* (Palo Alto, Cal.: National Press Books, 1971), p. 234.

[47]Melvin Le Baron, "New Perspectives Toward More Effective Local Elected Councils and Boards," p. 237, in Robert T. Golembiewski and William Eddy, editors, *Organization Development in Public Administration*, Part 2 (New York: Marcel Dekker, 1978).

[48]Meg Greenfield, "The Kennedy Puzzle," *Newsweek*, November 6, 1979, p. 82.

[49]Jesse L. Jackson, "Blacks' Political Salvation," *Atlanta Constitution*, October 1, 1979, p. 5A.

[50]As Loren Baritz so artfully reminds us in *The Servants of Power* (Middletown, Conn.: Wesleyan University Press, 1960).

[51]Singer and Wooton, *op. cit.*

[52]Robert Ross, "OD For Whom?," *Journal of Applied Behavioral Science*, Vol. 7 (September 1971), pp. 581-582.

[53]Herbert Kaufman, *Administrative Feedback* (Washington, D.C.: The Brookings Institution, 1973).
Parenthetically, consultants can be very useful in developing opportunities for input by low-power groups, which can become "foul-weather friends." See Ray H. Mac Nair, Russell Caldwell, and Leonard Pollane, "Citizen Participants in Public Bureaucracies," *Administration and Society*, Vol. 14 (February 1983), pp. 507-524.

[54]Edward B. Klein, Claudewell S. Thomas, and Elizabeth C. Bellis, "When Warring Groups Meet: The Use of A Group Approach in Police-Black Community Relations," *Social Psychiatry*, Vol. 6 (No. 2, 1971), pp. 93-99.

[55]Cecil H. Bell, Jr., and James R. Rosenzweig, "OD in the City," *Southern Review of Public Administration*, Vol. 1 (March 1978), esp. p. 435.

[56]For a review and synthesis of Project ACORD in the U.S. Department of State, see Donald P. Warwick, *A Theory of Public Bureaucracy* (Cambridge, Mass.: Harvard University Press, 1975).

[57]Joseph L. Bower, "Effective Public Management," *Harvard Business Review*, Vol. 55 (March 1977), p. 136. More broadly, see Gordon Chase and Elizabeth C. Reveal, *How to Manage in the Public Sector* (Reading, Mass.: Addison-Wesley, 1983), esp. pp. 145-175.

CHAPTER VIII

SEEKING GUIDANCE FROM EXPERIENCE AT THE INTERFACE II: INTERVENTION GUIDELINES RELATING TO INTERVENOR BEHAVIOR

"When in Rome, do as the Romans do." This piece of common wisdom often serves well, for those who seek to enter a social system without making waves.

OD intervenors need to respect a far-more difficult dictum, while at least threatening to make waves via posing definite choices or by working toward specific changes. They need to adapt their presentation-of-self to the public sector, all the better to transcend it. Intervenors need sufficient access to social systems in order to facilitate choice, and possibly change, by members of those systems. The fine-tuning centers on being sufficiently *within* a system to understand it and appear credible, but *not* so much a part of the system as to be socialized to it or deadened by it.

I. GUIDELINES PRESCRIBING INTERVENOR'S BEHAVIOR

Guidance in this subtle business will again be sought from experience at the public-sector interface, just as in the preceding chapter. Describing the texture of that interface constitutes the basic focus of that prior chapter, although some implications for the intervenor's behavior also were developed there. Here prescription takes center-stage. Given the public-sector environment, what rules-of-thumb seem reasonable for the intervenor seeking to work toward OD values in the public-sector?

Guideline 1. *The most powerful intervention at the interface involves the intervenor saying: No.* Expressed in another way, the intervenor at the interface should be especially careful to bias his choice of intervention-loci to maximize the chances of success. This counsel applies quite generally, but its salience seems greatest at the interface.

From one point of view this may seem curious, even reprehensible, but consider these three points. First, this bias is associated with increasing the probability of meeting a felt-need, and of doing so as to maximize the chances of psychological success of participants because they own the associated processes, overcome the risk involved in the intervention, and take responsibility for personal involvement as well as for outcomes. From an important point of view, then, this guideline represents a version of the traditional advice to interventionists: OD should gravitate to problem-situations that involve obvious pain or trauma for those involved. The hurt will help mobilize energies toward problem-resolution.

Second, the public-sector interface provides splendiferous opportunities for things to come undone, so the intervenor is well-advised to remember the usual advice, and then turn-up the dials by 50 or 100 per cent.

Third, the present advice does not imply pessimism. Contrary to popular opinion, as preceding chapters demonstrate, numerous OD applications in the public sector do exist and their success-fail ratio is quite attractive.[1] So this guideline prescribes intelligent caution rather than immobilization:

- Be smart. Pick strategic spots to intervene—where things work for you rather than against you.

- Generally, better no application than one with a low probability of success.

- Remember that the public-sector interface has little tolerance for experiments, except in deep extremis, when it often is too late.

- The interface seldom has any tolerance for experiments that fail, whatever the conditions.

- There is plenty of work to do that has a high-probability of success.

Specifically, how does one go about loading the dice in these qualified particulars? And what defines a high-probability situation? Each case will have unique features, but consider the case of North Carolina, which hosted a robust set of OD activities.

An incoming governor wishes to distinguish his administration—as a "real team" that is open and responsive—from its predecessor. That predecessor represents a very different set of interests and alliances; is characterized by a set of more or less conflictful departmental baronies, some legally independent; and follows the "old ways." Moreover, success in that differentiation will increase the probability that the new administration will gain a unique prize. For the first time in modern history, a sitting governor could succeed self.

The premium in North Carolina obviously was on the quick development of an executive team, early and substantial agreement about policies and objectives, and so on. Such conditions raise the probability of successful OD applications in the public sector.

Guideline 2. *The OD consultant should work for "the system," not specific units or individuals.* The objective dilemma should be obvious. Intervenors will work with and through individuals or groups; and yet essential guidance comes from accommodating a sense of the possible to some concept of the ideal at a systemic level that transcends individuals and groups. Phrased another way, intervenors are well-advised to represent and comport themselves as "third-parties," not as somehow above having an interest in the outcomes but as having *different* roles and interests. This concept has proved variously serviceable, as in the case of OD teams working with joint union/management efforts to improve the quality of working life.[2]

The advice applies quite broadly but with special urgency at the interface. The same overall sense of "out-ness" leavened by a degree of "in-ness" characterizes private-sector consultation, of course. But the pushes-and-pulls to me seem different or at least greater in the public sector, on balance. If nothing else, the usage puts on definite warning those officials who might be encouraged to use interventions in narrowly-manipulative or contraceptive ways. These are special dangers at the interface, as several parts of the following discussion should make clear enough. The intervenor may lose business because he is not "our guy," but that generally will be good business to lose.

Two derivative needs require underscoring. Paramountly, this second guideline requires that the intervenor variously help groups and individuals develop a sensitivity to systemic needs, which is to say that intervenors often will be encouraged to take perspectives and positions contrary to their own immediate individual or group interests and traditions, for which contrariness they may receive mostly psychic gratification. Operationally, moreover, OD intervenors at the interface needs a well-developed system of values, a philosophy for action which they can make substantially clear to others and which can be applied to many sets of operating conditions. Also important, but in a secondary role, the OD intervenor will be expected to have a model of how some major desired effects can be attained in organizations. Clients at the interface typically do not demand perfection in knowledge or control of reality, but they usually do require consistency in articulating and working toward some relatively clear goals in relatively effective ways.

Guideline 3. *Public-sector intervenors, and especially at the interface, must be energetic mobilizers of commonalities—shared affinities, preferences, interests, and so on.* The role is familiar in many contexts—e.g., T-Group trainers mobilize commonalities when they ask simply: "Now, how did all of you react when Jack did X?" Sharing such commonalities, in effect, does multiple-duty: participants disclose aspects of themselves, which implies vulnerability but can pay dividends in terms of interpersonal closeness and valid information; the processes of dealing with differences as well as similarities can provide practice with and trust in processes relevant to effective decision-making; sharing commonalities and working through differences can heighten cohesiveness; and so on.

The present point applies with particular force at the interface, even as it applies everywhere. An illustration will serve as a place to start to develop the full sense of this introductory conclusion, deriving from a management problem:

> Federal authorities were notified; ameliorative actions were begun; and local opinion expected some definite retribution against responsible parties. An in-house group was formed to recommend internal action, independent of whatever external authorities might impose and yet relevant to such imposition.

> An intervenor worked with both the recommending group and several possible affected parties, before and after the disclosure that had great no-win potential for all concerned. The general strategy sought to mobilize commonalities, as far as that was possible.

> Intervenor sought to encourage discussion of the multiple and mutual responsibilities, most often in sessions involving only the committee but at times also a key individual. The essential results? This process drew a previously-polarized committee away from two positions: fire the individual in question; or fire some lower-level employee(s). And the individual came to agree that some action against self was in the cards, indeed, that it was

politically necessary. But the committee bogged-down on the issue of what specific action to recommend.

Intervenor helped break the log-jam by encouraging exploration of what came to be generally seen as another commonality, if one arrived at by very different routes. Full details would be onerous, but the commonality essentially developed around a contractual agreement negotiated earlier by the individual, but not widely known. Both the individual and the committee came to agree that the contract was politically awkward, and its renegotiation constituted a major deprivation of the individual even as it avoided a potential political embarrassment for the organization and major actors in it.

Such mobilization of commonalities implies at least six useful features of the intervenor's role. *First*, "working for a healthy system" from the start makes it far easier to function in the required way. In the case above, for example, basic loyalty to either the committee or the individual probably would have limited the intervenor's flexibility and usefulness to both parties. A committee loyalty would have encouraged a bias toward firing the individual, or (more likely) some lower-level officials. Loyalty to the key individual might have forfeited raising the issue of renegotiating the agreement.

But did all of this really serve systemic needs? That is a tough question, obviously, to which no certain answer exists. Participants did generally accept the resolution, although it did not meet all priorities equally. The intervenor was especially sensitive to the possible political liabilities of the original agreement, but most participants agree some liability did inhere in the document. So change in those conditions was at once a punishment of the individual, as well as a finesse of a possible future problem. Beyond this, practical and ethical conditions commingle in subtle ways that come to this bottom-line: some wing-clipping of the individual seemed appropriate, and external publics expected some action; but firing was too much. In part, this was due to the undoubted contribution of the individual over time; and in part this bottom-line also derived from the very troublesome issue of who would replace that individual if he were removed.

Second, the intervenor should have a long and active memory, which operates on multiple tracks, as it were. That is, the sources of commonality can be diverse; they can simultaneously relate to multiple domains (e.g., managerial and political in the case above); and they can often go unrecognized by direct actors, in large part because they are so close to the action that they lose perspective on possible ways out of binds. In the present case, those directly involved initially did not recognize the potential political difficulties in the original agreement. Intervenor emphasized the possibility, and actors eventually checked-out the possibility with selected power-figures who had not known about the agreement. Most contacts expressed surprise that those conditions had been negotiated, and some even predicted dire consequences.

Third, the intervenor should be pro-active in seeking and suggesting possible bases around which commonalities might develop. In my experience, participants often profit from such stimulation. This may be because the intervenor is freer to take the risks in suggesting resolutions, needs to be less concerned about saving-face, and so on.

Fourth, this implies that the intervenor's role will contain major aspects of idea-generation or alternative-generation. The intervenor needs to be a "facilitator" in an augmented sense, then. This adds a strong substantive element to the process-oriented facilitation that often defines the intervenor's role.

Fifth, the energetic mobilization of commonalities has a unique salience in the public sector, more generally, because of the more common and pressing need there to relate multiple domains which strongly tend toward fragmentation or balkanization. Thus in the case of medical centers, Weisbord isolates three systems—governance, task, and identity—each of which has its distinctive characteristics, pace of change, and mode of operation.[3] Similarly, Human Service Organizations have been viewed by others in terms of three simultaneous overlays: policy, management, and service levels.[4]

Some such distinctions are applicable to all organizations, but with vastly-different loadings. The general point can be sketched in a number of related ways. For example, many private-sector organizations can be thought of as having a high if incomplete congruence of governance, task, and identity systems, while greater fragmentation characterizes the public sector. Alternately, the "task" or "management" domains can be viewed as dominant in many private-sector organizations. In the public-sector, in approximate but useful contrast, any of the three domains may be "hot" at one time, or all three may be active at the same time; and the domains can become salient in various combinations under a broader range of conditions than in the private sector.

In terms of domain theory, to illustrate, the example above deals basically with the interaction of policy *and* management domains. If the issue were in either the policy *or* management domain, it would be far easier to deal with. This implies a useful simplicism: the more elemental and congruent the domain(s) in which decisions/actions take place, the easier it is to mobilize forces sufficient to take necessary actions with the degree of ownership needed to make those actions stick. Looked at from another point of view, what seems to be delay in the public sector can be creative waiting. Waiting for what? In domain terms, actors could be waiting for one of two things. Thus actors could be waiting for fewer domains to be relevant, which simplifies decision and action. Or actors could be waiting on the conditions under which the demands of several domains could be met, more or less simultaneously.

Sixth, and perhaps paramountly, the intervenor at the interface must apply great energies toward what DeLuca calls "strategic orientations" to the socio-political context—or SPC, conveniently. DeLuca isolates four levels of these strategic orientations, whose major elements are abstracted in Exhibit 7. A Level 0 also can be distinguished as a possible intervenor mode:

Level O:
Narrowly-Helping Only

1. SPC seen as distal to change effort, if not irrelevant to it

2. Intervention methodologies seen as paramount

3. Practitioner focuses on individual and small group dynamics

4. Role of practitioner is to respond competently to process and the here-and-now; the client focuses on SPC

5. OD process is critical to ensure *good* products

Exhibit 7 permits a variety of useful perspectives on the role of the OD practitioner. Most elementally, many public-sector interventions really operate at Level 0: the intervenor acts basically independent of the SPC, or relies on the client to make the appropriate adjustments. Reliance on the client has much to recommend it, of course.

Over-reliance is not only common, however, but also potentially treacherous in that even simple OD designs have political components and implications to which a client-in-need may not be sensitive. For example, even enhancing the openness of a system via improved feedback is a political act that can influence the distribution of power in a system.[5] Momentous effects can occur in public organizations.

EXHIBIT 7. Four Levels of Strategic Orientation to A Socio-Political Context

Level I:	Reaction	1. SPC seen as *separate* from change effort
		2. Intervention methodology seen as *prime* component of change attempt
		3. Practitioner seen as having *no control* over shift in SPC
		4. Role of practitioner is to respond completely to shifts in SPC
		5. OD process important to ensure good *products*
Level II:	Forecast-Reaction	1. SPC seen as *separate* from change effort
		2. Intervention methodology seen as *prime* component of change attempt
		3. Practitioner seen having *no control* over shifts in SPC
		4. Role of practitioner is to
		a. collect imformation on SPC
		b. forecast potential shifts in SPC
		c. shape change effort to take into account potential SPC shifts
		5. OD process important to ensure good *products*
Level III:	Forecast-Pro-action	1. SPC seen as *significant component* of change effort
		2. Intervention methodology seen as *prime* component of change attempt
		3. Practitioner seen as being *able to influence* the nature of and shifts in SPC
		4. Role of practitioner is to
		a. collect information on SPC
		b. *forecast* potential shifts in SPC
		c. *influence* SPC openly to benefit change effort
		d. shape change effort to blend with nature of SPC and its shifts
		5. OD process important to ensure good *products*
Level IV:	Steering	1. SPC seen as the *prime component* to change effort
		2. Intervention methodology seen as *secondary* component of change effort
		3. Practitioner seen as being *able to influence* SPC
		4. Role of practitioner is to coordinate and direct various SPC forces in order to incorporate a new *value system* into organization
		5. Good products important to ensure continuation of OD *process*

From Joel R. DeLuca, "Developing Strategies for Dealing with the Socio-Political Context of Planned Change Efforts," p. 4a. Paper presented at Fall 1979 Conference, OD Network.

Many intervenors may see such designs as mere "openers" toward the kind of cultural change characteristic of comprehensive OD efforts, but, for public administrators and their publics, such "openers" may seem revolutionary.

Moreover, the OD intervenor has to be very conscious of which strategic orientation is operative at any time, as well as very concerned about the perception of others as to the operative level or levels. This makes life complicated, if not treacherous, for public-sector intervenors. Not only must intervenors be aware of their levels; and not only must they labor incessantly to gain understanding of others concerning their intent. Two plain facts enormously complicate the obvious difficulties. Thus the several levels are seldom easy to distinguish, especially when multiple issue-areas are involved. Moreover, many opponents will seek to portray even the most narrowly-helpful intervention as "steering."

These considerations at once underscore both the general wisdom and the specific impracticality of the public-sector OD intervenor presenting self as "helper" or "reactor" only, and especially at the interface.

Finally, although intervenor may seldom function at the "steering" level, and then only after having gained the confidence of broad ranges of actors in a system, that level has a critical significance. If nothing else, to explain, OD interventions do imply the energizing of a value system that is different from that which exists in most public organizations. This crucial point may be in the background, as in the case of OD interventions such as flexible workhours. Or that crucial point may be up-front and stage-center, as in major structural changes. But the point always applies, and can be neglected only at great peril.

Guideline 4. *Intervenors at the interface, even as they adopt a systemic orientation that seeks to encompass the public sector's multi-levelledness, must acknowledge and cope with some complex trade-offs inherent in that systemic bias.* As the preceding discussion suggests, by way of introduction, taking the systemic view at the interface does not constitute an easy piece. The intervenor straddles a major fault-line, where attitudes of despair or resignation often will dominate. And the intervenor's theory/philosophy also must be substantially complete and compelling as to both substance and salesmanship. And even where the intervenor can come through in these senses—as if they were not challenge enough—clients often will charge that a consultant is "playing God" by insisting on a systemic perspective, and some clients with parochial loyalties and identifications may seek to clip his wings. This restraint is likely to be all the more insistent to the degree that the OD intervenor acts impactfully, some reasons for which will be explored at several points below, especially in the discussion following Guidelines 12 through 14 below.

By far the greatest difficulties with taking a "systemic view" inhere in determining just what that is. Intemperately interpreted, such a view could provide a rationale for whatever an intervenor prefers—for "whatever my gut tells me." That is not the prescription here. Along with the liberal dollops of realistic humility and a passion for testing, in contrast, the organizationally-relevant literatures provide major perspective for seeing the forest as well as the trees. For example, the huge literature on the behavioral and attitudinal consequences of alternative structural arrangements can provide invaluable guidance concerning the structural roots of many organizational problems. Moreover, even though that literature is far from complete, it implies numerous approaches to restructuring that help explicitly choose those problems to be dealt with, and those to be avoided.[6] Similarly, an intervenor in a team-building experience would do well to keep in mind the substantial knowledge we have about phases of group development, among other relevant knowledge.[7]

The emphasis on cognitive knowledge and theory will not come easily. In fact, the tension between "action" and "research" often is very real, even when it does not merely provide an excuse for those who have not disciplined themselves to learn the literatures or to appreciate their underlying methodologies. Consider the common advice that the OD interventionist's most powerful weapon is his or her "warm body"—sensitivity and responsiveness to what is going on, prudent courage, and so on. That advice is at once profoundly correct in some senses, and impossibly empty in others. The prescription here does not undervalue the "warm body," but it proposes its linkage to a "good head," or a well-stocked information system.

Moreover, on a case-by-case basis, I believe that one can usually make major progress toward distinguishing the more-systemic from the less-systemic perspective. This manuscript contains several such examples, as in the illustration provided by the second point immediately following.

1. *Three Motivators to Cope Systematically.* By far, the advantages of

a systemic bias clearly carry the day. Three points illustrate the broader possible supporting argument. *First*, the systemic orientation avoids tiresome issues of "who is the client?" When only individuals or small groups are involved, clarity about "who is the client" patently is useful and even invaluable. At the politics/administration interface, however, the client is typically Janus-like with multiple and competing interests. Preoccupation with trying to define "client," then, may be paid for in terms of cultivating local loyalties and loss of systemic impact. The consultant should busy self with helping to seek/solve problems rather than with defining sponsorship, while being as clear as possible about whatever multiple clients are being served by any single intervention.

Obviously, the freedom to act in such ways implies major trust in the intervenor. Such trust does not get extended automatically, of course.

A chief executive had decided on a major appointment, he informed an OD consultant. The proposed appointee was saleable for various reasons, but (it soon became clear) had the basic attraction of being no threat to the chief executive. In fact, the CEO was bypassing an individual with better credentials for the job, but who also posed a greater threat to the CEO.

The appointment might be good "ward politics," the consultant agreed, but its systemic implications were serious. To illustrate, the CEO over time had importuned several subordinates to develop "strong back-ups," for all the usual public reasons but also to make it easier for the CEO to reassign and terminate employees. CEO encouraged others to "put it on the line," but when he had his chance he—like they—was motivated to take the easy way out. Few would be fooled, the OD consultant guessed.

The CEO reconsidered his choice, and discussion soon shifted to the topic of highlighting how the CEO had "bitten the bullet to set an example for one and all." This would be "good medicine for the system." Besides, the CEO concluded, the odds were better than ever that the new appointee soon would "dig his own grave with his mouth."

When informed that the OD consultant thought it wise to spend some time with the new appointee, the CEO first balked but finally agreed, in terms I found realistic although lacking in charity. "If you can help him, that will help me, if I play it with any finesse. And if you mess him up, or can't help, that also will help me."

This prescription for a systemic orientation may seem to increase the consultant's vulnerability, *second*, and it apparently clashes with the reasonable advice that the change-agent needs *a client*, first and foremost. But recall that I write here only of the politics/administration interface. Tactics well-designed to secure and safeguard *a* client, in short, often are counter-productive for maintaining a systemic role. I have become quite fatalist in this regard, and assign a very high probability to one of three outcomes in cases of interstitial consultancy:

- either the consultant comes into a situation in which a balance-of-power exists among actors, which balance recognizes the value of some external playing an interstitial role

- or the consultant quickly can encourage such a balance-of-power

- or the consultant is very unlikely to ever become effective in trading back-and-forth across the politics/administration interface

The need to legitimate the interstitial role quickly at the politics/administration interface rests on numerous considerations, two of which have a distinct prominence in my experience. Unless that occurs quickly, the consultant likely will either come to be—or come to be seen as—identified too closely with one of the sub-systems to be a credible interstitial player. One system member put it directly in observing that, although I "didn't work for him or his colleagues," I had a way of involving myself and being accepted (sometimes even welcomed) in their affairs. He noted:

> "Each one of us here, at one level or another, knows how important you have been—mostly in cases where we need help in getting together, breaking through barriers, but where we are too proud or too something to ask for help. You have a way of jumping in and fading out."

> "Although you don't work for any one of us, no one of us wants to shut you out, *or* to negotiate about specific sponsorship of your services. That's strange, given the way we do business—we like to own people. I guess we all know if anyone of us really had a lock on you, we'd all be worse off."

> "So we bitch some that no one really controls you, and especially [X, who authorizes payment for consulting services]. But we let it go at that because we have come to know that you aren't just working [X's] agenda for him."

Moreover, appropriate balances of power at the interface typically are temporary, which also seems generally true of lateral or horizontal linkages between separate units of organization at more or less the same level.[8] So the premium definitely is on getting something done quickly. This implies a certain disciplined boldness. To some, no doubt, this suggests a bull in a china shop. Most clients get the fuller message, quickly. Examples of both kinds may be consulted conveniently in other sources.[9]

Celerity also is appropriate in the third case above. "Getting out quick" when a supporting balance-of-power does not exist, or when it cannot be quickly induced, often will enhance a consultant's credibility as well as his leverage when the situation changes, as it almost certainly shall. "This just is not a propitious moment," the OD intervenor announces, in effect. "There will be other times, better times."

Third, an intervenor's focus on "the system" can be a damn good thing for, far more often than not, few others at the interface will be either equipped or motivated consistently to understand or evaluate systemic issues. The specialization prevalent at the interface inhibits such a view, for example. Thus "politicals" may be very active in developing the kind of agreements we call "policy," and they later may get involved in episodic casework for individual constituents but—beyond that, more than likely—their attention will be spotty. The usual preoccupation among politicals—even among those in executive or managerial roles—is to get reelected or reappointed, not to manage some system. Their focus likely will be segmented and superficial—that is, centered around those interests which can be welded into a *sufficient constituency*, no less and usually not much more.[10] For them, the OD intervenor can be useful in reminding them about what they are so likely to forget or undervalue. Note that developing "a sufficient constituency" is no mean feat. Indeed, it may be the quinteseential social act. And getting too far out ahead of a constituency can be a direct form of political suicide. But these factors merely heighten the responsibility implied above; they do not somehow pardon politicals from attending to that responsibility.

Professionals also may need systemic help, if for different reasons. Thus they often specialize in a function, in contrast to the specialization of politicals in stages of the policy-making and implementation cycle. That functional specialization may constitute a trained-incapacity, and its effects are perhaps most clearly seen in the budget process. Each functional specialty tends to fight for its own programs, which are particularistic but intensely advocated. Politicals may exacerbate these ubiquitous tendencies, moreover, as in playing favorites so as to guarantee access or to provide open lines of communication. Powerful members of Congress, for example, may use such an approach for dual purposes: to help control the presidency or political appointees; and to facilitate agency response to interests important to legislators.

What with nature being so amply aided by institutions and willful people, conflict-resolving designs between functional groups are a mainstay for the OD intervenor at the interface.[11] There will be many occasions when both politicals and professionals argue their often-different agendas with more zest than systemic consideration.

The intervenor also typically has experience in many more organizations than his client, whether political or professional. And intervenor's reading/study should be broader still. Such experience/knowledge—which by design is unfettered by day-to-day operating problems—often permits the consultant to sensitize clients to what may be "around the corner" so as to anticipate and prepare for it, or perhaps even to encourage them to venture beyond their probable vested interest in what exists today.[12] For example:

> A mass urban transit agency over a 5-7 year period would cycle through several identities—design, real-estate acquisition, construction, testing, and operations—so effort was channeled into continuous fine-tuning of policies, people, and structures so as to facilitate transitions from today to tomorrow. Hence the worst possible outcome was that the agency might define itself as a "design agency," or whatever, with serious consequences down-the-line.

> Conscious balancing and sequencing consequently got priority attention, which often conflicted with strong desires toward stability and standardization. Major changes in structure and style were often appropriate, as were some changes in persons. The organization was not allowed "to set," and intervenor's major role was to try to reinforce action looking ahead a year or so, while helping maintain an institution flexible enough to do today's job while anticipating tomorrow's demands.[13]

For organizations that are more stable and have simple products or services, this early-warning function is less useful, and may even be a nuisance to those at the politics/administration interface.

Guideline 5. *Contracting is always a double-edged sword, and especially at the interface.* My recommendation has schizoid qualities. I recommend far more specificity than is common in some regards, and far more open-endedness in other particulars than is usual.

1. *Open-endedness in a Central Particular.* I am mindful here of those fateful words in an otherwise-specific job description: "or other duties, as the supervisor may prescribe."

OD contracts could well have a similar quality, albeit a multi-lateral one. I do not here disparage the general value of the usual view of contracting by OD intervenors: who does what, when, for how much, and for whom?[14] But such SOP can have self-defeating consequences everywhere, and particularly at the interface. The mercurial quality of life there—the rapidity with which the "in" can become a "no, no," the serpentine ways in which even the same strategic objectives often have to be pursued tactically, the ways in which clients-of-the moment can come and go in the dynamics of seeking systemic goals, and so on—encourages a kind of basic "freedom clause" in OD contracts.

These and the many other features of the environmental texture of the public-sector interface detailed in the previous chapter make life difficult for the OD intervenor, as well as for members of the target-system. An open-ended contract will be helpful in responding to the character of the territory, and it will have two emphases:

- Intervenor contracts to do A, B, and C, within a specified time-frame, with certain specific likely effects

- Intervenor and target-client recognize that things can quickly change, and thus their contract reflects two basic commitments:

  — both intervenor and target-client propose to track developments closely so that appropriate adaptations can be made to the original contract, *as far as possible* on the basis of discussion and mutual agreement. Such reactions to fast-changing conditions should be the general expectation, in fact.

  — it is understood that in exceptional circumstances—which cannot be defined in specific terms—intervenor may in good faith make adaptations to the original contract when prior discussion and agreement is not possible, due to urgency or unavailability of client

2. *Toward Greater Specificity, Wherever Possible.* This notion picks up on a major element in the first contracting emphasis, which urges

greater specificity concerning the probable effects of an OD intervention. "Urge" seems the very most appropriate verb. For the greater specificity advocated here seldom gets attention, even though that specificity has important self-regulating consequences in enhancing responsibility, accountability and, hence, credibility.

For example, I utilize this general format in a standard team-building design. First, diagnostic interviews permit a judgment as to whether a crisis of agreement or disagreement constitutes the basic problem. More will be said about this crucial distinction later, be it noted.

Second, *given a diagnosis of disagreement*, I distribute Exhibit 8 to team members, with some such instructions:

> If you like to experience the effects indicated in Exhibit 1, for the six dimensions described there, I recommend a standard design.
>
> Experience indicates that the predicted effects will occur in 8 or 9 of 10 cases. So surprises can occur, but not often.
>
> I'll answer any questions you like now, and then I'll retire and let you decide on whether or not you'd like to go ahead. Call me back when you decide.

Third, the prognosis for a diagnosis of agreement is more complicated and problematic, and gets no further attention here.

Fourth, data concerning the predictions are then fed back to participants at various points to reinforce learning. Exhibit 8 provides one set of results from one such team-building experience. Those data represent typical effects. Note that the numbers in parentheses represent team members. As the reader might expect from the predictions in Exhibit 8, team member #8 in Exhibit 9 is the supervisor.

Guideline 6. *From the intervenor's point of view, being comfortable with "marginality"—even lusting after it—will be extremely valuable at the public-sector interface.* Being "marginal" here refers to having a "foot in two or more camps"—somehow psychologically straddling two or more groups that have differing value systems, goals, and behavior patterns. Specifically, the intervenor needs to be comfortable in living in two often widely-discrepant worlds: the client culture, and the OD profession.[15]

The marginal person, by hypothesis, can serve as a kind of linking-pin to help reduce any discrepancies, whereas "low marginals"

EXHIBIT 8. Predicted Effects of Standard Team-Building Design, Using Friedlander's Group Behavior Inventory

Group Behavior Inventory Dimensions	Predictions after Team-Building Experience
I. Group Effectiveness high scorers see creative and realistic team effort in problem-solving	I. most members will report *higher* scorers
II. Approach *vs.* Withdrawal high scorers see leader as approachable, as one with whom an unconstrained and comfortable relationship can exist	II. many members will report *higher* scores, but leader is a probable exception as are those who tried "approach" but saw it as not working or were punished for their try
III. Mutual Influence high scorers see themselves and others as having influence with others and Jim	III. will *increase* for most members, with probable exception of leader and the "exception(s)" described under II
IV. Personal Involvement and Participation high scorers are those who want, expect, and achieve active participantion	IV. will *increase* for all members, with possible exception of leader
V. Trust *vs.* Competitiveness high scorers are a group whose members have trust and confidence in each others	V. will *increase* for all members, with possible exception of leader
VI. General Evaluation high scorers see group as good, valuable, or pleasant *vs.* bad, worthless, unpleasant	VI. will *increase* for all members, with possible exception of those scoring lower on II-V

For details, see Robert T. Golembiewski, *Approaches to Planned Change* (New York: Marcel Dekker, 1979), pp. 323-339.

EXHIBIT 9. Typical Effects of Standard Team-Building Design

Actual Results of AT&T Team-Building
at T_1 = 1 and T_2 = 30 days

I.	Group Effectiveness	7 score higher (1, 2, 3, 4, 5, 6, 7)	1 scores same (8)	
II.	Approach vs. Withdrawal	4 score higher (1, 3, 5, 7)	3 score same (2, 4, 6)	1 scores lower (8)
III.	Mutual Influence	5 score higher (1, 2, 5, 6, 7)	1 scores same (3)	2 score lower (4, 8)
IV.	Personal Involvement and Participation	7 score higher (1, 2, 3, 5, 6, 7, 8)	0 score same	1 scores lower (4)
V.	Trust vs. Competitiveness	6 score higher (1, 2, 4, 5, 6, 7)	2 score same (3, 8)	
VI.	General Evaluation	5 score higher (2, 4, 5, 6, 7)	1 scores same (1)	2 score lower (3, 8)

would more likely become captives of one of their reference groups. "Marginality," in this sense, has long been recommended for the OD intervenor.[16]

My view is that this personal quality is especially critical in the public sector where powerful forces urge joining the client system—"going native," if you will—and/or despairing that pollyannish OD values have any chance with things as they are. Much of the surrounding discussion suggests the power of these two sets of forces at the public-sector interface.

Research on this central issue is just beginning,[17] but it does nothing to undercut the position here. Quite the opposite, in fact. Ther personal qualities associated with marginality are not firmly in-hand, but they seem to include open-mindedness, adaptability, low dogmatism, and so on. Note also the apparent usefulness of the simple approach to estimating an individual's marginality illustrated in Figure 7.

(For the curious, the high-marginal person would put his Y either smack *between* the square and the triangle, or *inside both* figures. A low marginal would put his Y inside one of the figures.)

The argument for conscious marginality—or interstitiality, if you will—can be made even more sharply. It is often dangerous to seek to

FIGURE 7. A Topological Approach to Marginality

Instructions: The triangle and square within the rectangle below each represents a group of people you associate with. The small circles represent other people. Draw a small Y to sant for *Yourself* anywhere in the rectangular space below.

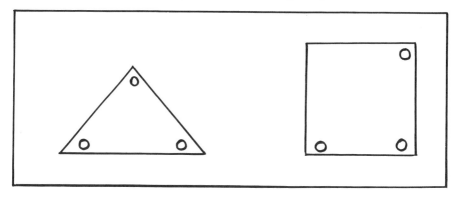

Based on R.C. Ziller, *The Social Self* (Elmsford, N.Y.: Pergamon Press, 1973), esp. pp. 46-57.

attach self—or to be content with having attached self—to a limited set of actors near the politics/administration interface. For political officials are vulnerable; and changes there typically result in several rounds of changes in immediate subordinates, among both patronage and career employees. Since OD programs can have long lead-times, establishing a tie with "the system" vs. a specific regime is not only difficult but may be necessary.

> The demise of Project ACORD in the U.S. Department of State can be traced quite directly to its basic attachment to the office of the deputy undersecretary for administration, with much less support (and even opposition) at two superordinate levels. When the undersecretary left, other departures followed, and Project ACORD soon folded although major effects persisted.[18]

Guideline 7. *I find serviceable a relaxed or flexible approach to confidentiality with members of the client system.* This might be seriously inappropriate in some settings, as in personal counselling. But at the interface, determined confidentiality can work to the significant detriment of the OD intervenors, as well as curb their systemic usefulness.

What approach is suggested here? I seldom agree to "keep this to yourself." Rather, the general contract has this flavor:

"If you tell me something, you'll generally have to rely on my discretion as to whether and when I'll mention it to others, or allude to it. Generally, also, my definite bias is to get the involved people talking about the issues, and complete confidentiality doesn't help."

"When an absolute confidence is required, which should be necessary only rarely, an explicit agreement should be made."

"What goes for me goes for you too, of course."

Confidentiality norms cover a vast range. I believe Drucker observed that: "I never talk about my clients." For him, that no doubt works.

My experience at the politics/administration interface is contrary, however, for several reasons. First, "leaking" or "inside dopestering" is a basic mode of political life. My contacts at the interface tend to regard substantial confidentiality with amused incredulity, and evidence of complete confidentiality is met with the awe reserved for those rare ascetics who shun strong drink, crude talk, fast women, big money, and (above all) power over others. "We couldn't do business that way," one official told me. "Information is our currency. It is often all we have. Having information I can't share is like having money I can't spend. Not much damn good when I need it, which is like right now and not bye-and-bye."

Second, to put it mildly, those at the politics/administration interface have been known to use confidentiality to control others. A well-chosen revelation can immobilize, as was true in my case even though I see myself as seldom immobilized. "You ought to know that X's wife is alcoholic and has been committed several times," I was told by an inside dopester before I could stop him. "That will help you understand some of the strange things that X does. But if you ever tell X, I'll deny I said it."

Why the immobilization? Let me sketch the pushes-and-pulls acting on me. Clearly, my preference would be to go to X, to test the point, or at least to share my concern. But my failure to reasonably resolve at least five points to my satisfaction inhibits me:

- There seems previous little sense to me in going to X and, in effect, saying "somebody, but I can't tell you who, is saying things about your wife."

- Suppose I identify the inside dopester, who then denies the conversation, as he promises he will do if I ever mention it? That may put me, as the politicals put it so directly, in a pissing contest with a skunk.

- Suppose I identify the inside dopester, who denies the conversation and, further, charges or implies that I would be so reckless only because of our differences (real enough) on other issues?

- Is X's affirmation or denial relevant for the organization and its agents, assuming no performance problems? I doubt it.

- My relationship with X has been kept free—deliberately on his part, I believe—of references to his non-work situation. Is it my obligation to expand the zone of our relationship? I see no present reason to do so, although I can easily envision circumstances that would impress that responsibility on me.

This is a still-unresolved issue for me, and it festers because I believe I am experiencing precisely the multiple-binds that my "helpful" informant may have intended.

Third, substantial confidentiality can forfeit major opportunities to make a difference, particularly when systemic matters are at issue. Confidentiality is a simpler matter in other cases, as when one acts as a personal adviser to a senior executive, or when one acts as a sounding-board against whom someone can bounce their ideas or concerns for a disinterested reaction.

Fourth, the OD intervenor need not devote much attention to fostering closedness, secrecy, distrust, suspicion, and so on, which overuse of confidentiality can breed. Those will no doubt have been well attended to, by masters at their craft.

In sum, both benefit and cost inhere in a relaxed concept of confidentiality. Taking advantage of systemic opportunities strongly encourages running the inevitable risks.

Guideline 8. *Whatever the point of entry, the consultant should from the start reveal the intent to work toward multiple access.* Multiple access permits more synergistic and systemic interventions, and it may even mean greater consultant freedom. The danger is that the OD consultant may get heaved and hauled in opposite directions, as by the possession of information that creates double-binds.

> I worked over a long period of time with a CEO as well as with his active board, with the knowledge of both parties, including a period when the board was considering how stringent their evaluation would be of the CEO's performance. I found more opportunities for two-way aid and direction in this arrangement than for double-binds and conflicts of interest. My role was to help read reactions in both directions, as it were, given my experience with both parties and their lesser experience with each other. I performed as go-between, while being explicit with both parties as to the temporary character of the arrangement.

Patently, a systemic orientation argues for multiple access, although it is not likely to come easily. Specific clients may wish to privatize their relationship; and clients must agree that they gain more than they lose as the consultant gains multiple access. I prefer bold signals, both at early stages and late, to make the point. To illustrate:

> "I will typically say to one chief executive with whom I have established a confidential relationship: "You say this business with X is not troublesome for you, now. I haven't had much contact with X, and I know your interests and his often conflict."

> "But I believe that this business can be a source of difficulty for the whole system, and thus in the long run for you as well."

> "Unless you object strongly, therefore, I propose to . . ."

As the intervenor brings home the bacon a few times, the leash may become longer.

Issues of confidentiality will arise, of course, but I have a standard position on the point. "I will always try to keep a confidence," I say. "But, in general, I am more comfortable if you only share that information which I might at my discretion communicate to others, if that seems appropriate. The same goes for anything I might say to you. We can go off the record occasionally, but that will require a special signal when we do."

As earlier comments imply, my experience here has been quite definite. Pledges of confidentiality can be used to control, as when people feel free to tell you something but pledge you to a secrecy they did not apply to self. If you are consistent, moreover, clients soon come to understand and to value the interstitiality, which will be impeded by firm (but usually unrealistic and unkept) pledges of confidentiality. From one perspective, confidentiality is a good way to miss systemic opportunities, as well as to model norms of anti-openness and anti-trust.

> In a formal setting, one member of a legislative group spoke to me: "We understand, Dr. Bob, that you have been working with [X, the agency head] on regular performance appraisals for his major subordinates. I understand some of these sessions have been very profitable, both to X and his subordinates. Would you recommend something similar for us and X? And would you help?"

This could either be a welcome or a highly-loaded request. If loaded, the request may seek to test whether I really mean my words about systemic concerns, or whether I am protective of a specific individual. Some actors at the interface may even intend the request to pose a no-win dilemma: If I overly-privatize my relationship with one individual, that makes me closed, secretive, non-helpful; if I deal publicly with aspects of that relationship, that may seem to make me loose-mouthed or even disloyal; and if I equivocate that makes me indecisive and perhaps evasive. As an opportunity, the request in effect offers multiple access and a chance to apply OD values at multiple levels.

As usual, the best safeguard against surprises is to anticipate the range of possibilities. In this case, X and I had an understanding about the implications of his using performance appraisals for his own subordinates. I did not have to guess about the motives of the legislators, even though I had no confidence I knew what they were:

> I replied: "You have an intriguing idea there, which I like. X and I have spoken about the desirability of such periodic meetings to clear the air.
>
> "I'm sure you don't want me to speak for him. But I believe he is receptive to the general idea.
>
> "As for my involvement, I'd be a hypocrite to see much difference between X appraising his subordinates and you appraising X. I have some ideas about which ways to go, so that also encourages my wanting to be involved. Having worked both with X and you, I might be useful in the first go-round or two.
>
> "We can re-evaluate my further participation at that time. I hope I won't be needed long. But let's wait and see."

Guideline 9. *The consultant typically should operate to expand the "range of credible discretion"* *for individuals and groups.* This represents the orthodox view, of course,[19] but it has some interesting applications at the politics/administration interface. For the CEO, for example, the associated ideal organization is one containing meaningful representatives of a diverse range of opinion, so as to maximize the range of available information and policy alternatives. In my opinion, "fostering conflict" thereby poses fewer risks than striving for a feigned consensus and/or vigilantly suppressing even timid discouraging words. Moreover, should the CEO have to act like Solomon and make the final decision when major disagreement exists, his ability to be both credible and yet consider a range of positions probably will be greater in direct proportion to the diversity of opinions and perspectives introduced.

Intervenors can work toward expanding the range of credible discretion in many ways. For example, the typical team-building effort devotes major attention to legitimating inputs by opinional deviants. Or intervenors may expose examples of Jerry Harvey's "crisis of agreement," first referred to as the "Abilene paradox": all or many members go along with a less-preferred or unpreferred choice because individually each member believes self to be the only deviant, when in point of fact all or many members share the same "deviancy" but none feel free to express it publicly.[20] Occasionally, also, a consultant with multiple-access will be able to increase the range of credible discretion by helping bring together two or more individuals or groups whose interests seem opposed but who in fact share significant interests and identifications, or can come to share them.

> An agency and a prestigious interest group had begun to take increasingly polarized positions on a technical issue, reinforced by mutually-perceived differences in background, attitudes, and policy styles.
>
> I learned independently from each party of separate efforts to test the superiority of their opposite technical positions, about which each side had made untested assumptions. I was also intrigued by the essential personal and style similarities between major decision-makers on the two sides, despite general agreement about the profound differences between them that contrasted "good old boys" and "silk stocking types."
>
> Both sides agreed to mutually test the sets of assumptions, after complex negotiations that I encouraged. Political loss-of-face was a powerful restraint

for both parties, but both soon came to appreciate the greater pain of the two alternatives: not testing the assumptions at all; or independently testing the assumptions.

Working toward an expanded range of credible discretion at the interface is often difficult and problematic. First, sauce for the goose may seem poison to the gander. For example, one CEO eventually accepted regular performance appraisal meetings with his subordinates because—despite its demands—he got more out of it than he put into it. But he was troubled initially—even hurt—when his governing body wished to apply the same technique to him. Fortunately, he had been urged to wrestle with that possibility before holding appraisals for subordinates. The OD intervenor should emphasize the implications for self of what is done unto others, early and late, even to the point of being pesty. Symbolically, persistence about such equal treatment can be very powerful.

Second, many decision-makers at the interface simply do not want an expanded range of discretion. Most are confident, if not opinionated; habitually, they tend to seek converging support for a position they somehow already favor, in contrast to divergent data that expands the range of credible decisions. They often want to build corrals, that is, not expand horizons. And when they are not building corrals for others, they often seek to avoid being corralled by others. Consider that a special interest important to an official may pressure him to take a position which is defensible only if some relevant data are kept suppressed. For such an official, expanding the range of credible discretion will be appealing only if he wishes to buck that interest.

Third, there are times when decision-makers cannot far enough or fast enough expand their area of discretion. When some issue is politically hot, a standard approach involves proliferating sources of data—multiple committees, commissions, study groups, and so on. Typically, the goal here is to escape the heat entirely, or at least to buy time while a bargain is struck among the central actors. Intervenors can be used to play this game, for it seems consistent with their preferences but is not. A certain native cunning about not being used in such elemental ways can go a long way toward earning some credibility for the intervenor at the interface.

Guideline 10. *Intervenor from the onset should announce his intent to work toward multiple public channels of information and evaluation.*

This is an orthodox OD notion, which seeks to increase the probability of reliable and valid information. The point intended here applies more broadly at the interface than in most OD formulations, as two emphases show.

1. *Multiple Channels Within A System*. The OD intervenor at the interface should strive to develop and maintain multiple channels of information and evaluation within *a system*. This parallels common efforts in the private sector, of course, although with a unique twist or two.

Paramountly, the politics/administration interface is infested with numerous "inside dopesters" having information of very diverse quality, as well as a penchant for creating their own reality, even one that departs wildly from what most actors know or believe to be true. These are always among us, of course, but nowhere more so than at the interface where inside-dopesters can have independent power-bases. This increases their influence or relevance, many fold. For having such a power-base variously insulates them from retribution or discipline, whatever the quality of their information. Moreover, developing/maintaining that power-base often will require (or encourage) presenting different views of reality—if not patent falsifications—as the overt reflections of basic differences in policy preferences or in supporting constituencies. In addition—and this for some takes getting used to—many actors at the interface have a genuine acceptance of "doing what has to be done," by themselves or others, no matter how discrepant the action from their perceptions of the situation or their preferences. "That's just politics," goes the typical evaluation of such flexibility concerning the truth, with the flavor that to see the game you have to pay the price of admission. The first rule, maybe the only rule, is: "Stay alive." Finally, the number and diversity of expressed interests is likely to be far greater in the public sector.

The intra-system usefulness of multiple channels of information and evaluation rests on a transparent rationale, especially in high-technology efforts, and much experience exists concerning their development. Team-building or survey/feedback designs clearly have such an objective. Occasionally, organizations will make concerted efforts to develop multiple channels for performance appraisals; and a few organizations will seek to build multi-channel networks into the very fabric of work.[21]

Such intra-system efforts often cut several ways at the

politics/administration interface. The benefits include those contributing to the sense of "self-forcing, self-enforcing" systems.[22] The costs include the possibility of a kind of Alphonse/Gaston mushiness in decision-making and action-taking.

> A governing body much desired to fire an executive. But that board also had supported an OD-inspired multi-channel system of reports, briefings, appearances, etc., before diverse public and private audiences. The board supported that strategy because of its managerial advantages in cross-correlating information, providing a general data-source for evaluating performance, spotlighting problem areas, encouraging mutual discipline among operating officials, and so on.
>
> The major untoward effect was that the target-executive had gained major support because of his prowess in this multi-channel system.
>
> The executive stayed. As much as the legislative group wanted his scalp, they wanted more to preserve the integrity of their multi-channel system.

Note that the OD intervention in this case clearly was "in politics," even as it encouraged a different kind of evaluation system than often exists. And the board clearly "lost," in the short run, although the system may be better off for their caution re unbuckling the executive and for their care in preserving their evaluation system.

2. *Multiple Channels Between Systems.* Without denigrating the usefulness of intra-system efforts, the OD consultant at the interface will find the richest opportunities in helping develop channels of information and evaluation *between* large systems, and especially those which are antagonistic. Major increments in cooperation may result. Moreover, given the delicacy of the effort, it may also be possible to induce competitive forces to alleviate the critical productivity crisis in government. Anti-trust laws often preclude similar inter-systemic efforts in the private sector.

> The governing body of Agency A had divided but intense opinions about whether or not efforts before the legislature would be made by one member—the head of Agency B with a competitive jurisdiction—to take over some activities of Agency A. Speculation also was rife among employees of agencies A and B. Complex issues were involved, for the two agencies had very different support groups—one rural and white, the other urban and black, to write in simplified but revealing terms.
>
> I was consultant to the governing body, but I felt more opportunity than

danger when I learned about the talk. Extensive conversations were held between the head of Agency A and the member of the governing body who was head of Agency B. Those conversations developed three major points of agreement. First, it might come to pass that Agency B's support groups would try to absorb Agency A. Second, the head of Agency B would neither initiate nor actively participate in such an effort. Third, both heads came to agree that—with some mutual care and cooperation—the possibility of a take-over might stimulate useful effort in both agencies to control costs and improve services so as to make better respective claims for each agency, if push came to shove.

In quite specific terms, these results were shared with managerial employees in both agencies, with special emphasis by both CEOs on the usefulness for each agency of a competition based on "fair play," performance, and ambition to cooperate.

Guideline 11. *Intervenors and interventions at the public-sector interface should be responsive to the special texture of the arena, which is in some respects unique but at least differs in noteworthy degree from the private-sector arena.* There is no definitive way to express the sense of this global point but, for openers, many public agencies reflect conditions or stages that do not permit unqualified acceptance of Shepard's[23] usually-appropriate counsel that OD interventions should build strength and build on strength. Roughly, there are some systems that cannot lose for winning; and there seem to be others that cannot win for losing. At the risk of being merely precious, the latter cases do not permit building strength and building on strength. Rather, the orientation may be to inspire some hope—even by risking dependence of the client on the consultant—while building on acknowledged and pervasive weakness, if not perversity.

How to distinguish such conditions or stages, specifically? Many approaches might be taken. Elsewhere, I try to differentiate "regenerative" from "degenerative" systems,[24] with the latter being characterized by low degrees of openness, owning, and trust, along with high degrees of risk. From a different but related perspective, Harvey[25] distinguishes crises of disagreement from those of agreement. For some important purposes, organization hosts with one condition or the other will differ. For example, the same data generated by the same OD design could have such profoundly different effects in the two systems:

• "Oh, so that's what's wrong. How can we remedy that?"

- "Yes, I know that's what's wrong. There's just no way to change that around here. It'll always be that way, or at least so long that I'll never live to see it change."

The image is that of a one-dimensional hill. Depending upon which side of the hill on which you find yourself (A or B), going the same distance in the right-ward direction will either get you closer to the peak (A') or still further away from it (B').

Diagnosis about whether an organization is at A or B cannot yet be precise. For example, I distinguish regenerative from degenerative systems mostly in my bones. More usefully, Harvey provides guidelines for determining which patterns of response imply agreement or disagreement.[26]

I have elsewhere detailed the kinds of distinctions between organizations that will be required for sensitive diagnosis and prescription,[27] so let me take a more general position here. Despite major problems, I am nonetheless convinced about three points: distinctions between kinds of organizations are critical; clues about the conditions usually are available; and public agencies are far more likely than private-sector organizations to have crises of agreement and advanced degenerative features. I cannot strictly prove my contentions, but I can easily illustrate the symptoms I have in mind as well as suggest evidence as to their public-sector pervasiveness. Let me try to be parsimonious and illuminating. I need search no farther than the lead-story on the first page of the newspaper which deals with teachers fleeing the classroom. One explanatory vignette must suffice here to illustrate degenerative systems and to suggest their growing pervasiveness. "This job is getting worse and worse every year," one ex-teacher reports. "No one seems to care anymore, not the parents, not the teachers. It's very depressing."[28]

In such systems, a key issue—perhaps *the* issue—then becomes how the *hope* of remedial change can be nurtured in the face of massive squelchers of that hope. Somehow, that hope might get kindled by itself; or a determined politico in high office may come along—as seems to be the case with Governor Hunt of North Carolina—who was seriously bent on renewing the state administrative system, and who could successfully avoid the charges of empire-building. Short of those happy happenstances, the analysis below has two emphases. A first emphasis considers some things an OD intervenor consciously can try in a degenerative system that might be ill-advised in a regenerative one. The second emphasis seeks to generalize implications for the OD intervenor's role.

1. *Some Personal Experience.* What kinds of things have often worked for me? Without prescribing them for any other OD intervenor, let me sketch a brief catalog of five semi-particulars. These five points do not exhaust what could be done, but they do illustrate what has been done.

First, consider the point-man notion. Plainly put, I have found that more personal risk-taking by the intervenor seems appropriate in degenerative systems. Instead of being personally up-front—to develop the point by contrast—the usual prescription for the OD intervenor-as-facilitator sagely encourages getting clients to own attitudes and behaviors, to express themselves openly, etc. To which many public-sector clients will respond: "That's easy enough for you to say, but very much harder for us to do." And so it is. One way to generate hope that regenerative features can be built into an organization is for the OD intervenor to be the "point-man," relying on infantry jargon. If the point-man lives, as it were, that implies some safety for others and all can advance.

A strong case can be made for using the OD intervenor as point-man although—as with any good thing—one can easily make too much of the notion. The "facilitative role" often will be helpful but, on many occasions, insistence on maintaining that role simply means that matters will fall between the cracks. Surely the point is one of fine-tuning. But public-sector applications often will profit from an intervenor's open and definite risk-taking. Why? The reasons are numerous, including a diversely-rooted caution—by those up for election, short-term political appointees, or shell-shocked career employees—about being up-front and active. As in the private sector, it is lovely to get the overt and active support of top-dogs in the public sector. But constancy often will be an unrealistic expectation for those actors at the public sector, even for officials who desperately want to support an OD effort. Moreover, having a point-man is often part of the culture of degenerative systems and, beginning from where the system is, typically constitutes good advice and sound practice. Moreover, the risks for the OD intervenor are in the general case far less substantial than for system members; and some pump-priming may be helpful symbolically, while any associated modeling may be useful to all concerned.

Since the danger surely exists, what safeguards inhibit unwise extensions of the point-man role? That is, the point-man may result in building dependence—thus standing Shepard's advice on its head, as it were—and it clearly builds on the "weakness" of suspicion, mistrust, and so on. And these represent conditions that are better avoided. Extended too far, relishing the point-person role may reveal more about the person than about OD intervention. I have heard, for example one intervenor note:

"I know I am helping people when they hurt me."

After some reflection, the intervenor sagely questioned: "Who do I think I am, Christ?"

A good question, that. The point-person role should stop well before an intervenor has to ask that question.

How to be a reasonable point-person, then? Basically, the OD intervenor must take the point in special senses only—as the conscience about the set of OD values as well as the technical expert on how to approach those values while also achieving political objectives. Very often public-sector clients will employ terminology expressing the blend-at-issue, as in referring to the change-agent as a "guru." This implies one who will show clients "a new way"—with potentially serious implications for what goes down and how—but also one who is not merely another competitor in the usual game of power.

I have found that my point-man posture most often is directed at some power figure, say a CEO or an executive, with a reputation for staunchness if not insensitive autocracy. If we can make it, as it were, subordinates may feel a glimmer of hope. Whether we make it or not, however, the signals can be very revealing to others.

> A powerful staff executive and I got into an animated discussion about leadership styles in the very early stages of mutual consideration of the usefulness of team-building for him and his immediate subordinates.
>
> In the heat of those early moments, he jerked a marking pencil from my hand, and sallied forth to cover several pages of newsprint, lecturing me and his subordinates.
>
> I grew resistive after 15 minutes or so, and consciously debated a deliberately-facilitative but avoiding comment like: "Now, Ernst, it might be helpful at this point for us to review people's reactions to the last few minutes to see if they're getting what they expected from this meeting."
>
> Rather, given my guess that his subordinates would not take that bait, I noted: "It's clear to me that either you have not understood what I tried to say earlier, or that I did a very bad job of it. And your knowledge of the research literature on leadership styles seems very weak to me. Give me the marker, Ernst, and I'll start again if the misunderstanding is general."
>
> The room grew very quiet. Ernst returned to his seat and, very revealingly, said: "I deserved having my chain yanked. That was good for me—I was beyond my depth." "But"—he added with no smile at all—"only one time this week."
>
> Ernst had saved everybody much time, and some possible grief. There would be no team-building, we all seemed to recognize at once, especially since Ernst would be retiring in less than two years. One week between feedback efforts is a long, long time.
>
> There would be a better time, and soon enough.

Second, the prime implication of the present characterization of the public-sector arena is that OD interventions appropriate to one organizational condition or stage might be inappropriate at another, perhaps even seriously counterproductive. Consider the decreased usefulness at the interface of such public interventions as group confrontations between hierarchical levels,[29] or various "mirroring" exercises. Their results in public agencies might only confirm a basic fact that everyone already knew: that the system is pervasively degenerative, which means essentially—openness, owning, and trust being so low, and risk so high—that candidness about the system permits only one conclusion. Conditions will not be changed by anyone, even given herculean effort and uncommon good fortune. Things are seen as so bad that publicly acknowledging the point only makes matters worse, simply deepens despair.

Let me briefly illustrate what I mean by proposing that group designs are less useful in what I consider degenerative systems. I tend to deal far more than in the private sector with single individuals, personally and as a go-between, with parties mutually aware of my role, and especially so when some new issue is being worked. Other localized or privatized designs—such as third-party interventions and role negotiation exercises—also can prove very useful.[30] Patently, this approach reduces the risk for principals, and permits face-saving should things not work out. Typically, when things do work out, success does not want for parents. After a successful iteration or so, actors at the interface typically take up-front positions.

> In one case, political officials were cautious about confronting a CEO with their view that he required a strong back-up. They did not want to offend the man, nor to reduce his clout by too-obvious demands that he acquiesce. The politicals did feel the need for greater confidence that a capable replacement was in the wings, but they wished to proceed with no public notice. The CEO wanted to appear neither obdurate nor a patsy for a possible take-over by training his own replacement. I was invited in by one side, but soon was accepted by the other.

> I traded back and forth, carrying information, but also contributing to strategy and tactics. I also strived to build as much openness as possible into a situation that had very narrow parameters, as by helping those involved articulate and share the political implications of the transaction, as well as their emotional reactions to it, although in most cases at a distance through me as an intermediary.

> Once that issue got worked through with minimum dislocation, the political officials sought similar action by other key executives. "We'll use the [CEO] model," I was told, "so we won't need you." And that pleased me.

Third, derivatively, interventions at the interface must be sensitive to short time-frames, with stops and starts. Hurry up, then wait: this characterization of military life well-suits the interface. One "hurries up" to nourish the faint bloom of hope; and one "waits" when attention suddenly shifts to other agendas, as can mercurially happen, and often does.

Hurry up and wait, of course, imply inconsistent demands. How to cope with them? Some things can be done, although each has mixed consequences and each requires some comprehensive and tough planning. For example, the prudent OD effort at the interface carefully builds around several stages, each with specific go/no-go choice-points. Progress might be followed by a resting period, that is, with subsequent design elements ready for picking-up when the environment again becomes propitious. This is good advice for all OD, but its relevance is greatest in the public sector. Relatedly, and especially early-on, public-sector interventions should tend toward limited-purpose designs, as contrasted with comprehensive social contracts pointed toward broad cultural change in organizations. Skill-training and coaching/counselling activities best represent limited-purpose designs of the interaction variety; and flexible workhours programs illustrate structural and policy OD variants that imply minor costs, skills, and training. Team-building is intermediate in its demands on time, energy, and commitment. System-building or system-renewal activities have the longest time-frames and the greatest energy requirements, but they also promise the greatest pay-outs.

Fourth, interventions at the interface must emphasize policy or structural interventions far more than is presently the case, because much of the degenerative quality of the public-sector arena has its roots in policy and structure. The point has long since been made in the literature.[31]

Overkill on the point must be avoided, however. I do not argue here that interaction-centered designs deserve neglect. But they should at least be based on careful diagnosis, with as specifically-limited a contract as possible; and I also propose that interaction-centered designs can be seriously counter-productive at the interface. To illustrate, interaction-centered designs can reveal a "new and satisfying way" for relating to others, a relevation that may merely aggravate dissatisfaction about how things "have to be" because of the legal-procedural features of the public sector that often defy modification or change. These features may derive from inflexible rules applicable throughout a jurisdiction, promulgated by a centralized personnel agency, and enacted by a distant legislature intent as much (or more!) on preserving its own avenues of access as on enhancing the efficiency/effectiveness of administrative units. In effect, technostructural activities can provide valuable reinforcement for behaviors and attitudes consistent with OD approaches. Moreover, technostructural rigidities may contraindicate a range of interaction-centered OD designs—except as explicit band-aids and cooling-out for policies, structures, and procedures that cannot be changed and will continue to produce negative effects in system members.

One illustration establishes the hardiness of policies/structures in public service, and how they can overwhelm even the firmest resolve generated in interaction-centered designs. Flexi-Time has been applied pretty much world-wide for over a decade. The first substantially-documented application in American industry goes back approximately 9 years,[32] and the intervention's overall record of positive effects seems undeniable, perhaps even incredible.[33] Although fewer public-sector applications have been attempted to this time,[34] the record for useful effects is not distinguishable from private-sector experience. Incredibly, however, Congress only in 1978 passed a law providing for a 3-year evaluation of such innovations in workhours, and the Office of Personnel Management in 1979 just began gearing-up to do that round of studies.

Fortunately, the intervenor often will experience more leeway in restructuring public-sector work and responsibilities. In some agencies, indeed, reorganization all but constitutes a way of life. These opportunities seldom get exploited, however, since reorganizations typically rest on a structural model and a mode of implementation inconsistent with OD values.

Fifth, the view of "the system" as inhibitor raises serious issues for the intervenor, in at least two major senses. Thus the accusation may only be alleged in cases, rather than established. Vigorous testing alone can establish whether the allegation reflects reality or constitutes a self-fulfilling prophecy. The system-as-inhibitor also implies serious dilemmas when the intervenor is urged "to do something" even though "the system" cannot be modified in any relevant particulars.

Consider the first of these two cases. The intervenor only by aggressive testing can zero-in on the issue of whether "the system" is as wicked as advertised. Very often, considerable "wriggle room" can be shown to exist, even if highly-specific and localized. In other cases, the essential cause may lie in some unapproachable, unalterable, and unavoidable policy or structure. Here the intervenor may resort to worst-case analysis. The focus here is on the basic question: "What would be the worst possible outcome if you (or your agency) did X?"

Sometimes "the worst" turns out on inspection to be pretty mild stuff; or various ways of blunting the effects of "the worst" might be brought to life. It might even be possible to work toward changing "the system."

But cases clearly exist in which the worst consequence of evasion is very wicked, while "playing the game" is costly for participants. Here intervenors face a dilemma. Should they be content with Band Aid interventions, as in cooling-out designs for disaffected participants? Or should they do nothing? Or should intervenors, with highly-probable futility, push for preventive interventions that reduce or eliminate the source of disaffection? The issue re cooling-out is particularly troublesome, for many OD interventions (like confrontation designs, or team-building) can create an era of good feelings and comraderie. And some managers use them to buy time, with little or no expectation that they will be more than "ventilation sessions" that "permit blowing-off some steam."

There are no general answers to such questions. But appropriate design-elements can help guarantee that it is not all amelioration and no prevention.

In one case, I agreed to an ameliorative-only effort by a CEO, whose basic style involved a preference for laissez-faire but included a quick reliance on potent authoritarianism when things did not go well in his eyes. I suspected he periodically built-up concern and even hostility in his subordinates, although his timing in scheduling "ventilation" sessions was pretty good. He would then drive the resulting "era of good feelings" into the ground, I feared, with no lasting change in his behavior.

I shared my concerns with him. I did not want to be prissy, I noted, but I simply had no time for ameliorative-only designs. "Now that's the kind of openness I want," he said. "If you can only get my colleagues to do half as well, we might generate some lasting changes."

I agreed to serve as the intervenor, but only if I could state my concerns to the troops and if I could so design the session as to dramatize the possibly-contraceptive character of the intervention. CEO agreed.

In the opening session, I noted my concern that the CEO could be a "cast-iron sponge," who would obligingly allow all feedback to pass through him but would respond to little or none of it. I explained the design thus would have two components: a confrontation phase between CEO and the group of his subordinates; and a contracting period, when CEO and they would bargain about what one party wanted the other to STOP, START, or CONTINUE. I advertised my major interest in seeing that any contracts would be met, but emphasized that there might be no contracts.

The CEO smiled benevolently. "Just what we need," he said, "agreements arrived at in public we can all share—both in formulating and enforcing." He later joined in enthusiastically, agreeing to "start" a major policy in return for an agreement by his subordinates to "stop" something they were doing. CEO was surprised by the issue, as was the intervenor.

CEO agreed to a major change in policy, after extended discussion and emotional exchanges. Both employees and CEO considered the experience a smash success.

About a week later, the CEO gave a party for me and several others he saw as central. At the party, I learned that the CEO had changed his mind about the major policy he had agreed to "start." The change would be communicated to others at "some later date."

The CEO asked each guest to speak briefly and, of course, I opened my remarks by saying: "I resign." CEO had made the agreement in public session and, if a change were unavoidable—which I doubted—then that arena was the one in which the change should be considered. And if his employees were as incensed as I about the surprise change, I concluded ominously, there would be trouble.

"Bob G raises a point we neglected," said the CEO, unruffled. "Day-to-day pressures encourage one to neglect the fine points. We shall reconsider. Good gurus are hard to find, you know."

A week or so later, I learned that the new policy, almost rescinded privately, was reinstated the same way. I worked with the CEO over several years—often intensely, but always at arm's-length to protect myself from being his foil and (I hope) especially to avoid compromising his subordinates.

Indeed, I am certain only of one thing in cases of "the system" as inhibitor. I think little of the OD intervenor who in effect says: "Look how easy it is to thumb your nose at your system. Why don't you try it? It's fun." The consultant might only precipitate clients into harmful situations, whose effect the consultant might experience in only attenuated degree, or escape altogether.

2. *Some Implications for the OD Role.* These samples of personal behavior imply some useful generalizations. Better put, perhaps, those

behavioral samples should be viewed *only* within a context which distinguishes three intervenor roles:

- generating the *need for change*

- *implementing* a program of change after system members perceive the need for change

- *modeling* aspects of the kinds of behavior appropriate to some needed change perceived by system members

The illustrations above of behaviors that have worked for me in seriously-degenerative systems should not relate to the first role-component. In my view, the client system usually must come to perceive that need. In certain exceptional cases, the intervenor may adopt such a role. But intervenors should do so with full recognition that this will probably disqualify them from either implementing or modeling roles, when and if some systems come to recognize the need to change. An intervenor's enthusiasm about a need for change also may pose serious risks for system members. They may find it awkward or even dangerous to buy into an intervenor's concept of the need for change. The issue will be especially real in autocratic organizations with a history of harsh treatment of deviants.

Notice a major qualification. Intervenors should not be timid about raising issues about which *choices* might need to be made, or which issues need to be explored to determine whether choices need to be made. Several guidelines above—e.g., 2 and 3—encourage just such energetic attention to strategic or likely choices. But change and choice are viewed very differently here. The intervenor who highlights choices performs a valuable service, in general. Intervenors who insist on change can be bothersome; and they may precipitate clients into situations for which they lack preparation or enthusiasm. Occasionally, insistence on change even might be dangerous for participants.

The illustrations above of behaviors that have worked for me in advanced degenerative systems argue that OD intervenors should do more modeling of behaviors appropriate to some needed change *perceived by a client.* Very often, the intervenor's role is perceived to be that of a facilitator who only enters a system, helps highlight the need for change, and perhaps provides appropriate skill-training. The illustrations above go beyond the intervenor playing the role of cheerful facilitator or (worse by far) of "cruise director."

Guideline 12. *OD consultants at the interface unavoidably find themselves actors in the "network of power": they are advocates concerning the allocation of values within the system, even though they often will play other strictly-facilitative or helpful roles.*

1. *Interventions as Politically-Charged.* I would argue that interventions, broadly conceived, are always politically-charged. But the interface seriously exacerbates issues that can be more easily managed in most private-sector loci, or even finessed there. Operating at the interface, the OD consultant may strive for a politically-neutral role; he may plead he only advises; or he may more justifiably say his goal is maximum ownership by all involved of any changes or choices. And these common restrictions will often make much sense at other loci, but not at the interface. For there, almost by definition, *any* significant intervention is politically-charged.

Hence the usual verbalisms that often usefully restrict the intervenor's role are mostly beside the basic point at the interface, and they seldom will disabuse anyone who counts of the typical reality *and* perception of the effective intervenor's role. Look at the point another way. Like it or not, the public-sector intervenor often will be operating in multiple domains—e.g., technical *and* political—or may act in them at any time, without notice or even awareness.

And what is that typical reality/perception? Effective OD ideology and designs applied at the politics/administration interface will impact directly on organizations whose structure, policies, and procedures derive in large part from some multiple, extra-organizational authority—complex legislative constituencies, for example—which may be difficult or impossible to reach, and which may have the capability of disciplining those perceived as somehow out-of-line. So OD efforts not only can have serious political implications in affecting constituencies, legislative access, and so on. But the OD intervenor can be more vulnerable when an intervention "succeeds" than when it "fails," in substantial contrast to the private sector.

This imbeddedness of public agencies in a broad and pervasive legal/institutional context puts them in a class by themselves, compared to even the largest and most centralized of private-sector organizations, although the gap is narrowing due to EEO, OSHA, and so on. Change can be herniating in the public sector, especially because the common derivative ethos may be described as one of "legal rational formality [which] creates an organizational climate that is conservative and careful, where conflict-avoidance is a way of life, whose employees have little ability to influence their reward system by their productive or collaborative behavior, and where win-lose dynamics characterize the nature of relationships within and among organizations."[35] The weight of previous and broad-ranging political agreements can be great, in the general case. "I have the feeling I am trying to lift the entire federal civil service," one official put it, "when I try for even minor innovations in my agency." That weight also can be brought to bear on anyone or anything disturbing today's delicate balance.

Let us narrow the present discussion to one illustrative focus. What Virginia Schein calls the "politics of implementation" will be significant in all efforts toward systemic change in all organizations. But no situation rivals the politics/administration interface in that significance. Consider one case—the providing of aid and comfort to enemies of a change-effort, enemies that may not only be numerous, but who have independent power-bases and more often than not answer to no common discipline or authority. Actors without experience at the interface may be surprised, for example, at the complex dynamics that may be induced by what seems like a simple authoritative order. Truman caught much of the flavor of the situation in predicting difficulty for the newly-elected President Eisenhower, whose experience in the military would ill-prepare him for the untidiness of politics, which lacked the discipline, definite career patterns, and established ways of doing things characteristic of the military in which Eisenhower spent virtually all of his adult life. "He'll sit there," Truman predicted, "and he'll say, 'Do this!' *And nothing will* happen. Poor Ike—it won't be a bit like the Army. He'll find it very frustrating."[36]

What can the OD intervenor do in the face of the difficulty of making things happen in the public sector? The OD intervenor at the interface really has no great range of choices. Following Schein,[37] again referring only to the unavoidable politics of implementing OD efforts in terms used earlier:

- the OD intervenor can conceptually "play down the politics of implementation and deny the pervasiveness of political behaviors in organizations," thus avoiding any direct confrontation with prevailing OD values as to openness and trust. The price may be ineffectiveness or failure, as the intervenor's ideology provides inadequate real-world guidance, especially with respect to systemic change which, of course, is crucial at the interface.

- the OD intervenor can acknowledge the potential conflict of OD values and the politics of implementation and, by conscious choice, restrict self to interventions in which conflict is least likely. This may be reasonable, but it patently forfeits most opportunities for systemic change. And it may relegate intervenor to Band Aid or cooling-out activities, which may be important but are self-limiting in crucial senses and (more significantly) can induce organization members to unwisely expose themselves when prudence calls for secrecy and deceit.

- the OD intervenor can conceptually acknowledge the potential conflict of OD values and the politics of implementation, all the better to consciously face the trade-offs that often will be required for effective implementation.

There should be little question about the bias advocated here, in the general case. The OD consultant at the interface must resolutely help induce an *alternative system of power*. That makes the OD intervenor an advocate, of course, and a probable-target for those with an interest in what exists. But little is lost thereby, because at the interface any significant intervention is by definition "in politics," or can easily and quickly become so, and no virtue inheres in trying to neglect that fact. Intervenors can more toward *their kind of power* (among other ways) by helping generate reliable and valid information, by working effectively in groups, by illustrating the central role of trust in making intended things happen, and by having a sure grasp of the literature relevant to the character and consequences of common organization structures and policies. That is, power has multiple bases, and it does not have to be coercive. To illustrate, an OD consultant may derive influence from expertise, access to information, political insight and sensitivity, status or stature, and group support.[38]

2. *Intervenor's Presentation of Self.* In my experience, the OD intervenor at the interface can help gain credibility in these regards by special presentation of self. For example, shunning the broader political arena seems comforting to participants. That is, this implies

that consultant is not "ambitious" in the political sense, that he will not without the greatest provocation seek to usurp the roles of others in communicating with visible externals, and that (perhaps primarily) he really means it when he proclaims emphasis on the health of the target system as contrasted with making it in the broader political arena. Similarly, it is most helpful if significant actors do not see the OD consultant as a direct competitor *for* their authority, even if a person is concerned with *how* that authority is exercised.

How does an intervenor go about this potent but non-competitive presentation of self? The approaches are as diverse as consulting human-kind, but they all involve a basic innoculation against "capital fever." This narrative will illustrate these approaches briefly:

> "One reason you pay me so well," I might express one aspect of this point, "is to make it financially unattractive for me to want to do any other job but my own. Like yours, for example."

> Similarly, hosts might be happy to learn that a commitment to research provides the major motivation for a consultant's involvement. And some are anxious for verification that "only a fool would leave the cushy university job of mine for the doubtful privilege of getting peppered from all sides."

What are signs that a consultant presents self in intended ways? Again, this discussion offers an illustration rather than a catalog. As a place to begin, the intervenor would do well to analyze the symbols generated by hosts that refer to consultant's interstitiality and relate to the normative thrust of the intervenor. These symbols may be tinged with admiration, hostility, or some envy that the consultant is in substantial degree free from normal hierarchical orpolitical controls; and they can provide useful clues as to the consultant's perceived role. Consider three examples:

- "Guru" is one such usage suggesting at once an extra-hierarchical plane as well as advocacy of a "new way." I consider that a good mix. Some intervenors find "guru" distasteful in its implication of dependence but, when I hear it, the word typically has enough playfulness or hostility associated with it to preclude any fear of over-dependence.

- "The ghost" is another usage, and here the emphasis clearly is on sudden comings-and-goings. This symbol suggests a desire for greater contact, notice of appearance, and perhaps mystery/fear/inquisitiveness about who is seeing whom. Analysis of this metaphor prompted executives to share an index card listing all external appointments for the next day, so that non-appointees could touch base if they wished and all would know when consultant/client contacts were made.

* "Digger O'Dell" implies more concern still, the reference being to radio's "friendly undertaker," the "last to let you down." Consultant was involved in many discussions with and about those having performance problems. Hence the usage, clearly referring to an external agent, occasionally useful and even necessary, but whose appearance was not a signal for rejoicing and would (by definition) come too late for the person most directly involved!

These several metaphors all impute a kind of other-worldliness yet potency for the OD intervenor, and I like to see both elements attributed to my role, although the latter two metaphors clearly encourage some fine-tuning. The former emphasis I take as one effort to deal with interstitiality of the intervenor's role and to symbolize its freedom from normal constraints; and the latter component (I hope) contains elements of reality as well as of wish. Illustratively, actors are more likely to deal with me when I am seen as potent but not as narrowly-competitive. Then, they are more likely to provide me that piece of information that they would love to test but do not want to (or cannot) risk testing, for they know my role permits testing such information with those who matter.

Guideline 13. *The consultant will earn most strokes for his ameliorative successes, but both professional and systemic considerations urge substantial and growing attention to preventive efforts.* This is not simply a way of encouraging consultant suicide, although that may occur. The basic motivation inheres in the harsh reality that sometimes, perhaps often, risking that unhappy outcome can be a very good thing at the interface.

1. *Ameliorative or Band Aid Interventions.* Let the present point be put in balance. Major attractions urge ameliorative interventions, patently. OD interventions are best applied when the hurt is obvious to the client, who can ask for help, participate in diagnosis and

prescription, feel the relief of any successful interventions, and experience the increments in self-esteem associated with psychological success in these regards. Relatedly, intervenors seldom will succeed if they raise merry hell with an authority system by seeking to remedy evils and rectify wrongs that have priority only (or largely) within their own framework for interpreting reality and defined by their own values. Moreover, patient helpers-on-the-sidelines can be significant resources when an organization becomes polarized by conflict or whatever. Comfort and safety often inhere in being able to call on a third-party who has no obvious ax to grind.

2. *Preventive Interventions.* Equally weighty considerations encourage a strong emphasis on preventive work, however, on the general principle that avoiding a mess is often preferable to merely tidying-up afterward. Ameliorative-effort-only also can imply a puny role for the intervenor; and it can pose ethical dilemmas relevant to cooling-out those disadvantaged by organization processes, by professionals acting with full knowledge that those processes will not be changed. As our knowledge of organizations and behavior increases, so also will it be ethically and professionally more difficult to "stand by." Too colorfully perhaps, the ameliorative OD intervenor is, at best, like a traffic engineer who can prescribe traffic lights at an intersection only after several accidents or deaths occur. At worst, the ameliorative OD consultant is like the traffic engineer who can only catalog the carnage, and who must await the next "accident" without even comforting the grieving survivors.

In sum, the OD intervenor everywhere does well to give growing attention to preventive interventions, and perhaps especially at the politics/administration interface. Perhaps even more so than in the rest of life, politics is far more reactive than pro-active, and this bias at least deserves highlighting. Moreover, "politics" is an invention for dealing with facts and especially values that are in conflict. Enough issues in doubt usually exist without creating additional ones. OD certainly is no replacement for politics; but OD consultants help clarify the issues in doubt by preventive interventions, or at least can help by educational efforts concerning the value of specific preventive efforts. This is the case even though preventive efforts

- may not induce great managerial enthusiasm, e.g., as they impact on the authority system or imply changes in standard procedures and policies

- have effects that are difficult to ascertain, especially in the sense that only vulnerable arguments support the position that some specific stimulus X inhibited some outcome Y which never occurred

- present intervenors with substantial opportunities for self-delusion about what needs doing, and about the impact of their interventions

- often constitute no-win situations in that intervenors not only are rightly criticized for ameliorative interventions that fail, but their successful interventions also can be dismissed by the assertion that experience simply proved that no intervention was necessary

One point deserves emphasis, although it may be obvious. Band Aid interventions often will be interaction-centered, as in ventilation sessions. Quite often, in contrast, preventive interventions get deeply involved with changes in structure, policy, or procedures.

Guideline 14. *When in doubt, despite the danger, the intervenor should work toward OD values and emphasize systemic and preventive interventions.* This does not seek to provide encouragement for the power-hungry, or for those desperate to make an impact. Simply put, other perspectives on more parochial issues typically will have numerous proponents. Few participants will have either the motivation or the relative safety to take a systemic and preventive perspective.

Typically, precious little reason urges fear that OD intervenors at the interface can "make things happen" and hence should consciously restrict self lest they compromise voluntarism, owning, and so on. The politics/administration interface is no T-Group, where concerns about "making things happen" vs. "letting them happen" can be appropriate. Typically, OD values at the interface do not have a prayer, unless they are somehow very right and fit other needs. As one observer commented about Carl Rogers' position that an increased concern with human relationships was *the* prerequisite for effectively managing our institutions:[39]

> Though I agree with [Rogers] heartily, I have some very strong questions about whether, indeed, this kind of future is in the cards for us . . . in the basic decision-making that takes place, the values Dr. Rogers and I hold dear have an extremely low priority. Indeed, the old-fashioned concerns with

power, prestige, money, and profit so far outdistance the concerns for human warmth and love and concern that many people consider the latter extremely irrelevant in the basic decision-making. Sadly, it is my feeling that they will continue to do so.

1. *Implications for Intervenor.* In short, OD intervenors may make a pain of themselves by prattling about OD values, systemic perspectives, and preventive interventions. But they are very unlikely to somehow catapult a large organization into humanist orbit, or into disaster either, although they may generate some trouble for themselves.

Consider the case in which a CEO from the start had given such overt and unqualified support to an executive that the latter fixated on his mission and created problems for his fellow executives. The fine-tuning dilemma for many was real: how to curb the favored executive without significantly reducing his ability to get a needed job done?

As the OD consultant, I pieced together my diagnosis. Several executives, possibly by design, adopted a strategy of "let us hold your coats while you fight" toward the favored executive and one of his colleagues, a new man on the team whose work was significantly impacted by the executive's single-minded rush to completion. I guessed that the older hands had themselves failed in efforts to control the operating executive. The new man respected the operating executive's competence, liked him as a person, but came to be suspicious of "his numbers."

I agreed that curbing the senior executive probably would be useful, but I did not like the scenario. I discussed the problem with the new executive, and he concurred that it was both serious and growing. I learned that the new executive was unwilling to involve the CEO, except indirectly, for at least two reasons. He wanted to solve his own problems; and he did not want to be seen as a tattle-tale who succeeded by highlighting the failure of others. He also realized that the CEO might be one of those wishing for a fight—not being willing to curb the executive personally but desirous that it be done by someone. Moreover, the new man wanted to avoid this central question: the operating executive or me?

Although I had to be careful not to substitute my analysis for that of the CEO or the new executive, I did not feel the proposed fight would be useful for the system. Indeed, I forecast such a clear victory for the operating executive that he would be even more unresponsive to the needs of others. In short, I concluded a fight might raise some hell, but little else.

I confronted the CEO, and expressed my concerns. I got a double message: he denied any intent to use the new executive to discipline the senior man (for reasons I found credible enough), while noting that he saw no real problem between the two men (which I found hard to believe). I expressed my incredulity, and outlined my desires to work toward a collaborative resolution of the issues between the operating executive and the new man.

I received no great encouragement from the CEO, but no clear wave-off either. So I went ahead.

Details would be onerous here, but part of the effort involved an "interface meeting" of all executives, whose purpose was to check the adequacy of collaboration among departments. Although the CEO warned that he did not "want anyone picked on," to make a two-day story short, the operating executive heard a chorus of complaints, for the first time in common session, and apparently concluded he had been pushing his luck.

Shortly thereafter, the three of us—the operating executive, his new colleague, and I—got together, and attention focused on an unusual way the operating executive chose to report some critical data. The suspicion about "his numbers" soon evaporated into bemusement as to why and how that particular convention came to be relied on, since it might inhibit early awareness of potential cost over-runs. The convention was changed soon thereafter, quietly.

In my view, the early results were mixed: +1 for the system; -1 or less for RTG (the intervenor). The required job got done, without major warfare. The new executive took pains to feed my self-esteem. Moreover, some of the perceived instigators later came out of the closet, and they did not seem terribly out-of-joint. "It was a long shot, anyhow," one of them told me. "And the two guys seem to be making progress, although slower than I like." But the CEO and the senior operating executive showed no early enthusiasm for what happened. Several weeks later, in fact, I got a note and enclosure from the CEO, sent with the sparse comment: "I believe you would want to see this." The enclosure was a Xerox of another consultant's resume, sent to the CEO by the senior operating executive in question, on which the latter had written: "Now here's *MY* kind of consultant!"

There are no certain guides for proceeding here. What I did in this case was to meet with the CEO, and share with him my perception that for the first time in awhile we seemed far from being on the same wave-length. And I had pushed hard enough and I might be undermining his strategy with the senior operating executive. I asked whether he wishes:

- to revise my contract, which gave me great leeway within the agency

- to consider termination, if we were far enough apart.

He encouraged me to "let things simmer" with the operating executive. Beyond that, he added: "When you started on that venture, I was skeptical. I have come to appreciate somewhat more what was involved, but I still believe you overreated."

Things do appear somewhat rosier in the longer-run. Perhaps two months after the reporting convention was changed, a major potential cost overrun was highlighted by the new convention for reporting data. This occurred at least 6 months sooner than if the old convention had still been in-place. The CEO observed: "We of course always believe in getting such possibilities out in the open to do something about them. Or at least in time to give fair-warning to our various publics, to show we are on top of things."

Longer-run score: + 2 for the system; + 1/4 for RTG.

Guideline 15. *When in doubt, the OD intervenor should work toward OD values, emphasizing individual and systemic development as contrasted with political or power considerations.* Generally, the intervenor is poorly-advised to tether his recommendations to the political environment, as in guesses about "what will go down." This may seem .to save-face all the way around, but that convenient assumption often will be wrong.

So let the intervenor emphasize individual and systemic development. Again, numerous others are very likely to espouse other perspectives; again, also, this prescription requires that the intervenor risk in major ways. Having substantial "money in the bank" with the client seems a prerequisite for attempting what often needs doing.

The conflict between personal development vs. political leverage constitutes a common specific case-in-point. Take the situation of the female executive secretary, who had the opportunity to take on managerial responsibilities but also was attracted to another similar but somewhat better-paid secretarial position, in another office, in which she could be of great aid to her present boss because he had continuing difficulties with that office. She also envisioned returning to her present job when relationships improved with that other office.

Clearly, the woman's boss (also my direct employer) strongly preferred that she take the secretarial role. She also felt such strong loyalty that she announced for that role, despite some attraction to the managerial job.

On my initiative, and with her present boss' unenthusiastic sufferance, she and I held several career planning sessions to clarify needs, pay-offs, etc. She was willing at first, but became obdurate as the choice-point drew near.

> She decided to take the new secretarial job, after some major struggles between her needs and her loyalty. "It would have been easier," she observed, "if you just let me alone. I knew what I had to do."

> My relationship with her had cooled somewhat, although her boss is more ambivalent. "I know you really had to do it, so I didn't tell you to buzz off. I end up respecting you for doing a dumb thing, from my perspective. That's how it all comes down."

Guideline 16. *It will sometimes be the case that differences in values between the intervenor and actors at the interface will be great but inconsequential; at other times, even apparently-minor differences can be profoundly significant.* Value congruence between client and intervenor is no necessity in OD efforts; but value sensitivity always is.

Take the first case, which advises against stiff-neckedness. Intervenor and others at the interface need not always read from the same text of preferred behavior. Sometimes, even radically different texts pose no problem. Recall an earlier example, in which a CEO promoted a possible competitor, and then agreed to my suggestion to help the new man in these pragmatic terms: "If you help him, that will help me, if I play it with any finesse. And if you mess him up, or can't help, that also will help me." Clearly, we were coming from very different directions, even though it was possible in this case to go hand-in-hand, at least for a bit.

But happy parallelisms-in-practice from very different value or ethical bases should not induce intervenor euphoria. Joy about making collaborative progress can be sweet; but it should not lull one to neglect realities. Basic value differences must be made explicit and kept in mind, for they might later become consequential. "Never smile at a crocodile," advises one of our children's songbooks. But also search for agreement and even partial parallelisms, I urge.

How can the intervenors avoid stiff-neckedness without unduly sticking-out their necks or that of clients? I believe the basic bind here for OD intervenors inheres in the common overemphasis on interaction-centered designs. Here the intervenor properly stresses "working things through," and coming to some basic reconciliation of different values and preferences. There will be much room for such interventions at the interface, but one can easily make too much of a good thing. In many cases, for example, those at the interface typically and sharply differentiate between more or less stable personal values or preferences, and positions that are variously politically possible, expedient, or even necessary to preserve one's power-base. The latter can change in quick-silver fashion, and most at the interface will acknowledge the "correctness" of even substantial "flexibility." Too much concern about "working things through" may not only be inappropriate, but could be seriously counterproductive, as by inducing guilt in those who personally would like to agree but politically cannot.

The phenomenon clearly is not limited to the public sector. The "political" component exists in all organizations, generally enlarging as one ascends the hierarchy. My experience indicates that the associated dilemmas do exist in the private sector—but with less frequency, with reduced virulence, and with involvement by narrower ranges of an organization's members.

An unstable normative environment does not preclude all interventions, but it encourages two biases—toward localized or privatized interaction-centered designs, and toward structural or policy interventions. There will be numerous cases in which agreement on structures/policies/procedures can be achieved even when values differ. For example, an OD intervenor may see flexible workhours in the context of increasing employee freedom, while a manager may see it as simply a low-cost way of gaining some chips for later bargaining. Here the OD intervenor needs to keep two points in mind: the incongruence should be made explicit, for unappreciated incongruence can be troublesome later; and the intervenor should be convinced that, on balance, the structures/policies/procedures will serve OD values. [40]

At other times, very rigid stiff-neckedness will be appropriate when values conflict. Consider the common issue of encouraging greater openness in an autocratic organization. Consider also these six possible motivations which might encourage a manager to employ a team-building design, and which imply values variously congruent with OD values:

- "I am really concerned about my managerial potency, about my confidence and ability in making decisions. Team-building seems like a good way to share the burdens, to lighten my responsibility, and perhaps to avoid criticism or blame if things go wrong."

- "Joe Wright did some team-building, and he tells me it was great. I admire Joe more than my father."

- "Many other managers in my organization are into team-building, and a guy has to adapt to organization fads, however curious they may be."

- "I am an unreconstructed autocrat, but a clever and devious one. My young guys want team-development; I'll given it to them. I'd promise them anything to get them to produce more."

- "I have a new team, and I want us to get to know one another quickly, and to get some vital work done more expeditiously. My supervisory style is mildly autocratic, and I intend it to remain that way. But you can't work fluidly with people you barely know. So I'm for team development, up to a point."

- "I'd like for the rest of my team to learn what an incompetent rat Joe Brown is. He's slippery enough to play one person off against another. I want to nail him in a group situation, where his incompetence and duplicity are there for everyone to see.

The degrees of incompatibility with OD values clearly range all over the lot. I would be particularly cautious in cases 4 and 6, as well as cases 2 and 3 for very different reasons. Case 5 presents the best fit, with case 1 being intermediate between case 5 and the incompatible cluster.

Although value-compatibility rankings by others may differ for the six cases, the point remains. Value congruence will be variable and complete matches are not essential. Indeed, much of the intervenor's usefulness at the interface will be determined by the success of dealing with those whose values or behavior widely diverge from OD values, but where parallelisms exist.

Guideline 17. *More so than in most private-sector applications, an OD intervenor's effectiveness at the politics/administration interface will be determined by management of an inevitable tension—between those high vs. low on status, on influence, and so on.* If nothing else, the OD intervenor often will be seen as encouraging or even permitting some voice or influence for the deviant, some minority, and so on. This patently occurs in many interaction-centered interventions, as well as in team-building designs.

The interface provides a particularly inhospitable home for such influence-equalizing tendencies of OD interventions. Basically, public officials at the interface tend to be close-to-the-vest types, keeping "short chains" of command, encouraging or forcing decisions to be made at their own level. And the primary motives are likely to be care, caution, the short tenure of political appointees, the consequent lack of trust of many career personnel deriving from lack of common experience, the need for swift and sudden response to often-hostile legislators, the media or other interests, and so on.

Relatedly, perhaps the prototypical derisive description at the interface is: "He/she doesn't count." Many officials there take a dim view, if not a vindictive one, toward those low on the totem pole. That is not unique to top-level public officials, of course. In my experience, however, public officials in general seem to have less tolerance for, and greater suspicion of, those who are not among the loyally effective or the effectively loyal. To much the same point, I have been impressed by the starkness of the fast fall from power of public officials, of how quickly they "die," get "put in the deep freeze," and so on.

> Picture an exit interview involving a public executive, a non-civil service subordinate only-just-released, and myself. I encouraged the meeting, hoping that both parties could gain greater perspective on what went awry, and might even agree on details about the ways in which the two men could still help themselves and each other.

> Very quickly, the interview turns into a monologue by the executive, who in quick sequence expresses solicitous concern over the subordinate's passing, hopes that the subordinate didn't take it too hard because things didn't quite work out, wonders whether emergency plans had been made, and so on.

> After several such comments, I interject: "Well, why don't you ask him? He's here, although I'd never know it. You talk about him like he's dead, although he's just to your left."

> "And so he is," the executive replies, with a steely glint in his eyes that suggests that the "is" referred to both being here *and* to being dead, and could as easily apply to me as to the departing subordinate.

This unredemptive character of public-sector management implies serious issues for the OD intervenor, four of which get some attention here. In sum, these points advise intervenor about what should be anticipated and avoided.

1. *Avoid Being Someone's Hit Man*. At the very least, OD intervenors should make every effort to check for "walking dead" prior to any conventional design such as team-building, which may be counterproductive if it includes one or more examples of this kind. Subtle executives have been known to inaugurate team-building for the very purpose of inspiring peers to give "marching orders" to those whom the executive already has decided must go. The executive may prefer a kind of firing squad of peers rather than being his own trigger-man. In my experience, this is a far more likely danger in the public sector, perhaps because of the often-greater difficulty of removing public officials, whether political appointees or career types.

The effective OD intervenor should have ambitions far beyond being careful about acting as someone's hit man, however. Basically, top officials must come to see that—within quite wide limits—a viable minority can expand their range of credible discretion, as well as add potentially-vital inputs of information and values. This lesson definitely goes against the grain of most of those with whom I have worked at the politics/administration interface. Their operating rule is more likely to be that the best way to treat minorities is to make certain they never exert any influence. The vernacular puts it directly: the goal is to "cut their throats" rather than to given them "a pulpit to preach from." This school of thought urges that "the best enemy is a dead one," although impotent and quiet ones will do nicely.

2. *Avoid Being Seen As Narrowly Competitive*. The intervenor will likely experience public-sector difficulty, further, because the intervenor is a special case of another someone who may exert influence. Consequently, intervenor's treatment may be interestingly different in the public sector, in general. Certainly my experiences have been interestingly different. Consider two examples, the first of which has happened to me in substantially the same form a number of times at the public interface, but never in a private-sector intervention.

The first typical setting is the post-intervention euphoria, where all sides agree that major progress has been made and where plans are being made for another meeting. "How does that date fit your schedule, Bob?" someone may ask.

I have learned to delay an answer at the interface. Quite often, I hear the sense of this message from a colleague to that friendly questioner, if not these very words: "What's the matter? You afraid you can't do it without him?"

That counter-question suggests important aspects of the common culture at the politics/administration interface. The *machismo* is dominant, but suffused with caution about adding a potential new competitor or at least an additional resource for an old competitor. Also prominent is the trigger-quick ownership of something that *has worked*. Should the original intervention have failed, or still be in doubt, the follow-on meeting would have old Bob prominently associated with it, that is far better than a 50/50 bet.

A second example is more elaborate, but also more revealing of the texture of events common at the interface. The example is quite explicit in how a public agency sought to cushion itself from the impact of outsiders. Even though the interface culture is seldom so explicit, its dominant themes are similar.

In an agency with a very prestigious technical reputation, the rare consultant was introduced carefully. Typically, consultants were invited by those well down in the ranks, even when they were to eventually see senior people. In effect, consultant "worked his way up the hierarchy," talking with several people of increasing rank, finally "meeting" the advertised client, almost as if by accident. On the first visit, the process was very time-consuming. The warm-up time diminished on subsequent visits, but the pattern remained for a long time.

The procedure apparently reinforced the integrity of the chain-of-command as ritualistic preparation for possible/probable influence by an "outsider," who by definition is less subject to the command structure. Moreover, the process effectively located any risk at low levels, should a consultant "bomb out," while also sharing any possible blame quite widely. People in the organization referred to it as "sending the baby after the moonshine," the implication being that organizational "parents" could slake their thirst while being saved from "arrest," but only by risking their "child's" welfare.

Apparently, agency norms also implied concern that reliance on consultants might be seen by monitoring legislators as a sign of internal ineptness, so consultant only "met with" executives but "worked for" lower-level personnel.

Finally, the process was in effect a quick socialization that provided low-pressure introduction to agency ways. For example, no ashtrays were visible in any office, because the CEO did not smoke. Early on his first visit, consultant would be tutored on the point (although the rationale therefor would not be discussed), and made aware of "safe zones" if desperation set in. Progressively more detailed instructions also alerted the consultant to other folkways, saving potential mutual embarrassment and also freeing other agency personnel from instructing/disciplining any unwitting norm-breakers.

3. *Avoid Being Silent Servant.* Beyond such exotica, I am impressed with how much more often in the public sector: the intervenor is encouraged to become "silent servant" reporting only what client already knows and merely wants reinforced by an external; or the intervenor must work through a kind of adversary stage with the client. Both reactions suggest the delicate equilibrium at the interface. "Silent servant" patently does not disturb that equilibrium. An intervenor who will not play that role threatens those who do not wish to risk some re-equilibration, or those who just feel their comfort-level has been lowered by the interloper.

Evidence supporting these two tendencies could be marshalled from various sources. For example, the careful reader of signs should be impressed by the fact that the private-sector literature on consultancy is large, varied, and also emphasizes the helping, diagnostic, or truth-seeking aspect of the relationship with the client. The similar literature developed by those with a major public-sector identification, in revealing contrast, is quite skimpy, stereotypic, and emphasizes (a la the renowned Machiavelli) the hierarchy-serving if not sycophantish aspects of consultancy. Of course, the advice of the renowned Machiavelli has well served some in the private sector. When that happens, revealingly, observers in the private actor probably will report with disapproval: "That's politics."

4. *Anticipate Power-Related Issues.* Let us return to the two probable consulting modalities I see at the interface. My own behavior plays a part in this but, as a general rule, I find far more authority- and power-related issues in my public-sector consultancy. Typically, I refuse to play silent servant. For most private-sector clients, that poses no problem. In the public sector, that helps establish a reputation for "rocking the boat," which often is seen as bad by "them" and a sign by me that public-sector clients often want a validator or confirmer more than a consultant or intervenor.

A substantial contrast summarizes my experience. Even though consulting contacts in the private sector do generate opposed client/consultant interests, adversary episodes there for me are likely to be brief, only periodic, and of low intensity. In the public sector, however, the adversary stage often gets intense, complicated, and may even remain difficult or impossible to resolve. This difference derives from historical and institutional features that are unique or that differ in degree, I hypothesize. The difference, I also suppose, is intensified by the fact that many OD interventions at the interface will probably go against the grain of practices and traditions concerning authority. And public-sector actors seem to have a greater need to even the score, sometimes in non-organizational ways.

In the course of team-building, a CEO was bombarded with criticisms of his suspiciousness, lack of trust, failure to delegate, and so on.

After a particularly trying day, he challenged me to a series of footraces—eventually negotiated at 40, 50, and 60 yards, at my insistence. He was well over 6 feet tall and 185; I was 5'10 and 245; our ages were comparable. He was a college track man, and he knew I had played football, but was unaware I had been a sprinter of sorts. I made no effort to advise him thereof.

Nobody was much fooled by the CEO's intent. I was going to get "the treatment" for my infernal OD designs, subordinates chortled. The "boss would get even," and I would be "smart to run as slow as I looked I should run." Dinner time was laugh-time.

I was concerned that team-building progress might be lost on a track, but I was caught between a rock and a hard place. If I begged-off or if I lost, that might signal to the subordinates that they also would get theirs later for being open and taking risks in the team-building. The night before, I ruminated on the several possibilities, but gave up because—although I knew my current best times for those distances down to the tenths of a second—I had no idea of how fast he was. He did look fast, I worried.

I found out, quickly, the next morning before all the assembled subordinates. They had a stop-watch, judges, and (for a trophy) a gussied-up beer can. The subordinates also presented several cheers, designed just for the occasion, which are too ribald to describe here, or almost anywhere, to those of any sensibility or compassion for their fellow person.

I won handily at 40 yards, and then by a narrower margin at 50. I lost at 60 yards, decisively.

The CEO read my mind. "Did you throw the last one?" he asked. "I gave it some thought," I admitted, "but I did try my best."

"This approach didn't settle much, in any case," the CEO noted. "But I believe you, and I see how hard it is for me to share authority or influence, how I have to even-up with those I see competing for what I usually try to monopolize. God knows how many times in the past I read 'competition' when someone was just trying to get involved or contribute. That's some progress in 150 yards of running."

The story of *the* race was often repeated, for awhile. The message was clear to all. Challenges were OK; performance and not rank was central; there might be some adverse reactions, anger, or whatever; but, given enough goodwill, it will be possible to talk things through, to get in touch with feelings, even after precipitously acting out. The symbolism of the race was most useful. When the CEO would dig in his heels on an issue that someone suspected was related to his ego or concept of authority rather than to the problem, that person might say: "Time to lace up my running shoes, I suppose."

Guideline 18. *The linkage between internal and external intervenors has often been emphasized as useful, and many see it as ideal. That ideal linkage will tend to be both more useful and more problematic in the public sector, and especially at the interface.*

The underlying argument has two basic parts. *First*, for a variety of reasons, intervenors internal to the public-sector host will be less available and less potent. In part, this is due to historical accident—to the earlier development of OD in the business sector. In part, also, this is due to the lack of public-sector enthusiasm for even potential disturbances of power balances, as the previous guideline proposes.

Second, internal intervenors can be especially useful in the public sector, as in reading the socio-political context in which an agency exists. Hence the cultivation of internal resources should receive priority attention, and on multiple fronts. Thus external intervenors should seek to establish mentor as well as collegial relationships with insiders, with a determination even greater than in business organizations—where the same commitment is important enough. Also of special note, attention can usefully be given to "pull-back strategies" for internal intervenors in the public sector. Directly, such intervenors may be vulnerable, given the general disinclination in the public sector to own or be associated with failure or even "controversial" outcomes. And much time and energy by both internal and external intervenors often can be well-spent on getting and staying straight about the torturous issues that can be involved.

Guideline 19. *The OD intervenor at the interface is safest when setting realistically pessimistic aspirations for the pace and extent of change.*
The institutional and historical features reflected at the interface tend to have profound mirror-effects far down the hierarchy, effects which can be summarized briefly and with basic accuracy. Except for occasional "conversions" by officials, of which I am generally suspicious, most officials at the politics/administration interface behave in ways sharply at odds with OD values when it comes to sharing influence, information, and so on. The reasons vary, but the tendencies are similar and a standard deviation or more beyond private-sector standards. The common consequence: the pace and extent of change probably will be moderate, if not snail-like.

Those who worked in Project ACORD, for example, were impressed with the still-potent impact on many State Department personnel in the late 1960's of the harassment by Senator Joseph R. McCarthy in the 1950's. Closedness and low risk-taking were the norms, apparently as safeguards against the worst happening again. Scrutiny by multiple congressional committees, a press often hostile to the "fudge factory," and the need to make decisions whose effects might not be obvious for decades or even generations, in the face of shifting political priorities and changing political appointees: these objective factors illustrate the far-broader family which reinforced the protective and defensive tendencies encouraged by McCarthyism.

Similarly, city managers constitute a class for which there is no private-sector analog: made suspicious by long experience; with short tenures; subject to vagaries of electoral shifts; and cautious about delegation because subordinates they train may become their replacements.

As for police, one has to be impressed with the fact that when they play "How I see myself," the two most-common adjectives are "suspicious" and "paranoid."

Looked at from another perspective, since public-sector issues can be profoundly divisive and deep-rooted, "success" comes in protean forms. Consider the targets of some public-sector efforts at change:[41] to ameliorate Protestant-Catholic conflict in Ireland; to work on relationships between Jews and Arabs in Israel; to facilitate accommodations between the races in schools; and to work toward resolution of a border dispute in Africa. What constitutes "success?"

Clearly, the once-and-for all-time resolution of the issues would qualify. Just as clearly, however, that would be a wildly-idyllic single measure.

What more modest measures of progress toward the OD ideal would be reasonable and meaningful? That is a tough one, and has no general answer. Suffice it to note here, however, that both theory and experience are growing as to what can be expected of various learning designs under conditions that are specified with increasing precision.[42] The choice, then, takes on some such form:

> We know that interaction-centered designs tend to have such-and-such a range of effects on interaction and trust *in the learning environment*.

> We also know that transfer of learning to the back-home site can be problematic, with (for example) the probability of transfer being increased by periodic reinforcement and by providing back-home "support groups."

> Should we, then, chance (for example) a learning design in small groups intended to reduce the conflict between Irish Catholics and Protestants via an emphasis on appropriate attitudes and skills?

> No guarantees exist, but the stakes have a certain clarity.

> We can reasonably predict changes in the interaction of the trained population. But we also can predict re-entry problems, as when back-home zealots threaten physical harm to learners who would collaborate with their enemy.

> And this judgment will be mightily influenced by other details; e.g., by what can be reasonably predicted if *no* intervention were made; by practical considerations as to whether enough of the appropriate people can be trained to make a difference; and so on.

So deciding on criteria for "success" requires the discipline of still-developing theory and experience. And what do we know of public-sector interventions? Whatever the historic or institutional roots, some general features seem clear enough. Especially for those at the interface—but extending far down the hierarchy as well—their "primary behavioral systems" emphasize suspicion rather than trust, a protective closedness as opposed to a vulnerable openness, a basic preoccupation with winning-and-losing versus giving-and-sharing, and so on. This behavior focuses dominantly around power rather than affect, around aggregations of capital far more than human needs, around top-dog status or at least survival as contrasted with sharing influence. On the latter point, indeed, most of those at the politics/administration interface seem most interested in one kind of sharing—sharing blame—and then only when they cannot avoid it altogether. As for success, so many claims are likely to be put forward that the real parents can go unnoticed, especially if they are modest or even truthful.

> My favorite war story in this regard comes from early in a team-building experience in the 1960's, when a design based on the Jo-Hari Window[43] was being used to encourage safe sharing of initial feedback and disclosure. Anonymously, participants were to submit on notepaper examples of the two kinds of information which they had not shared publicly, and which were generated during the present team-building session. The presenter gave a brief theoretical rationale for the design, explaining that each example submitted would be read and briefly discussed as to its implications for the communication network which had repressed (or at least did not encourage) its sharing.

> Almost always, the design is both revealing and hugely entertaining. Not this time. War comes closer to describing what happened.

> As fate would have it, the first example of disclosure on which my eyes fell said simply, "I play the banjo."

> I remember a momentary tingle of amusement. Someone in this large group of bright, well-educated, and successful people had not heard the instructions. Moreover, no wonder that this disclosure had not been made. The agency prided itself on its cosmopolitanism and sophistication, it recruited very selectively with almost-exclusive preference for loci where banjos were not mainstream, and the agency was so up-tight about rigid up-or-out personnel policies that the universal approach was to take a low profile even with respect to trivial matters that might suggest difference, let alone "flakiness."

> No wonder, then. But how sad it was.

> My amusement-cum-sadness was short-lived. The accusations thundered in a room of white-knuckled participants (my words are in parentheses):

> - "You planted that." ("No, I didn't.")

> - "You're trying to embarrass us and the agency." ("It's not my note. One of you wrote it. Ask him or her about its intent. I can only speculate. What do you think it means? It's obviously important to everybody here, or almost everybody.") "Fat chance of getting anyone to own up now. We may be paranoid, but we're not stupid!" [Uproarious laughter.]

- ("How do you feel now?") "Mad." "Used." "I want to leave."

- "Who wrote that note?" [No one volunteers.] "There, that proves it was a plant!"

- "You said this was a here-and-now experience. You sneaked in that back-home garbage. You broke your own rules." ("OK, assume that I did, even though I didn't. The banjo is now here-and-now, however it got introduced.") "There you go again, twisting our words and the rules."

The accusations diminished after awhile, and the symbolism of the banjo was explored. Stereotypes were offered, their significance for agency operations was established, and most acknowledged how furiously repressive their system could be. "I guess we showed what happens to the fool who tries to swim upstream in this outfit." But learning was very difficult and—even though some agency policies and procedures were changed, in part as a result of the incident—suspicion and mistrust still dominated. "That was a great learning design," one official recalled very much later. "But to this day I don't believe there was a banjo player in the room. Our selection procedures were fool-proof! We talked about the incident for years."

The present conclusion—and its accompanying example-in-extremis—may seem dark ones, but they mirror a central tendency for behavior which does not necessarily mean despair about making progress. Let me make five points. *First*, I have been careful here to talk about central tendencies in *behavior*, for I believe those at the politics/administration interface generally have *values* consistent with OD. "It's a damn shame," goes a typical refrain, "that the world isn't a different kind of place. But I have to deal with it as it is." OD interventions can build on such normative preferences for a different world, if slowly and carefully.

Second, this tension between value and behavior—unlike the tension in the similar formulation of Argyris and Schon[44]—is likely to be conscious. The politics/administration interface is simply that kind of turf: it can be treacherous. As one public official told me: "When you have been harpooned as many times as I have—and then had the wounds salted, peppered, and sandpapered—you tend to grow a thick protective skin." This consciousness constitutes both an opportunity for, as well as a challenge to, OD interventions.

Third, however—and this is a crucial however—selective and sometimes dramatic progress can be made toward decreasing the value/behavior gap, as well as in overcoming harsh past experiences.

Multiple levers can motivate a closer congruence of behavior and value. Actors at the politics/administration interface do have needs for affection, for example, although those needs *in role* often seem to be a standard deviation or so less strong than for most people. These actors also can see the value of valid and reliable information when the other guy deals in suspicion, mistrust, and duplicity, although they realize that such information can curb their own style when they find it necessary or convenient to deal from "under the table." And these actors—like all of us—also need to know how they are valued by their peers, and they know how important it is to be able to communicate clearly about what they would like to be valued for.

Examples of these points-of-leverage for increasing the congruence of behavior and values could be multiplied, but they imply progress is possible even if modest expectations about the extent and speed of that progress are appropriate. Witness the success with team-building among elected public officials.[45] Using designs common in the laboratory approach to OD, resource persons at the University of Southern California have been able to design learning environments in which officials tend to come to a significant conclusion: that important pay-offs *to them*, on balance, can derive from reducing the behavior/value gap. As Le Baron explains:[46]

... local officials live within a dichotomy of power and trust; they are more familiar with—and therefore, more capable of handling—power than trust. Power is inevitable to someone elected to local office and its appearance cannot be avoided. Politics is the struggle for power . . .

[This emphasis on power-bases for individuals can be seriously dysfunctional when elected officials must act together, as on a board or council.] Power, in a group situation, often blocks as much [progress] as it creates. It also tends to prevent council/board members from seeing their own humanness, and blinds them from the human qualities in others. We have found that council/board members recognize, once their attention is diverted from a strict power orientation, that trust is the cosmic glue which holds a relationship together. The foundation may be power, but the support structure is trust.

. . .

The movement from power to trust is accomplished through communications. Particularly, communications which release some of the unnecessary unknowns in the relationships of council/board members.

All this is to say that I expect a low congruence between OD values and the behavior of officials at the politics/administration interface; but I also know that greater congruence is possible, and especially as experience grows that useful bottom-line effects can be achieved. Indeed, I strongly suspect ardent and generalized support of OD values in the absence of clear-cut evidence that OD values have met some official's pressing problems. Hardball politics is the art of the practical, and strong suspicion therefore attaches to any ardent support that is not reality-based. Such support may only mean that the official has either lost his power-base, or is in the process of so doing, or sees the OD technology as a short-run expedient for gaining an advantage over others.

Although the orientation here could encourage cop-outs, the discussion above implies that the OD intervenor should expect that progress usually will come in dribs and drabs, although great leaps forward may occasionally occur. Anecdotal evidence suggests that many intervenors with mostly private-sector experience find it difficult to cope with different standards in the public sector.

- In Project ACORD in the State Department, one intervenor— several days into a "cousin T-Group"—grew so frustrated at the closedness of participants as to burst into tears.

- In one southeastern city, OD intervenors were so concerned about lack of progress by employees in a mass team-building design that their anger erupted in outbursts of profanity, much to the delight of the local press.

- One distinguished intervenor left a senior group of civil servants—all on detached duty from their agencies to seek ways of greater inter-departmental cooperation—walking out in disgust during the third day of meetings. "These guys had to call their departments to see if they could go to the bathroom," he complained. "I was just wasting my time."

I know of only very scattered incidents of the same kind in private-sector OD experiences.

Fourth, I have come to expect a yo-yo effect at the interface, far more so than in the private sector. Using a range of indicators, regression at the interface seems more likely after real progress has been made. So OD intervenors can profit from a certain elasticity of spirit, as well as a sense of what I take to be the related ebbings and flowings of the political tides.

One can interpret this yo-yo effect in several ways, the most congenial of which to me emphasizes the interaction-oriented character of most OD interventions in the public sector. Briefly, such interventions are able to temporarily reduce symptoms but commonly do not have much effect on their often-institutional causes. I have no problems with such pressure-reducing interventions, if one recognized their character and consequences as being puny in comparison to the inducing cause—"something out there that is bigger than all of us." Periodic ventilation can have much to recommend it, indeed, but the effects will be short-lived.

Fifth, both boon and bane, OD effects in public agencies can have long lead-times. Interventions may not be wasted, in sum, even though no effects appear immediately. I believe such an effect characterized Project ACORD in the State Department, for example, although alternative explanations of the delayed effects have been offered.[47]

Guideline 20. *Public-sector OD interventions often will be used to test mutual intent, or degree of resolve, relevant to some specific issue by participants who have not the least interest in "getting together" in any sense, who have no desire to "work through the issues," let alone to seek to reduce differences.*

This case severely complicates measuring the results of OD interventions. Frequently, in fact, an OD intervention might have a limited but important outcome, even as the participants have a real and expressed fear or even abhorrence of "getting together." Polarization, in short, may be the key to retaining their power-bases, which the parties choose not to threaten by even intimations of reduced polarization. For example, some black/white issues get framed in just such terms.[48] I repeat here an illustration used earlier—a design involving the unlikely combination of local police, Black Panthers, and a White Citizens' Council:

> The design had none of the usually-desired objectives or effects: the three groups were not "brought closer together," did not develop collaborative norms, etc.
>
> However, the design was right-on for the limited political purpose in

> question: to have the parties mutually convince one another of their individual
> preparedness and resolution to wage urban war, to more accurately estimate
> the costs/benefits to each of such an outcome, and to discuss the conditions
> that could lead to that consequence.

Both simple and subtle rationales can be used to support cousinly OD interventions having little or no intent to reduce polarization. Consider the comment of a minister who on Sunday stirred his congregation (and me) with a version of Buber's I/Thou concept and its implications for the community of humankind. On Wednesday of the same week, the minister as a political representative of a particular community group expressed his definite reservations that a confrontation meeting "could go too far in creating a community of common interest" between *his* support groups and *theirs*. Buber or no, the preacher's political powerbase ultimately depended on there being *his* group and *their* group.[49] Moreover, "community" might only complicate the single-minded scuffling for scarce resources which the preacher would prefer to capture for *his* group.

Whatever the full explanation, the preacher clearly saw the differences and tensions between the two roles. "One's preaching, the other's politicking," he explained.

More complex rationales for sharply-bounded OD interventions also exist. Consider a need to preserve a separation of powers between legislative and executive, for example. Some distance and even enmity can be seen as appropriate reinforcers of an important institutional difference that should not be cushioned by socio-emotional closeness or shared interests. Even in such cases, a need may surface to experience a limited design for restricted purposes, as in testing whether that "distance" is too great.

I have no objection to such bounded OD interventions, although unclarity about goals can lead to disillusionment, or worse.

Guideline 21. *The intervenor's life at the interface is simplified in a critical particular: very often, some realistic and workable balance-of-power is not only the most that can be achieved, it is the ideal.* Put otherwise, not only will "success" often be out-of-reach for the public-sector intervenor who gives primacy to truth/love *and* who persists in that mode. But that unrelieved mode can be seriously counterproductive. As background for making these crucial points, the reader can refer back to the contrast of truth/love and advantage/power, sketched in guideline #6 in the previous chapter.

This argument is a difficult one, and especially so for someone who—like myself—wants with every fiber in his being to accord primacy to truth/love whenever and wherever possible. But the reality underlying this argument can be avoided, at best, only in those cases at the interface where the objectives are quite narrow and get very substantial support. Generally, those conditions do not describe the interface.

So what constitutes a realistic and workable balance, to begin? Major caveats are in order. Thus the details will vary widely from case to case; and substantial doses of truth/love often will enlighten and ease the effort to build and maintain a useful balance of power. In general, however, I apply such criteria, among others, to estimate the realism and workability of a balance of power.

- a substantial degree of congruence exists between the private reality of actors and their public actions and statements

- alternative public forums exist in which divergent opinions get expressed *and* responded to

- actors have the regular opportunity to get to know one another's reactions, and to distinguish them—e.g., as personal, political or technical—without having to guess

- the trust-level is sufficient to induce actors to hold their fire until issues-in-doubt can be clarified

- goodwill and mutual acceptance are such that the initial prejudice generally goes to the fellow actor until issues can get addressed face-to-face, as in such significant benefits-of-a-doubt: that fellow actors had a good reason to do what they did; that they meant no harm even if they were palpably foolish; and so on

- actors have only a gentle "background fear" that expression of deviant opinions risks the loss of psychological membership

- votes or choices-of-record show diverse distributions, avoiding both general surface-unanimity as well as skin-of-the-teeth margins

- "the majority" varies—in size, in membership by issue-area, and over time

- actors honor the need, within limits, for colleagues from time to time to "speak to their separate constituencies," even in ways incongruent with the messages exchanged among actors

- norms develop that permit acceptance, even honor, for "the happy warrior" who often finds self among the minority, in sharp contrast to those cases in which opinional deviants risk scapegoating

- the realization exists that a viable minority role need not only be tolerated, but can be valuable, as in

  — providing an impetus and vehicle for change

  — acting as ombudsman for those aggrieved

  — inhibiting the corrupting influences often associated with political near-monopolies

  — helping induce the sense and reality of choice-taking from a range of alternatives

These may seem reasonable enough criteria for a "balanced system," but the guideline to which they relate can still induce major complaint. Basically, this guideline implies that interventions at the interface seldom can *resolve* issues—in any sense, let alone in terms of a truth-love model. Indeed, even very successful interventions often will only clarify the features of the dissensus, or mobilize a heretofore quiescent minority, or develop norms that reflect mutual forebearance if not a positive conviction concerning the synergy that can derive from a viable balance of power.

This constraint can constitute a harsh message for intervenors, especially for those who emphasize interaction-centered designs. The dominant verbalisms underlying such designs—"working through an issue," "a community of co-learners," "coming to closure," "acting on the basis of general consensus," "getting together," and so on—do not apply nicely and completely to a balance-of-power orientation. Indeed, they may not apply at all.

To suggest the contrast, an intervenor over several years has worked with both a CEO and his governing board to develop and maintain a reasonable balance of power. For the CEO, applicable rationales emphasize the degree of personal and institutional freedom that can derive from such a balance on the board. For the board, rationales vary. Vignettes implying such rationales accompany several guidelines above—specifically, guidelines #3, 4, 8 through 12, and 19 in this chapter; and guidelines #9 and 10 in the preceding chapter.

In many cases, a rationale attractive to the governing board emphasizes such a quid pro quo: a tolerable balance reduces the probability of "surprises." Thus valid and reliable information will be more available if most actors see an acceptable balance; decisions are less likely to come unravelled after being "made;" and actors often will feel freer to share personal reactions to one another, which serves the need to test for one's competence as well as to equilibrate one's perceptions with those of central others.

For a variety of reasons—after several years of efforts to create and sustain a balance, including an early revolt against a once-dominant majority—it seemed probable that a very dominant board majority would develop.

What was intervenor's strategy? He urged caution in discussions with the board and the CEO. The CEO's discretion could be limited; or board/staff distance could increase, with board "attack" being met by staff defensiveness and protectionism.

The board held a retreat, whose bottom-line was that constituency pressures were such that reasonable alternatives to a probably-emerging dominant majority were quite unlikely.

At CEO's invitation, then—and with board knowledge—the intervenor met with the CEO and his staff to try to gear-up for "new board/staff relationships." Topics included: the greater pressure that might be applied by the board's new dominant majority, and how to handle such pressure—issue-area by issue-area—in ways responsive to the board and yet not divisive of CEO/staff or intra-staff relationships. The goals sought to emphasize the common fate of staff, as well as to develop a sense of agreement about and ownership of coping strategy and tactics.

It is possible to provide some perspective on why such efforts to work toward a rolling balance can be significant. Two perspectives must suffice here. A balance-of-power often will be the most that can be achieved, goes one theme. Moreover, such a balance may even be *the* ideal.

Why is some acceptable balance-of-power often the most that can be achieved? Four points suggest the broader response that might be made. *First,* the achievement is far from trivial. More so even than most of us—who have the same tendency in ample degree—politicos do not like to lose, and especially publicly. So inducing a real balance goes against the grain: many are the 6-4 decisions that get tallied as 10-0, in the absence of major effort.

> "It is far better politically," one actor at the interface notes, "to be on the wrong side of issues, as events later determine, than to be on the losing side when decisions get made.

> "Politics hates a loser, especially one who turns out to be a correct loser. If he was so smart to begin with, why did he lack the skills to bring others into light from darkness?"

Hence, I propose, the common "surprise" about newly-emergent coalitions. Their real strength gets understated by common accommodations to avoid being a "loser," as when the "outs" vote with the "ins" simply because the former can count.

Second, many decisions at the interface get made in terms of the prevailing *zeitgeist*—on the basis of what will wash today. The "politically acceptable" can be quite definite and unavoidable, even if people see it as limited or even perverse. This feature makes life difficult for minorities who wish to be credible, and who also want to avoid being seen as common scolds.

Third, such general anti-minority forces can be truly overpowering when reinforced by social forces centered around acceptance and membership, as when what Janis calls "groupthink" dominates.[50] Here membership is so valued that no one wishes to risk it for fear of being the only deviant from an assumedly otherwise-unanimous opinion; and here also no legitimate ways exist for publicly testing such assumptions. As Janis and others show, many 6-4 or even 2-8 distributions of opinion can get distorted into 10-0 decisions.

Fourth, the pressures from constituencies often are such that actors had better remember that a political consensus does not and perhaps cannot exist. Even seeking consensus can be dangerous to the political health of actors, in short. For example, team-building at the interface on the truth/love model can fail for participants even as it succeeds. For participants know that their power-base often rests on dissensus between the several constituencies, and this base can be threatened by building "too much" trust and cohesiveness in their "team" which may encourage some buffering of constituency demands or interests. I have in mind a major official, once a labor leader, who took a post of public trust and helped move the organization to unexpected achievement. But that very organizational effectiveness deprived labor unions of leverage with the agency. The consequence? "[The organization]," the ex-labor leader reports, "cost me my identity."

The argument favoring an emphasis on a reasonable balance of power can be extended. Such a balance might even be *the ideal*, for at least three reasons. First, constitutional and legal provisions often separate powers, even as practice requires that they be shared. The tension in reality can be real enough to preclude "community" or "consensus;" and many would argue this is the way things should be. Adversary relationships may serve as surrogates for "the truth," in short, at least to a substantial degree.

So practical and theoretical competence in helping build and maintain separate and shared powers via a balance-of-power has much to recommend it. The point applies even in the private sector, for example, where the early focus of OD at managerial levels constitutes a "most favorable case" of shared interests and identifications. Those seeking evidence supporting the point need only refer to the more difficult OD experience at labor/management interfaces, which raise many of the issues of concern here.[51]

Second, the emphasis on balance-of-power is consistent with the usual methodology in popular government for knowing "truth" of certain kinds. The trick—as an earlier guideline notes—involves distinguishing at least four truth-realms and dealing with the complex interactions that exist between them. These truth-realms are: the political, the personal, the technical, and the ethical-moral. A balance-of-power mode can be dangerous in seeking technical or scientific truth,[52] even as it well suits the search for "political truth."

Third, the sense of a rolling balance-of-power sits well with what may be called the common distribution of political opinions, or preferences re governance. Considering any one political issue-area, to simplify, at least three classes of support can be distinguished on the five positions A through E:

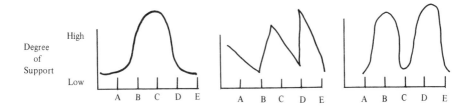

Given any substantial set of issue-areas, examples of all three kinds would be likely. Clearly, only a very complex balance-of-power approach could be fitted to such a common range of distributions of opinion on various issue-areas.

Guideline 22. *Finally, and perhaps paramountly, intervenors should try to focus on what they get done rather than on how long it takes.* This is usually good advice, although it can be hard to take for many reasons—lack of knowledge, failure of courage, need for fees, etc. But nowhere is the advice more apt than in the public sector. Opportunities may quickly come, but they also disappear mercurially; and although few public officials can give a clear go-ahead on anything, numerous veto-centers typically exist. Taking a long time to fail or make a little progress reflects no particular virtue; indeed, taking a long time probably will tilt the odds toward failure.

What "gets done" can involve serious trade-offs, of course. Consider the case of a large urban mass-transit project. Time-urgencies were great: a single day's delay would cost about $250,000 in additional debt charges only. Hence an elaborate set of OD interventions was set in motion to induce the development of several interacting teams, and cost and time targets were basically met.53 A retrospective view of the project revealed several significant costs of this success—personal as well as organizational costs.54 And there seem ways of reducing such costs in future similar efforts.55

This process—of reducing costs and increasing benefits or at least maintaining them—outlines the basic goal of OD. And this book hopes to contribute to this process—in some halting ways perhaps, but hopefully in significant particulars as well.

FOOTNOTES

[1]Carl W. Proehl, Jr., *Planned Organizational Change*. Unpublished doctoral dissertation, University of Georgia, 1980.

[2]Barry A. Macy, Edward E. Lawler, III, and G. Ledford, *The Bolivar Quality of Work Experiment* (New York: Wiley-Interscience, forthcoming).

[3]Marvin Weisbord, "Why Organization Development Hasn't Worked (So Far) In Medical Centers," *Health Care Management Review*, Vol. 1 (Spring 1976), pp. 17-28.

[4]James M. Kouzes and Paul R. Mico, "Domain Theory," *Journal of Applied Behavioral Science*, Vol. 15 (December 1979).

[5]Ken K. Smith, "What Constraints Limit Feedback and Disclosure?" in Robert T. Golembiewski, *Approaches to Planned Change* (New York: Marcel Dekker, 1979), Part 2, pp. 397-408.

[6]Consult Robert T. Golembiewski, "Structuring the Public Organization," in William Eddy, editor, *Handbook of Public Organization Management* (New York: Marcel Dekker, 1983), pp. 193-225.

[7]E.g., Robert T. Golembiewski, "Enriching the Theory and Practice of Team-Building," in D.D. Warrick, editor *Contemporary Organization Development* (Glenview, IL: Scott Follsman, 1984), pp. 98-113.

[8]Leonard Sayles, *Managerial Behavior* (New York: McGraw-Hill, 1964).

[9]Golembiewski, *Approaches to Planned Change*, Part 2, esp. pp. 455-462.

[10]Laurence E. Lynn, Jr., *Managing the Public's Business* (New York: Basic Books, 1981), esp. p. 7.

[11]See Richard Walton, *Interpersonal Peacemaking* (Reading, Mass.: Addison-Wesley, 1969), who reports on the evolution in the U.S. Department of State of "third-party interventions" for managing conflicts.

[12]For one example of an intervenor's effort to get a client to learn from the experience of similar others, see Robert T. Golembiewski, *Public Administration as A Developing Discipline* (New York: Marcel Dekker, 1977), Part 2: pp. 31-40.

[13]Robert T. Golembiewski and Alan Kiepper, "MARTA: Toward An Effective Open Giant," *Public Administration Review*, Vol. 36 (January 1976), pp. 46-60.

[14]Sheldon Davis, "An Organic Problem-Solving Method of Organization Change," *Journal of Applied Behavioral Science*, Vol. 3 (January 1967), pp. 3-21.

[15]Chris Argyris, *Intervention Theory and Method* (Reading, Mass.: Addison-Wesley, 1970).

[16]Davis, *op. cit.*

[17]Chester C. Cotton, Philip J. Browne, and Robert T. Golembiewski, "Marginality and the OD Practitioner," *Journal of Applied Behavioral Science*, Vol. 18 (October 1977), pp. 493-506.

[18]Donald P. Warwick, *A Theory of Public Bureaucracy* (Cambridge, Mass.: Harvard University Press, 1975).

[19]E.g., Argyris, *op. cit.*

[20]The basic theoretical distinctions are drawn by Irving L. Janis, *Victims of Groupthink* (Boston: Houghton Mifflin, 1972). See also footnote 25 below.

[21]E.g., Harvey M. Sapolsky, *POLARIS* (Cambridge, Mass.: Harvard University Press, 1972).

[22]Leonard Sayles and Margaret Chandler, *Managing Large Systems* (New York: Harper & Row, 1971).

[23]Herbert Shepard, "Rules of Thumb for Change Agents," *OD Practitioner*, Vol. 7 (November 1975), pp. 1-5.

[24]Golembiewski, *Approaches to Planned Change*, Part 1, pp. 48-50 and 163-169.

[25]Jerry Harvey, "Neurotic Organizations," pp. 16-34, in W. Warner Burke, editor, *New Technologies in Organization Development* (La Jolla, Cal.: University Associates, 1975).

[26]*Ibid.*

[27]Golembiewski, *Approaches to Planned Change*, Part 2, pp. 315-408.

[28]Stuart Emrich, "Teachers Becoming the New Dropouts," *Atlanta Constitution*, September 19, 1977, pp. 1, 14.

[29]Such designs have been used with good effect in public agencies, but their effectiveness seems greatest in "new" organizations as contrasted with those more set in their ways. For example, consult Golembiewski and Kiepper, "*MARTA*"; and R. Wayne Boss, "It Doesn't Matter If you Win or Lose, Unless You're Losing," *Journal of Applied Behavioral Science*, Vol. 15 (June 1979), pp. 198-220.

[30]This class of designs also has two features especially useful in the public-sector. Their "boundaries" are easier to delimit than those of group confrontational designs; and, relatedly, these designs tend to engage less status- or power-related dynamics. Other discussion emphasizes the public-sector difficulties with "drawing boundaries" and managing status/power dynamics.

[31]Robert T. Golembiewski, *Men, Management, and Morality* (New York: McGraw-Hill, 1965).

[32]Robert T. Golembiewski, Richard J. Hilles, and Munro S. Kagno, "A Longitudinal Study of Flexi-Time Effects," *Journal of Applied Behavioral Science*, Vol. 10 (December 1974), pp. 503-532.

[33]Robert T. Golembiewski and Carl W. Proehl, Jr., "A Survey of the Empirical Literature on Flexible Workhours," *Academy of Management Review*, Vol. 3 (October 1978), pp. 837-853; and Robert T. Golembiewski, Ronald G. Fox, and Carl W. Proehl, Jr., "Is FlexiTime for Employees 'Hard Time' for Supervisors?: Two Sources of Data Rejecting the Proposition," *Journal of Management*, Vol. 5 (Fall 1979), pp. 241-259.

[34]Robert T. Golembiewski and Carl W. Proehl, Jr., "Public Sector Applications of Flexible Workhours," *Public Administration Review*, Vol. 40 (January 1980), pp. 72-85.

[35]Richard Heimovics, Personal Communication (1977).

[36]Richard Neustadt, *Presidential Power* (New York: John Wiley & Sons, 1961), p. 9.

[37]Virginia E. Schein, "Political Strategies for Implementing Organizational Change," *Group and Organization Studies*, Vol. 2 (March 1977), pp. 46-47.

[38]A.M. Pettigrew, *The Politics of Organizational Decision-Making* (London: Tavistock Institute, 1973).

[39]Warren G. Bennis, "A Funny Thing Happened on the Way to the Future," *American Psychologist*, Vol. 25 (July 1970), pp. 601-602.

[40]Several chapters above provide relevant evidence.

[41]For a review of the several levels of outcomes of a number of such interventions, consult Gerald J. Miller, "Overseas Applications of Behavioral Science Technology," *Southern Review of Public Administration*, Vol. 4 (October 1980), pp. 229-252.

[42]E.g., see David G. Bowers and Doris L. Hausser, "Work Group Types and Intervention Effects in Organizational Development," *Administrative Science Quarterly*, Vol. 22 (March 1977), pp. 76-94; and William A. Pasmore and Donald C. King, "Understanding Organizational Change," *Journal of Applied Behavioral Science*, Vol. 14 (December 1978), pp. 455-468.

[43]Joseph Luft, *Group Processes* (Palo Alto, Cal.: National Press Books, 1963).

[44]Chris Argyris and Donald A. Schön, *Theory in Practice* (San Francisco, Jossey-Bass, 1974).

[45]Melvin J. Le Baron, "New Perspectives Toward More Effective Local Boards and Councils," pp. 235-253, in Robert T. Golembiewski and William B. Eddy, editors, *Organization Development in Public Administration* (New York: Marcel Dekker, 1978), Part 2.

[46]*Ibid.*, pp. 237-238.

[47]Consult Harry Levinson, *The Great Jackass Fallacy* (Boston, Mass.: Graduate School of Business Administration, 1973), pp. 143-158.

[48]Edward B. Klein, Claudewell S. Thomas, and Elizabeth C. Bellis, "When Warring Groups Meet: The Use of A Group Approach in Police-Black Community Relations," *Social Psychiatry*, Vol. 6 (No. 2, 1971), pp. 93-99.

[49]This crucial point often gets neglected, as do its significant implications for judging "progress." For example, DeMott generally comes to a pessimistic conclusion about the effects of "encounters" based on laboratory education principles that focused on federal educational policy, even though powerful interpersonal effects clearly occurred. He notes: "Sometimes the encounters marked the beginnings of talk between two parties of equal power passionately mistrustful of each other or suffering from image anxiety. (The far right and far left of the school board of a great Southwestern city, factions that, by their own admission, could never be seen together back home without losing their political power bases dined together and worked together in a small group . . . .) More than a few who participated in the sessions became so attached to coworkers and to the concept of the meeting that they shed tears at departure time." Benjamin Demott, "Hot-Air Meeting," *Harper's Meeting*, Vol. 251 (July 1975), p. 74.

[50]Janis, *op. cit.*

[51]Thomas D. Taber, Jeffrey T. Walsh, and Robert A. Cooke, "Developing A Community-Based Program for Reducing the Social Impact of A Plant Closing," *Journal of Applied Behavioral Science*, Vol. 15 (June 1979), pp. 133-155.

[52]For overwhelming evidence of the danger of such crucial carelessness, see David Joravsky, *The Lysenko Affair* (Cambridge, Mass.: Harvard University Press, 1970).

[53]Golembiewski and Kiepper, "MARTA."

[54]Robert T. Golembiewski and Alan Kiepper, "Perspectives on A Fast-Paced Public Project," *Public Administration Review*, Vol. 43 (June 1983), pp. 246-255.

[55]Robert T. Golembiewski and Alan Kiepper, "Lessons From A Fast-Paced Public Project," *Public Administration Review*, Vol. 43 (December 1983), pp. 547-555.

NAME INDEX

Adams, Bruce, 286
Akerstedt, Torbjorn, 128
Aldefer, Clayton P., 254
Allan, Kathryn H., 52, 68
Allan, Thomas K., 52, 68
Alinsky, Saul D., 288
Alsop, Stewart, 40, 286
Appleby, Paul, 149, 188, 197, 225
Argyris, Chris, 40, 41, 75, 117, 225, 226, 351, 362, 364

Bard, Morton, 52, 68
Baritz, Loren, 288
Barrell, R.P., 285
Beard, Charles, 160
Bell, Cecil H., Jr., 40, 52, 68, 71, 289
Bell, Robert L., 52, 68
Bellis, Elizabeth G., 56, 69, 70, 364
Benne, Kenneth, 226
Bennis, Warren G., 188, 227, 364
Bentley, Arthur F., 187
Berg, David N., 70, 80, 90, 254
Berg, Per Olaf, 90, 229
Berkes, Leslie J., 192
Berman, Katrina V., 226
Bernstein, Paul, 193, 199-205, 216, 219, 220, 225, 226
Berry, P.C., 193
Billingsley, Keith, 129
Block, C.H., 193
Blumberg, Arthur, 89, 90, 228
Bolman, Lee, 288
Bonsall, John, 127
Boss, R. Wayne, 52, 68, 363
Bower, Joseph L., 33-34, 41, 42, 289
Bowers, David G., 287, 364
Bowman, James S., 40, 191
Boyer, Ronald K., 55, 69, 71
Bradford, Leland P., 226
Brown, F. Gerald, 52, 53, 69
Brown, Juanita, 68
Brown, M. Craig, 189
Brown, Richard Harvey, 210, 227
Browne, Philip J., 362

Buchanan, Bruce, 192, 286
Bullock, R.J., 90
Burke, W. Warner, 4, 9, 74, 89, 285, 287
Byrd, Richard E., 53, 69

Caldwell, Russell, 288
Carew, Donald K., 53, 69, 71
Carrigan, Stokes B., 228, 229
Carroll, Sephen J., Jr., 285
Carter, Sylvia I., 53, 69
Chandler, Alfred D., 190, 192
Chandler, Margaret, 192, 363
Chandler, Ralph Clark, 229
Chase, Gordon, 40, 191, 289
Cherches, Chris E., 53, 69
Christian, George, 286
Cleveland, Sidney E., 52, 68
Cloonan, John, 103, 107, 110, 113, 127, 128, 129
Coch, Lester, 219, 226, 228
Coker, Francis W., 188
Cole, Muriel, 99, 126
Cooke, Robert A., 228, 364
Cornog, Geoffrey Y., 287
Corson, John J., 40
Costello, Timothy W., 68
Cotton, Chester C., 362
Couzens, Michael, 152, 188
Crawford, Robert Bruce, 98, 125
Crenson, Matthew A., 189

Dahl, Henry G., 226
Dahl, Robert A., 141, 146, 149, 152-154, 187, 188, 206, 209, 217, 218, 227
Davis, Sheldon, 240, 362
Dean, John, 286
DeLuca, Joel R., 297, 298
Demott, Benjamin, 364
Dempsey, John R., 41
Derr, C. Brooklyn, 53, 69
DeWolfe, A.S., 285
Djilas, Milovan, 186, 189
Dodd, Lawrence C, 40, 174, 191
Dow, Cabot J., 53, 69, 71

Drexler, Allan, 59, 71
Driscoll, James M. 54, 69
Duffee, David, 58, 71
Dunsing, Richard J., 54, 69
Dunsire, Andrew, 152, 188, 189
Dvorin, Eugene P., 186
Dye, Thomas R., 144, 145, 187
Dyer, William G., 227, 288

Eddy, William B., 31, 41, 68, 70, 229, 288, 362, 364
Elden, Max, 181, 183, 185, 192, 193
Elsworth, Rod, 101, 126
Emery, F.E., 192
Emrich, Stuart, 363
Everd, Roger D., 207, 208, 226
Ewing, David W., 225

Faison, Frank A., 57, 70, 71
Fischer, John, 171, 191
Fleischman, Edward, 229
Fletcher, Clive, 103, 127
Flynn, Wayne C., 54, 69
Finegan, James R., 98, 125
Finer, Herman, 169, 190
Finkle, Arthur L., 99, 125
Ford, Robert, 193
Forsyth, Douglas R., 56, 70
Fox, Ronald G., 91, 128, 129, 228
Frank, Linda L., 229
Freeman, J. Leiper, 191
French, John R.P., Jr., 219, 226, 228
French, Wendell L., 68
Friedrich, Carl J., 169, 190
Friere, Paulo, 226

Galbraith, John Kenneth, 147-148, 187
Gamache, Janice M., 53, 69
Gardner, Neely, 68
Garson, David G., 187
Gentry, Joe E., 54, 69
Giammo, Thomas, 99, 125
Gibb, Ack R., 222-223, 229
Gibb, Corinne Lathrop, 191
Giblin, Edwin J., 54, 68, 69, 74, 89
Gibson, Frank, 40, 287
Giegold, William C., 54, 59, 69, 71
Gluckstein, Norma B., 54, 69
Glueck, William F., 125
Goldman, Eric, 188

Golembiewski, Robert T., 7, 9, 39, 40, 44, 45, 55, 68, 69, 70, 71, 89, 90, 91, 124-25, 127, 128, 129, 138, 186, 187, 188, 190, 192, 193, 225, 226, 227, 228, 229, 256, 285, 287, 288, 307, 362, 363, 364, 365
Goodman, Paul G., 200, 227
Goodman, P.S., 129
Goodstein, Leonard D., 30, 33, 42, 55, 69, 71
Gosch, Martin, 288
Graf, Lee A., 127, 129
Graversen, G., 57, 70
Greenfield, Meg, 273, 288
Griffin, J.E., 285
Grizzard, Lewis, 286
Grodzins, Morton, 246-247, 287

Haase, Richard F., 56, 70
Hackman, J. Richard, 229
Halperin, Morton, 191
Hammer, Richard, 288
Hanson, Philip G., 52, 68
Hardiman, Rita, 53, 69
Hare, Garry, 58, 70
Harris, Joseph P., 40, 41
Harris, Reuben T., 227
Harrison, Roger, 228, 287
Hart, David K., 189
Harvey, Barron H., 99, 125, 126, 128
Harvey, Jerry, 285, 314, 318, 363
Hausser, Doris L., 287, 364
Heaton, Herbert, 166, 190
Heclo, Hugh, 41, 191
Heimovics, Richard, 363
Heisler, W.J., 188
Herring, Pendleton, 187
Hilles, Richard, 127, 128, 228, 363
Hofstadter, Richard, 190
Hopkins, Ronald H., 286
Hornstein, Harvey, 287
Houck, John W., 188

Jackson, Bailey W., III, 53, 69
Jackson, Jesse L., 273, 288
Janis, Irving L., 238, 286, 359, 362, 364
Jermier, John M., 192

Kagno, Munro, 127, 128, 363

Kaufman, Herbert, 20, 22, 39, 40, 41,42, 152, 172, 173, 175-176, 188, 191, 288
Kaufman, M. Frances, 68
Kelman, Herbert C., 177, 192
Kelson, Hans, 166
Kiel, David H., 40, 90
Kiepper, Alan, 55, 69, 71, 362, 365
Kilmann, Ralph H., 226
King, Donald C., 364
Klein, Donald C., 55, 69
Klein, Edward B., 56, 69, 70, 364
Klein, Lisl, 178-179, 192
Kouzes, James M., 258, 260, 262, 287, 362
Krocker, Larry L., 56, 70

LaBier, Douglas, 286
Lamb, Howard, 59, 71
Lampman, Charles M., 129
Lansky, Leonard M., 57, 70
Lawler, Edward E., III, 362
LeBaron, Melvin J., 56, 70, 272, 288, 352, 364
Leete, Burt A., 285
Lerner, Allan W., 286
Levin, Gilbert, 56, 70
Levine, Charles H., 68
Levinson, Harry, 364
Lewin, Kurt, 193, 226
Lindbloom, Charles, 142, 143, 144, 186, 187
Lippitt, Ronald, 193, 226
Long, Norton, 187
Lovrich, Nicholas P., Jr., 286
Lowi, Theodore, 187
Lubell, Samuel, 188
Luft, Joseph, 364
Luthans, Fred, 99, 125, 126, 128
Lynn, Laurence E., Jr., 362

Maccoby, Michael, 192
MacNair, Ray H., 288
Macy, Barry A., 362
Maiben, Dean H., 56, 70
Mann, Dean E., 40
March, James G., 189
Margulies, Newton, 226
Marini, Frank, 134, 135, 139-40, 149-50, 155-56, 158, 186, 188, 189
Marrow, Alfred J., 41
Maslow, Abraham, 75, 116-17
Mauer, Elizabeth H., 127
McCleod, Donald, 103, 127

McDuffie, James M., 287
McQuitty, L.L., 193
Meyer, Marshall W., 157, 158
Meyer, Robert G., 54, 69
Mico, Paul R., 258, 260, 262, 287, 362
Miles, Matthew B., 271-72, 288
Miller, Gerald J., 192, 364
Mills, Ted, 188
Mirvis, Philip H., 70, 90, 254
Mohrman, Susan A., 56, 70
Moley, Raymond, 155
Morrison, Peggy, 73-74, 89
Mosher, Frederick C., 128, 165, 166.167, 168, 169, 187, 190, 191, 225, 229, 251-52, 287
Mueller, Oscar, 99, 126
Murphy, Thomas P., 68

Nadler, David A., 228
Nelson, Michael, 186, 193
Nelson, Richard R., 70
Neustadt, Richard E., 191, 363
Nicholas, John M., 82-86, 90
Nightingale, Donald V., 192
Nollen, Stanley D., 90, 125, 128, 129
Novak, Jan F., 127

Obey, David, 287
O'Connell, Walter E., 52, 68
Olmosk, K., 57, 70
Osteen, Cicily P., 100, 126
Ostrom, Vincent, 134, 137, 149, 188

Packard, Ralph W., 54, 69
Paine, Frank T., 285
Parisi, Eunice M., 53, 69
Parker, Glenn M., 57, 70
Parkinson, C. Northcote, 2, 9
Pasmore, William A., 364
Patkai, Paula, 128
Paul, R. Shale, 40
Peabody, Robert, 189
Perkins, Dennis T., 228
Perkins, Richard E., 57, 70
Perkins, Richard F., 55, 69, 71
Perrow, Charles, 192
Perry, James L., 286
Pettersson, Kerstin, 128
Pettigrew, A.M., 364
Pfiffner, John, 256, 287
Pfister, Gordon, 58, 70

Pollane, Leonard, 288
Pondy, Louis R., 226
Porras, Jerry I., 73, 80-81, 89, 90,105-06, 127, 227
Porter, Lyman W., 286
Price, Don K., 163, 189
Primps, Sophia, 103, 107, 110, 113, 127, 128, 129
Proehl, Carl W., Jr., 65, 71, 79-82, 90, 124, 125, 127, 128, 129, 227, 228, 287, 362, 363

Raia, Anthony P., 226
Rainey, Glenn, 129
Rainey, Hal G., 177, 178, 192
Rapport, R.N., 226
Raven, Bertram H., 286
Ready, R.K., 57, 70, 71
Reddin, W.J., 249, 287
Reddy, W. Brendan, 57, 70
Redford, Emmette S., 135, 144, 145, 146, 151-52, 174, 186, 187, 188, 191, 197, 225
Reppucci, N. Dickson, 58, 70
Reutter, Mark, 100, 126
Reveal, Elizabeth C., 40, 191, 289
Rhinehart, Jesse B., 285
Riker, William H., 135-36, 186
Roberts, Nancy, 105-06, 127
Rogers, Carl, 335
Ronen, Simcha, 103, 107, 110, 113, 127, 128, 129
Rosenzweig, James E., 40, 52, 68, 71
Rosenzweig, James R., 435
Ross, Joyce D., 58, 70
Ross, Robert, 288
Rourke, Francis E., 40, 172, 189, 191
Rubin, Richard S., 95, 124, 128

Salvatore, P., 100, 126
Sapolsky, Harvey M., 363
Sata, Lindberg S., 58, 70
Saunders, J. Terry, 58, 70
Saunders, Robert J., 31, 41, 52, 53, 68, 69
Sayles, Leonard R., 192, 362, 363
Sayre, Wallace S., 30, 40, 171, 191
Schamie, Charles F., 54, 69
Schein, Virginia E., 127, 214, 227, 330, 363
Schlesinger, Arthur, 40
Schmuck, Richard A., 58, 70, 228, 271, 288
Schoeck, Helmut, 243, 244, 287

Schon, Donald A., 351, 364
Schott, Richard L., 40, 174, 191
Schulman, Jill E., 101, 126
Schwabe, Charles J., 56, 70
Scott, William G., 189, 225
Sebring, Robert H., 58, 71, 248, 287
Shaffer, Paul L., 286
Shakoor, Muhyia A., 59, 71
Shellow, Robert, 59, 71
Shepard, Herbert, 285, 318, 321, 362, 363
Sherwood, Frank, 256, 287
Shipel, George A., 68
Shipp, Bill, 287
Simmons, Robert H., 186
Simon, Herbert A., 188, 288
Singer, Ethan A., 288
Singer, Henry A., 59, 71
Sink, David, 68, 71, 89
Skowronek, Stephen, 189
Slater, Philip E., 188, 227
Slevin, Dennis P., 226
Smith, Ken K., 213, 227, 362
Snow, C.P., 34
Spaner, F.E., 285
Stein, David D., 56, 70
Stevens, Errol D., 101, 126
Susbauer, Jeffrey C., 227
Susman, Gerald I., 207, 208, 226
Svyantek, Dan, 90
Swart, J. Carroll, 101, 126, 128

Taber, Thomas D., 228, 364
Tannenbaum, Arnold S., 225
Tanner, W. Lynn, 59, 71
Taylor, Donald W., 193
Taylor, Frederick W., 189
Teahan, John E., 59, 71
Terpstra, D.E., 90
Thayer, Frederick C., 40, 149, 150, 188, 182, 225
Theobald, Robert, 226
Thomas, Claudewell S., 56, 69, 70, 289, 364
Thompson, John T., 59, 71
Thompson, Victor A., 29, 30, 155, 188-89, 286
Thornton, L.V., 101, 126
Thorsrud, Einer, 192, 193
Truman, David, 14, 187

Uhlmann, Gary J., 102, 126

Vaill, Peter B., 226
Van Riper, Paul P., 41, 191, 288
Verba, Sidney, 179-80, 192
Vieth, Warren, 102, 127

Waldo, Dwight, 164, 165, 186, 187, 189, 190, 227
Walker, James, 103, 127
Walsh, Jeffrey T., 228, 364
Walton, Richard, 193, 362
Warwick, Donald P., 128, 289, 362
Warrick, D.D., 362
Wayson, William, 228
Weber, Welford, 228
Weisbord, Marvin, 30, 31, 32, 41, 59, 71, 257-59, 260, 287, 296, 362

White, Robert K., 193, 226
Wildavsky, Aaron, 41, 187, 229
Wilson, John Rowen, 190
Wilson, Woodrow, 155, 164, 165, 168, 189, 190
Wolf, Lawrence, 129
Wood, Richard D., 42
Wooten, Leland M., 288
Yale, Donald A., 286
Yates, Douglas, 70
Yeager, Samuel, 127, 129
Young, Marjorie, 226

Zeigler, Harmon L., 144, 145, 187
Ziller, R.C., 309

SUBJECT INDEX

"Abilene paradox," 314
Action research, 206-210
  as contrasted with positivist science,
    206-210
  features of, 206-209
  in OD, 209-210
Administration, as separated from
  Politics, 149-150, 158
Administration, three couplings of
  Democracy with, 136-186, 195-229
  Democracy *and* Administration,
    136-138
  Democracy *vs.* Administration,
    138-186
  Democracy *within and through*
    Administration, 195-229
Advantage/power as intervening mode,
  271-274
Aggression, varieties of, 117
Agreement, crisis of, 88-89, 306-307
  features of, 89
  in public-sector OD, 88-89, 306-307
  in team-building, 307
Atlanta Regional Commission, 109

Bureaucracy, 138-186
  and control of technocrats, 162-164
  costs of, 170-186
  in Democracy *vs.* Administration,
    138-186
  features of, 150-151
  and merit system, 167-170
  in Marxist thought, 160-162
  rationale underlying use in public
    administration, 151-170
  as undercutting democratic ideals,
    178-186
Business/public sector differences,
  259-262, 318-329

Career planning, 221-222
Central Intelligence Agency, U.S., 196
Change, organizational, 1-6, 13-129
  233-365

and diagnosis, 31-33, 75, 117, 256-263,
  306-308
and features of public sector, 233-365
and flexible workhours, 93-129
and "hard" indicators, 82-86, 115-124
and measured productivity, 115-124
optimistic view of, 2-6
pessimistic literature, 1-2
public-sector constraints on, 13-42, 45-71
and success rates, 74-91, 94-229
and types of conflict, 88-89
Climate or atmospheres,
  organizational, 222-223
Coaching/counselling activities, 75
Confidentiality, relaxed attitude toward,
  309-311
Constraints on public-sector OD, 13-39,
  47-66
  in all settings, 63-66
  and characteristic cultures, 34-39
  conclusions about, 66-67
  and "habit background," 23-30
  institutional, 13-23
  at management levels, 30-39
  testing for incidence of, 50-66
  types of, 47-50
  in urban settings, 52-63
Contracting for team-building, 304-308
Control, patterns of, 200-202
Countervailing powers, theory of, 147-148

Decisions, bases for, 270-279
  and advantage/power vs. truth
    love, 271-272
  implications for OD, 272-273
  and "the political," 274-279
Degenerative interaction systems, 318-320
Democracy, three couplings with
  Administration, 136-186, 195-229
  Democracy *and* Administration,
    136-138
  Democracy *vs.* Administration, 138-186
  Democracy *within and through*
    Administration, 195-229

Democratic forms or levels, 141-153
    committee, 141-142
    kinds of, 141
    polyarchical, 141-148, 152-153
    referendum, 141
    representative, 141
Democratic ideals, 179-186, 195-229
    and political socialization, 179-180
    role of worksite socialization in, 180-185
    as supported by OD, 195-229
    as undercut by bureaucratic model,
        178-186
Democratic theory, classical, 134-138
    naivette of, 139-148
    properties of, 134-136
    and theory of countervailing powers,
        147-148
    view of administration congenial to,
        136-138
Designs for OD, 60-89, 93-129, 207-220,
        233-365
    eight classes of, 74-76
    flexible workhours, 93-129
    and forms of democracy, 216-220
    interaction-centered, 75-76, 118
    and polyarchical democracy, 216-220
    and public-sector features, 233-365
    structurally-oriented, 75-76
    survey/feedback, 67
    and types of crises, 88-89
    in urban settings, 60-77
    and values, 207-215
Diagnosis, 31-33, 75, 117, 256-263, 306-308
    in flexible workhour applications, 117
    models for, 31-33
    in team-building, 306-308
    and types of crises, 88-89, 306-307
    usefulness of overlays in, 256-263
Disagreement, crisis of, 88-89
    features of, 89
    in public-sector OD, 88-89
Domains, multiplicity of in public
        sector, 255-263
    and general overlays, 256-257   265-275
    implications for OD, 260, 262-263
    and more specific sub-systems, 257-261
Dr. No syndrome, 36-39

Elite theory, 144-146

Emotional tone in public sector, 236-245
    and despondency, 236-237
    and fear, 237-245
    supporting factors of, 238-245
Envy, role of, 243-244

Fear, motivators of, 238-245
Federal Bureau of Investigation, 196
Federal Executive Boards, 19
Federalist Papers, 139-140
Fixation, 117
Flexible workhours, or Flexi-Time, (F-T),
        85-129
    available public-sector studies of, 98-106
    effects of in public sector, 95-124
        on attitudes, 106-111
        on behaviors, 111-114
        on measured productivity, 115-124
    features of, 93-94
    in private sector, 94-95
    success rates with, 85-86, 93-129
    underlying theory of, 116-117
Frustration, effects of, 116-117

Governance, cycles of, 22-23
"Groupthink," 238
"Growth psychology," varieties of, 116-117

"Hard" indicators, OD effects on,
        82-86, 115-124
Hierarchy of needs, Maslow's, 116-117
Humanism, organizational, 197-225
    and action research, 206-210
    approaches to via OD, 216-225
    and consistent values, 210-215
    and enacted consciousness, 203-206
    and patterns of control, 200-202
    and ways of responding to employee
        needs, 197-200
Human Service Organization, or HSO, 32-34

Interaction systems, types of, 318-320
"Interest-group liberalism," 146-148
    features of, 146-147
    problems with, 147-148
Intervening in public sector, guidelines for,
        233-285, 291-365
    and definition of success, 263-270
    and features of interface, 233-234
    guidelines for, 291-365

and texture of control, 234-285
bases of decisions, 270-273
content of "the political," 274-279
and difficulty of drawing boundaries,
279-281
emotional tone, 235-245
loosely-bounded, 253-255
multi-leveledness, 245-253
and role of media, 283-285
and rogues or renegades, 281-283
Intervenor behavior, guidelines for, 291-365
and aspirations re change, 348-354
and balance of power, 355-361
and confidentiality, 309-311
in contracting, 304-308
as different in business sector, 318-329
in expanding range of credible
discretion, 313-315
in managing effects of status, 341-347
for internal/external intervenors, 347
in mobilizing commonalities, 294-299
in "network of power," 329-333
in picking OD targets, 291-293
and preventive efforts, 333-335
in relation to marginality, 306, 308-309
and strategic orientations to socio-political
context, 297-299
and systemic identification, 293-294,
299-304, 335-338
and values, 293-294, 329-333, 338-341
working toward multiple access channels,
311-313, 315-318
Interventions as politically-charged, 329-331
"Iron quadrangle," or "little groups of
policy neighbors," 15-16

Job enrichment, 85, 221-224

Loosely-bounded or under-bounded
systems, 253-255
as characteristic of public sector, 253-255
features of, 254
implications for OD, 254-255

Marginality, 306-308-309
Measured productivity, OD effects on,
115-124
Merit system, 166-175
and bureaucratic model, 166-170
features of, 167

and "program politics," 170-175
Motivators vs. satisfiers, Herzberg's, 117
Multi-leveledness in public sector, 245-253
as encompassing politicals and
professionals, 251-253
and range of interventions, 249-251
and republican governance, 246-248
and theoretical comprehensiveness,
248-249

Navy, U.S., 2
New Public Administration, 134
North Carolina, as strategic OD target,
292-293

Office of Personnel Management, U.S.,
95, 171
Organization Development (OD), 3-5,
13-42, 60-124, 133-365
and action research, 206-210
and approaches to organizational
humanism, 197-200, 216-225
constraints in public sector, 13-42
definition of, 4
designs for, 60-76, 88-89, 93-129,
207-220, 233-365
effects on "hard" indicators, 82-86,
115-124
and forms of democracy, 216-220
and frustration, 116-117
and measured productivity, 115-124
and "growth psychology," 116-117
guidelines for improving success
rates in, 233-365
objectives of, 24-30
and political theory, 133-229
and polyarchical democracy, 216-220
and sensitivity training, 40
and success rates, 3-5, 74-91, 94-129
as value-loaded, 210-215
and values, 180-182, 197-200, 207-215,
320-322
"Overhead democracy," simple model of,
151-152
Overlap for diagnosing organizations,
256-261

"Participatory consciousness," 203-205
Pluralism, 144-145
"Point-man" intervening mode, 320-329

as conscience about OD values, 320-322
and intervenor roles, 327-329
some OD design implications, 322-327
Polyarchical democracy, 141-186, 195-229
compatible model of Administration,
195-229
features of, 141-148
and Democracy *vs.* Administration,
148-186
and Democracy *within and through*
Administration, 195-229
and OD designs, 216-220
and Organizational humanism, 197-225
Politics, as separated from Administration,
149-150, 158
Positivist science, as contrasted with action
research, 206-210
Process analysis, 74-75
Productivity, 82-86, 115-124
and frustrating stimuli, 117
and "growth psychologies," 116-117
OD effects on, 82-86, 115-124
"Professional" vs. "political" roles,
251-252, 303
"Program politics," 170-175
Project ACORD, or Action for Organization
Development, 16, 66, 236, 283, 289,
309, 353-354
Public/business sector differences, 259-262,
318-329

Quality of Working Life, or QWL, 180-185
and authority structures, 182-185
values underlying, 180-182

Regenerative interaction systems, 318-320
Regression, 117
Research, types of, 105-106
assessment, 106
evaluation, 106
implementation, 105
theory-building, 106
Resignation, 117
"Rogues," or "renegades," 281-283

Self-actualization, Argyrian dimensions of,
117
Sensitivity training, 40
Skill-building, 75
Socio-political context, five intervenor

orientations toward, 297-299
"Spoils politics," 137-138
State, U.S. Department of, 16, 66, 236,
283, 289, 309, 353-354
Success, organizational, in public sector,
263-270
features of, 264-266
implications for OD, 266-270
Success rates in OD, 76-89, 93-129, 234-365
in applications throughout public sector,
78-86
with flexible workhours, 85-86, 93-129
guidelines for raising, 234-365
with flexible workhours, 85-86, 93-129
for "hard criteria" only, 82-86, 115-124
implications for enhancement of, 8-89
for measured productivity, 115-124
in urban applications, 76-78
Survey/feedback designs, 218-219
System-building, 75

Team-building, 75
contracting for, 306-308
success rates in, 75
and types of crises, 306-308
Technostructural change, 75, 83-86, 93-129,
219-224
and flexible workhours, 93-129
and measured productivity, 115-124
in organizational humanism, 219-224
success rates in, 85-86
Theory, political, 134-148, 175-186, 197-200
classical democratic, 134-138
democratic ideals in, 178-186
and organizational humanism, 197-200
and polyarchies, 141-148
as supporting OD, 195-229
Theory Y vs. X, McGregor's, 117
Truth/love as intervening mode, 271-274

Values, 149, 180-182, 197-200, 207-215,
320-322
in action research, 207-209
and science of administration, 149
for guiding OD, 197-200
and intervenor as point-man, 320-322
in OD, 210-215, 320-322
and organizational humanism, 210-215
in QWL efforts, 180-182

Whistle-blowing, 40
Worksite democratization, 197-225
  approaches to via OD, 216-225
  and action research, 206-210
  and consistent values, 210-215

and enacted consciousness, 203-206
and patterns of control, 200-202
and ways of responding to employee
  needs, 197-200